OXFORD CONSTITUTIONAL THEORY

Series Editors:
Martin Loughlin, John P. McCormick, and Neil Walker

Post Sovereign Constitution Making

OXFORD CONSTITUTIONAL THEORY

Series Editors:

Martin Loughlin, John P. McCormick, and Neil Walker

Oxford Constitutional Theory has rapidly established itself as the primary point of reference for theoretical reflections on the growing interest in constitutions and constitutional law in domestic, regional and global contexts. The majority of the works published in the series are monographs that advance new understandings of their subject. But the series aims to provide a forum for further innovation in the field by also including well-conceived edited collections that bring a variety of perspectives and disciplinary approaches to bear on specific themes in constitutional thought and by publishing English translations of leading monographs in constitutional theory that have originally been written in languages other than English.

ALSO AVAILABLE IN THE SERIES

Popular Sovereignty in Early Modern Constitutional Thought
Daniel Lee

The Cultural Defense of Nations
A Liberal Theory of Majority Rights
Liav Orgad

The Cosmopolitan Constitution
Alexander Somek

The Structure of Pluralism
Victor M. Muniz-Fraticelli

Constitutional Courts and Deliberative Democracy
Conrado Hübner Mendes

Fault Lines of Globalization
Legal Order and the Politics of A-Legality
Hans Lindahl

The Cosmopolitan State
H. Patrick Glenn

After Public Law
Edited by Cormac Mac Amhlaigh, Claudio Michelon, and Neil Walker

The Three Branches
A Comparative Model of Separation of Powers
Christoph Möllers

The Global Model of Constitutional Rights
Kai Möller

The Twilight of Constitutionalism?
Edited by Petra Dobner and Martin Loughlin

Beyond Constitutionalism
The Pluralist Structure of Postnational Law
Nico Krisch

Constituting Economic and Social Rights
Katharine G. Young

Constitutional Referendums
The Theory and Practice of Republican Deliberation
Stephen Tierney

Constitutional Fragments
Societal Constitutionalism and Globalization
Gunther Teubner

Post Sovereign Constitution Making

Learning and Legitimacy

Andrew Arato

Dorothy Hart Hirshon Professor of Political and Social Theory, The New School

OXFORD
UNIVERSITY PRESS

OXFORD
UNIVERSITY PRESS

Great Clarendon Street, Oxford, OX2 6DP,
United Kingdom

Oxford University Press is a department of the University of Oxford. It furthers the University's objective of excellence in research, scholarship, and education by publishing worldwide. Oxford is a registered trade mark of Oxford University Press in the UK and in certain other countries

First Edition published in 2016

Published in the United States of America by Oxford University Press
198 Madison Avenue, New York, NY 10016, United States of America

British Library Cataloguing in Publication Data
Data available

Library of Congress Control Number: 2015960808

ISBN 978–0–19–875598–2

For Jean and Julian

Preface

This book is third in a series of studies dealing with the new world of constitutional politics that opened with the Spanish transition to democracy and became more universal in the 1990s. In the first, *Civil Society, Constitution and Legitimacy* (2000), I focus on East Central Europe, while in the second, *Constitution Making Under Occupation* (2009), I examine the perhaps unlikely case of Iraq under American rule. The present volume resumes the study of the former state socialist countries, with the case of Hungary, as well as the Middle East with an extended study of constitution making in Turkey. Its purpose is not only comparative, but primarily theoretical. It seeks to better understand the new paradigm of constitution making that I call post sovereign, focusing on its achievements in two areas: the generation of political legitimacy and the facilitation of legal and political learning. In order to fully assess these desiderata, I very much focus on the slightly idealized South African case, one which I consider the most complete and normatively distinguished realization of the paradigm organized around the institution of round table negotiations. Contrasts with the alternative democratic models, the constitutional convention invented in North America, and the sovereign constituent assembly pioneered in France help me thematize the gains involved, as well as possible losses and difficulties.

In this work I also consider how the post sovereign process can fail, as in Hungary, and conversely, how insufficient learning from it can lead to a severe constitutional crisis, the case of Turkey. As in any properly theoretical work, I build on and debate with the conceptions of others. My sources go back to the great democratic revolutions, where I find anticipations of the new paradigm in French theory, as well as American practice. I found some of the legal theorists of the French Third Republic especially helpful in evaluating the grave problems with constitution making and altering in France. In the world of the older German theory, I have been most influenced by Hannah Arendt, while my critical debate with Carl Schmitt runs through the whole volume. Among contemporary theorists, my debt to Claude Lefort and Jürgen Habermas should be obvious throughout, but the conception has been most directly influenced by the recent work of Ulrich Preuss, Bruce Ackerman, and János Kis. There are also theorists who serve as both important sources and debating partners, in particular Stephen Holmes, Ernesto Laclau, Ran Hirschl, Tom Ginsburg, and the authors of the collective volume *The Paradox of Constitutionalism*, especially Hans Lindahl.

There are also other debts I need to mention. I am grateful to Johan van der Walt for organizing two seminars around my work in Glasgow (2009) and Johannesburg (2010), and for the School of Law of the University of Witwaterstrand for having supported me with the prestigious Bram Fisher Honorary Professorship for a period beyond the duration of the latter. Similarly, I wish to thank Pierre Rosanvallon for having invited me to give four lectures at the Collège de France (2012), which enabled me to write materials incorporated in this volume. I thank several organizations for allowing me to repeatedly come to Turkey. In particular I thank Levent Gönenc for inviting me to two seminars with TEPAV in Ankara, during the second of which I had a chance to meet and discuss with members of the parliamentary Constitutional Reconciliation Committee. Fuat Keyman and Ayse Kadoglu have been instrumental in inviting me to two sessions on the constitution at Sabanci and Koc Universities, and similarly Aysen Candas and Ayse Bugra at Bogazici University. Giancarlo Bosetti and Nina zu Fürstenberg have been kind enough to invite me to several conferences of their journal Reset in Istanbul, and I thank Osman Kavala for two serious seminar discussions at his "public restaurant." In Hungary my debt is not only to László Majtényi for having invited me to an important seminar on the constitution in 2004, but to all my discussion partners in Budapest, Miklós Haraszti, András Bozóki, Gábor Halmai, Zoltán Miklósi, Kriszta Kovács, Gábor A. Tóth, and of course János Kis. Further, I am grateful to the US Department of State for having sponsored me as a democracy lecturer focusing on constitution making in Nepal (2006) and Zimbabwe (2010), and in particular to Sharon Hudson-Dean, the officer in charge of Public Affairs at each of these US Embassies at the time of my visits. In both countries I had the pleasure of meeting politicians as well as civil society activists engaged in constitutional issues. Finally, but not least, I thank my Turkish students for teaching me a great deal (never enough) about Turkish constitutional politics, in particular Ertug Tombus, Aysel Madra, and Bahar Tabakoglu. I also thank another student of mine, Anna Matthiesen, for editorial work on this volume.

As always, I am very grateful to members of my family, Jean Cohen and Julian Arato, who have helped me with many theoretical and legal matters, given me a great deal of emotional support, and to whom this volume is dedicated.

Contents

Introduction: Beyond the Paradox of Constitutionalism

I THE PARADOX OF CONSTITUTIONALISM

Constitutionalism, the most important modern safeguard against tyranny, is now commonly said to be paradoxical.[1] Its key idea of a democratic constituent power, long assumed to be the foundation of two-track or dualistic constitutionalism, is often shown to be circular or self-contradictory and for two reasons. First, the constituent power that has always been posited as the (legitimate) source of the constitution seems to come into being only as its result. The postulated extra-constitutional author, *the people*, gains its identity as well as ability to act only in the basic law or rather the constituted regime. Yet, although constituted by the constitution, the constituent power is uniquely understood as sovereign in the traditional sense of being unlimited, or "in the state of nature." The famous circle of constituent power is noted by Hannah Arendt, recognized even earlier by Hans Kelsen, and then much later by Jacques Derrida, and is thus the first dimension of this paradox.[2] Even Arendt tries to escape circularity only by relying on a form of American exceptionalism that implicitly conceded the more general "solution" to Kelsen, namely that (almost all) actual beginnings are linked to dictating violence and can have no normative justification.[3]

Today, interpreters seek to escape this version of the paradox by a theory of imputation that is itself very Kelsenian, according to which the unitary and unified people as the constituent power is indeed not the origin of anything, but instead a result of the constitution, a *constitué*, but to whom the *pouvoir constituant* can then be ascribed.[4] But this leads only to the second, more fateful

[1] See the editors' "Introduction" to M. Loughlin and N. Walker (eds), *The Paradox of Constitutionalism* (Oxford: Oxford University Press, 2007) as well as Walker's own essay in the same volume: "Post Constituent Constitutionalism? The Case of the European Union."

[2] "Introduction" in Loughlin and Walker, *Paradox of Constitutionalism*. See H. Arendt, *On Revolution* (London: Penguin, 1990); Hans Kelsen, *General Theory of Law and the State* (Cambridge, MA: Harvard, 1945) 261; J. Derrida, "Declarations of Independence 1" (1986) 7 *New Political Science* 1 7–15.

[3] R. Carré de Malberg, *Contribution à la générale Théorie de l'État* (first published 1920, Paris: Dalloz, 2004) 497.

[4] The constituent power thus becomes a substitute for the Kelsenian *Grundnorm*. See H. Lindahl "Constituent Power and Reflexive Identity: Towards an Ontology of Collective Selfhood" in Loughlin and Walker, *Paradox of Constitutionalism* 13, 19.

dimension of the paradox, namely the survival of the *constituant* in or under or next to the *constitué*, in the form of an extra-constitutional popular sovereign within the constitutional form and superior to it in principle.

The paradox of constitutionalism is a deeper version of the counter-majoritarian difficulty, one that has long dominated American discussions of judicial review, and has not been laid to rest despite the important efforts of authors such as J.H. Ely, John Rawls, Bruce Ackerman, and Jürgen Habermas. The new version is more fateful because it weakens other dimensions of constitutionalism, for example entrenched amendment rules and the separation of powers, in addition to the constitutional court. As for the amendment rule, one side of the paradox, the popular constituent implies not only a higher level of change, one not bound by eternity rules or basic structures, but also the idea that insistence on the *formal* amendment rule is nothing but mere legalism. As for the separation of powers, the constituent power is not believed to be one of them, and, well above all the rest, it is not supposed to be limited by the famous checks and balances. As for judicial review, the other side of the paradox, the idea of the constituent power *as result* weakens the key defense of constitutional invalidation of laws since Hamilton and Marshall, namely the idea that the constitution represents higher law because of its origins and foundations in a democratic constituent process.

The paradox of constitutionalism is often supposed to be redeemed by a piece of political theology. It is emphatically theological to say that something that has never come to be nevertheless continues to exist, and survives as an uncontrollable and unlimited form of power.[5] And as readers of Carl Schmitt know, or ought to know, such a survival represents a sword of Damocles hanging over constitutional, and I would add: democratic, government.[6] The attempt to domesticate Schmitt by, for example, absorbing him in Kelsenian imputation, as by Hans Lindahl, cannot succeed. While on the one side he notes, implicitly in the path of François Furet and Claude Lefort, that all claims on behalf of the people can be challenged by other claims, Lindahl also posits that constituent power as "normative innovation and rupture . . . proceeds from a radical outside no political community succeeds in domesticating."[7]

It is true: readers of Lawson and Locke,[8] as well as Jefferson, Condorcet, Sieyès and even *The Federalist*, will certainly point to survival of the constituent power under constitutional structures as nothing else than the revolutionary right of a political community to alter or replace its form of government. This right, however, in all of these great authors was tied to the demand of justification, one that could eventually in turn be linked to procedural requirements and tests concerning *who* had the right to speak in the name of *the* people and *when*

[5] Ibid. 17. [6] Walker, "Post Constituent Constitutionalism?" 248.

[7] Lindahl, "Constituent Power" 22–4.

[8] See M. Loughlin, "Constituent Power Subverted: From English Constitutional argument to British Political Practice" in Loughlin and Walker, *Paradox of Constitutionalism*.

as well as *how*.[9] The Declaration of Independence contains just such an attempt at justification. Condorcet's famous constitutional draft of 1793, in this respect followed by later two or three track amendment rules, went on to postulate the relevant tests and procedures.[10] But combined with populist ideas of the unitary people as embodied in one of its parts,[11] a group or an individual, the notion of the imputed constituent power leads to the outcome that the extra-constitutional people, even if it has not existed before the constitution, under or next to a constitutional regime is nevertheless unlimited. Its actions expressing the highest form of democratic self-determination need therefore no additional justification. I believe it is this idea of the unitary popular sovereign as the constituent power that is the main source of the paradox of constitutionalism, whether expressed as a myth of origins, imputation, or even the denial of the constituent power as a relevant category.

It is not surprising that some interpreters take a step in Kelsen's direction, even further than Lindahl, and seek to get rid of the notion of the constituent power altogether.[12] This move seemingly eliminates the paradox.[13] But the heavy price they must pay is the adoption of a Hobbesian perspective: that it does not matter how constitutions are actually or empirically made, because in any case they are ultimately based on fear. This was a price that even Kelsen as a political thinker, rather than the theorist of "pure law," refused to pay.[14] I would like to think that he implicitly understood that the Hobbesian perspective leads to an unacceptable equalization of the procedural methods of constitution making. David Dyzenhaus, for example, treats the very different constituent processes in the United States in 1787 and in Germany and Japan after the Second World War and South Africa recently as if they all represented simply alternative forms of imposition, by internal elites or external powers.[15]

Yet the idea that the method of constitution making does not matter very much is also supposed to be confirmed by large-scale empirical research. Thomas Ginsburg and his collaborators seem to have come to this conclusion after having examined and compared supposedly 460 cases.[16] But what is it that they

[9] Walker explicitly thematizes the normative requirements that have to be fulfilled when the constitutive power is invoked. He mentions the "who" and the "how" to which I add the "when" that was explicitly stressed by Lawson and Locke.

[10] A. Arato, "Multi-Track Constitutionalism Beyond Carl Schmitt" (2011) 18 *Constellations* 3 324–51.

[11] See Chapter 6 below.

[12] See D. Dyzenhaus, "The Question of Constituent Power" in Laughlin and Walker, *Paradox of Constitutionalism*; and his "Constitutionalism in an Old Key: Legality and Constituent Power" (2012) 1 *Global Constitutionalism* 2 229–60.

[13] So would sociological reductionism or realism, paying the same price. See Walker, "Post Constituent Constitutionalism?" 261.

[14] See, for example, Kelsen, *General Theory*, where he speaks, inconsistently in terms of the pure theory, of a democratic way of making constitutions.

[15] Dyzenhaus, "Constitutionalism in an Old Key" 12.

[16] T. Ginsburg, Z. Elkins, and J. Blount, "Does the Process of Constitution-making Matter?" (2009) 5 *Annual Review of Law and Social Science* 5.

really have proven in this endeavor? On the one hand they show that the formal organization and inputs of popular participation do not seem to produce more legitimate or supported constitutions than processes that lack this kind of involvement. On the other hand, they show that using normal legislatures as opposed to constituent assemblies does not affect the powers of parliaments or legislatures in the new constitutions. I think both of these arguments are flawed, in part because of their adherence to two populist assumptions about participation and democracy that, in whatever version they are presented, are at the very root of the paradox of constitutionalism. While assuming that the plebiscitary mobilization seen in cases such as Eritrea and Ethiopia is genuine participation,[17] they claim that participation does not matter, whereas the results of tabulating two of its forms, genuine (in South Africa) and manipulated (further north), may have only resulted in cancelling each another out. As they assume (although do not actually claim) that constituent assemblies are supposed to be better embodiments of the people than the normal parliaments seen as organs of government, Ginsburg et al. are surprised by their apparently similar outcomes. Here too a conflation may play a role between non-sovereign conventions of the U.S. type and French-modeled sovereign constituent assemblies.[18] Admittedly, these empirical results are important, but as materials for the critique of populist assumptions, rather than for their thesis that methods of constitution making do not matter.

How and why do first-rate legal analysts come up with skeptical conclusions regarding process, flying in the face of more closely examined historical realities, to reach conclusions that they would never recommend as expert advisors to actors engaged in constitution making? Does the paradox of constitutionalism explain this conclusion, whereby one is forced to choose either a populist position based on popular sovereignty or a narrowly result-oriented, liberal one based on constitutionalism? I strongly believe that the dominant version of the paradox is rooted in or linked to the plebiscitary populist conception of Carl Schmitt (or rather his particular interpretation of Sieyès[19]). Accordingly, the paradox of constitutionalism consists of the tension between the extra-constitutional unitary sovereign called the nation or the people, which is the revolutionary source of constitutions, and the constitutional form. In this conception, the people, as a procedurally and substantively unlimited actor, is not only superior to the constitution including its revision rules, but can choose to act under constitutional forms (as an electorate or a public) or outside and

[17] I have experienced what so-called participation can be like during a brief trip to Zimbabwe in 2010: http://harare.usembassy.gov/andrew_arato.html accessed October 16, 2015. On this issue also see A. Saati, *The Participation Myth: Outcomes of Participatory Constitution Building Processes on Democracy* (Diva Portal, 2015) comparing Zimbabwe and Kenya.

[18] On the fundamental difference see Chapter 3 below.

[19] Most follow this interpretation. For alternatives, see P. Bastid, *Sieyès et sa pensée* (Paris: Hachette, 1939) and P. Pasquino, *Sieyès et l'invention de la constitution en France* (Paris: Odile Jacob 1998); as well as Chapter 1 below. Also see my (forthcoming) *Adventures of the Constituent Power.*

against them. Interpreters who assume that the *pouvoir constituant* implies such notion of the people are left with the bad choice of either trying to domesticate Schmitt in some way or to abandon the notion of the constituent power and along with it any interest in the processes of actual constitution making, their possible justification as well as criticism.

This claim is easily demonstrable for many, perhaps most of the authors collected in the volume, *The Paradox of Constitutionalism*. It is entirely clear that Dyzenhaus' polemic is directed at a Schmittian conception of the constituent power, even as he tries to root the origins of the notion in the dualism of politics and law, which he in fact cannot eliminate as an empirical matter. On the other hand, Ulrich Preuss, whose earlier post Schmittian turn has influenced me greatly,[20] obviously returned to an earlier Schmitt-Marx synthesis, according to which constituent power is possible only in revolutions led by a vanguard actor. After some cogent remarks on the difficulty of identifying the people as the carrier of the constituent power, and the need for normative rules of recognition, he proceeds to nevertheless find this subject in the actions of a revolutionary vanguard, a minority, acting through constituent assemblies or referenda through pure majority rule, and its complement, Schmitt's tacit consent.[21] In this context Preuss also repeats the Schmittian claim that "the people cannot discuss, negotiate, and make compromises like a parliament . . . it can only say yes or no"—although it is a great mystery in light of history why constituent assemblies, or town meetings in the American processes of ratification are not supposed to be capable of just these types of parliamentary action.[22] Of course, Preuss claims the constituent power is sovereign, apparently fashioning that concept through the example of a unitary monarch, and he might answer that all the assemblies I have in mind (along with his previous co-author Elster!), those that deliberated, bargained and compromised, and decided by qualified majority, were either not sovereign at all or did not embody the people as a whole. In light of these considerations, it is not surprising that he does not find constituent power at work in East and Central Europe.[23] As he has come to understand the concept, there was none to be found.

According to Preuss, in Central and Eastern Europe something like the universal class of the young Marx was absent, a class or a stratum and a group that could ("rightly") identify its particular interests with the interest of the whole.[24]

[20] See U. Preuss, *Constitutional Revolution* (first published 1990; Atlantic Highlands, NJ: Humanities Press, 1995) and Chapter 2 below.

[21] U. Preuss, "The Exercise of Constituent Power in Central and Eastern Europe" in Laughlin and Walker, *Paradox of Constitutionalism* 211–19.

[22] See J. Elster, "Arguing and Bargaining in Two Constituent Assemblies" (1999) 2 *University of Pennsylvania Journal of Constitutional Law* 345.

[23] Though in contrast to his previous work he now deems 1989–90 as revolutions, without any previous clarifying adjective. See Preuss, *Constitutional Revolution* 8, where in 1990 he spoke of a non- or even anti-revolutionary spirit.

[24] Ibid. 214–15, 223.

More surprisingly, he laments the fact that actors in transition from communism were forced to act under the veil of ignorance in producing new constitutional arrangements, whereas vanguard revolutionary parties presumably could establish the political order corresponding to their interests. Nevertheless Preuss is right on one point. Where the structure of the state was tied up with the old Communist regime, as in the German Democratic Republic, Yugoslavia, and even Czechoslovakia, the collapse of existing states made the task of constitutional creation much more difficult. He rightly criticizes the rise of nationalist actors in some of the countries, though it is entirely unclear why a nationalist vanguard could not play the Schmittian constituent role that Preuss seems to restrict to class-based minorities. I, of course, do agree with his earlier view: a Schmittian notion of the constituent power was indeed absent in the self-limiting revolutions or changes of regime of the late 1980s and 1990s. That was the point of the round tables about which Preuss was enthusiastic in 1989, and whose normative authority to initiate pluralistic constituent processes he once applauded.[25] Now, after the failure of the East German Round Table at which he participated, he has returned to the conception of Carl Schmitt, whose shadow hangs over all populist theories of constitution making.

Admittedly, the debt to Carl Schmitt is not always this close or explicit. For some authors, the Schmittian conception seems to work only teleologically. Starting with the emphatically non-Schmittian (in its practice if not always in theory: non-sovereign, not unlimited etc.) model of the American constitutional convention,[26] Steven Griffin winds up with the acts of the contemporary American presidency in emergencies as the exemplification of popular constituent power in the United States. The fact that acts of presidents can informally change the constitution, generally with help from other branches, is undeniable, and has been known since the work of Georg Jellinek at the latest.[27] We see an especially radical such de facto attempt to change the constitution in Turkey today. Yet the legitimacy of these acts from a normative point of view may be doubted or at least seriously questioned, and in the United States were so questioned by the Hamdi and Hamdan courts. Similarly, Lucien Jaume seems to be aware of the differences between the theories of a Condorcet and perhaps even (the antinomic[28]) Sieyès and the populist insurrectionary conceptions already present in the French Revolution. Yet, after lamenting the long (supposed) absence of the constituent power especially under the Third and Fourth Republics,[29] Jaume speaks of its apparently salutary return under the plebiscitary

[25] Ibid. 94–6.

[26] Schmitt's inconsistency on this point is interesting, but in the end he saw the making of the Federal constitution as a status contract of a *Bund*: C. Schmitt, *Verfassungslehre* (Berlin: Duncker & Humblot, 1928) Chapters 29–30.

[27] G. Jellinek, *Verfassungsaäderung u. Verfassungswandlung* (Berlin: Häring, 1906).

[28] On his antinomy, see more in Chapter 1 below.

[29] It was certainly present on the doctrinal level under the Third Republic, see further on Carré de Malberg and Hauriou in Chapter 1 below. As to the Fourth, its origins represented a form of creative adoption of the notion

transformation engineered by de Gaulle in 1958 and 1962. What is astonishing in the two presentations by Griffin and Jaume is that they do not even take notice of the dramatic transformation of the notion of the popular constituent power from democratic to plebiscitary modalities, from assembly-based to executive-centered politics. This oversight is only possible on the bases of assumptions such as Schmitt's, according to which the constituent power of the people is tied to no particular procedure, and can act through a variety of procedures or none at all.[30] It is just this idea that is at the basis of the paradox of constitutionalism.[31]

Most interestingly, for me, Christoph Möllers identifies that paradox as the antinomy or conflict between "constitutional populism" and "constitutional form," deriving the first concept, remarkably enough, from Ernesto Laclau's *On Populist Reason*.[32] He defines this constitutional "populism" in the non-"pejorative" sense, differentiated from populism as such, as a democratic politics "specifically orientated towards constitutional orientations and procedures without formally being part of them." This would correspond to what has been long understood as the politics of civil society, whose outer limits are represented by civil disobedience.[33] But in the historical presentation of Möllers the protean character of "the people," as under Laclau's concept of the "empty signifier," reveals itself as such well beyond the constitutionalist definition. The distinction between populism and constitutional populism is not maintained, and neither is the limitation to informality. The shadow of Schmitt's idea of the popular constituent power that cannot be limited to any specific actors or procedures lingers over the whole analysis.

While isolating the paradox as it rightly appeared to Schmitt under the Weimar Republic involving the tension between plebiscitary elements of the constitution (the directly elected presidency with emergency powers, and the importance of referenda) and parliamentarianism, Möllers seems to project it both backwards and forwards in German history to fully generalize the tension between politics and law, legality and legitimacy as understood by populism. Thus the Reichstag, elected by universal manhood suffrage under the *Kaiserreich*, is said to be a populist organ (similarly to the European Parliament now!), the National Socialist revolution institutionalized in the dual state (following Ernst Fraenkel) represents the triumph of "populism," while the *Grundgesetz* and the regime of the *Bundesrepublik* are depicted as the triumph of the

that Jaume either discounts, because of the element of limitation of the two constituent assemblies, or ascribes the originality entirely to de Gaulle, who was in fact quite dissatisfied with this process, which excluded the executive in constitution drafting.

30 See C. Schmitt, *Verfassungslehre* 82 and *passim*.

31 As Paolo Carrozza demonstrates, A. Negri's multitude is equally protean, and has entirely parallel difficulties, even if we forget its violence-prone vitalism. See P. Carrozza, "Constitutionalism's Post-Modern Opening" in Laughlin and Walker, *Paradox of Constitutionalism*.

32 Christoph Möllers, "We Are (Afraid of) the People: Constituent Power in German Constitutionalism" in Laughlin and Walker, *Paradox of Constitutionalism* 87. This derivation works only for the period of the Weimar republic, and for the rejection of plebiscitary democracy under the *Grundgesetz*.

33 A. Arato and J. Cohen, *Civil Society and Political Theory* (Cambridge, MA: MIT, 1992).

Rechtsstaat over democracy, as hostile not only to plebiscitary populism but to popular government as well. Yet under the *Bundesrepublik*, the *influence* of civil society and the public sphere, that at times is exactly what Möllers means by constitutional populism, always was and hopefully will be an important dimension of politics, potentially even on a constitutional level. The reference to Habermas' *Structural Transformation of the Public Sphere* (1962) as a call for constitutional populism under a German regime that excludes it is quite misleading, since that author, who has never been any kind of populist, has since radically revised the thesis of decline, as Möllers admits.[34] But then the latter's thesis concerning the *Grundgesetz* excluding extra-institutional democratic politics should have also been revised.[35]

Of course the assumption that all extra-institutional democracy is populism was also a foundation for the conservative politics in Germany after the Second World War. In Möllers' presentation this political perspective led traditionally to resistance to referenda as part of the European treaty-making process. Later it blocked the making of a new constitution under article 146 of the Basic Law (Grundgesetz für die Bundesrepublik Deutschland, 1949) after what was called the East German "revolution," assumed to be populist.[36] Unfortunately, he himself seems to share the same assumption, although it is clear that the identification of populism with democratic constitution making did not help the cause of those who, like Preuss, in his capacity as a jurist, rightly sought a new constitution under article 146's original promise. I note that such an effort could have remained under the supervision of the Constitutional Court under the eternity clauses (articles 1–20 as entrenched by 79), and thus need not have endangered the achievements of the *Grundgesetz* as conservative opponents often claimed. Möllers, perhaps not aware of the relationship of constitutional courts as mediators between interim and final constitutions in Hungary, as well as in South Africa, seems to resist the very plausible idea that the *Verfassungsgericht* could have protected the eternity clauses even in an article 146 procedure, indeterminate as that was under the *Grundgesetz*.[37]

[34] Indeed Laclau and Habermas are entirely incompatible as theorists of democracy, as both of them have fully realized.

[35] On how the idea of the co-originality of rights and democracy in Habermas is supposed to resolve the paradox of constitutionalism, see R. Nickel, "Private and Public Autonomy Revisited: Habermas' Concept of Co-originality in Times of Globalization and the Military Security state" in Laughlin and Walker, *Paradox of Constitutionalism*.

[36] Möllers, in "We Are Afraid (of the People)" 99, cites the famous "Wir sind das Volk" and omits the later but equally famous "Wir sind ein Volk" that together show in a limited setting the protean character of the people or *das Volk* as Laclau's "empty signifier." For more doubts about the revolutionary character of the Central European changes of regime, see not only my work but also János Kis, "Between Reform and Revolution" (1998) 12 *East European Politics & Societies* 2 300–83 but also Preuss, *Constitutional Revolution*.

[37] Möllers, "We Are Afraid (of the People)" 96–7.

None of the authors cited here is a populist politician.[38] However, the paradox of constitutionalism does have political consequences, and it can lead in the direction of populism. A case in point is the work of Joel Colón-Ríos, who is inspired not only by Schmitt's conception of the constituent power, but also by Latin American populist experimentation.[39] In Chapter 6 I will return to a critique of his conception and of his politics, which, in the version of Antonio Negri at least, transcends the limits of democracy by potentially valorizing the overthrow of constitutional democratic regimes by mobilized violent minorities. This explicitly populist conception represents the polar alternative to a liberal politics that proposes the suppression of the idea of the constituent power altogether. If Colón-Ríos seeks to establish revolution as permanent, Dyzenhaus tries to banish it by philosophical fiat at least from the normative universe. Neither of them can move beyond the rigid alternative of revolution and reform, which it is possible to transcend, as I will try to show. Thus one conception is normatively untenable, while the other is easily falsified by empirical reality.

In between these two options lies a stress closer to my own, emphasizing the importance of popular participation in constitution making. In its current form this perspective is less inspired by the populist projects of the Andes than by contemporary experiments with institutionalizing popular inputs in Ireland, Iceland, British Columbia, and, on the level of proposals, even in the United Kingdom and especially Scotland.[40] At their weakest, the interpretations of these projects imply *both* a hopeless search for a subject that incorporates the authentic or genuine "people" *and* an equally mistaken neglect of the problem of power, which is as necessary for establishing constitutions as legitimate authority is. At their most convincing, the projects and their interpreters seek to pluralize the legitimation sources of constitutional authority, by including channels rooted in civil society in addition to the role of actors of the established political systems. While this second type of interpretation comes close to what I mean by the post sovereign paradigm, the likely oscillation between the two interpretations is due to assumptions drawn from the populist source of the paradox of constitutionalism. It is very difficult in other words to give up unitary visions of "we the people."

[38] In a contextually surprising twist, Möllers refers to previous bouts with (constitutional?) populism as the darker side of German constitutional history: ibid. 104. Thus he needs to construct yet a new concept, namely that of "a constructive form of constitutional populism" (ibid. 100).

[39] J. Colón-Ríos, *Weak Constitutionalism* vol. 1. (London: Routledge 2012)—"weak" because of the ever presence of a superior popular constituent power. Carrozza, in "Constitutionalism's Post-Modern Opening," uses the concept of "weak constitutionalism" in a partially different sense, with globalization and courts being responsible for the weakening of the two-track structure.

[40] cf. Silvia Suteu, "Constitutional Conventions in the Digital Era: Lessons from Iceland and Ireland" (2015) 38 *Boston College International & Comparative Law Review* 251; Z. Elkins, T. Ginsburg, and J. Melton, *A Review of Iceland's Draft Constitution* http://comparativeconstitutionsproject.org/wp-content/uploads/CCP-Iceland-Report.pdf accessed August 31, 2015.

Fortunately, there is an alternative. A reflexive appropriation of the experience of the several cases of post sovereign constitution making can be of great help in alleviating the stress on democratic participation from its populist burden.

The last sentence describes my project. In the chapters below, I will argue on prudential bases first that the method of constitution making does matter, and second that in particular what matters is the type of legitimacy and the mechanisms of learning a given method can generate. I will also argue that while models are not in themselves decisive, and in any case seem to be path determined, it is nevertheless of great importance that there is a new paradigm of constitution making, beyond the antinomies of revolution and reform as well as populism and liberalism, one that without forgetting the issue of power generates more legitimacy for constitution makers and their product than other historical paradigms. I will maintain not only that even in the midst of contemporary revolutions and comprehensive reform attempts it is possible to learn from post revolution, but also that because of the globalization of constitutional ideas its principles of legitimacy are already present even where the paths do not allow or require the paradigm to be adopted.

I call this new method the post sovereign, post revolutionary, round-table-led, and multi-stage paradigm of constitution making. I believe that this paradigm is able to overcome the paradox of constitutionalism in both of the senses introduced here. It is able to rely on normative rules that help construct the actors and justify their action in the period of constitution making without their being under either the old or the new constitution. And, while the constituent power implied by the paradigm survives as part of the new regime, this survival does not in itself represent a threat to constitutionalism. All this is possible because of a new though not unanticipated conception of the constituent power that has emerged, to use an expression of Frank Michelman: one always under law. In other words the constituent power survives under constitutions but as a post sovereign, pluralistic, always limited power whose authority is due to both its legitimacy and, even during legal breaks, its legality.

II THE POST SOVEREIGN PARADIGM

I use four related terms above to describe the new paradigm of constitution making. I call it "post sovereign," to focus on the key theoretical issue of the exclusion of any single agency, institution, or individual that claims to embody the sovereign power and authority of "the constituent people." But I also refer to it as "post revolutionary," to recognize that radical changes are accomplished beyond the old antinomy of reform or revolution. Focusing on the central institution of the paradigm, I speak of round-table led constitution making. Finally, concentrating on the process and the key role of interim constitutions, I also use the adjectives "two" or "multi-stage." Each of these terms highlights a different feature of the paradigm.

I consider the new method the most important alternative to populist ideas of the constituent power, and of the process of constitution making. The origins of the latter can be traced back to the English, American, and French Revolutions, and they are still dominant in many regions of the world. Chapter 6 of this volume presents my objections to populism as it pertains to constitution making: I reconstruct that approach as a political theology with authoritarian implications. More positively, the purpose of the bulk of the book is to focus on the gains of the new paradigm in terms of legitimacy and learning. As for *legitimacy*, I argue that unlike revolutionary and reformist projects of constitution making, the post sovereign process reflexively thematizes its own legitimacy problems and seeks to mobilize pluralistic forms of justification relying on multiple values: plurality, inclusion, publicity, fairness, compromise, generosity, and legality—including even the application of constitutionalism to the very process of originating constitutions.

As for *learning*, I see this occurring on three levels. First, the new paradigm incorporates aspects of other methods pioneered in the democratic tradition of constitution making, while consciously abandoning the populist features that have had repeatedly negative consequences. The paradigm inherits from revolution the stress on the importance and the enhanced legitimation requirements of new foundations or re-foundations of polities. From reiterated reform, the new paradigm has learned the importance of the expansion of the time of the constitution-making process, even if, more critically, the need for temporal closure has evolved as a differentiating feature with respect to open-ended process. Second, learning is involved as the method developed through several country experiences. In particular, the mechanism of the round table itself, though absent in Spain, was added in Poland, and detailed rules for final constitution making not yet there in the Hungarian case were incorporated in South Africa, addressing thereby the dangers of an entirely open-ended, multi-stage process. Third, the multi-stage aspect incorporates learning within the method itself. Specifically, operating under an interim constitution allows experimentation with forms that could still be discarded or replaced. The transitional use of consociational devices is a case in point, allowing power sharing at times of extreme vulnerability without freezing a form that could later become extremely rigid and burdensome. Indeed the previously under-studied aspect of time dimension in constitution making is a central concern and feature of the new model.

In spite of its great advantages, I have already come to recognize the path-determined aspects of post sovereign constitution making in my previous book on Iraq (*Constitution Making Under Occupation*.) Upon further reflection, first on the case of Turkey (Chapter 5), and later in comparing Egypt and Tunisia, I have nevertheless come to the conclusion that aspects of the post revolutionary, post reformist model are applicable also in revolutions, as well as under comprehensive reform attempts. This book explains why. In analyzing the early successes of the model, one might try to focus on the legitimating principles that could be effectively utilized under different settings. Or one might examine the role of structural elements that could be partially taken over from the new paradigm. I have realized, however, when considering the cases of Turkey and Egypt, that both under reform and in revolutions there would likely be a veritable "horse race" between paradigms, one in which the older models of sovereign constitution making would have the advantage, and where the presence of elements of the new may play a destabilizing rather than a constructive role.

This horse race between paradigms is also present in the classical round table countries, though here at least the post sovereign version has the initial advantage. I demonstrate this with the case of Hungary, where most liberal democratic observers admit that the constitution-making process has taken a very negative turn. From the outset, projects of constitutional reform as well as revolution were present in Hungary, and did not disappear after quite successful round table negotiations and the crafting of a substantively viable, liberal democratic interim constitution. Revolutionaries on the political right depicted that process from 1989 on as a betrayal of genuine regime replacement and the preservation of the power positions of the beneficiaries of the old regime—the latter objection not without substance. At the same time, constitutional reformists, often on the left, both before and after the round table considered top down reform, whether initiated by the government or carried out by the powerful constitutional court, as adequate alternatives to the creation of a fully legitimate permanent constitution, one putting a definitive end to the constitution-making process. Unfortunately, in this case the very architects of the interim constitution opened the door to revolutionary and reformist alternatives by neglecting to enact rules and procedures for the legitimate ending of the process and for the making of a permanent constitution. An attempt to enact a permanent constitution under new consensual rules failed in 1996, among other reasons because the interim constitution represented a fall-back position that seemed to satisfy liberal democratic desiderata. Thus, after the initial drafting of the interim constitution in 1989, between 1990 and 2010 the Hungarian process can be characterized as piecemeal reform steered alternately (and in uneasy alternation) by the regular amending power and the Constitutional Court. In spite of its occasional hegemonic claims, that Court never put an end to the abuse of the amendment rule that any two-thirds of the single chamber parliament could control. That rule, as I have repeatedly maintained, was especially dangerous in the context of a highly disproportional electoral rule. When revolutionary rhetoric and reformist practice were successfully combined by the FIDESZ government, which was elected in 2010 with a two-thirds parliamentary majority, a new constitution was enacted in a process and with results in deep disharmony with the round table paradigm.

The purpose of my analysis is not only descriptive. It is rather to intervene in an intellectual, ideological, and political problem. As those involved in the relevant processes well know, constitution making and remaking pertains to the highest level of law making, the political design and allocation of power within a polity. How one understands the process, its structure, participants, and purpose matters a great deal and the stakes are high indeed.

III STRUCTURE OF THE BOOK

The book is divided into three sections. Part I focuses first on historical, then on theoretical issues that will help me locate the new paradigm, and explicate the need for it given the problems of its forerunners. The opening chapter examines the concept neglected by most students and advocates of the *pouvoir constituant*, namely constituent authority. After a critique of the neglect or misunderstanding of authority in Carl Schmitt and legal positivism as well as their attempted synthesis, the chapter goes on to try to reconstruct the concept through the legal philosophies of Maurice Hauriou and R. Carré de Malberg, and the political theory of Hannah Arendt. Regarding the history of constitutionalism, particular attention is paid to the earliest attempts in both France and America to move beyond the sovereign conception. In France this happened mostly on the level of theory, while in America it was the practice of "conventions" in the post 1780 version pioneered in Massachusetts, which anticipated elements of the post sovereign idea. I end the chapter by arguing that the post sovereign model makes an important contribution to solving the problem of authority. Chapter 2, "Constitutional Learning," proceeds to examine the introduction of the post sovereign paradigm in recent constitution-making experiments. In particular it stresses an innovative combination of forms of legitimation and learning that is generated within the new paradigm. Chapter 3, "Conventions, Constituent Assemblies, and Round Tables," attempts to systematize the contrast between convention, constituent assembly, and round-table led forms of constitution making. Here, I pay particular attention not only to constitution-making form, but also to normative theory, presenting the normative gains and possible losses involved in the adoption of the new paradigm. On balance I will strongly argue in its favor, both because of its synthetic nature preserving some of the institutional achievements of the older models, and especially the greater richness of its normative content.

Part II of the volume turns to cases. The focus on Hungary (Chapter 4) is easy to justify, and not only because it is here that I have the requisite experience and language knowledge to rely on some directly empirical presentation. Hungary is a classical round table country, with an interim constitution, and thus represents a good case for testing the new paradigm and its main features. But it also provides, unfortunately, a much-needed lesson that a structurally open-ended process can begin democratically and end up with a much more authoritarian outcome. Here comparisons with Poland, Bulgaria, and South Africa will help to make the argument, since each of these countries provided for the process of making a permanent constitution on the interim constitutional level. The bulk of the chapter focuses on what went wrong in Hungary, and the rest attempts a reconstruction of FIDESZ's illegitimate reform, including the major challenge it faced: the temporary revival of the conflict between government and Constitutional Court.

I should also explain the choice of Turkey for this volume (Chapter 5). It is a test case for the possible application of my conception to a country undergoing a long-term reform process. Moreover, Turkey is eminently suitable for purposes of comparison with Hungary. Interestingly, in both countries the democratic order is currently under analogous threat. But there is more they have in common: both formally inherited an authoritarian constitution as the source of serious legitimation and even structural problems, and both have undergone incremental constitutional change, Turkey since 1987, and Hungary in 1988–89 and again after 1989. They both demonstrate the hazards of an open-ended process, in which there has been insufficient attention paid to dealing with time in a reflexive and planned manner. In both, there was a horse race between government and constitutional court, which, in contrast to India, was won by the political branches.

Turkey is a country of long-term, incremental, reiterated reform that nevertheless incorporated the consensual practice of the post sovereign model in the 1990s. Here too the failure to establish a timetable for the process, along with incentives and sanctions, has exerted a price even if in distinction to Hungary an authoritarian last stage based on majority imposition has also not been formally accomplished. Not yet, I should add, for two reasons. First, the danger persists in the context of a highly disproportional electoral rule that could make a simple majority—or even a minority—into a constitution-making majority, something that the previous Turkish government desperately sought to accomplish in the elections of 2015, though for the moment in vain. Behind the desire to control a constituent majority similar to that of FIDESZ lies a different, if scarcely disguised, project of replacing parliamentarism with a hyper-presidentialist form. Second, the case also shows that even if a constitution-making majority is not attained by the governing party, it seems very possible to rely on the partially reformed practices and institutions inherited from the original imposed constitution of 1982, along with plebiscitary potential of the new position of a popularly elected presidency for the same end. Disturbing steps have already been taken toward the informal establishment of a semi-authoritarian system resembling in many areas the practice of the earlier military-imposed regimes, if now in an Islamist rather than an aggressive secularist form. The recent turn to the foreign policy option of destructive warfare, after an unsuccessful parliamentary election, shows the potential of combining the two factors, inherited and plebiscitary authoritarian patterns.

Part III of the book turns to the political stakes of paradigms of constitution making. It presents a critical theory of the contemporary populist challenge, the most important and seductive alternative to my approach. Populist projects of constitution making were of course strong in both Colombia and Venezuela, but led to different processes with different outcomes. Less obviously, the recent constitutional developments of Hungary and Turkey demonstrate the range of populist politics well beyond Latin America. Thus, the last chapter implicitly tries to answer the obvious question: "How do they get away with it?" In it I focus on a theoretical reconstruction of populism, through a critique of one of its most important exponents, and go on to consider one theory of populist constitution making, drawing on the political theological version of Carl Schmitt developed in the 1920s.

The book deals with constitutional theory as well as practice, with history of the past as well as the history of the present. I firmly believe that in the countries discussed, and in many places elsewhere, the options presented and criticized here remain on the agenda. Though I stress the need for completion with respect to the new paradigm, no constituent process can or should ever be considered entirely finalized. Even in cases where I stress the success of the process, as in South Africa, the dangers otherwise depicted here remain present, though in different guises. While the paradigm I present has built-in learning processes—which, aside from generating a plurality, forms of legitimacy are its great advantage—as we have seen in Hungary there is no guarantee that what has been learned cannot be unlearned. Conversely, however, even in settings not conducive to internal learning, such as radical revolutions, and top-down reform processes, it is possible to consciously appropriate many elements and resources from the new paradigm. This book tries to show that such cross-paradigm learning is possible in the case of long drawn-out reform processes. A subsequent volume will attempt to show the same in the more difficult contexts of radical revolutions. There, focusing on issues of time and sequence, and relying on a comparison between Tunisia and Egypt, will allow me to analyze some of the preconditions under which the lessons learned from the new method could be productively utilized even in revolutions.[41] In analyzing the prospects of both reform and revolution, I am guided by the idea that in some small but significant measure political freedom in the future will depend on constitutional learning.

[41] See A. Arato and E.H. Tombus, "Learning from Success, Learning from Failure: South Africa, Hungary, Turkey and Egypt" (2013) 39 *Philosophy and Social Criticism* 4; A. Arato, "Review of Books on Iraq by Zaid al Ali and Haider Hamoudi" (2014) 12 *International Journal of Constitutional Law* 3; A. Arato "Time and Sequence in Changes of Constitutional Regimes" http://www.iconnectblog.com/2014/06/time-and-sequence-in-changes-of-constitutional-regimes/ accessed August 31, 2015.

PART I

HISTORY AND THEORY

1

Toward a Theory of Constituent Authority

I INTRODUCTION

In current discussions about constituent power one sentence is often repeated, with only slight variation: "the event of the foundation of an order is not part of the founded order" or "the act that gives rise to a legal order is not itself part of that order."[1] If this means that the legal order to be established cannot supply binding rules for the process of its own creation, the sentence is trivially or even tautologically true, and one needs no reference to medieval political theology, Bodin, Rousseau, Heidegger, Schmitt, or Kelsen, or for that matter post structuralist philosophy, to justify it. The most famous statement remains that of Sieyès, who put the nation, as the *pouvoir constituant* "in the state of nature," and hence not just free of the normative order to be established, but arguably subject to no rules or norms of any kind.[2] This idea, contradicted by another definition of nation by an antinomic Sieyès,[3] re-affirmed by Carl Schmitt, and then

[1] See H. Lindahl, "Sovereignty and Representation in the European Union" in N. Walker (ed.), *Sovereignty in Transition* (Oxford: Hart, 2003, 2006) 103–4, where the same idea is translated as "not mandated" and even as "irreducible groundlessness." See also H. Lindahl, "Constituent Power and Reflexive Identity: Towards an Ontology of Collective Selfhood" in M. Loughlin and N. Walker (eds), *The Paradox of Constitutionalism* (Oxford: Oxford University Press, 2007) 17. That is apparently accepted by N. Walker in "Post-Constituent Constitutionalism? The Case of the European Union" in the latter volume. I too once made the same point, namely that where there is no democracy one cannot begin democratically, but I did not mean one cannot begin legitimately: A. Arato, "Forms of Constitution Making and Theories of Democracy" in A. Arato, *Civil Society, Constitution, and Legitimacy* (Lanham, MD: Rowman, 2000).

[2] It is, however, an equally plausible interpretation that Sieyès considered natural rights to bind even the constituent power. See P. Bastid, *Sieyès et sa pensée* (Paris: Hachette, 1939), which consistently stresses a liberal and even Lockeian interpretation of Sieyès. Nevertheless, the most important interpretations of his work have stressed the notion of absence of any limitation. See C. Schmitt, *Verfassungslehre* (Berlin: Duncker & Humblot, 1928) and H. Arendt, *On Revolution* (New York: Viking, 1965).

[3] "What is a Nation? It is a body of associates living under a *common* law, represented by the same *legislature*," writes Sieyès in his pamphlet, *What is the Third Estate?* See M. Sonnenscher (ed.), *Political Writings* (Indianapolis, IN: Hackett, 2003) 97. Claude Klein in *Théorie et pratique du pouvoir constituant* (Paris: PUF, 1996) 16–17 presents Sieyès as antinomic, but in my view sees the antinomy not quite in the right place, between an unlimited constituent power and a constrained amendment rule. The amendment rule Klein has in mind, that of the Constitution of 1791, was adopted against Sieyès' efforts that involved calling a new convention, in a rather Jeffersonian style, whenever constitutional conflicts required it. This view was presented in his essay on the royal veto, "Dire sur le véto royale" in R. Zapieri (ed.), *Ecrits politiques* I (Glasgow: Gordon and Breach, 1985) and the

seriously questioned by Hannah Arendt, also provides a necessary warning: if not yet being under the new legal order (or no longer being under the old one) is supposed to mean that a beginning cannot therefore take place governed by rules or any other normative standards at all, then the idea is false, and the following attempt to derive a theory of constituent *authority* from the best theories of constituent power will try to show how we might transcend it.[4]

But let me jump ahead for the moment, way ahead. A more obvious refutation, to which I will dedicate some considerable space in this book, lies in recent history. To begin with, under liberal democratic political orders, entirely new legal orders can be made under the constitutional rules of the existing system. Though exceptional in the eighteenth century, this happened in some American states[5] (on the Federal level the rules of change were violated), and today it has become commonplace. It may seem right to say that Sweden before 1974 (when a new constitution was made under the existing rules) and after remains under the same legal order, but it would be the height of Kelsenian doctrinaire thinking[6] to suggest that a legal transformation of authoritarian or dual states[7] into constitutional democracies would leave in place the same system. That system replacement occurred within legality and legal continuity is obviously true in the cases of regime change or coordinated transition, using the terms of Janos Kis,[8] where the amendment rules of Communist and, later, apartheid regimes were used to abolish the old political order and establish the new one, which in South Africa also included the creation of new amendment rules, hence resulting in "the revision of the revision."

If cases of legal continuity could still be used, in a very doctrinaire way, to argue that they indicate no changes of legal orders, this is not possible where there is a legal break, as in the case of the move from the American confederation to a federation. As some of the strongest advocates of an interpretation stressing illegality have come to realize, however, violation of some rules need

debate was fully reconstructed by A. Esmein already in his seminal *Éléments de droit constitutionnel français et comparé* (first published 1903, Paris: Pantheon-Assas, 2001) 572–3; as well as E. Zweig *Die Lehre von Pouvoir Constituant* (Tübingen: J. C. B. Mohr, 1909) 277–309 and K. Loewenstein, *Volk und Parliament* (first published 1922, Munich: Scientia, 1964) Chapter 4 and especially 304. Klein attributes the same perception of the antinomy or mystery of Sieyès to Olivier Beaud, but regarding the latter's *La puissance de l'état* (Paris: PUF, 1994) 228–9 he is clearly mistaken.

[4] A non-antinomic or sovereigntist Sieyès is still insisted on by Lucian Jaume in his recent fine essay "The Constituent Power in France: The French Revolution and *Consequences*" in Laughlin and Walker, *Paradox of Constitutionalism*.

[5] Jefferson's *Notes on Virginia* were directed against one such attempt. Note that he did not object to legal continuity, but only to an ordinary assembly legislating constitutional rules. On all this see R.R. Palmer, *The Age of the Democratic Revolutions* vol. I. (Princeton, NJ: Princeton University Press, 1959); and G. Wood, *The Creation of the American Republic* (Chapel Hill, NC: University of North Carolina Press, 1969).

[6] For two critiques see my "Revolution, Restoration and Legitimation" in Arato, *Civil Society, Constitution and Legitimacy*; and, even better, J. Kis, "Between Reform and Revolution: Three Hypotheses about the Nature of Regime Change" (January 1995) 1 *Constellations* 3 and "Between Reform and Revolution" (Spring 1998) 12 *East European Politics and Societies* 2 300–83.

[7] See E. Fraenkel, *The Dual State* (Oxford: Oxford University Press, 1941).

[8] Ibid.

not have meant and did not mean violation of all legal rules, or a legal vacuum, and above all did not mean an absence of political legitimacy that the American framers both inherited and were capable of generating. As a result Bruce Ackerman goes so far as to suggest that in the American case *instead of* constituent power, one should speak about constituent authority.[9] As this chapter will argue, given the irreducible role of political power in constitution making, that move would be a half a step too far away from an ethically salutary political realism. Constitutions can never be and never have been established without or in a vacuum of (state) power. Thus, I would rather speak of constituent power *and* authority.[10] Moreover, Ackerman's theory is divided against itself, reflecting the antinomies of the framers in both America and France. On the one side, he has indeed recovered a concept of constitutional authority, one that depends on elements of legal continuity, a plurality of sources of legitimacy and an absent sovereign. On the other side, he still clings to a strong notion of embodied popular sovereignty, at least in the constituent process, one that implies a fundamental legal rupture. As Hannah Arendt realized, this can easily imply the derivation of "power" and "authority" from the same ultimate source.

Against Arendt, who distributed its two poles between the two sides of the Atlantic, I would argue that this antinomy lies deep in the political theory and practice of *both* the American and French framers. In America, the sovereign conception appeared mostly in theory, and the post sovereign version mainly in the practice. Conversely, in France, post sovereign reflection on the American pattern was mainly theoretical, in intellectual tension with more dominant theories insisting on embodied forms of popular sovereignty, while the practice on the whole reflected ideologies linked to the latter conception. Elsewhere, I will attempt to "liberate" the post sovereign dimension through immanent criticism of both American and French traditions. Here I would like to do the same for the concept of constitutional authority.[11] I hope to make the reader conscious of the destructive potential inherent in reductionist treatments of authority, present on both sides of the Atlantic, if in very different forms and at very different times: constitutional change without authority (or reduction of legitimacy to power) and a frozen constitutionalism (or reduction of legitimacy to legality.) I believe that a rediscovery of the problem of constituent authority could lead to a form of constitutionalism that would resemble parts of the early (1780–88) American practice, one that relied on power, legitimate authority as well as (elements of)

[9] See B. Ackerman, *We the People. Transformations* (Cambridge, MA: Harvard University Press, 1998) vol. II, 11. Ackerman has anticipated the contrast of constituent power and constituent authority. I think the stress is new in his second (1998) volume, as against his more Schmittian approach in the first one (1991). See also R. Kay, "Constituent Authority" (2011) 59 *AJCL* 1, 715, 743–55. Kay's views are very different than mine, because of his insistence on legal rupture, and the rigid differentiation of constituent and constituted powers.

[10] One consequence for Ackerman is an under-emphasis on the role of power in constitutional change, especially obvious in his treatment of the U.S. Civil War, where he insists a little too strongly that the guns had little to do with constitutional change.

[11] On all this see my forthcoming book, A. Arato, *The Adventures of the Constituent Power* (Cambridge University Press, 2016).

legality. More importantly, such a constitutionalism could hopefully provide an adequate theory for the new paradigm of constitution making available from the 1970s, pioneered in Spain, practiced in Central Europe and perfected in South Africa. Without adequate theory or theoretical self-reflection, many of these experiments are open to destructive challenges that can lead, if successful, to more authoritarian polities. The current constitutional development in Hungary indicates what the dangers are, as yet without adequate response.[12]

Here, I will engage in theoretical reflection on the relation of constituent power and authority. The tradition of theorizing that most clearly began to reflect on the problem of the reduction of authority I have in mind was European. Hannah Arendt's argument is the best known, but even before her, French public law of the early twentieth century thematized and attempted to transcend the deformations caused by sovereignty in the constituent process. Most certainly, it was the destructive course of the French Revolution in the constitutional dimension that led to these critiques. Many of these theorists, perhaps surprisingly, shared Arendt's appreciation of the American Revolution. However, unlike her, they fortunately believed that its normative lessons for a theory of the constituent power could be applied more universally, beyond the original exceptional conditions.

I would like to show that we should be able to speak of authority and power even in the hardest cases, of which the American Revolution is not one. By that I mean cases of revolution (not revolutionary reform, regime change, or coordinated transition[13]) when both inherited legitimacy and legality are broken, as in the French as opposed to the American Revolution. In the latter, only a part of legitimacy, the imperial, was replaced by those of independent states, entities that retained their own legitimate institutions and practices.[14] What I will try to show is that a strong case can be made that, even in radical revolutions, the problem of authority, or at least that of the legitimate creation of the new, cannot be entirely suppressed. To be sure, radical revolutions have rarely shown[15] that the beginning can be saved, in Arendt's words, from its own arbitrariness—that is from the force of dictating violence.[16] What the great revolutions in the tradition of the French have failed to achieve has been more attainable in cases of regime change and radical reform. But since revolution remains an important fact of the modern world, it remains worth asking whether their legitimacy problems can be solved, and if so how. Thus, my aim here is to move the concept of constitutional authority from the American exceptionalist limits of the

[12] See Chapter 4.

[13] See Kis, "Between Reform and Revolution: Three Hypotheses" and Kis, "Between Reform and Revolution"; see also my "Conventions, Constituent Assemblies and Round Tables" (2012) 1 *Global Constitutionalism* 1 as well as chapter 3, below.

[14] See A. Buchanan, *Secession* (Boulder, CO: Westview, 1991) 49, 69, where the origins of the United States are depicted as secession, rather than revolution.

[15] One possible exception is the Tunisian Revolution of 2011 and after.

[16] Arendt, *On Revolution* 212–13.

analysis of Arendt's and even Ackerman's to a place where it can become part of a more general theory of constituent "power."[17]

II POWER "OR" AUTHORITY

I begin with a German sentence hard to translate into English:

> *Verfassunggebende Gewalt ist der politische Wille, dessen Macht oder Autorität imstande ist, die konkrete Gesamtentscheidung über Art und Form der eigenen politischen Existenz zu treffen, also die Existenz der politischen Einheit im Ganzen zu bestimmen.*[18]

This is the second of three texts in *Verfassungslehre* where Carl Schmitt recognized the role of authority in the creation of constitutions, though the grammatical form "power *or* authority" seems to indicate that the constituent power (is a will that) can exert itself and accomplish its mission through *either* of these two "channels."[19] The important choice we are given by Schmitt is signified by the word "or." Similarly, earlier in his work, but perhaps more confusingly, *verfassunggebende Gewalt*, that is, the *pouvoir constituant*, was even identified as *Macht oder Autorität*, again as a choice. However, a footnote indicating Schmitt's precise knowledge of the Roman distinction between *potestas* and *auctoritas* says the contrary: "Both power and authority are alive and active next to one another in every state"[20] and we know that the constituent power presupposes for Schmitt a state or a political entity that gives itself "Art und Form" through a constitution.[21] However, as it turns out Schmitt sometimes does treat this matter as a question of choice, and authority, seemingly reduced to a kind of atavism,

[17] Such an effort was apparently begun but then abruptly discontinued by E.-W. Böckenförde, "Die verfassunggebende Gewalt des Volkes – Ein Grenzbegriff des Verfassungsrechts" in *Staat, Verfassung, Demokratie* (Frankfurt: Suhrkamp, 1991). After indicating that the concept of the constituent power should be understood in terms of legitimacy rather than decision (in my view: correct), as a *politische Größe* (political entity or magnitude) rather than retroactive legal imputation (also correct) he then proceeds, on the evidence of constitutional preambles no less, to resurrect the whole Schmittian conceptual mythology concerning the constituent power of the people along with all its organizational forms including the plebescitary Bonapartist one.

[18] Schmitt, *Verfassungslehre* 75–6. My emphasis is on the first phrase, which has three terms *Gewalt, Macht*, and *Autorität* for which the English has only two: power and authority, since evidently the author, in the usage of the German *Staatslehre* does not mean to use *Gewalt* in the sense of force or violence. The three French terms, *puissance* for *Gewalt*, pouvoir for *Macht* and *autorité* as established by translators of Jellinek or by Carré de Malberg would seem to serve better here, accept for the fact that *verfassunggebende Gewalt* is itself a translation of *pouvoir constituant* that Schmitt still preferred to use directly in the French in *Die Diktatur*, 2nd edn. (first published 1923, Berlin: Duncker & Humblot, 1928).

[19] Through a curious linguistic inversion characteristic of the language of the German *Staatslehre* (state theory or public law), *Macht* means raw power here, and *Gewalt* contains the possibility, obviously, also of legitimate use of force. For reasons unknown to me since I am not German and have not studied law in Germany, Böckenförde in "Die verfassunggebende Gewalt des Volkes" says "Kraft und Autorität." (94) Does that mean legitimacy is included in *Kraft*, as against *Macht*? I need help, what is more legitimate, *kräftig* or *mächtig*, or conversely, authoritative, *Gewalt, Kraft*, or *Macht*?

[20] Schmitt, *Verfassungslehre* 75.

[21] For example, ibid. 21–2; 78–9. E.-W. Böckenförde, "Der Begriff des Politischen als Schlüssel zum staatsrechtlichen Werk Carl Schmitts" in E.-W. Böckenförde, *Recht, Staat, Freiheit* (Frankfurt: Suhrkamp, 1991, 2006) 351–2.

receiving only a minor role in the development of his concept of the constituent power. Yet there are key moments when it returns, and when Schmitt then faces the prospect of turning his abstract theory into a political program, in particular in 1932 in the pamphlet *Legalität und Legitimität*.[22] What I would like to show here is that Schmitt's theory of the constituent power, still the major reference point for many serious students of this topic,[23] has two diverging positions on the question of authority, neither in my view attractive.

The surprise appearance of the concept of authority in *Legalität und Legitimität* is anticipated by both presences and absences in Schmitt's more theoretical work, *Verfassungslehre*. In the latter, explicitly, authority reappears for one last time in Schmitt's treatment of the derived, unstable, and inconsistent form of the constituent power, the monarchical one. Suddenly, we hear of the power *and* (rather than *or*) the authority of the *verfassunggebende Gewalt*[24] that must be recognized for a constitution to be *legitimate*, both juxtaposed to the legality of the procedures of its making that is necessarily absent. For a moment then it looked as if the legitimacy of the constitution depended on its origins in both power and authority. In fact, we still seem to be given a choice, this time in concrete historical-political terms: there are according to Schmitt *two types of legitimacy*, a democratic one based on power (itself linked to popular sovereignty or *maiestas populi*) and a dynastic one based on authority defined as "prestige based on continuity" as "tradition and persistence," in other words as *traditional legitimacy*.

The cursory presentation of the authority of the monarch is nevertheless important and supplies some important clues. Crucially, authority and power not only have different foundations, but are applied differently. Authority can authorize, mere power cannot. The monarch as constituent power, in spite of the self-contradictions involved in a constituted dynasty having this role, has one obvious advantage: he or she can clearly articulate a will and is capable of making commands.[25] The monarch has *both* the (state) power and the (politico-religious) authority to enact a constitution. The contradiction that Schmitt sees is that, while the authority in the monarch's case can genuinely authorize, this happens to be pre-constituted. Thus the monarch (or the dynasty) is a *constitué* that acts as a *constituant*. The contradiction may be inherent in having brought attention to authority, as well as power, in the first place in the very definition of the *verfassunggebende Gewalt*. It could be removed in two ways. One is by relativizing the differentiation between *constituant* and *constitué*, an option Schmitt will staunchly reject. The other is by reducing the constituent authority of the

[22] Berlin: Duncker & Humblot, 1932.

[23] See, for example, J. Colón Rios, *Weak Constitutionalism* (London: Routledge, 2012); A. Kalyvas, "Popular Sovereignty, Democracy and the Constituent Power" (2005) 12 *Constellations* 2, and even Lindahl, "Constituent Power and Reflexive Identity."

[24] Schmitt, *Verfassungslehre* 87.

[25] Ibid. 76, 82.

monarch to a historical, and post revolutionary atavism, and banishing the concept of authority from the theory of the modern *verfassunggebende Gewalt*. It is the latter option that seems to be chosen by *Verfassungslehre*, but this leaves the shadow of an absent authority over the work.

The point is crucial, because Schmitt defines constitution making, at least under a popular *pouvoir constituant*, as *sovereign* dictatorship;[26] and all dictatorship in his theory involves by definition a commission given to an agent (here: an assembly or a man) having all the requisite power to accomplish the goals (producing a constitution) of the commissioning subject. We do not know how this can happen without an authorizing subject that has either a physical or legal existence, or with a subject like Schmitt's "people" that is said to be formless, amorphous, and whose will can be and is even likely to be unclear and systematically hindered.[27] He goes on to say that the expressions of the will of the people can be "easy to mistake, misinterpret or falsify," even if he also says that "even the silent agreement of the people is always possible and easy to recognize."[28] It is even more difficult to think of a subject as an "author," over whom its supposed agent exercises the very dictatorship that is supposed to be an instrument of the subject.[29] Schmitt's "people" cannot advise, deliberate, discuss, rule, administer, norm, nor even participate in Renan's famous daily plebiscite of the self-constitution and re-constitution of the nation. It cannot even choose the questions for organized referenda to which a yes/no answer can indeed be given.[30] Finally, we do not know how a subject such as the people can be identified and express itself without procedures[31] that define the decisional outcome as legitimate even if not legal.[32] This is so indeed for the referenda or plebiscites that Schmitt considers possible, but apparently not in any way preferable to other forms of mass (or tacit!) acclamation.

Nevertheless, Schmitt seems to be concerned about avoiding an interpretation of the constituent power as merely a question of raw power.[33] Even with

[26] The monarch is sovereign, and thus his constituent power does not need a temporary sovereignty, a sovereign dictatorship for its operation. As Schmitt explained in *Die Diktatur* (134, 140) the nature of popular sovereignty is such that it requires a "commissioner" to actually exercise sovereignty, thus the sovereign dictatorship.

[27] Schmitt, *Die Diktatur* 6th edn. 140; 141–3.

[28] Schmitt, *Verfassungslehre* 83, 91.

[29] Schmitt, *Die Diktatur* 6th edn. XIX.

[30] Schmitt, *Legalität und Legitimität* 86.

[31] This point is clearly sensed even by a left Schmittian such as Böckenförde, who seems to think that the priority of the state over constitution solves it. See "Begriff und Probleme des Verfassunssataates" in *Staat, Nation, Europa* (Frankfurt: Suhrkamp, 1999) 137. As far as Schmitt was concerned, the insistence that no prior procedures or meta-procedures can define democratic constitution making is repeated (*Verfassungslehre* 82, 84, 90–1), even if there are occasional procedural criticisms of some historical efforts (80), for example 1789–91, turning "aristocratic" by adopting representation and eschewing a referendum.

[32] See my essay, A. Arato, "Good-bye to Dictatorships?" (2000) 67 *Social Research* 925–55. One answer that Schmitt gives is that the constituent power of the people can serve this purpose because of its very formlessness. It thus cannot bind the dictator like an absolute monarch could, and yet, because of its earthly quality does not involve the impossible distance of a divine creative power. This claim perhaps seeks to open the door to a theory of (sociological) legitimation that is not (legal) authorization. Schmitt, *Die Diktatur* 6th edn. 134–5.

[33] "bloße Machtfrage": Schmitt, *Die Diktatur* 6th edn. 134.

respect to legality, he is constrained to argue that though dictatorship ignores law, it is in order to defend, actualize, or establish law. Moreover, the constituent power as the foundation for dictatorship presupposes a minimal constitution, one that, even if it is not constituted constitutionally, is nevertheless a basis for some kind of order, for example, a democratic order in the case of a democratic constituent power.[34] Only it is not clear if this presupposition has any implication for the constitution of a (provisional) government by the agent of the constituent power, who in Schmitt's depiction is rather free to create any type of governing mechanism, as long as the initial foundation is preserved.[35]

Schmitt identifies the minimal constitution of the constituent power as the foundation of the legitimacy of constitutions, one that distinguishes the basic law from a merely factually enforced order.[36] Having elsewhere[37] freed the concept of legitimacy from its positivist identification with legality, or even with Weber's legal rational legitimacy, there was apparently still the requirement to ground the normative validity of constitutions, even in the context of legal breaks. Thus the emphatic rejection of the grounding of the new constitution in the legality of its predecessor need not have meant according to him that it was grounded in nothing but factual power. And indeed, the sovereign dictator that dictates to the entity that supposedly commissions it nevertheless does not cease to legitimate itself and its actions by reference to that entity, the sovereign people.[38] We have apparently moved from authority to the wider concept of legitimacy.[39] According to Schmitt, repeatedly, in the modern age legitimacy can only be a democratic one.[40] But how does that legitimation supposedly work?

Schmitt's theory has been recently reinterpreted as a theory of democratic legitimacy, and I will concede that this is a possible interpretation of his abstract consideration of the constituent power and the nature of the modern constitution in *Verfassungslehre*. The problem with this side of his thought would be the reduction of the problem of democratic authority to popular plebiscitary power. But there is a less reductionist, but more authoritarian other side, actually grounded in *Verfassungslehre*,[41] even if in sections that are under the *constituted* powers. In line with the earlier footnote on Roman concepts of *auctoritas* and *potestas*, Schmitt here insists on two fundamental principles, "identity" and "representation," whose combinations yield the various basic forms of the state: democracy, aristocracy, and monarchy. Regarding constituted government at least, he insists that *identity*, the democratic principle (understood as that of

[34] Ibid. XVIII, 146. [35] Schmitt, *Verfassungslehre* 94–5. [36] Ibid. 87ff.

[37] Admittedly later (1932): Schmitt, *Legalität und Legitimität* especially Introduction 10–14; but the Weberian distinction seems implicit all along.

[38] Schmitt, *Die Diktatur* 6th edn. XIX; Schmitt, *Verfassungslehre* 23ff and *passim*. For those who think sovereign dictatorship in the name of the people is no longer central in *Verfassungslehre*, see 59–60ff.

[39] More on this in my *Adventures of the Constituent Power*.

[40] C. Schmitt, *The Crisis of Parliamentary Democracy* (Cambridge, MA: MIT, 1985) 22ff; C. Schmitt, *Political Theology* (Chicago: University of Chicago, 1985) 51.

[41] Schmitt, *Verfassungslehre* 204ff; 208ff.

collective *power*) is defined as the immediate presence of a people that is capable of action because of its high level of homogeneity, firm natural boundaries, or whatever other reason, but is impossible to find in a pure form. It always must be complemented by representation, evidently the principle of authority, where an individual or group symbolically and personally embody the absent people in their unity and totality. As he says very clearly and, as often, entirely bluntly: "In every state there must be individuals who are able to say: 'L'état c'est nous.'"[42] For Schmitt, even direct democracy involves representation, of the absent by the present, of the young by the mature, or even the whole person by the citizen capacity. Moreover, in his Hobbesian model of representation, the representative has absolute authority to act in the name of the represented. The pure concepts of identity and representation point, however, to an ideal typical analysis of actual states of affairs. Existing state forms are said to be mixtures of identity and representation, as in that footnote where all states were said to involve both power and authority. Identity and representation are then the deeper level, from which power and authority are generated with the proviso that legitimacy can supposedly be based on either.

Here is where we get to the second option within Schmitt's theory of constituent power, at the level of its foundations. Given the fact that the constituent power presupposes the state in his theory, we have no reason whatsoever to assume that the dualistic conception should not apply to it as well. Indeed, Schmitt tells us specifically that the two relevant subjects of the constituent power, people and monarch, "are located between the two opposite principles" of identity and representation.[43] According to the logic of this argument, empirically neither can attain the pure form. The constituent power of the people means that the identity pole has become dominant, and it is obvious that where the constituent power of the monarch is relevant, the pole of representation is the key factor. But neither can exist alone, according to the logic of the analysis. Accordingly, he states that in his spectrum of possibilities, plebiscitary forms are defined as the most extreme of identity, as against representation.[44] This I think should be interpreted in terms of the line in *Political Theology* that defines popular sovereignty, or its subject as the instance(s) "that can *identify* [distinguished from actual identity in an essay on Parliamentarism!] themselves with the people without contradiction."[45] We are not directly told what contradiction (*Wiederspruch*) would mean here. Does it mean logical, factual, or political contradiction, with the latter requiring someone, or more likely more than one person, saying (*dictio*) something against (*contra*) the claim in a way that can practically refute it? But we have seen that even here, the asking of the question presupposes a representative, or trusted, or authoritative person or persons. Victory in a plebiscite is the operational definition then of non-contradictory

[42] Ibid. 206. [43] Ibid. 205. [44] Ibid. 207.

[45] See Schmitt, *Political Theology* 10; Schmitt, *Verfassungslehre* 205; and especially Schmitt, *The Crisis of Parliamentary Democracy* 15–17; 26–31, which makes Schmitt's view of democracy quite clear.

identification, where the proposal or candidate has not been successfully contradicted, or *wieder-gesprochen*. Yet neither the actor that has asked the question, nor the the candidate if there is one, is the same as the people. They are at least two different actors, and this means representation of one by the other. The acclamation means both identification and the acceptance of being represented by a trusted authority. It is hardly superfluous to stress that representation here is absolute representation[46] and the public status it requires is that of the so-called representative, that is, non discursive public sphere, where the symbols and insignia of power are exhibited to other public holders and the subjects of power.[47]

While Schmitt insists that representation and identity are always present, in all states and in all constituent processes, the pure types appear in very different mixtures that can be dominated by either one extreme or the other. It may be that the radicality of the constituent process pushes mere mixtures toward one of the extremes. Thus, on an abstract level he feels apparently justified in neglecting the side of representation (and in criticizing Sieyès for relying on it) when he develops the notion of the constituent power of the people. This in turn means a corresponding de-emphasis of authority and even legitimacy (in either a political-normative or sociological-empirical sense) in Schmitt's constitutional theory.[48] Accordingly, the commissioner of the constituent power exercising sovereign dictatorship not only cannot be legalized, but at least in one version of the argument, need not be authorized by (an entity having) any other form of legitimacy. There is to be sure such an entity, or rather imagined actor, the so-called subject or carrier (*Subjekt, Träger*) of the constituent power, and it can have two types of legitimacy: monarchical or democratic. But having this legitimacy again only means the minimal constitution, namely that a political entity that is to be given a constitution *exists*, and the subject (monarchical, democratic) *can* determine the "Art und Form" of this state, that is, give it a constitution. The act needs no justification beyond an actor's ability to accomplish the task, least of all a normative one.[49]

Two things should be well noted. First, though Schmitt refers to the proprietor of the constituent power as its subject or carrier, in his concrete depictions it is always a self-authorized agent, such as an assembly or a man, actually carrying out the act of constitution making in the name of the people. In his view, elections make little difference, and if anything, in this context, representation

[46] See H. Pitkin, *The Concept of Representation* (Los Angeles, CA: University of California, 1967) for this concept, which she calls the "authorization view of representation" and the contrast with other forms.

[47] Schmitt, *Verfassungslehre* 208–9. Also J. Habermas, *The Structural Transformation of the Public Sphere* (Cambridge, MA: MIT, 1989) and particularly Chapter 2 for the concept of the "representative" public.

[48] This is because in the end, he considers most forms of legitimacy other than legal and democratic to be merely historical and obsolete, and understands the latter form, democratic legitimacy, only in terms of a plebiscitary version the weak democratic credentials of which are apparent to him.

[49] Schmitt, *Verfassungslehre* 88–9.

only establishes an aristocratic gulf between people and representatives. Second, while his argument began by trying to distinguish legitimacy from a factual state of affairs, it ends by reducing it to exactly that. In fact, Schmitt concedes that he only spoke of legitimacy of a constitution and distinguished between monarchy and democracy for historical reasons, and that otherwise it would have been better to speak, apparently, of the constituent power as the self-justifying form of existence underlying the validity of the constitution.

That argument may carry weight with some in the case of democracy, democratic legitimacy, or a democratic form of existence. Only we do not know if even the democratic dimension of the model is democratic at all on the grounds that Schmitt offers. He provides us with several ideal types of constitution making, ones that apparently qualify for the label democratic legitimacy or form of existence. Two out of three are, however, severely deficient, even in his own presentation. The model of 1789–91 involved a self-authorization of the Estates General to speak in the name of the French people, whose democratic credentials Schmitt thinks would be mere legalism to contest[50] but whose turn to representation and avoidance of plebiscitary ratification he condemns as aristocratic. (He should have had it the other way around, perhaps, as did Sieyès, who defended representation but had qualms about the form of election.) Thus, in his scheme of ideal types involving identity and representation, 1789–91 moved too far toward the latter, and thus an aristocratic model. Schmitt sees as much more democratic the Bonapartist models that he himself describes as self-authorized (i.e. not authorized) with heavily constrained and manipulated referenda. On the other hand, two sets of convention models involving the election or delegation by elected officials of extraordinary assemblies, and the subsequent popular ratification of their product are not considered superior to either the deficient or the Bonapartist type, because of the way the makers of the constitution have been elected, selected, or authorized.[51] If they are superior at all, in Schmitt's general balance sheet, it is only to the one model without any subsequent popular ratification. Thus, and *most crucially, in the end, the mode of election and mode of drafting do not seem to matter.* All we are left with on a theoretical level is bland statements like "the people exercise their constituent power through any kind of recognizable expression of its common will."[52] Beyond this we are told only that the "natural form" of this exercise is the acclamation, or the yes/no declaration of the assembled multitude, which in modern states takes the form of "public opinion."[53] The conception is unclear, in that we do not know whether the emphasis is on diffuse acceptance, or formal plebiscites. Either way, nothing in this conception distinguishes between free and manipulated opinion or acclamation.

We are ready to sum up the present analysis of Schmitt. After having raised the problem of constitutional authority, ultimately on the bases of his theory of identity and representation, he seems to have had two theoretical options. He

[50] Ibid. 82, 87. [51] Ibid. 85–7. [52] Ibid. 82. [53] Ibid. 83–4.

could either throw authority on the dustbin of monarchical legitimacies and focus on power alone, or end up reviving the same authority as the king's, only in a modern, secularized, no longer traditional form.[54] He winds up oscillating between these choices. Generally, therefore, in his dramatic and influential treatment of the problem, *verfassunggebende Gewalt* is either treated as only power, or even more as a will or source of action prior to any possible differentiation between power and authority. In either case, the independent role of authority disappears; and that of its initial stand-in, legitimacy, winds up oscillating between success, and a normatively undemanding plebiscitary acceptance or acclamation. Theoretically, however, his conception was and remained dualistic. Thus, he wished to expand on what bases the president of the republic, only a commissarial (under the famous Article 48[55]) and not a sovereign dictator, nevertheless was supposed to represent parts of the Weimar constitution (*Regierungsstaat*; state of the government, i.e. the executive) against other parts (the parliamentary state and *Rechtsstaat*) and not be limited to defending the whole against its enemies. When he found the plebiscitary power of the people unable to alone justify this jurisdictional expansion, he resorted to authority once again, quoting Sieyès: "authority from above, trust from below."[56] Only this was a third Sieyès, one that I have not yet introduced, the organizer of the coup of the 18th Brumaire of Napoleon Bonaparte. Schmitt explains quite correctly that "Plebiscitary legitimacy" "needs a government or some other authoritarian instance that can be trusted to pose the right question in the right way, and not to misuse the great power that lies in posing the question."[57] Such an authority can come, according to him, from either political success or the prestige of pre-democratic times or that of a non-democratic elite, and it is clear that what he has in mind is the revival of either a traditional authority, the establishment of a modern dictatorship, or their combination. It is also clear that he has reabsorbed raw power in his concept of authority, as his references to "success" and non-democratic elites (the administration or the military) indicate.

In the end then, Schmitt's theory of constituent power is either a mythological conception of the popular *pouvoir constitutant* without authority (and with a greatly reduced concept of legitimacy), or a conception of constituent authority, relying on both state power and a combination of traditional authoritarian and democratic-plebiscitary legitimation.

III SCHMITT AND POSITIVISM

I will for the moment disregard this obvious authoritarian turn or, more correctly, the authoritarian dimensions in Schmitt's thought, and his other

[54] As to the latter, his discussion of the thinkers of the counter-revolution who had to renounce monarchy and opted for dictatorship instead seems to indicate his own basic choice. Schmitt, *Political Theology*, Chapter IV.

[55] Art. 48 of the Weimar Constitution (Die Verfassung des Deutschen Reichs 1919).

[56] Schmitt, *Legalität und Legitimität* 87. [57] Ibid.

strong methodological and political disagreements with positivism. Focusing on the aspect of his thought that does without authority, the populist side, the level of overlap with many positivists on the question of original constitution making seems impressive. The views of Kelsen, Schmitt's famous antagonist, are most striking here. In Kelsen, the foundations of a constitution are split into logical and empirical dimensions. Logically, the validity of the constitution is based on the postulate of a *Grundnorm* or basic norm—that is the transcendental condition of possibility of a hierarchically structured legal order already in operation, with a constitution as its most fundamental legal rule. All basic norms say one and only one thing, in various wordings: "behave as the individual or the individuals, who laid down the … Constitution have ordained" or "act as the absolute monarch commanded, or the constituent assembly determined."[58] Here is where the empirical dimension comes in: the framer of the constitution, always in a revolutionary process of the overthrow of an old constitutional order, can be anyone, "an individual usurper" or "some kind of assembly" or as above "an absolute monarch" or a "constituent assembly."[59] The empirical model of founding, however, is said to have no normative consequences, "the historical events are only the *conditio per non* (necessary conditions) not the *conditio per quam* (sufficient condition) of the legal ought."[60] Thus there is no way to express normatively grounded preferences among them; and even applying the label "democratic" to one, as Kelsen sometimes does, is misleading from at least the legal point of view understood in terms of the pure theory.[61] In full agreement with Schmitt, no founders can operate, by the very definition of a revolution,[62] under the rules of the previous system, nor under those of the new one, not yet established, for that matter. And they cannot be judged by either set of standards. And this is because the authorization of the power that makes the constitution is self-authorization, which in reality is not authorization at all.[63] The term usurpation in fact applies not only to one, but to all of Kelsen's

[58] H. Kelsen, *Das Problem der Soveränität* (Tübingen: J.C.B. Mohr, 1928) 97; H. Kelsen, *General Theory of Law and the State* (Cambridge, MA: Harvard, 1945) 115–16.

[59] Schmitt also generally operates with these two alternatives, monarchic or democratic constituent power, though faithful to the Aristotelian theory he also mentions all three of the classical types of founding (monarchical, aristocratic, and democratic).

[60] Kelsen, *Das Problem* 97, 105.

[61] Kelsen, *General Theory* 267. And indeed elsewhere Kelsen does not distinguish between a usurper or a constituent assembly, at least not from a legal point of view. They are all usurpers … that is, first traitors, and then founding fathers. Ibid. 115, 117.

[62] Ibid. 117.

[63] See H. Lindahl, "Constituent Power and Reflexive Identity: Towards an Ontology of Collective Selfhood" in Loughlin and Walker (eds), *Paradox of Constitutionalism* 11. Lindahl (relying on H. Kelsen, *Allgemeine Staatslehre* (Berlin: Springer, 1925) uses the terms empowerment and self-empowerment with the same meaning, and interchangeably with authorization.

empirical models of change.[64] But there is one requirement, namely political success—otherwise the usurper is merely a traitor, and does not become a "founding father." In order to establish a new and legitimate constitution any of the various sorts of framers have to be *successful* by establishing a legal order (defined minimally by one rule of legislation or change) that is an effective one.[65] Success, or effectiveness, are again said to be only necessary rather than sufficient conditions of validity (119), its condition rather than its reason. But the reason of validity is the *Grundnorm* that is imputed on the basis of the successful, prior establishment of a new legal order.[66]

As already shown, Schmitt starts out saying that mere factual success is not enough for constitutional legitimacy, but ultimately is not able to complete the argument and demonstrate on what basis he makes this claim.[67] What is behind this unintentional convergence with Kelsen is a deeper theoretical affinity than usually realized: the basic norm, shared with Schmitt the idea that a democratic constituent power indicates an authority that does not and cannot authorize. Or, to make the distinction clearer, in Kelsen we encounter an equally problematic, retroactive act of authorization without an authority. Common to both is the broken link between authorization and authority. It is of course true that because of a difference in philosophical perspectives, the emptiness of the basic norm directs the interpreter or the judge back to the constitution, where the empirical founder has no status. In Schmitt, there is also the postulate of the existence of a diffuse and latent power next to and above the constitution itself, one that can challenge its legal interpretation and produce serious constitutional conflicts and crises. However, one thing is identical in the two views, if openly admitted only by Kelsen: nothing in the mere process of founding can be a source of authority, and the legitimacy of the constitution is based on either something after its making, or a mythical subject that is claimed to be prior. To Kelsen, that posterior thing can simply be the operation of the legal system established by the constitution, namely the acts of enforcing and obeying its rules. Schmitt's dominant argument, however, as we have seen, is linked to acclamation or ratification, something more active on the part of an undetermined portion of the popular constituent power. But these acts too are posterior to the making of the constitution, to the extent that they cannot alter or amend the

64 I disregard his idea of the domestication or legalization of revolution, as a form of constitutional revision under international law (Kelsen, *General Theory* 221). International law, as he initially saw it, was interested only in the successful exercise of state power and prescribed no method or procedure for fundamental internal change.

65 Kelsen, *General Theory* 118–19, 368–9.

66 I disagree with Lindahl's implication ("Constituent Power and Reflexive Identity") and subsequent argument that there are normative preconditions for Kelsen himself for a *Grundnorm* to be able to initiate a legal order. Actually even the term initiate is misleading. It is the legal order that comes first, and the *Grundnorm* is a transcendental rather than historical condition of possibility.

67 Probably similar qualms about the genetic fallacy did lead Kelsen to a whole train of argument not shared by Schmitt, of course, whereby success becomes a normative criterion of legality under international law. Kelsen, *General Theory* 220–1, 368–9.

text in any way, and especially the rules defining the operation of referenda or plebiscites.[68]

On a formal level at least, Kelsen could neither exclude nor require such plebiscitary reinforcement as part of his scheme. Yet reference to the people involved shows that a crucial difference remains between the two views, and it lies in Kelsen's demythologizing thrust. In other words, although he agrees with the realistic side of Schmitt's conception, Kelsen rejects clothing it in a conceptual myth of the people. He refuses to posit an identity that in its mere existence also carries normative validity or legitimacy. According to Kelsen, when a constitution, its preamble, and, by implication, a constitutional theorist such as Schmitt, attribute the origin of the constitution to "the people," they imagine a source that is in fact, or rather "in law," solely a product of the constitution itself. In the case of the making of a new constitution, the claim is meaningless legally, and though of course it is possible "politically," Kelsen should have said ideologically or rhetorically. But the latter case almost always refers only to minorities. It is by implication only subsequently that the law for the first time enables the majority to participate, or allows for majority rule.[69] Strictly interpreted, this criticism should apply even to Kelsen's own previous formulation: "that if a State is created in a democratic way, the first constitution originates in a constituent assembly, what the French call *une constituante*."[70] With an old constitution and its procedures dead, and the "first" constitution and its procedures not yet made, "democratic" should make no more sense than "people," at least on the level of Kelsen's supposedly pure legal theory. It will be the burden of the whole argument here, however, to show that both his defense of democracy and demystification of any kind of populism can be upheld, and that the notion of a "democratic" or at least legitimate procedure, if not its popular, unitary subject, can be made sense of in between constitutions, even if not in terms of a pure theory of law or the traditional model of the sovereign constituent assembly.

To repeat: if one overlooks the demythologizing project of Kelsen,[71] it is the compatibility of his theory of constituent power and constitutional origins with Schmitt's that comes to the fore. This affinity is shown indirectly by recent attempts to synthesize the views of the two authors, which often work all too well, at the expense of taking the actual processes of constitution making and

[68] Technically, a ratificatory referendum or plebiscite is still within the constitution-making process since a draft is enacted only through these acts of consent. But who is to ratify, under what rules is often determined by the constitution itself (e.g. even Article VII of the U.S. Constitution) with the aim of facilitating enactment. Moreover, many plebiscites are constrained either by use of force or by the voters being given an unfair choice, as in Chile and Turkey in 1982.

[69] Kelsen, *General Theory* 261.

[70] Ibid. 259.

[71] It may sound strange to accuse Lindahl of such forgetting after his critique of the metaphysics of presence in the already-cited article, and in the earlier "Sovereignty and Representation in the EU" in Walker, *Sovereignty in Transition*. He uses this critique effectively to criticize Schmitt's postulate of the popular sovereign as the author of the constitution.

their legitimation problems seriously.[72] In place of Kelsen's *Grundnorm* and Schmitt's democratic constituent power, in Hans Lindahl's synthesis there is a democratic basic norm that can be imputed to a constitution if the requirements of a successful legal order, but here also of a basic democratic arrangement, are satisfied, creating an order in which it makes sense to speak of the people as the source of the state's unity.[73] With all the improvements this entails regarding the original, undemanding positivist scheme of what constitutes a legitimate constitution, the cost is a re-affirmation of mythology in the retroactive form that ultimately came also to dominate Schmitt's thought, though in his case in a plebiscitary version: "By exercising their constitutional rights, they retroactively take up the first-person plural perspective of a 'We' that has (already) enacted a constitution in its interest" and "The collective self must rely on a present that never has been present and a future that never will become present."[74] This is a pretty suitable depiction of the temporal status of mythology: a present that never is a past or a future.

Ultimately, one could say that the attempted Schmitt-Kelsen synthesis sacrifices Schmitt to Kelsen, and thus the constituent power to the *Grundnorm*, except for the fact that one of the possible outcomes of Schmitt's own theory is being drawn out. Lindahl rightly calls attention to the "irreducible passivity" at the heart of Schmitt's doctrine of the constituent power, though he wrongly wishes to canonize this conception and draws the highly counter-intuitive conclusion that "the constituent power comes second, not first."[75] While an attempt to relativize the strong differentiation between *constituant* and *constitué*[76] makes sense, the idea that "an act of constituent power gives rise to the legal order only retroactively ... when it is viewed as an act of the constituted power," offered as an interpretation of the "remarkable insight" of Kelsen's *Grundnorm,* is not only not Kelsen,[77] but is also self-contradictory.[78] An entity can be its own creator only in mythological time.

[72] Lindahl's "Constituent Power and Reflexive Identity" rightly summarizes Schmitt's critique of what would have been Kelsen's theory of constitutional origins, if he really had one.

[73] As Lindahl does.

[74] Lindahl, "Constituent Power" 20; the same argument based on tacit consent is in fact there in Schmitt, *Verfassungslehre*.

[75] Lindahl, "Constituent Power" 21.

[76] This is explicitly stated by Walker and Lindahl in the already cited articles and by B. van Roermund, "Sovereignty: Popular and Unpopular" in Walker, *Sovereignty in Transition*, but was also a point made in my book, Arato, *Civil Society, Constitution and Legitimacy* Chapter 3 (originally "Dilemmas Arising from the Power to Create Constitutions in East Europe," *Cardozo Law Review* 14 (Fall 1992)). Also see Schmitt's concept of the monarchy in *Verfassungslehre* and Arendt's reconstruction of the constituent power at least in America, and Ackerman's *We the People* vol. 2. All share this relativization. Thus it seems very strange for some authors to continue to rigidly insist on the sharpest distinction between *constituant* and *constitué*.

[77] Thus I also disagree with O. Beaud, *La puissance de l'état* (Paris: PUF, 1994) 212–13, that Kelsen became more open to the notion of the constituent power in later works. I detect no such change in *General Theory* or in *Pure Theory of Law*, where the term never appears.

[78] As Lindahl "Constituent Power" 19 reveals, "an act of constitution making can only be viewed retroactively – and provisionally – as an act of the collective." I too would stress the parenthetical phrase "provisionally,"

Lindahl's implicit abandonment of the idea of the constituent power confirms what is ultimately a common prejudice of Schmitt and Kelsen: there can be no normative theory of the origins of constitutions. In the terminology I would like to introduce here, this move can be an abandonment only of the originating *authority*, but certainly not the *power*. It is simply false that the power comes second in this process.[79] Even if unauthorized in the given historical time, someone with power must begin in order for there to be a beginning. But, by implication, it does not matter how one begins: "Someone must seize the initiative" according to Lindahl. However, when put this way, the gap between sovereign and sovereign dictator cannot be bridged in Schmitt's or Kelsen's terms: the authority ascribed to the *Grundnorm* can be given no historical shape. Initial constitution making can be nothing other than dictatorship, usurpation, or perhaps prophecy.[80]

This corresponds to the verdict of Raymond Carré de Malberg: that "there is no place in the science of public law for a chapter consecrated to a legal theory of coups d'état or revolutions and their effects."[81] Thus he recommends leaving to the side the study of the constituent power in its original or primordial forms, and concentrating solely on the amendment rules,[82] what later come to be called the "derived constituent power." It is a recommendation that, luckily for us, he did not keep.[83] And the reason is obvious. Carré de Malberg thought there was a fundamental choice between force and right, and as his great text repeatedly shows, he did not wish to confine that choice to the binary of peaceful revisions, or events that almost never happened in France, as opposed to re-foundations, events that took place very often in his country. As his critics pointed out, in France, by that time having been under ten to eleven constitutions, the legal

which in this context, however, makes no sense at all. Provisionality points to linear, forward-looking time being able to alter the status of the constitution, and presupposes something that is unfinished. A thing retroactively legitimated must be by its nature complete, and can be altered only as a whole, not as part of an open-ended process. To refer to some of our most important political acts as "irreducible passivity," as does Lindahl, is deeply unfortunate, however brilliant the analysis of Schmitt's fictions may be.

[79] As Marx and Lenin well knew, and as Schmitt too always understood. See, on the Frankfurt Assembly of 1848, K. Marx, *Articles from Neue Rheinische Zeitung*, 1848–49 (Moscow: Progress Publishers, 1972); V. Lenin's 1905 "Two Tactics of Social Democracy in the Democratic Revolution" in *Selected Works* vol. 1 (Moscow: Progress Publishers, 1970) 494ff, 555ff.

[80] N. Machiavelli, *Discourses* Chapter IX: "It is well that, when the act accuses him, the result should excuse him; and when the result is good, as in the case of Romulus, it will always absolve him of blame." See also Madison, *Federalist* 41; for whom arguing from the result is only one of the arguments, one to use if all other methods of justifying the actions of the framers fail. In a contemporary version: See J.H.H. Weiler, *The Constitution of Europe* (Cambridge: Cambridge University Press, 1999) Introduction. Weiler's biblical allegory assumes that the actors that are given the constitution are slaves or have the mentality of slaves.

[81] R. Carré de Malberg, *Contribution à la générale Théorie de l État* (1920) (Paris: Dalloz, 2004) II 497.

[82] Ibid. 493, 496–7.

[83] Klein, *Théorie et pratique* 14, 82, for a moment seems to realize the tension between what Carré de Malberg says and does, before he treats him as an analyst merely of the *pouvoir constituant derivé*, or amendment rules (187–8). Beaud, who altogether disregards the issue of the Americans, also takes the jurist of the Third Republic at face value, as if he really did not study original constituent processes. (*La puissance de l'état* (Paris: PUF, 1994) 210ff, 212ff).

amendment rules were hardly ever used successfully (just three times in total), while the replacement of these constitutions classically took place through revolutions and coups.[84] Carré de Malberg himself in fact spent an enormous amount of time studying these dramatic changes of constitution, and not merely as a historian but as a legal and political theorist. His theory of national sovereignty was derived from the critique of the first such effort, the great revolution. Equally important here, his warnings about *constituants* or constituent assemblies were based not on malfunctioning amendment rules, but on original constitution-making efforts that, in his estimation, went astray and were ill-conceived. And while these were supposedly (if hardly convincingly) negative lessons only for the construction of future amendment rules, they would be senseless if the two types of constitution making, what the French call *originaire* and *derivé*, could not be analyzed and evaluated by the same theoretical and normative standards.

Below, I will try to show that, inconsistent in his positivism, Carré de Malberg did in fact have a normative theory centered around the concept of national sovereignty, one that allowed him to develop a legal analysis of original constitution making, and in particular of its authority structure. While he did not yet develop a theory of legitimate constitution making, he took some important steps toward it. However, as a positivist, Carré de Malberg could only draw the already-stated conclusion that no such analysis or theory was possible. If all legitimacy is legality, and all law is state law, two premises that he continually affirmed, then there can be neither legality nor legitimacy in the midst of breaks between constitutions.

IV POWER "AND" AUTHORITY

Under positivistic assumptions, then, one could not discover authority and legitimacy during constitutional ruptures, nor during the creation of entirely new constitutions. In this section, I will present two attempts to re-introduce normative foundations in foundings, one based on a conception of legal norms outside the law of the state, and the other ultimately settling on procedures justified by reference to their own discursively justifiable principles. These approaches will be presented through the relevant works of Maurice Hauriou and Hannah Arendt. In my view both offer something important and can be seen as complementary. Without justifiable principles, the stress on non-state law can fall back into a species of customary or traditional legitimacy that is hard to rely on in the midst of revolutions. But without normative references to a political culture established by a history of custom, previous legality, and institutional life, it is

[84] For example, M. Hauriou, *Précis de Droit Constitutionel* 1st edn. (Paris: Sirey, 1923) 281.

equally hard to see how a mere discursive justification can motivate political obligation.[85]

Juridical or normative theories of original constitution making are indeed easier to conceive when based on non-positivistic dualistic foundations, where law itself is not identified with the law of the state. Such a theory was anticipated by George Lawson,[86] who postulated a double doctrine of state and popular sovereignty in opposition to Hobbes, the common root of Schmitt and positivism. There is no need to return here to Lawson, whose importance for the history of the concept of the constituent power has been made clear by J. Franklin, E. Morgan, A. Kalyvas and M. Loughlin.[87] Maurice Hauriou's important work, reflecting on the same dramatic historical experience as Carré de Malberg, is not well known, however, outside France. Hauriou is especially significant here because of his attempt to get out of the positivist straightjacket by reflecting on the normative and political foundations of law, which he tried to conceive beyond the state centralized norm-sanction model characteristic of both Kelsen and Carré de Malberg. Anticipating Arendt and other critics of positivism, in a historical-institutionalist tradition, Hauriou understood law to be based on both coercion and cooperation. He tried to conceptualize two types of law, state-coercive and social-customary, and even two types of sovereignty based on these foundations, which he also placed at the origin of all state-type formations beyond tribal organization. It is possible that Hauriou's legal dualism, closely akin to E. Ehrlich's pluralist sociology of law,[88] could be reformulated and defended in more modern terms, such as the dualities of primary and secondary rules (Hart), or law as system and law as institution (Habermas), but the reformulation of the foundations of law cannot concern us here. Nor can the highly interesting consequences Hauriou, as well as Ehrlich, drew out for the grounding of the legality of international law. More important here is the doctrine of two sovereignties, admittedly unusual, that Hauriou placed at the very center of the theory of the constituent power, which was no longer formulated in terms of the mythology of the "people" still present in Lawson. In my view, this doctrine can be translated in terms of the duality of power and authority being examined here.

Hauriou is simultaneously a realist and a normativist. To simplify his conception, during the earliest foundations of modern law, more primitive legal forms based on coercion and on association or consent were both required to create

[85] The need to combine norms that justify and norms that motivate was developed by Jurgen Habermas in his distinction between the moral and the ethical in his *Theory of Communicative Action* 2 vols. (Boston, MA: Beacon, 1984, 1987).

[86] See my forthcoming *Adventures* Chapter 1.

[87] J. Franklin, *John Locke's Theory of Sovereignty* (Cambridge: Cambridge University Press, 1981); E. Morgan, *Inventing the People* (New York: Norton, 1988); A. Kalyvas, "Popular Sovereignty, Democracy, and the Constituent Power" (2005) 12 *Constellations* 2 223–44; M. Loughlin, "Constituent Power Subverted" in Loughlin and Walker (eds), *Paradox of Constitutionalism* 38–40; and my Chapter 2 in the forthcoming *Adventures*.

[88] E. Ehrlich, *Fundamental Principles of Sociology of Law* [1913] (New Jersey: Transaction, 2002).

early state forms, and in his view both are still needed to create and maintain the modern state.[89] Perhaps without knowing it, his analysis parallels a version of Weber's theory of domination and legitimacy or legitimate domination, albeit somewhat disguised by a form of presentation drawn from ancient history and anthropological research then at a relatively early stage. What is especially valuable for us is the application of this "normative realism" or "realist normativism" to the problems of the constituent power. The link between the concept of law and constituent power (that Carré de Malberg tried to break) is sovereignty, but it is interpreted in a dualistic form entirely unacceptable to the positivists. As in Lawson's model, sovereignty is not one but two: that of the government and that of the national community.[90] The first is based on coercion, the second on the associative, consensual, federative element of law, or type of law. Thus contrary to Lawson and even Locke's idea of supreme powers, Hauriou's model does not assume two potentially incompatible coercive powers.

According to Hauriou, harmony and unity between the two "sovereignties" is possible in what could be called state (he calls it "ideal" or "republican") sovereignty, and it is this form that has the full characteristics of domestic unity and supremacy needed in international affairs. A successful constituent process presupposes the coming together of the two sovereignties in a contractual form.[91] But conflict between the two more fundamental sovereignties is also possible. In periods of stability the coercive element comes to the fore, and may become repressive, even despotic. The typical state form of this is a government dominated by the executive. In revolutionary periods the consensual element, resisting all coercion, may become more important, the typical state form being assembly government. In this argument, both forms of one-sided sovereignty tendentially weaken the ideal one, the third type, and in revolutionary periods this is the explanation of the empirically well-known oscillation between assembly and executive forms of dictatorship.

According to Hauriou, by its nature the constituent power belongs more to the democratic form, national sovereignty. But the need to establish a form that is stable, binding, and coercive requires a governmental role. Thus, successful exercise of the constituent power requires the limitation of each sovereignty by the other, a combination of governmental and popular roles. For Hauriou, the famous problem of the sovereign's self-limitation is not a problem at all, because in his view it is these two sovereign powers that limit one another. And it does not require a valid constitution to accomplish the limitation of sovereignty, because their ability to limit one another is based in the coercive power of existing institutions (and an ethics of consequences) in one case and a customary law (modernized as an ethic of freedom) in the other.

89 M. Hauriou, *Précis de droit constitutionnel*, 2nd edn. (Paris: Sirey, 1929) 86.

90 Ibid. 86–9.

91 Thus for Hauriou not only federations but all legitimate constitutions have a contractual beginning, even as the contract is transformed into an institution. He believed moreover that the origin of the state everywhere involves the moment of "federation," not of individuals so much as chiefs. The contrast with Schmitt's view is striking. See Beaud, *La puissance* 247ff.

Of course, Hauriou was not operating in an intellectual vacuum. A. Esmein, and following him, Carré de Malberg, had already pointed out the role of inherited state institutions in almost every French Revolutionary episode of constitution making. Nevertheless, in each case Carré de Malberg was constrained to stress that none of these institutions (the Estates General of 1789, the Legislative Assembly of 1792, or the Councils of 1799, for example) was able to follow the existing constitutional rules in creating new constitutions. This was a very important point, given the traditional insistence inherited from Sieyès, later re-emphasized by Schmitt, that the constituent power was supposed to be in a state of nature. Without referring to Esmein's evidence, likely obvious in France at the time, Hauriou focuses instead on the indispensable role of these inherited institutions in the making of the new, helping to generalize a merely historical observation, and potentially, as we shall see, allowing us to overcome the American exceptionalism inherent in a similar observation by Hannah Arendt. Consistently sociological and institutional, Hauriou believed in the availability of far broader and pre-existing normative foundations for the constitutive act. As already indicated, he argued that any legal order contains two types of law, enacted and customary law. The former, small differences aside, is the law of the positivist: enacted law gaining its force from governmental command and enforceable sanctions. Customary law gains its strength from tradition, and enforcement through diffuse societal institutions. Such tradition can be recent, and indeed could have its origins in enacted law. This is what happens, for example, in two possible cases Hauriou stresses: the individualism of the modern legal order never explicitly enacted, but institutionalized along with formal provisions of modern French constitutions and legal codes; and fundamental rights, enacted during the Revolution in the famous declarations, but no longer formally present in the constitution of the Third Republic. As in the doctrine of two sovereignties, the functioning of a legal order depends on the coherence of the two types of law, customary and governmental. More importantly here, the collapse or rather rupture of governmental law, even in revolutions, does not leave or create a legal vacuum. The other law, customary law, is there to fill the space. Interestingly, for Hariou revolutionary popular sovereignty is itself based on such customary law, revolutionary customary law. Thus the rights of popular forces come to the fore in revolutionary breaks. Because it is based on law, popular law making itself is legally bound, by its own and other customs, to the legal principles of a historical community. The legitimacy of a revolutionary constituent effort will depend on its adherence to and ability to draw on legal norms, on the process of legitimation in the sociological sense.[92]

To that issue I will return in more detail when returning to Carré de Malberg's theory. For now, it would certainly seem that, for the domestic system,

[92] Hauriou's dualistic theory, including the idea of pre-existing normative foundations for even revolutionary law has been recently renewed by Olivier Beaud, though his far greater debt to Schmitt has helped to obscure this. Beaud too speaks of a double sovereignty, more traditionally as state and popular. Beaud, *La puissance* 208f, 217, 224ff.

what Hauriou had in mind would have been better elaborated not by a doctrine of two sovereignties, but as a duality between domination and legitimacy from the point of view of sociology, and between power and authority when it comes to constitutional theory and analysis. So reinterpreted, the advantage of Hauriou's conception remains not only that at the times of revolutionary breaks in the law of the state it gives us the normative dimension of another "law" uncoupled from sovereign power, interpretable as principles of potential legitimacy that can lend a new construction its authority. He is also able to point to constellations of power capable of backing up and being legitimated by the normative claims. Similarly, in the domain of international law, the conception can give us guidance to understand another type of law, based on custom and voluntary co-operation, rather than, obviously, command or centralized enactment. In both cases, the theory remains staunchly realistic, in that for Hauriou power can be limited only by power.[93] What remains to be seen is whether the idea of limiting the constituent will work if we conceive of it entirely outside the doctrine of sovereignty.

Hannah Arendt provides the alternative to Hauriou's roundabout way of establishing the independent foundations of authority through a dualistic sovereignty in her depiction of the challenge in modern republics to any internal role of the sovereignty doctrine. In the study of constitutional origins, the dualistic perspective of power and authority, anticipated by Rousseau[94], has no more distinguished representative than the Arendt of the great essay, *On Revolution*. Her interpretive approach reconnects us to all the relevant starting points: political theology, the conception of the two contracts, a dualistic notion of law, the political philosophies of the American and French Revolutions, and even their political histories. Granted, this pluralism of repeated re-starts leads to a conceptual apparatus that is somewhat mixed and difficult to analyze. While less pressing in the statement of the problem, the need to separate "power" and "authority" in the foundation of republican constitutions, as well as within them, her pluralism does culminate in eclecticism when it comes to solutions, and ultimately produces a rather weak outcome stressing American exceptionalism. But that is still a small price to pay for a rich restatement of the fundamental issues.

Although her persistent dialogue with contemporaries like Kelsen and Schmitt can only be assumed, not proven, Arendt begins by apparently conceding that "it is in the very nature of a beginning to carry with it a measure of complete arbitrariness."[95] Contract theories in the end confirm this claim, seen in the case of Hobbes and Locke, who both allow conquest and (in Hobbes' case tacit) consent to replace genuine agreement.[96] According to Arendt, attempts to

[93] With Hauriou's double sovereignty in effect reduced to that of an organ, it is unclear how the limitation of that organ by elements of normative regulation is supposed to work in the way that Hauriou intended.

[94] On this see my forthcoming *Adventures*

[95] Arendt, *On Revolution* 206.

[96] See Chapter 1 of *Adventures*.

remove "complete arbitrariness" or "foundational violence" run into two vicious circles, those of law (we might call it: "the Kelsen circle") and politics ("the Schmitt circle").[97] Arendt's fundamental difference from the positivists, now the followers of Derrida, and also ultimately even from Schmitt as presented here, is that for her the act of beginning *can be nevertheless made* legitimate in strong normative terms.[98] This was already the project of contract theory, with its implicit stress on the imputation from ideal to actual foundings. But Arendt is interested in historical beginnings, and not in mere retroactive imputation.

Thus much depends on whether Arendt can actually deliver on her belief that a new and different theory of constitutional beginnings is available to us. She knows the stakes as well as Schmitt, namely that she is not dealing with merely an epistemological or logical problem, but that the problem of beginning a new political order raises the question of "foundational dictatorship," whether Sulla's and Cicero's *dictator rei publicae constituendae*, Harrington's "sovereign legislator," Robespierre's "despotism of liberty" or (unsaid because of some apparent taboo) Schmitt's *sovereign* dictatorship.[99] And foundational dictatorship opens the door in her view to dictatorship as a more permanent political regime, as in the case of the short transition from French *gouvernement révolutionaire* to the Napoleonic dictatorship.[100]

The problem of foundations is explored repeatedly from the point of view of the duality of power and authority. What she calls "power," "the capacity to band together with others" more precisely refers to the generation of the identity of the holder of power, and she generally neglects all the questions as to what makes such an actor "powerful" (i.e. resources such as numbers, organization, skills, and money).[101] "Power" in this sense arises from individuals or groups, hitherto separate, coming together and learning through communicative action to act in concert.[102] While she cannot in all consistency avoid normative questions (and thus legitimacy, if not authority) when speaking about the emergence of power[103] she is relatively insistent in arguing that the power position is an existential one, and cannot ground normative rightness, legitimacy or authority. The results of the use of power are factual, not normative.[104] This does not mean, however, that acts of power are somehow self-legitimating, even in the case of the constituent power, as we will see. How the new power holder should act, what power should "do" or "produce" allows for alternatives. Her conception does not allow us to say that anything the right "power" wills or does is right (as in Rousseau's general will, for example, which may nevertheless be in

[97] Arendt, *On Revolution* 161. [98] Ibid. 212. [99] Ibid. 207.

[100] Ibid. 163; see my two essays, the "Schmittian" one, Arato, "Goodbye to Dictatorships" 67 Social Research 4 (2000) and the more "Arendtian" one: A. Arato, "From Dictatorship to Totalitarianism" (2004) 69 *Social Research* 2.

[101] For a thorough critique: see J. Habermas, "Hannah Arendt's Communicative Conception of Power" (1977) 44 Social Research 3.

[102] Arendt, *On Revolution* 160–70. [103] Ibid. 158, 166–7. [104] Ibid. 174.

error); but rather that beyond the identity of the actor, *the who*, there is also another question, or two rather, *the how* and *the what*, and none of them should be reduced to the other. As this was clearly Arendt's position, the question of authority arises for her both in relationship of the "what" and the "how" of the process of using power in processes of constitution making. The "what" question reduces to the following: does the constitution found a system of new power and authority that preserves hopefully public, and at the very least, private freedom? But even this formulation does not solve for her the question of how, as it would for Kelsen and some of his followers.[105] She considers it essential to ask (and try to answer) whether the constitution makers had legitimate power and authority to establish their constitutional product, and if not thereby eliminating the arbitrariness of the break, or breaking the vicious circles of foundations and law making, then at least making them "legitimate."

Unfortunately, the concept of authority is ambiguous in Arendt's work, as she herself realizes, but nevertheless is unable to do anything about.[106] On the one hand, authority is defined, analogous to Schmitt, and close as well to Weber's idea of *traditional* authority, as a form of legitimating command and obedience by reference to a past that has been "sacralized," or at least made strongly binding in the normative sense. It involves both nonviolent but also unquestioning recognition of a reputation or dignity of a higher person or an office,[107] thus quite fundamentally of a hierarchy, one recognized as *legitimate* by both the higher and the lower. Authority in this meaning (and authoritarian rule in the strict sense, as against something resembling it that rests on force that is defined, classically, as tyranny) is thus always legitimate. Its legitimacy rests on two possible sources "both outside the reach of sphere of power of those who possess the means of force" either a super-personal law that was not enacted by men, or "ancient usages, hallowed by tradition."[108] One is tempted to argue that both can be reduced to Weber's traditional legitimacy,[109] because natural law has to be interpreted, and its interpreters are almost always "authorities" whose right to do so is dynastic or religious. Her first impulse is to treat this type of authority as a thing of the past, gone with religion and tradition, the other two pillars of the "Roman trinity."[110] But a second concept of authority, "authority in general," both resembling a more modern theory of legitimacy and moving toward Weber's use of the two terms as synonyms, causes her to partially revise this

[105] Even the theory of Rawls is based on imputation.

[106] H. Arendt, *What is Authority?* (New York: Viking, 1961).

[107] H. Arendt, *On Violence* (New York: Harcourt, 1970) 45.

[108] Arendt, *What is Authority?* 92–3 and *passim*. See also H. Arendt, "Macht und Gewalt" in *Zwischen Vergangenheit und Zukunft* (Munich: Piper, 1994) 46–7.

[109] Weber always considered natural law separately, as a substantively but not formally rational scheme of legitimation. This violates his three-part format, and thus he may have thought of it as a mixed type, partially traditional because of its link to dogmatic interpretation, and partially modern because of the possibility of its legal systematization.

[110] Arendt, *What is Authority?* 94, 120ff; Arendt, *On Revolution* 117–18.

view of obsolescence, even though she thinks legitimacy too is in crisis with modernity.

The difficulty arises here because when Arendt speaks about the rebuilding of authority, we never really know whether it is the traditional and quasi-religious type involved, or if she merely refers to a new legitimacy that has arisen after earlier crisis and collapse. Power in her understanding requires legitimacy, but can only take the form of authority.[111] In *On Revolution*, for example, we are told that revolutions (logically: in their phase of liberation) presuppose the collapse of authority (and this means obviously the traditional form), but in their phase of constitution they then require a new if difficult reconstruction of authority.[112] This leaves open whether the reconstructed authority in question could only be a type that has an element of the traditional or the religious attached to it, or if it might also be based on a new type of legitimacy. The former would necessarily assume a person with authority behind normative validity, an author, while the latter would ground even the authority of persons in norms that do not have an explicit author at all. In principle, either form could supply the form of justification needed to escape the vicious circle of higher law making, or to make the arbitrariness inherent in it legitimate. Yet it would seem to matter a great deal which of the two forms is recommended and available to modern constitution makers.

What is central to Arendt's own thesis is that she makes a determined effort to insist on the desirability of separating the sources of authority from those of power, and vice versa, following the classical Roman model that focused on separate institutions (Senate and popular assemblies) altogether.[113] At times this is articulated in terms of the separate sources of law and power,[114] but the idea remains the same—at the very foundation of law there must be a legitimate authority that authorizes the first lawmaker. Nevertheless, when it comes to historical analysis, her attempt to show that such separation is fully possible succeeds only for settled constitutions, where one can point to a (supposedly[115]) powerless Senate (Rome) or a ("least dangerous branch") Supreme Court (United States) that nevertheless has tremendous political influence. This can be seen in her discussion of American constituent power, which, unlike the French (in the version of Sieyès) was supposedly not said by anyone (she is mistaken here) to be in the state of nature, but was based on organized bodies. As a result,

[111] Arendt, *On Violence* comparing 52 vs. 46. The distinction between legitimacy and justification is an artefact of defining legitimacy by reference to the past, and justification, to the future.

[112] Arendt, *On Revolution* 115ff, 118, 160.

[113] Ibid. 178.

[114] For example, ibid. 156, 165.

[115] As Polybius already showed there were important resources of power controlled by the Roman Senate, indicating how misleading Arendt's theory power can be. But that does not affect the argument here. See Polybius, *Histories* (Cambridge, MA: Harvard, 1922) Book VI.

the example of American constituent power, as opposed to the French, is construed as legitimate and authorized, or, as in a later phrase of Frank Michelman[116] "always under law."[117] Arendt quotes Madison to the effect that the American Constitution derived its "general authority ... entirely from subordinate authorities," which are in fact equivalent to the constituted powers, powers on which, according to her, the American constituent power was supposedly based.[118] Unfortunately, the fundamental question of authority she focuses on was not solved by mere reference to "subordinate authorities": the authorization to be the agent (or as we will see in the American case: the agents) did not reach so far as to authorize any particular way of proceeding, or any specific constitutional outcome.

Bound up in all this are not merely questions of definitions, and conceptual groundings, but high political theory. The baseline is the absolute monarchy, interpreted in terms of the doctrine of the king's two bodies, and therefore a personalized institution, outside and above the legal order (*legibus solutus*), in which power and authority, though also derived from different sources (dynastic and religious) were united in the same will incorporated in a physical body.[119] While the doctrine of the two contracts[120] sought to re-separate these sources (as did dualistic legal theories challenging the command-sanction model) positivist attempts to keep them united under the monistic model of state law were greatly favored by the key modern doctrine of sovereignty. According to Arendt, it was under the influence of that doctrine that Sieyès (who himself originated the famous metaphor, unbeknownst to her[121]) put the nation or the people in place of the king, as the source of *both* power and authority.[122] However, the American case revealed that the sovereignty doctrine could be entirely transformed. According to Arendt, the Americans "consistently abolished sovereignty within the body politic of the republic."[123] This formulation should be definitely translated as a discovery, that sovereignty could be maintained and reinforced externally, while abolishing it internally.[124] This indeed was the very purpose of building a federal republic in a world of states.

[116] F.I. Michelman, "Can Constitutional Democrats Be Legal Positivists? Or Why Constitutionalism?" (1996) 2 *Constellations* 3 293–308.

[117] Arendt, *On Revolution* 163, 165.

[118] Note that the quotation actually goes too far in terms of other Madison texts (the eclectic justifications he offers in *The Federalist* 40 and 43).

[119] Arendt, *On Revolution* 156.

[120] Ibid. 169ff.

[121] "Opinion de Sieyès sur plusieurs articles de titres IV et V du projet du constitution," speech at the Convention, 2 Thermidor, Year III (July 22, 1795), in *Ouevres de Sieyès* (Paris: EDHIS, n.d.).

[122] Arendt, *On Revolution* 146–7, 151, 186.

[123] Ibid. 153.

[124] Ibid. 152: that is, Montesquieu's project to "reconcile the advantages of monarchy in foreign affairs and republicanism in domestic policy." See my essay with Jean Cohen: A. Arato and J. Cohen, "Banishing the Sovereign" (2009) 16 *Constellations* 2.

In the context of constitution making, the banishing of sovereignty seemed to have meant two things for Arendt: that the source of even the highest, constituent power had to be under and constrained by law, and that this highest power and, implicitly, even its initial terms of authorization, could not be the source of the authority of the whole constitution-making process and its result. And this is so because the constitution is to be understood as man-made higher law,[125] one that is to transcend and be protected against ordinary legislation, namely acts of republican power of future generations. If authorized merely by one political power, why should the authority of the succeeding one not be sufficient enough to change or replace it? Resting on nothing but popular power, such a constitution would be, and was in France according to Arendt, a construct resting on quicksand.[126] But with religious justifications gone, where is this authority to come from if not from the constituent power?

We will not find the definitive answer to Arendt's own question in her work—or rather, we find she toys with too many answers. The authority of the higher law is said to rest on the constitution itself,[127] or on its key authoritative institution, the court,[128] or on its ability to amend and change itself.[129] All these features may very well demarcate the system of authority within a constitution, but do not solve the problem of the legal vicious circle, namely its initial source of authority. This is unless we solve this problem though a Kelsenian retroactive imputation, to which Arendt, hardly a Kantian, showed only slight inclination. There is also the more obvious candidate of natural law in the form that both American and French constitution makers adopted: natural rights.[130] Arendt is deeply skeptical of their efficacy, as is well known, and specifically in relation to constitution making for the additional reason that she thought the primary task of the process was to establish rather than to limit power. She did not seem to actually know that the religious reverence for the U.S. Constitution, which was also one of her minor arguments here,[131] began only with the adoption of the Bill of Rights. Most people would undoubtedly regard arguing authority from tables of rights to be arguing from results. This, however, would be false reasoning, for two reasons: one relating to France (though possibly some of the U.S. states as well), and, more relevant to theory, the other relating to America and significant for practice. By putting the Declaration of the Rights of Man and of the Citizen before the first constitutions, the Assembly and the Convention sought to indicate that there were transcendent principles the constituent power could actualize, but never violate or abrogate. This admittedly would not have been a very meaningful source of authority and authorization for Arendt, any

[125] Arendt, *On Revolution* 161, 182, 184. [126] Ibid. 163. [127] Ibid. 190. [128] Ibid. 192.

[129] Ibid. 194.

[130] M. Gauchet, *La Révolution des pouvoirs. La souveraineté, le peuple et la représentation 1789–1799* (Paris: Gallimard, 1995) 7 and 55. For Gauchet the reference to the Declaration solves at least the problem of the origin and authority of law, but not that of power.

[131] Arendt, *On Revolution* 191.

more than divine and natural law, interpreted and enforced by the absolute monarch, could be counted as an independent source for his authority. In the American case, however, the adoption of the Bill of Rights was the function of a particularly exemplary process.[132] Although Arendt chose not to focus on this, it is essential in offering more meaning to the final answer she gives to her own question.

That final answer was that it was neither anything prior nor posterior to the act of foundation, but that the act itself was the source of the authority for what was done.[133] Arendt seems to return to Schmitt's self-justifying existential posture, but in fact she has something different in mind: not a beginning without a normative principle, but "a beginning ... that carries its own principle within itself."[134] Thus Arendt can be safely acquitted from the charge of having abandoned normativism after all, in favor of Schmitt's existentialism. But that does not mean that she escapes another ambiguity, that between a traditional concept of authority very much like Schmitt's and a concept of legitimacy linked to her own communicative conception of the political, one which is diametrically opposed to Schmitt's, in effect the idea that the new principle contained in the act has two interpretations, consistent with the two meanings of authority in Arendt's work. The first is the authoritarian rendering, with the framers seeing themselves through the eyes of future citizens[135] as founding fathers.[136] Here their authority comes from the revival of a successful revolution of the Roman tradition of *patres patriae*, as people with great reputation who managed thereby to focus on their own role as they consciously founded a civil religion of the constitution. As correct as this reconstruction may be in the context of an occasional famous utterance, such as Madison's call for sacralization of the constitution[137] as he successively attacked the Pennsylvania censors and Jefferson's idea of frequent conventions (two ideas Arendt liked[138]), and for America's subsequent religion of the constitution,[139] this analysis does not explain how, in the midst of harsh controversy, the process and the result came to be accepted in the first place. Arendt, however, has another line of analysis that points in a different direction. Instead of basing the principle in question on a hierarchical relationship of fathers and people, this analysis focuses on the horizontal relationship of mutual promise and common deliberation.[140] According to Arendt, it was this idea that freed the Americans from the specter of dictating violence, which turned out to be avoidable in foundations and in revolutions after all.

[132] This process started under Art. VII with the ratificatory state conventions, many of which demanded the addition of a bill of rights to the constitution, continued with the first congress, and ended with the state legislatures under Art. V.

[133] Arendt, *On Revolution* 205–6. [134] Ibid. 206. [135] Ibid. 190. [136] Ibid. 195–6.

[137] Madison, *The Federalist* 49. [138] Arendt, *On Revolution* 223 and 226–7. [139] Ibid. 191ff.

[140] Ibid. 205–6.

Deliberation, or deliberative democracy as the foundation of constitutional authority is important; but it does not seem to be enough. I think it rightly throws focal interest on the question of procedure, but ultimately does not reveal very much of that procedure, and as we know, given the many compromises involved, this notion of founding very much idealizes what actually took or takes place. Moreover, there was just as much deliberation at the French Constituent Assembly, a body that in Arendt's view failed to establish a new constitutional authority. Here her reply would be that it had no power, or rather that its power had no legitimacy, since it was not based on constituted bodies. However, her idea that in France there were no constituted bodies, and therefore the Estates General could not express them, is itself not defensible.[141] The French constituent power was also based on constituted entities, even if these were linked to privilege. And even if the illegalities that created the Constituent Assembly as a new body (and the resulting legal break a vacuum) were certainly greater than those in the case of the Federal Convention, the significance of the difference is hard to evaluate, since Arendt, amazingly enough, leaves the actual procedures out of her account.[142]

Arendt thus leaves us with a great puzzle. If it sounds rather convincing that the procedures of American constitution making (something one could learn from generally) made a great deal of difference for the constitution's subsequent authority, her two or three lines on how this supposedly worked definitely do not make the case. They do, however, help to flesh out Hauriou's conception of authority, with its stress on customary norms, that lacked the modern dimension present in Arendt's deliberative model. But this model, based on the specifically American history and on the existence of "small republics" prior and during constitution making, throws us back to historical determinism and exceptionalism (from which there is little to learn).

V AMERICAN EXCEPTION OR FRENCH FAILURE? THE CLASH OF INTERPRETATIONS IN AMERICA AND FRANCE

The aim of this section and the following is to explore how a focus on the actual processes of constitution making in America may lead beyond what is an ultimately sterile exceptionalism. I believe that Arendt's emphasis on *how* the constitution was made in America, without actually elaborating on the method of constitution making, tends to throw her back to the *exceptional* institutional inheritance of the Americans, namely the power of small republics, the governments of the states, and in some states all the way down to townships. While she

[141] See R.R. Palmer, *Age of Democratic Revolution* vol. I (Princeton, NJ: Princeton University Press, 1959) on whom she otherwise relies.

[142] See Elster for a cogent comparison: J. Elster, "Arguing and Bargaining in Two Constituent Assemblies" (1999) 2 *University of Pennsylvania Journal of Constitutional Law* 345; for the best discussion of illegalities Ackerman, especially in the second version: *We the People* vol. II.

at times seems to imply that the French made tremendous mistakes, her emphasis clearly seems to be on the fortunate historical givens of revolutionary America, as well as the unfortunate institutional inheritance of France, and even of the modern world. According to Arendt, the shaking off of religion and tradition in modernity clearly seems to have the general consequence that authority as well as power can win their reality only from "the political." Sieyès and the French were not alone in this, and Arendt's republican emphasis forbids her to argue, following in the path of J.E. Mounier or Edmund Burke, that they should have built upon their constituted powers, kingship, and the society of orders to generate a British type of political compromise order. The statement that only the Americans were fortunate enough to have true constituted bodies reduces to the view that only they had republican ones.[143] Thus, by implication, one must have a republic before one can have a republic: a superfluous demand where applicable, and a senseless one where it is not. Moreover, it seems that, according to her, the attack on monarchy and privilege did put France into a state of nature, in reality and not only in the theory of Sieyès.[144] But if this is the case, the American theory was not a theory of the constituent power, but instead, as in Schmitt's thought, only a limited version where the real stake was formation of a federation from already constituted units. This is in a way analogous to his conception of the post revolutionary monarchy as a constituted constituent.[145] And if this latter view is clearly mistaken in relation to the constituent processes of the individual states, these too could still be said to refer to the rather exceptional cases of constitution making, where the problem is the transition from one republican form to another. But in France, at issue was the transformation of an absolute monarchy (and a society of orders) into a republic and a civil society. Indeed, Hannah Arendt repeatedly suggests that it is very likely that this particular historical origin and inheritance could only lead to the doctrine of absolutist popular sovereignty, one which then ruined everything else by appearing as the only possible source of law and power, and became a stable foundation for neither.[146]

More recently, in a highly interesting analysis, Marcel Gauchet has strengthened Arendt's exceptionalism thesis, upholding it in spite of the superiority he ascribes to French theorists like Sieyès and Condorcet (whose American influences he does admit). According to Gauchet, the Americans succeeded in establishing a regime of representation based on popular sovereignty (here he differs terminologically from Arendt) because they managed to establish a system of division and separation of powers.[147] They inherited the burden of neither the prerogatives of a political body, one and indivisible (i.e. the absolute monarchy) nor the privileges of aristocratic society. This much was of course in Hannah

[143] Arendt, *On Revolution* 156–7ff. [144] Ibid. 154.

[145] Schmitt, *Verfassungslehre* 8: ii 2 and iii 4, b and c (77–8, 85–6). The point is made initially only with reference to the state constitutions, but is meant to apply also to the Federal Constitution, if the priority of Sieyès is to be maintained.

[146] Arendt, *On Revolution* 174–5. [147] Gauchet, *La Révolution des pouvoirs* 9–11.

Arendt's work, and earlier in R.R. Palmer's *Age of Democratic Revolutions*, and even the French thinkers of 1789 were clear about this difference. But Gauchet goes further, even further than E. Morgan in a similar context. The failure of the French revolutionaries is rooted from the outset in having created an omnipotent assembly, and this failure was due not only to their odd combination of Rousseau and representation,[148] but to a situationally determined combination of radicalism and moderation. Because the revolutionaries were rejecting monarchical sovereignty, they needed an alternative, powerful, unitary vision: thus their particular conception of popular sovereignty. But because they kept the king in his symbolic place, as well as occupying the place of the executive, two other things had to happen. First, they needed to keep the powers of the executive weak. Second, they needed to erect an actual, operative power, one capable of being counter-posed to the monarch who could always revive his traditional claims. Both moves led to an assembly government centering in a sovereign legislature. It makes little difference whether the advocates used a single- or dual-bodied version of popular sovereignty (without or with referenda for some issues; without or with a so-called "an appeal to the people"). Thus assembly government, along with sovereign constitution making in two single-stage versions became the fundamental French formula, one which even the Napoleonic episodes and the Restoration did not replace with a democratic or constitutionalist alternative.[149] To Gauchet, apparently, the real alternative had to wait for the Fifth Republic.

This elegant argument proves a bit too much. In the transition from monarchy to republics, in all the modern revolutions the fear of restoring the power of "the one" seems to have been almost as great as in ancient Rome, at a time shrouded in myth. Weak executives were created everywhere in the first round,[150] and assembly government or tyranny was said to be the danger everywhere. Jefferson's *Notes on Virginia* is a famous testimony referred to by *The Federalist Papers*, and some of the French framers knew both of these texts. Indeed, Gauchet provides a great deal of evidence that many in France, starting with Sieyès (and even Mounier) were at least as fearful of unchecked legislature threatening the other branches, the people, and the constituent power, as was Jefferson.[151] Yet where the Americans succeeded in limiting the legislative power the French attempts all failed, and here Gauchet's argument does seem to work, if slightly differently than he intended. In France it remained possible to attribute political malfunctioning to the badly designed constitutional structure and the element of moderation within it, namely, having kept a king who admittedly worked to sabotage the structure. It was impossible to say the contrary, as in

[148] See Chapter 2 of forthcoming *Adventures*.

[149] Gauchet, *La Révolution des pouvoirs* 56–61ff.

[150] Wood, *The Creation of the American Republic*; see also Victoria Crespo's new book, *Del rey al presidente* (Mexico: El Colegio de Mexico, 2013), which I had the pleasure to read in English as a New School dissertation.

[151] Gauchet, *La Révolution des pouvoirs* 61–79.

Virginia, New York, Massachusetts, and elsewhere before the Philadelphia Convention, namely that part of the problem came from the weakness of the executive in the place that the king (there: the king's governor) once occupied. Thus, where in America the constitution of 1787 strengthened the executive, in France, the constitution of 1793 or the revolutionary Convention Government further diminished the formal powers of the executive, even as the latter body actually fell entirely under the dictatorship of its own executive committee.

If Arendt and Gauchet were entirely right, their combined lesson of exceptional American success and inevitable French failure would be a somber one for most other settings facing the problem of producing democratic or liberal or republican constitutions. Fortunately, French theorists, from Sieyès and Condorcet to Carré de Malberg and Hauriou, were not interested in admitting American exceptionalism on the basis of iron-clad historical givens in the two countries. They had good reason to learn very specific legal and procedural lessons from the American experience, whatever the difficulties of transferring options between such different contexts. From Carré de Malberg on (and his views go back to Mounier and Lafayette)[152] there is also a distinct tendency to claim that "we, the French, did not learn even what we could and should have learned." Interestingly, in the case of a doctrine that may have been so learned, Carré de Malberg claims the concept of national sovereignty for the French. This concept was based on the negative principle that sovereignty, the mutually dependent domestic supremacy and international equality of a power[153] belongs to the community as a whole, the nation, or the state, and that no single organ of the state can assume it as a whole without usurpation, or any of its powers without express delegation.[154] Applied to the organ(s) exercising constituent powers, this means expressly a non-sovereign status.[155] This conception follows the German *Staatslehre* of the time, and possibly the work of Georg Jellinek, but Carré de Malberg's criticism of organ sovereignty, namely the identification of sovereignty with a state organ exercising some fundamental state powers (*Staatsgewalten*), is much more insistent. Showing some patience regarding Bodin's failure to distinguish between monarchical organ and state, Carré de Malberg regards subsequent popular or populist revivals of organ sovereignty as indefensible, and increasingly as usurpations pointing toward dictatorship.[156] In his view, the French revolution discovered the alternative, national sovereignty,

152 Carré de Malberg, *Contribution* II 512, 535 (on Lafayette) and 535 (Mounier).

153 Ibid. I 70–1.

154 Ibid. II 167–70. Carré de Malberg considered the innovation as French, in spite of the fact that in effect he himself rediscovered it in America, where in the end he spoke of popular sovereignty cum judicial review as the functional equivalent of national sovereignty (ibid. II 167, 546–8). Actually, Americans generated this then new concept of sovereignty to account for the possibility that there could be sovereignty on both state and national level, thus as an interpretation of federalism. See D. Elazar, *Exploring Federalism* (Tuscaloosa, AL: University of Alabama Press, 1987) 230–1.

155 Ibid. II 505–6.

156 Ibid. I 76ff; regarding dictatorships 79–88; plebiscite as confiscation of national sovereignty II 499.

though it quickly relapsed into a form of organ sovereignty of its own: "popular sovereignty."

Carré de Malberg interprets Sieyès as the founder of a rival doctrine, that of a constituent power based on "popular" rather than "national" sovereignty.[157] His antinomies are occasionally noted, but are not taken seriously. Sieyès is also depicted, following the claims of his enemy Lafayette, not as the discoverer of the *constituant-constitué* distinction ascribed to the Americans, but as the one who "confounded and ruined everything" in this very conceptual move.[158] The key to Carré de Malberg's critique of Sieyès, and even revolutionary public law, lies in the link between popular sovereignty and representation.[159] However, it is interesting to note here that his critical presentation of Sieyès happens, strangely enough, in relation to original constitution making that Carré de Malberg previously excluded from the purview of juridical science. Perhaps he is speaking as a historian and a political philosopher, but, as we will see, the legal theorist will draw quite specific and important consequences from his critique.

According to Carré de Malberg, rather than adopting the new revolutionary principle of *national* sovereignty, one more linked ultimately to Montesquieu's separation of powers, the adoption by Sieyès of Rousseau's *popular* principle entailed the imagining of a positive subject of sovereignty, "in the state of nature," unstructured, unlimited, and unitary, yet capable of action and a single will. It was this entity, the "nation" or the "people" that was said to have the constituent power. Since there is not, never was nor will be such an entity, the harm was done really only when "illogically," the unRousseau-like concept of representation was added to the original one, creating a body indeed capable of willing, unlike the primordial people, with all the attributes of the latter transferred to the former.[160] While the primordial people were not an organ, nor a *constitué*, the use of representation meant that unlimited constituent powers were transferred to a specific body of representatives, and indeed with them all other powers that it wished to exercise as the full stand-in for the people or the nation. Rousseau's direct democratic conception could not entertain the distinction between constituent and legislative power, and this obliteration of one side of the double differentiation between constituent and legislative powers, ensuring that neither was to assume the function of the other, was supposedly taken over by Sieyès. However, this criticism fails to notice that Sieyès understood the acceptance of a legislative and governmental role for the constituent assembly as merely an emergency measure.[161] For Carré de Malberg, the extent to which a doctrine emanated from the constitution-making body or its ideologists was the extent to which it justified usurpation. This political form, created abstractly, was exactly what Schmitt was to call sovereign dictatorship, but the French jurist

[157] Ibid. II 487ff. [158] Ibid. II 535. [159] See my forthcoming *Adventures*.

[160] Carré de Malberg, *Contribution* II 488–9.

[161] Sieyès, *What is the Third Estate?* 139, 142–3; "Préliminaire de la constitution" *Écrits politiques* (Paris: EAC, 1985) 192.

shows that this charge was anticipated already in 1789 within the Constituent Assembly itself.[162]

Carré de Malberg does not really seem to grasp the American influences on an antinomic Sieyès.[163] While he does glimpse elements of the theory of Sieyès that indicated "double differentiation," he thinks these are all vitiated from the very beginning by the peculiar version of Rousseau, which entailed the definition of the sovereign in positive terms by allowing embodiment and the transference of all its powers without limit to representatives. But without defending Sieyès, for which there is no need, the question should be asked: to whom should the deputies of the Estates General or the Constituent Assembly have ceded legislative and executive powers under the French circumstances, when all older powers in the state were initially arrayed against even moderate change? Mirabeau's failure to get royal cooperation in a national program of moderate monarchy was a case in point.[164] One cannot move beyond Arendt's American exceptionalism without asking these questions. It is demonstrably the case that the American examples from the individual states (which were hardly characterized as a group by the double differentiation Carré de Malberg took as canonical) were taken extremely seriously by the important French protagonists, from Mounier and Lafayette on one side to Sieyès and Condorcet on the other. Yet under French circumstances it was extremely difficult to apply the lessons of, for example, Massachusetts or New Hampshire without creative reinterpretations, of which signs were to be found only among radicals like Sieyès (and Condorcet). This is the problem that Hauriou's parallel critique of the French revolutionary model of the constituent power encounters as well.

As we have seen, Hauriou does not reject a juridical treatment of original constitution creation, and thus does not contradict himself as he examines the model of the French revolution. While his understanding of national sovereignty is closer to standard views of popular sovereignty, his notion of two sovereignties allows him to come to similar conclusions as Carré de Malberg. In all politics including the constituent process, the achievement of a normatively desirable overarching form of sovereignty requires that neither governmental nor popular sovereignty should dominate. In revolutions and revolutionary constituent politics, because of the revolt against previously oppressive forms of governmental power and the special normative relationship of the democratic type of sovereignty to the production of a nation's fundamental rules, the danger is that it will be popular sovereignty that will threaten to subsume everything. Hauriou calls this the emanationist model of sovereignty, meaning that "the nation" is not merely satisfied with "taking possession" of sovereignty, but

162 Carré de Malberg, *Contribution* II 535. O. Beaud is right, however, to point out the duality of constituent authority and constituent power in Rousseau, implied by the role of the legislator to recommend and the popular assembly to enact (*La puissance* 234ff).

163 See Arato, *Adventures*.

164 F. Furet, "Mirabeau" in F. Furet and M. Ozouf (eds), *A Critical Dictionary of the French Revolution* (Cambridge, MA: Harvard, 1989) 270–1.

seeking to exercise all of its powers as well.[165] This effort must ultimately fail, because, according to Hauriou, the majority is never in position to take initiatives. But it can be and was tried in the French Revolution, with an attempt to reduce all governmental power to a mere emanation of popular power. In the absolutist manner, sovereignty was thus pronounced as one, but in the popular rather than governmental form, and no body or individual was said to be allowed to exercise authority except by express delegation by law. Instead of interpreting this formula as a means to block organ sovereignty, Hauriou proceeds to give the equally plausible interpretation that this part of the Declaration of Rights establishes the complete supremacy of the legislature over all other branches of government—and thus the dictatorship of the assembly.[166] But he goes further: because legislative power too was supposed to be a delegation or emanation, the same intellectual and political logic also established the primacy of the electorate, or the street, over the assemblies, and the resulting political convulsions invited yet another dictatorship with plebiscitary support: that of the hitherto suppressed executive.

For Hauriou there is an oscillation in French history between these phases, with each phase having its own type of constitution making. The project of popular constitution making represents yet another example of this emanationist logic, with popular power seeking to take over this most fundamental power in the state, which then becomes the foundation for its future dominance. However, fully popular constitution making turns out to be either an illusion, or part of the process destabilizing a particular form of the state, including even a revolutionary state. As Esmein noted well before Arendt, it is a project of permanent revolution.[167] In the case of even relative success, governmental and national "sovereignty" must both play a role, with the latter confirming the initiative of the former as the last word. The role of inherited governmental institutions in constitution making is thus hardly accidental, according to Hauriou. It is rather a condition of possibility of even relative success.

Interestingly, in the second volume of *We the People*, Ackerman also comes around to stressing the role of inherited institutions in the American constitutional moments, but now speaking more of revolutionary reform rather than revolution, and of legitimate "constituent authority" rather than by earlier implication "sheer acts of will" (or: illegal constituent power).[168] Though the participants are still seen as violating some legal norms, they are nevertheless now depicted as respectful of legal forms in general. Lawbreaking is not necessarily lawlessness.[169] In particular, the American framers relied on some legitimate institutions of the established order: not only ones they wished to build on, like Arendt's small republics, the states, but also some they planned to entirely

[165] Hauriou, *Précis*, 1st edn. 222–3, 224ff.

[166] Ibid. 227.

[167] Esmein, *Éléments de droit constitutionnel*.

[168] Ackerman, *We the People* vol. II. 11.

[169] See my Chapter 4 in *Civil Society*; originally in (1994) 1 *Constellations* 1–2.

displace, or "re-organize," such as the Confederation Congress.[170] They gained the assent of pre-existing institutions to their own reorganization. While Ackerman says that this type of negotiation and coming to agreement "vastly enhanced their claim to speak in the name of the People," the meaning of "People" suddenly changes in this version of the presentation. In reality, the argument disorganizes his earlier claim, with its focus on extraordinary assemblies supposedly embodying the People, that now no single institution or organ is said to be able to represent. In this new version, it is a plurality of old and new institutions that together enhance the right to a popular identity, throwing doubt on whether or not any of them could make the type of claims Ackerman earlier ascribed to conventions.

However that may be, this co-production, based on self-organized popular forces involved in revolutionary extra-legality and with inherited state institutions the legality of which is assumed, was fully anticipated by Hauriou's insistence on the need for governmental and popular power to be involved together in constitution making. This corresponds to the aforementioned French analyses of Esmein and Carré de Malberg: contrary to the assumption of total revolutionary breaks, most of the time French constitutional politics has been based on the active role of inherited institutions, such as the Estates General, the Legislative Assembly, the two Councils of the Directory, Napoleon's Senate, and so on. But the theoretical problem is not thereby solved, because as Carré de Malberg shows,[171] the illegalities involved in each case were drastic, usually more so than in the American case, the role of force was much more significant. With the exception of the Legislative Assembly that was hampered mostly by an impossible amendment rule, the old institutions in question were not suitable partners for the erection of the type of rule the new forces fought for without radical reconstruction. Thus the very similarity of Hauriou and Ackerman's later conception on an abstract level once again throws us back to the kind of exceptionalism that Arendt could not transcend. Apparently, reliance on inherited institutions works only in exceptional circumstances, that is, with the availability of republican institutions.

VI FROM HISTORICISM TO QUESTIONING THE MODEL: *IL Y A CONSTITUANTES ET CONSTITUANTES*

The further exploration of a possible improvement in methods of constitution making by Carré de Malberg, and less reluctantly by Hauriou, points beyond historicism or historical determinism. Carré de Malberg is especially interesting for us, because while his interest in actual history and politics breaks through his positivist bias, that very bias leads to a productive stress on amendment rules. Yet the conceptual frames stressing the preservation of national sovereignty (Carré de Malberg) and the balanced relationship of the two sovereignties (Hauriou)

[170] Ackerman, *We the People* vol. II.

[171] Carré de Malberg, *Contribution* II 496–7.

are quite parallel. What is important here is the common use of the problem of amendment rule design to make a theoretical point that goes beyond that issue, to the original constituent power. I start with Hauriou's somewhat earlier and less developed conception, one more forthright in its legal treatment of revolutionary constitution making.

Hauriou considered the distance between original constitution making and amendment rules as great in principle as Carré de Malberg, if for somewhat different reasons.[172] While neither is outside the law, foundations and re-foundations are oriented to revolutionary-customary law, while for amendment rules it is the law of the state that is decisive. Yet on pragmatic grounds, in the case of revolutions, and on normative grounds, in the case of functioning states, he considered the coordination of the two types of law as always desirable, and along with it the presence of the two types of politics in the constituent operation.[173] Disregarding Condorcet's great proposal of 1793, he takes for granted (in agreement with Carré de Malberg) that the initiative cannot logically come from below. In any case, in his mind, excluding the people from ratification amounts to a governmental usurpation of popular or national sovereignty. What about the process in between initiative and ratification? Here he extends Carré de Malberg's questioning to amendment rules themselves. In principle, a doubly differentiated, freely elected, non-sovereign constitutional assembly that will operate under prior limits and avoid usurping other powers is possible, but is not likely. Thus Hauriou (as a good man of the Third Republic, with its National Assembly formula that united the two ordinary chambers in one supposedly extraordinary one) warns against using this so-called primitive form: the national convention or the constituent assembly, replacing ordinary organs in the constituent operation.

While in the modern state the distinction between legislative and constituent power is fundamental, according to Hauriou it is extremely difficult to stop the primitive type of assembly from assuming the legislative role.[174] This argument, implying the danger of dictatorship, is supported by French historical examples (as well as the *decemviri* and other Roman ones). The fact that the American national conventions do not join the constituent and the legislative power is noted, and the French difference is then explained by the emanationist doctrine of popular sovereignty. Thus it is the combination of this doctrine and the primitive form that seems to be at the root of the problems. The encroachment on legislative power is really an attempt to subsume governmental power, parallel to the subsumption of the executive by the legislature.[175] Thus, if the revolutionary constitutions adopted the primitive form for their amendment rules in the interest of their own stability, they did so with precise procedures of separation and limitation of powers.[176] Even the adoption of referenda can be seen as a political check on omnipotent primitive assemblies. This is possible as long as

[172] Hauriou, *Précis* 1st edn. fn. 284; international law 285–6. [173] Ibid. 280ff, 282ff.

[174] Ibid. 287–8. [175] Ibid. 289. [176] Ibid. 291.

referenda are not interpreted in terms of the theory of emanation, or as the voice of the people as such. Hauriou notes a historical trend away from the primitive form of assembly, and he sees as confirmation the disregard of the convention option in Article V in the United States, widely feared because of the possibility of runaway assemblies. The popular element is better restricted to referenda, even if for the theorists of the Third Republic the recent Napoleonic practice had given these a bad name.[177]

The fear of "the primitive form" is also expressed in Carré de Malberg's phrase: "il y a Constituantes et Constituantes."[178] In other words, there are limited constituent assemblies and usurping constituent assemblies. Along with this worthwhile reminder, he invites us (or the French) to choose between national sovereignty and the use of force, and against the grain of French history between amendment rules and revolutionary re-foundations. In that history, rules tended to lose out to revolutions. But the invitation could also be reinterpreted as pointing to a choice, in both amending and original constitution making, between two types of foundational (or re-foundational) procedures. By the early twentieth century, the term *une Constituante* was commonly used in both revision and re-foundation, the exercise of both *pouvoir constituant derivé* and *originaire*, leaving behind such earlier terms as convention and *assemblée de révision*. This terminological overlap allowed Carré de Malberg to explore both issues more or less together. Note that the analysis relativizes the *constituant* and *constitué* distinction, because the amending power is a *constituant-constitué*, or a constituted form of the constituent power. Note also that the persistent use of the American model by Carré de Malberg[179] also focused indifferently on the convention form common in original constitution making and in many rules of revision: "in the United States ... *les Constituantes* cannot be considered sovereign assemblies." Or: (1) they do not have legislative power and (2) their decisions in the different states have to be confirmed by popular ratification. This is then counterposed to the French revolutionary doctrine of the omnipotent constituent assembly, whose difference here is not explained by its status as *originaire* but by the contradictory and irreconcilable combination of popular sovereignty and representation. They thus use popular sovereignty to make the assembly all powerful, and representation to exclude the people (and achieve the assembly's dictatorship). Fortunately, he argues (at least for legal theory) that the concept of national sovereignty has provided a way of thinking of *Constituantes* in line with the American conception.

This is even true in France, where, according to Carré de Malberg, amendment rules historically provide for a special organ or combination of organs with limited powers, restricted to constitution making, leaving in place the existing powers of government. No constituted organ alone was ever supposed to

[177] Ibid. 291–2. [178] Carré de Malberg, *Contribution* II 549.

[179] Ibid. 549, contradicting his notion (547–8), repeated even here, of the French origin of national sovereignty.

exercise the constituent function. Thus the requirement of double differentiation has been generally (though incompletely in the Third Republic) obeyed, at least in the constitutions.[180] According to Carré de Malberg, the amending power is logically the highest, because it can change all powers in the state and is in this sense supreme, but it is not a politically sovereign organ: it cannot command the other powers that stay in place. It is also not unlimited (e.g. the republican provision or the clause that entrenched it could not be changed even by the amending power of the Third Republic); nor is its word final in several of the versions, where popular ratification has been added.

At all points this survey by Carré de Malberg is guided by the need for double differentiation and his concept of national sovereignty that requires it. Thus, he approves the fact that the French constitutional texts (or most of them) seem to exclude a constituted power becoming the constituent organ.[181] The possibility that a governing organ might transform the state to its benefit must be excluded. Properly speaking, he also says, there are or should be no constituent organs, only constituted powers in the state.[182] While the point would not automatically apply to original constitution making, it is greatly stressed that all French constitutions, with the exception of the never-used one of 1793 (and he might have noted, also Condorcet's draft), had a role for constituted powers in constitution making.[183] The contradiction is then removed in the presentation in two ways: by pluralizing the constituent organ, first, and by using the words "ordinary" or "established," second. The first option would avoid "organ sovereignty" by creating a complex constituent organ in which different powers, including popular ratification are parts of a mechanism in which a plurality of actors must work together to alter their various jurisdictions or to create new ones. The British model of parliamentary sovereignty,[184] where the Commons has gained all the constituent powers and can "do anything," is entirely unacceptable from the point of view of the doctrine of national sovereignty. This is one side of the double differentiation, the thrust of which is to deprive above all the existing legislature of constituent powers, something that was incompletely realized in the Third Republic. Thus Carré de Malberg's remarks can be taken as a critique of parliamentary monism or assembly government.

The second option, and the second dimension of differentiation, has to do with Hauriou's primitive form, the classical constituent assembly in its French (and occasionally even American) form. Until 1875 at least, consistent with the principle of national sovereignty, all French constitutions assigned the task of constitution making to a specially elected assembly for that purpose and that purpose alone, *une Constituante*, in effect an American convention, under the changing names of assembly of revision, convention, and even senate under Napoleon. Again, consistent with the same principle, these assemblies, whether newly elected or not, would be "ordinary." This was to mean, without exception,

[180] Ibid. 506–7, 509. [181] Ibid. 506–7. [182] Ibid. 500. [183] Ibid. 510.

[184] Ibid. 541–5.

that they were to be limited in their powers, tasks, temporal duration, and, ultimately even in their ability to finalize the enactment of the constitution by leaving room for ratificatory referenda. Whatever the name, to Carré de Malberg such an institution is of American origin (to be put on the side with the French—actually Pennsylvanian—invention of the sovereign constituent assembly—for which the name *Constituante* established by the Assembly of 1789 is more suitable). In denying legislative and other governmental powers to the constitution-making assembly, its purpose is to block the road to the usurpation of sovereignty, or sovereign dictatorship.[185]

Given the absence of serious misuse in the history of the amending power in France until Vichy and then the beginnings of the Fifth Republic, and especially in America, Carré de Malberg's strong warnings about *Constituantes* may seem a little strange. The most natural way of reading these important passages is in terms of an implicit turn back to the processes of *original* constitution making in line with his critique of Sieyès, rather than recommendations about writing "safe" amendment rules. Of course, a theory of amendments is his guide in the effort. The warnings may seem more relevant to constitutional designers than to revolutionaries, but there is a category also between them: the designers of the process of design. And to them (or to both types of designer) Carré de Malberg, close to Hauriou but more detailed, says that a *Constituante* is naturally tempted to exaggerate its powers (even when they are formally limited). This is because asked to found all powers, such an assembly will easily imagine it possesses all in order to be able to give or delegate them. Where the ideology of popular sovereignty as a positive form is dominant, a *Constituante* (as in the best known version of Sieyès' theory) will feel empowered by the people's total power even as it cannot be controlled or limited by the same people.[186] Having power only provisionally, such an assembly will seek to extend its temporal limits if the time for constitution making proves too short or if there is a political emergency. The attempt to limit it to mere amendment may not succeed, and Carré de Malberg could have added that it did not do so even in the case of the American Federal Convention.[187]

Yet the American Federal Convention, clearly a run-away convention, was not a sovereign *Constituante*, and the Massachusetts (1780) and New Hampshire (1784) conventions that generated the model even stayed within the bounds of legality. Even the legal violations of the Federal Convention were limited to two, though admittedly very important, issues: replacement rather than amendment, and changing the rules of ratification. Certainly no usurpation was even attempted of the other powers of government in 1780, 1784, or 1787, which according to Carré de Malberg was "one of the greatest errors committed in France since 1789" by the Constituent Assembly, and even more so by the National Convention of 1793–95. Several key dimensions in the process of the

[185] For the latter concept, see Schmitt, *Die Diktatur* Chapter 4.

[186] Carré de Malberg, *Contribution* II 540, 549. [187] Ibid. 541.

making of the Federal Constitution that correspond to Carré de Malberg's theory of amendments (culled from French constitutional texts) are worth stressing here once again.

1. The plurality of participating actors: the initiating Annapolis Convention, the old Congress, the state legislatures, the Convention itself, the ratifying conventions and the new Congress. In the theory developed here such a plurality is assumed as desirable to guarantee 3 and 4 below.
2. Some of these actors, Congress and the state legislatures are already constituted; while others, the conventions, are extra-ordinary.
3. The non-sovereignty of any of the actors.
4. The limitation of the drafting assembly to the one task of constitution making.
5. The parallel functioning of other legitimate governmental powers.
6. The important legal continuity involved (despite the well known violations).
7. The multi-stage nature of the process, from the articles, to the new draft to ratification, to the ten amendments that produced the Bill of Rights.
8. The important role of elections between stages (two sets: for ratifying conventions; and for the new Congress/plus many of the state legislatures that will participate in the amending power producing the Bill of Rights).

The overlap of this historical model, subsequently adopted in different versions by some Latin American states, with a theory of amendments seems to indicate the applicability of both or their common principles to constitution making more generally. Of course, the use of the term convention in France, and the fate of this adaptation in 1793–95, was an example of "learning" that seemed to indicate more the recalcitrance of historical givens. The same case could be made about many Latin American uses of the American model. All the more striking, but perhaps still explicable, is the fact that French constitution makers, after doing things more in line with doctrines of popular sovereignty and omnipotent assemblies, would adopt amendment rules proposing restraint and limitation for future actors. One could say perhaps that each generation prefers to bind the next one rather than itself.[188] Yet binding future generations while not binding oneself in the present creates not only the long-running problem of generations explored by Jefferson in America and Condorcet in France, but also short-run legitimation problems for the present generation. By what right can unbound representatives of a generation (e.g. the Constituent Assembly of 1789–91) bind other representatives of the same generation (e.g. the Legislative Assembly of 1792)? Thus the question remains relevant: why did the French revolutionaries of each original round not follow the very well-known American example, which

[188] J. Elster, *Ulysses Unbound: Studies in Rationality, Precommitment, and Constraints* (Cambridge: Cambridge University Press, 2000).

implied that the principles of self and mutual limitation were applicable to original constitution making?

Given the overlap between the American example and the French theory of amendment rules, we can safely dismiss the act of original constitution making itself as the reason, and even less the justification for escaping all limitations of the constituent power. One possible answer already discussed is that the French revolutionaries tried to follow that example, but given the difficult circumstances either had to fail or, more likely, failed to discover the mechanisms by which they could do so. Another possibility is that though they occasionally did discover such mechanisms, the theory of popular sovereignty (the Rousseau dimension) was stronger in France than the theory of national sovereignty (the Montesquieu dimension), associated in part with the unfortunate historical givens of France. As a result they disregarded any such discovery.

Reluctantly, Carré de Malberg seemed to come to the last of these conclusions, without seeing the technical alternative already available, when he came to stress not revolutionary breaks as such but, more interestingly, the type of theory of sovereignty that informs the process. According to him, popular sovereignty leads to omnipotent *Constituantes*, and losing everything, whereas national sovereignty (or its American functional equivalent) leads to a constitutional amending power and to an American type of original process.

At issue is not abstract theory, but the theory actualized in the political processes. Carré de Malberg perceives the theoretical antinomies of the Americans without clearly thematizing them as such. On the one hand, their theory is popular sovereignty. On the other, their practice is a functional equivalent of national sovereignty. This was possible because of judicial review. But he is wrong, at least with respect to the founding. Judicial review came later, and the original constituent process nevertheless operated as if under the aegis of "national sovereignty," that is, without allowing the emergence of the sovereignty of an organ, the usurpation of sovereignty by a movement, an institution, or a person, in spite of the language suggesting popular sovereignty. Thus in this argument, while Ackerman is clearly right in discovering the strong intellectual tradition of popular sovereignty in America neglected by Arendt, it is striking that the conception did not lead to sovereign claims by the conventions he focused on, nor by any other constitution-making authority. The Federal Convention repeatedly stressed its right only to recommend, while the ratifying conventions were not given the power to draft. Undoubtedly, the new turn given to the Convention form, first in Massachusetts, has much to do with this achievement. But although this particular invention was parasitic on what Arendt discovered, namely the prior existence of republican institutions, it did not automatically lead to procedures of "double differentiation." Indeed, the Massachusetts Convention could share power with the General Court and the townships, and the Federal Convention with Congress and the states, because the traditional institutions themselves had an elective republican form. But it was equally important that in each case, a federal structure served to protect continuity in the midst of change, either the states in the case of federal constitution making, or the federation in cases of state-level efforts.[189]

What we have to realize is that on the theoretical level, the French too were challenged by the same antinomy within the theory of sovereignty as the Americans. One form this antinomy took was the conflict between the influence of Rousseau vs. that of Montesquieu, with the latter defeated, given his links to the society of orders and estates. But the models of the Americans really did have a chance against Rousseau, especially because representation could not be avoided. Yet representation could lead to either double differentiation or the postulate of a sovereign constituent assembly. Sieyès incorporated this very antinomy. Again, Carré de Malberg formulates the two terms as national and popular sovereignty, and attributes the two poles to public lawyers and politicians, respectively. He ascribes the ultimate choice in France to the dominance of the wrong theory, popular sovereignty, among the politicians. His solution (and in part Hauriou's too) was, then, based on the need to switch theoretical paradigms, a matter to which I will return by trying to evaluate the strengths and weaknesses of the doctrine of national sovereignty below. However, it is again instructive to compare this rather voluntarist view of the public lawyer blaming things on the politicians with Arendt, who was equally opposed to the doctrine of popular sovereignty in the internal life of the state, and who, as we have seen, tended to blame situational givens in France or the absence of the American situational advantages. Would the right theory have changed everything?

VII FROM EXCEPTIONALISM TO LEARNING AND INNOVATION

In my view, even situational disadvantages can in principle be compensated for by a combination of constitutional learning and invention.

This is demonstrated by the case of Sieyès, in spite of his antinomic position. On the purely theoretical level, he is rightly understood by Carré de Malberg to have been originally a follower of Rousseau much more than that of Montesquieu, and thus he is the main French revolutionary "politician" criticized. Yet he was already a public lawyer too, and from the legal point of view one aspect of the particular version of the Rousseauian position ascribed to him, perhaps his dominant perspective until the Terror, did trouble him. These were the obvious legitimation problems of the concept of the general will transposed to a sovereign representative legislature. In response to this, he was to formulate yet another of his very original ideas, a mostly neglected one, the provisionality of the "first constitution."[190] According to this idea, if double differentiation is not

[189] On the role of the federal form see Arato, *Adventures* Chapter 2.

[190] Ibid. In my interpretation, Sieyès and Condorcet were pre-eminent among those who actually learned something from the Americans, and managed to fashion their insights as new ideas, but what they learned has been lost for a long time.

possible in the case of the first constituent assembly, it may be possible in the case of the second one. Thus, he came up with the project of making the product of the first assembly merely provisional, so that the right formula could be followed the second time around, re-legitimating the whole enterprise.[191] Though no one ever seems to have noticed, this was an American-influenced idea of Sieyès, connected not only with the idea of a convention restricted to the task of constitution making, but also to calls for a second convention, both in Philadelphia and during the ratification debates.[192]

As far as I can tell, in recent French discussions only Olivier Beaud has pointed to Sieyès' argument concerning the provisionality of the first constitution, and its full import.[193] More importantly, though, this provisionality is central to his own conception of Sieyèsian constituent power, seen not in terms of an underlying antinomy but in two stages: destructive and constructive. According to Beaud's rather free reading, it is only in the destructive, *déconstituant* stage that the constituent power of Sieyès is unlimited in terms of the state of nature metaphor; in the constructive phase it can be limited in terms of Hauriou's normative universe[194] and analyzed, as against Carré de Malberg's dictum, by the instruments of legal science. But norms on their own do not limit, especially fragments no longer or not yet united into a legal order. So how is this limitation to be conceived? Here Beaud goes far beyond Sieyès, and offers a stage model of the constructive phase in terms of pre-constituent and constituent decisions. Pre-constituent decisions, themselves divided into two types, and the actors enforcing them then bind the constituent power. The interim constitution of Sieyès, rediscovered in France in 1945 and partially again in 1958, and then in the democratic transitions starting in Spain is the "modern" form that the binding takes: "prescribing the future constituent power, the forms (procedures and competence) and sometimes the fundamental principles." The interim constitution can organize, produce different versions, and link together the various stages of the second, constituent phase.[195]

Admittedly, Beaud is on to something important, however free his interpretation of Sieyès, who proposed stages not in general but only because of the special legitimation problems of the first constituent assembly in France. The legitimation problem involved, however, may relate to all new beginnings under

[191] Since the exercise of the constituent power (in the Constituent Assembly) "has not rigorously conformed to what the nature of that power requires ... the constitution ... provisionally obligatory ... will not be definitive till after a new constituent power is convoked in an extraordinary manner for that special object has given its agreement according to rigorous principles" (Sieyès, "Préliminaire" in *Écrits* 192); see also Sieyès, *What is the Third Estate?* 143, 151–2. Also Sieyès, "Dire sur la question du veto royal" in *Écrits* 239–40, where using the American term Sieyès is clear about the meaning: a national convention expressly convened and limited to this unique object.

[192] Curiously enough, this proposal is missing in the presentations of Schmitt and Arendt, and is misunderstood by those who think that Sieyès was only trying to combine a constituent assembly with a ratificatory referendum, namely the formula of the Convention Nationale of 1793–95 (cf. Jaume, "The Constituent Power in France").

[193] Beaud, *La puissance* 267–8.

[194] Ibid. 263–4.

[195] Ibid. 264–5 also 271, 272–6.

non-democratic regimes and also foreign occupations. While it is unconvincing to depict the first French *Constituantes* according to such a stage model, Beaud indeed makes a good attempt to begin to describe the most interesting contemporary constitution-making process, one that I have also repeatedly described in similar terms.[196] But many questions arise as he does this. For example: who does the binding, on what basis, who is bound, and can it work? And most importantly, is Beaud's theory the right one to sustain the description?

I start with the last question, one which becomes another: which theory? In the case of Beaud, the theory could be either the one he derives from Hauriou, or the Schmittian one in favor of which he abandons the former. Given his rejection of the doctrine of two sovereignties, which could explain how the constituent power might be limited, in my view Beaud has reason to leave Hauriou behind. But the Schmittian theory of unlimited constituent power, unlimited in all phases, ascribed to a unitary subject or carrier, a conceptualization present also in Sieyès before it was openly abandoned during Thermidor, fails to theoretically ground the second theory also derived from Sieyès, the one involving a provisional constitution and the desirability of double differentiation. So we are offered a very uneasy synthesis of a new theory where the constituent power has one subject *senso strictu* and many subjects *senso latu* (in the broad sense) whatever that ultimately means—and the meaning shifts I think as Beaud proceeds.[197] The subjects are so numerous—multiple and different *pré-constituant* and *constituant* instances, here called "authorities," where some have the competence the bind the others, and especially to limit the *constituent power properly speaking* that is said to be the last, the ratifying or sanctioning instance. With the power of decision assigned to those called authorities, the last thus may have the least power, yet it is very paradoxically the one pronounced as sovereign, or the sovereign.[198]

At this point, I think, the theory of sovereignty or sovereign constitution making can no longer carry the weight that is being assigned to it, and is open to all the objections of a Carré de Malberg, and even more to those of an H.L.A. Hart, who proved the superfluity of looking for the ghost of a sovereign organ in many or even most constitutional machines.[199] A charitable way of looking at Beaud's analysis is that, as in the case of Ackerman writing the second volume of *We the*

[196] Arato, *Civil Society*; Chapter 2 below (original version in (2005) 52 *Theoria* 106); and *Constitution Making under Occupation* (New York: Columbia, 2009) Chapter 2 and Conclusion. Aside from Beaud in *La puissance*, I know only of two other authors who have focused on this dimension, without, however, seeing the American roots: Ulrich Preuss, *Constitutional Revolution* (New Jersey: Humanities, 1990) and, in a general theoretical discussion of the relevant transition type, Kis, "Between Reform and Revolution."

[197] It would have been a little more clear to say the reverse: many subjects in the strict sense, one subject in the broadest sense, namely the political community on behalf of which the many subjects all act.

[198] Beaud, *La puissance* 266.

[199] H.L.A. Hart, *Concept of Law* (Oxford: Oxford University Press, 1961) Chapter IV. Beaud is even more vulnerable to Hart's critique for having adopted an obsolete theory of law, the command theory, in one of its least hospitable areas: constitutional law involving secondary rules. The two issues of organ sovereignty and command theory are of course connected.

People, we were catching him in the moment of shifting from one theory to another, most likely under the impact of the same historical events, for example, the radical but non-revolutionary forms of regime change from 1989 to the mid-1990s. All the same, his old theory still constrains him, as it also held Ackerman back. Unlike Carré de Malberg and Hauriou, Beaud does not generate a critique of the revolutionary model of convention government and, missing the clash over the interpretation of French revolutionary constitution making, attributes Schmitt's theory of sovereign dictatorship only to his experience with the Bolshevik revolution. He does not see the differences between American and French models, and retroactively links the new model, one that is incompatible with organ sovereignty, to the French revolutionary one that was based on it. He does not see the exceptional nature of Sieyès' proposal of provisionality in his context, or, if he does see it, he speaks as if it were actually adopted during the Revolution rather than being entirely disregarded.[200] As in Ackerman's case, it does not help to say that there is a beginning, middle, and end in each process, one that involves early as well as later "decisions." The real question is who is the agent at each stage, whether it is the same organ to whom sovereignty can be attributed or a set of agents that make such an attribution impossible. In line with this observation, it is a mistake to attribute sovereignty to either the beginning or the end of the process. The insistence on the subject of the referendum as the sovereign, rather than seeing even the referendum (which is not even necessary in the new model) as yet another counter against organ sovereignty means that in the end Beaud's new model is still open to authoritarian deformation and exploitation, as we have seen in the Iraqi case, actually one of the few "modern" cases after the French examples where the referendum was used in the new multi-stage model with an interim constitution.

As to the beginning, with its irreducible element of arbitrariness, when giving up on Hauriou's contract model in favor of Schmitt's denial of a plurality in the constituent power,[201] Beaud has deprived himself of a possible line of reasoning that could have made good use of this very notion. Beyond classical theories of the social contract, as in Schmitt's theory of the federation[202] contractual constitution making could be interpreted in terms of plurality and horizontality among agents that come to an agreement about the rules. As Hauriou anticipated, this idea could be generalized outside of federal settings, and indeed it was used by the famous round tables of the late 1980s and 90s, mostly in non-federal countries. As these show, even determining *legitimate* participation cannot be simply a sovereign decision, because political plurality carries its own weight in society, and, as countless historical examples show, either it is not up to merely an initial power holder to leave out other important ones from negotiations (examples include Inkatha in South Africa and Fidesz in Hungary), or if it is, the price may be political legitimacy (the Sunni forces and the Mahdi army in

[200] Beaud, *La puissance* 268. [201] Ibid. 251–2.

[202] Schmitt, *Verfassungslehre* Chapters 7 and 29.

Iraq; in Egypt: the democratic movements). Finally, even together the participants of a round table are not sovereign, because they cannot establish a new constitution on their own. The more legitimacy, the further the actors can go in entrenching their results, as the extensive thirty-four principles in South Africa show. By going too far, they invite their whole work to be legitimately repudiated.

Whatever its theoretical problems, Sieyès' idea of a provisional constitutional arrangement was no passing fancy, but an idea that found its way, as a minor theme at least, into French public law as an alternative to the doctrine of omnipotent original *Constituants* beyond a theory of mere amendment rules.[203] Let me sum up what I think were the tremendous potentials of the proposal:

1. A multi-stage, multi-actor model could be substituted for a single-stage, one-actor model.
2. The disadvantage of the French old regime and society of orders, stressed by Arendt, would be compensated for, by substituting at least in a significant part newly constituted actors for the privileged actors of the old regime and their normatively guided interaction for the legal state of nature of the revolution.
3. Part of the constitution-making process would be put under a constitutional rule, even if a provisional one. This would be an amendment rule of a constitutionalist constitution. Legal continuity would thereafter be maintained.
4. A doubly differentiated assembly could be set up restricted to a single task, serving together with a (provisional) legislative assembly itself created by the provisional constitution.
5. The constitution-making assembly could be put under limits, even though in Sieyès' theory this is strictly speaking not possible. Here the sovereignty doctrine was in the way of understanding how limitation could be possible. While the double differentiation he wished for would not always be possible, there could be functional substitutes as we now from South Africa.
6. There are free elections between the stages of constitution making, thereby also answering the important objection at least for the first assembly that subsequent electoral accountability does not play the role for a constituent assembly as it does for ordinary ones.[204]

Note the similarity of these potentials of the proposal to the American model as here depicted. My thesis again is not one of direct, linear influence of a model, but rather that the American concept of double differentiation, derived from Montesquieu, as I show elsewhere,[205] could perhaps motivate Sieyès to come up with a different and equally valuable alternative, the provisional constitution. Admittedly, his own doctrine of the constituent power, one which biased him

[203] Beaud, *La puissance* 276.

[204] Formulated by Beaud, *La puissance* 233.

[205] Arato, *Adventures* Chapter 2; and see especially Zweig, *Die Lehre vom Pouvoir Constituant* (Leipzig: J.C. B. Mohr 1909).

toward keeping constitutional politics open (as against the very difficult amendment rule being proposed and passed in the Constituent Assembly)[206] and his diagnosis of the legitimacy problems of the French process contributed to his hesitant proposal, twice, of interim arrangements that would be the foundation for a new and better process that just so happened in terms of its abstract principles to come closer to the American one than any in France, at that time or since. These were the principles that Carré de Malberg found in French amendment rules, and then re-derived from his normative concept of national sovereignty.

But was the normative concept of national sovereignty sufficient to establish the legitimacy of a structure of original constitution making that abstractly linked together the American model, French amendment rules, and recent multi-stage round-table-led experiments?

VIII RETURNING TO THE QUESTION OF AUTHORITY AND ITS FOUNDATIONS

The turn to amendment rules, and then back to original constitution making, reconceived as a multi-stage model via Sieyès, seems to be an excursus that takes us away from the problem of authority and legitimacy, the topic of this chapter. This is because amendment rules seem to be matters only of legality, a legal order the authority for which rests on the constitution. According to his positivist meta-theory, Carré de Malberg postulated that such a purely legal theory of authority is the best we can do within legal science. And yet the overlap between the American model of constitution making, with its extra legal aspects and the theory of amendments this particular theorist developed, suggests that a form of legitimacy is shared by both—the supposedly unique model of original and the more generally applicable though demanding versions of the derived constituent power. Admittedly, we have not fully articulated the meaning and the demands of this theory of *legitimacy* that on first sight may appear to be only the negative principle of non-embodiment and anti-usurpation. We need to articulate its positive content to show that constitution making and higher law can be *authorized* even when there are breaks in positive legality. Without such legitimate authority, extensive or significant though legal changes of the constitution through amending procedures of *Verfassungsänderung* (constitutional revision) or through other legal or extra-legal channels of *Verfassungswandel* (constitutional change) may be nevertheless deeply problematic.[207]

I distinguish between legitimacy and authority, though they are often overlapping categories. The distinction is not between normative and sociological levels. Both of these are relevant to legitimacy as well as authority, since in both cases the criteria of justice and validity philosophically considered, and the

[206] Zweig, *Die Lehre*; Esmein, *Éléments de droit constitutionnel.*

[207] Both points and their connection are anticipated by E.-W. Böckenförde's reinterpretation of the constituent power as a principle of political legitimacy. See Böckenförde, "Die verfassunggebende Gewalt des Volkes."

empirical beliefs of groups in a given form of justification can and almost always do diverge. Rather, in my view, legitimacy should be used in reference to principles that can justify processes, systems as well as the acts of political "officials," whereas authority requires leadership and, in a relative sense, at least a distinction between rulers and ruled. Authority requires an author;[208] legitimacy does not. Granted, there is legitimate authority, that is, when there are principles, sociological or normative, that validate or justify a leader or leadership. However, because of the problem of circularity, there cannot be authority all the way down. Legitimacy is ultimately always prior to authority, because pure self-authorization of a leadership is impossible to justify. In the cases of Weber's traditional or charismatic authority, sociological legitimacy is attained through either a tradition interpreted by others or charisma that must have emotional appeal to others if it is to exist at all. Finally, legitimation in the sociological sense is a more fluid category than authority. As in Hobbes, it can be linked to fear, or, as in Marx, to interest, and often it is impossible to separate fear or interest from normatively positive categories such as peace and wealth or welfare. Legitimation, moreover, unlike authority, can be negative. Often this too is linked to fear, to the fear of tyranny and usurpation, or fear of conditions even worse than the existing ones.

Such a negative legitimacy is at the heart of Carré de Malberg's national sovereignty, based on the fear of dictatorship, of which France had three variants at the time of his writing, each connected to at least one constitution-making episode. The negative idea of national sovereignty (close to Arendt's idea of banishing sovereignty) implies the restored sovereignty of the whole political community, one that ought not be confiscated or usurped by an organ, an institution, a branch of power, a body, or a single individual. It requires, moreover, that all branches of power respect the boundaries of one another, and a renunciation of the unilateral use of the constituent power that would allow self-authorized expansion of jurisdictions. All these, however, are negative principles, flowing from a reading of the doctrine of the constituent power in the spirit of Montesquieu, pioneered by Egon Zweig in 1906, continued by Carré de Malberg, and representing one side of Sieyès' thinking, originally the subordinate and thus less well-known one.[209] Narrowly understood, the principle of legitimation is only a pluralist one, which could be made consistent even with another facet of Montesquieu, the defense of the *Ständestaat* (or state of estates) that made his theory difficult to adopt at the time of the French Revolution. Broadly understood, as in America by the Federalist papers, the principle was of a modern constitutionalism where the separation of powers cum checks and balances and a written constitution as higher law mutually stabilized one

[208] See Pitkin, *The Concept of Representation*.

[209] Seen most explicitly in Sieyès, "Dire sur la question du veto royal" 239, where the two separations, executive from legislative and legislative from the constituent, are treated even in the same sentence, and also as deeply related; see also the post Thermidor speech: "Opinion de Sieyes sur plusieurs articles de titres IV et V du projet du constitution" in *Oeuvres de Sieyès* (Paris: EDHIS, n.d.) vol. III.

another. We can assume that this is part of the meaning of Carré de Malberg's "national sovereignty" applied to American "double differentiation," one that represents a political translation of his legal concept. But in that case national sovereignty when applied to constitution making as suggested here, either by American example, the model of amendment rules, or even Sieyès' precocious anticipation of interim constitutions, would be nothing more than the application of constitutionalism, usually understood in terms of the results of constitution making, to its very process.

In spite of the supposed contradiction involved,[210] I have noted this possibility on several occasions. Yet in view of the problems, I must again ask whether such a legitimacy can be enough? In light of the counter-majoritarian dilemmas raised in the case of already-authorized constitutions, although often resolved by pointing to the higher democratic pedigree and authorship of the constitution itself, is it sufficient to ground the authority of the constitution in the constitutionalist procedures of its own making (that can never be gapless or perfect in any case)? That again may be the best we can sometimes do, but it will immediately raise the problem of exclusion. We are thus back with the question of democracy, and my own earlier assertion that "where there is no democracy one cannot begin democratically."[211]

While it is true that legitimate authority begins with an existing principle of legitimacy, negative legitimacy does not in itself lead to any authority. It would be senseless to say, for example, that any plurality of actors is authorized by the mere fact of their plurality. That could still be highly exclusionary, as in an oligarchy overcoming the resistance of the excluded by sheer force. It is for this reason that I introduced the work of Hauriou, who aimed beyond the negative conception of the positivist. He too certainly shares the fear of revolutionary dictatorship and of governmental usurpation. But he thinks that revolutions always involve positive principles as well, ones that resist their own dictatorial tendencies. A theory of revolutionary authority first appears in the work of Hauriou, under the guise of another law, the law of freedom, which is somehow the heir of customary-associational law. The idea is that in the midst of revolutions, or rather liberation from an oppressive state legality, individual subjects recover what was always one of the two bases of law (next to coercion) before and under the state, namely association and consent. The modern state, however, positivizes that source, and Hauriou does not seem to claim that with the collapse of the state remnants of custom recover an independent legislative power. The most he ultimately says is that, in line with his theory, under the

[210] As articulated by the Hungarian right in the early 1990s, then led by István Csurka. The contradiction was supposed to be the application of constitutionalism when by definition it does not exist. As I repeatedly explained (Arato, *Civil Society*) the solution lies in treating the fictions of non-constitutionalist constitutions, its rights, and amendment rules in particular, as if they were real.

[211] A. Arato, "Forms of Constitution Making and Theories of Democracy' (1995–96) 17 *Cardozo Law Review* 2 191–225.

modern state the older legal source is transformed into a method of legitimation, based on tacit or explicit consent, and these sources can be attributed or denied to some old state authorities as well as offered to new revolutionary claimants that possess means of violence even before they have captured state power. We call the latter a revolutionary form of legitimacy, linked to a legal order of the future rather than of the past. But what are its bases, and how can it legitimate or help authorize the framers of that new legal order? What Hauriou offers in this context, tradition and liberation, is still too little. The grass-roots tradition of associationism he has in mind, if it was ever real, is vitiated in the modern world of societal complexity. Those who associate in a revolutionary movement tend to be a minority, and it is not clear why their consent should legitimate a project in the eyes of others.[212] And liberation itself is ultimately only a negative principle that unites only as long as the common enemy has not fallen.

Moreover, Hauriou's realism tends to vitiate even the little that he has accomplished. As we have seen, he lays great stress, following French and even American history, on the role of inherited state institutions if the emanationist vision of popular sovereignty is to be avoided. The point is important, because constitution making requires coercive power, and it is better when power holders are divided from the outset, and are forced to compromise. Accordingly, a participation of old powers as we have seen in the second version of Ackerman's argument (as opposed to the first) can help avoid a new power claiming to embody sovereignty. But this framework of compromise threatens to vitiate or at least weaken the idea of liberation implied in revolutionary legitimacy. And indeed, in all revolutions we should notice along with Tocqueville and Lenin the disappointment when people see the return of so many of the old guard in new power positions. The alternative in general being chaos is important for an ethics of responsibility, but does not help with the problem of identifying legitimate authority. Avoiding chaos or civil war too is an idea of negative legitimacy.

Fortunately, contemporary political theory can help us in bringing the negative and positive aspects of legitimation together. I have in mind the communication ethics of Arendt and Habermas on the one hand, and the theory of democracy of Claude Lefort on the other. As we have seen already in *On Revolution*, Arendt pointed to the fundamental communicative principle of making promises to one another that we are obliged to keep as the beginning that contains its own principle. Habermas has not only generalized this conception in terms of an expanded discourse theory of legitimacy, but has shown its modern roots, as opposed to traditional ones, in the enlightenment practice of the public sphere. Thus, the theory transcends the limits of a model of association and consent based on custom and tradition.

212 I think it is mistaken to imply as Z. Oklopcic does in "Three Arenas of Struggle: A Contextual Approach to the Constituent Power of 'the People'" (2014) 3 *Global Constitutionalism* 2 that it does not matter as long as the excluded are themselves not mobilized.

Converging with the efforts of Lefort, Habermas has redefined popular sovereignty beyond any form of embodiment in terms of an open-ended, critical communication process.[213] He identified the preconditions of this process in terms of procedural demands, requiring equality in discussion and mutual recognition of participants as full equals. These demands can admittedly seem idealistic and even tautological. Once again, as in the case of Schmitt's constituent power, they seem to treat the desirable outcome of a process, one that can never be fully realized, as the starting point. To me, however, they indicate only the difference between normative and sociological principles. In other words, the procedural model can be further developed in terms of sociologically and politically plausible desiderata. Instead of mere pluralism, one can insist on the inclusive pluralism of participation. Instead of the idealized societal public discussion of all concerned, one can demand public openness and participation by partial publics. Instead of absolute consensus one can attain relative consensus and fair compromise.[214] Instead of complete legal continuity, in revolutions one can try to restore the rule of law as early as possible. Instead of assuming the moral equality of previous oppressors with their victims, one can grant their right to participate through acts of generosity. That all these realistically tempered normative principles are possible is shown by the round-table-led constitution-making processes of the late 1980s and 1990s.

Admittedly, these processes involved intense conflict as well as agreement, and there is too little conflict in even a sociologically translated model of Habermas. It is here that the related, anti-embodiment model of Lefort becomes important. Lefort's well-known idea of democracy as the emptying of the space of power[215] on first sight resembles Carré de Malberg's negative idea of national sovereignty. Without necessarily being conscious of the connection, Lefort draws attention to it when he distinguishes between the idea of power "belonging to no one" and "being an empty place." The former, an idea rightly said to be that of (European) aristocratic society (thus with an opaque but still unmistakable reference to Montesquieu and the *Ständestaat*) means only that actors who separate or divide power deny one another the right or the ability to take all of it. The totality of power exists but in the middle, between them, and could still be assumed by the winner in the competition without destroying the social foundations of the given society.[216] To make Lefort's meaning clearer, we may point out that this is indeed what happened in the transition from *Ständestaat* to royal absolutism, explored from Bodin through Montesquieu all the way down to Tocqueville. However, when the place of power is empty, according to Lefort, this

213 J. Habermas, "Popular Sovereignty as Procedure" in J. Habermas, *Between Facts and Norms* (Cambridge, MA: MIT, 1996) Appendix I.

214 Habermas, *Between Facts and Norms* 165–7.

215 C. Lefort, *Democracy and Political Theory* (Cambridge, MA: MIT Press, 1989) 17ff; C. Lefort, *Writing: The Political Test* (Durham, NC: Duke University Press, 2000) 225ff.

216 Lefort, *Democracy and Political Theory* 226.

means that both external and internal foundations of unity, God or social totality, no longer exist or are even conceivable from the point of view of politics. Society's unity is symbolic in the sense that it is constituted through a fundamental division and conflict over its principles. In such a society separation and division of power are institutionalized much more deeply than in the version Montesquieu has analyzed. I would add with Sieyès that the distinction between *constituant* and *constitué* is just such a step of deeper institutionalization. But, as Hannah Arendt so well stressed, it raises new problems. With the backdrop of the totalitarian fusion of power, law, and knowledge, analogous to, but more far reaching than the French revolutionary attempts to derive law and power from the same source criticized by Arendt, Lefort's aim is to show how democracy blocks the road to all models of the embodiment of sovereignty, of putting the People-as-One into the empty place of the king.

So far, of course, Lefort's is only a more conflictual, more socially rooted and more secularized version of the theory here attributed to Carré de Malberg's concept of national sovereignty, and the jurist's important critique of organ sovereignty. But Lefort's theory is also more democratic. Although he stresses the negativity of the fundamental principle, in his theory this too would be open to questioning and contestation. Thus the appearance of popular sovereignty, and the antinomy it introduces into the foundations of legitimacy, is not a flaw or a recurring political-theoretical error, but a necessary consequence of both democracy and the conflict that belongs to its essence. The question of sovereignty should not be erased, he clearly states, in a purely negative model.[217] But no claim of sovereignty can go unchallenged without immense dangers. In my interpretation at least, Lefort's dynamic empty space, unlike Carré de Malberg's static national sovereignty, means that there will be claims to occupy it, immediately questioned, confronted, and challenged by counterclaims.[218] Until successfully challenged or replaced the claimants have authority. They become usurpers only when they capture all the power, including the power to question, making further questioning of their authority impossible.

I would not adopt an orthodox version of Lefort's position, one that neglects all consensus in favor of a conflict model. For the resulting serious conflicts to remain within the framework of *constitutional* democracy, I believe one needs a consensual minimum to frame them and the public sphere of questioning. As Habermas has realized, that is one function of constitutions and constitutionalism. The negative principle of national legitimacy with its important linkage between written constitutions and the separation of powers provides that minimum. But for constitutionalism to be *democratic*, such a constitution also has to be democratically made and renewed, and for that a negative principle is insufficient. In spite of its dangers, the principle of popular sovereignty, within the antinomy of the popular and national analyzed by Carré de Malberg for France, has been present from the outset and is not likely to disappear in favor of the

[217] Lefort, *Writing: The Political Test* 232.

[218] Morgan, *Inventing the People*.

negative pole of sovereignty. If the dangers of usurpation in the name of the popular sovereign are to be avoided, we need to rely on the sociologically translatable principles of plurality, inclusion, consensus, publicity, legality, and generosity.

One interesting historical example confirming a Lefortian version of how this takes place has been generated by F. Furet and E. Morgan, and has been confirmed by the studies of K. Baker and P. Rosanvallon on the French Revolution.[219] Combining their testimony (for England, America, and France), the principle of popular sovereignty seems to have been initially popularized, if not actually invented, by oligarchic power holders or claimants who sought a sufficiently great principle of legitimacy, capable of challenging and replacing the sovereignty of the king. But evidently the people's natural body could not be identified as easily as the king's: in this sense the famous, continually repeated transference from pope to king to people had to become diffuse and even threaten to break down when it came to the last term. This is of course the idea of democracy as an empty space. Yet bodies would emerge that claimed to speak in the name of the people or even to be the people's body and to exercise the people's will. Parliament, Cromwell's Army, the Third Estate, the National Assembly, Continental Congress, or state legislatures, even Wood's and Ackerman's conventions, La Convention Nationale, or the Paris sections would all be such claimants, each denouncing the previous one and being challenged by the next. Morgan rightly remarks that the counterfactual democratic norm itself changes in the process, is enriched, becomes more inclusive, and has such components as universal rights originally undreamt of. But unless the struggle is short-circuited and a successful usurper emerges, a plebiscitary dictator, for example, and this is a constant danger, it is the movement and questioning that is the essence of legitimation by popular sovereignty rather than one of its way stations in any kind of body, natural or artificial.

Just as Carré de Malberg's national sovereignty can be rediscovered in the American model of constitution making and in Sieyès' attempted innovation of the provisional constitution (which had to wait to bear fruit until 1945 or later) so can the model of popular sovereignty developed in the theoretical path of Lefort, as helpfully concretized by intellectual historians such as Morgan, Baker, and Rosanvallon. What I would stress in closing is the institutionalization in a single, multi-stage model of the assertion, challenging-questioning, and reassertion of authority based on popular sovereignty with ever-changing meanings of a multi-bodied people.[220]

Initially it must be a body with deficient authority that claims some kind of right to do something in the name of the people: the Estates General transmuted into a National Assembly; a convention whose members are delegated

[219] Ibid.; also see F. Furet, *Interpreting the French Revolution* (Cambridge: Cambridge University Press, 1981) 48–52, and Lefort, *Democracy and Political Theory* on this subject.

[220] See, for example, N. Walker, "Post Constituent Constitutionalism: The Case of the European Union" in Laughlin and Walker, *Paradox of Constitutionalism* 261–4.

rather than elected; or, looking into the future, a provisional government based on self-constituted councils, a round table based on parties co-opting one another and so on. In this assumption Lindahl is partially right, but only partially. Because it is deficient in legitimacy, this instance has only the right to recommend to others, as the Americans James Madison and James Wilson rightly admitted, thereby recapturing one aspect of Rousseau's legislator that allowed for the separation of authority and power. But that authority cannot be too deficient—it must be somehow justified or legitimated. Sieyès does this for the Third Estate quite obviously, as does Madison for the Federal Convention, both with pretty strong arguments, even though they also admit the deficiency. The same could be done, even more successfully, for the round tables based on plurality, inclusion, legality, and publicity. But it would be as great a mistake to focus on the deficiency alone as it would be to accept the justification as complete. In Sieyès' case the proposal of provisionality, the call for a second assembly freely elected on the one hand, and his insistence on the other that the initial national assembly nevertheless had the full right to pass a constitution (preferably an interim one), indicates that he was fully aware of both sides. The second assembly would be less deficient because it would be freely elected. Admittedly, Sieyès here did not go far enough to provide a proposal that was in any case not really on the agenda. Only if one either limited the authority of the second assembly in a procedural or substantive way, or added the requirement that its constitution too would have to be ratified in some additional process, would one be saying that even this assembly could not occupy the empty space of power or fully embody sovereignty.

This type of final limitation was indeed characteristic of the American example, as well as the contemporary round-table model. Admittedly, in America there was no need for an interim constitution because of the pre-existing constitutionalist context, though even here the Articles of Confederation arguably played such a role from the equally important point of view of learning. Here the attempts to limit the drafting Convention succeeded only very partially, in terms of its voting rule by states that, however, abandoned the earlier rule of unanimity. The Convention on the whole made its own rules. Yet it could not be said to be sovereign, as Carré de Malberg and Schmitt respectively noticed with the opposite evaluation, because the claim that the constitution was initially only a recommendation was not only technically but also politically justified. Had more than four states rejected the document it would have been null and void. However, it cannot be said that the ratifying conventions to whom the recommendation was made were therefore *the* sovereign people. This is because of their plurality, and because they were still acting as if they were making a new treaty on behalf of the peoples of ratifying states in the plural[221] and because they could say yes or no, but not amend, something the Anti-Federalists bitterly resented and even Jefferson at first criticized. Finally,

221 See Madison, *Federalist* 39 and Ackerman, *We the People* vol. II, 34ff.

the amending power, still arguably part of the original constitution-making process, that was to enact the Bill of Rights, was itself composed of two stages (moving through Congress and the states) and had to operate under strict rules not of its own choice. This amending power could be another stage in the process of constitution making, because there were already several stages whose status was always more akin to powers of revision than those of assemblies with sovereignty and omnipotence. The way was open to a future, open-ended constitutional politics, except for the fact, disguised by the relative ease with which the Bill of Rights was passed, that the new amendment rule of Article V was an extremely difficult one, with overly high consensus requirements.

While calling attention to the relationship of the American and round-table models of constitution making on the level of legitimacy and authorization, I do not wish to claim or admit identity.[222] In my view, the U.S. process of constitution making, whether in the key original states of Massachusetts and New Hampshire, or on the Federal level, was not post sovereign, at least not reflexively so. The ringing declaration of authorship in Philadelphia ("we the people"), the later debates until the civil war about the locus of sovereignty, and theories as late as Ackerman's in the 1990s, all testify to an antinomic model, in the context of the procedures of actual authorization just described. In other settings, these antinomies could lead either to one or another level claiming full sovereignty, or to dual power. Finally, rigid reliance on the American model, even if freed from some of its ideological baggage, would still make post sovereignty at best an exceptional phenomenon, presupposing the rare givens of pre-existing republican institutions stressed by Hannah Arendt.

On the contrary, the round-table paradigm does not presuppose pre-existing republican or even rule of law systems. In a post revolutionary atmosphere from the 1970s to the mid-1990s, sovereign claims were not made on behalf of any of the actors in the process. The danger of dual power was avoided by the treatment of the initial drafting instance as a private gathering outside the constitution and with even less power than the American drafting conventions based on state legislatures or townships. The American convention could easily be interpreted as a sovereign *constituant*, as happened in France in 1792–93, in Russia in 1993 where dual power did briefly emerge, and in Latin America repeatedly, most recently in Venezuela. Even if we were to represent the American convention as a forerunner of the multi-stage process led by the round table, it is only with the latter that the post sovereign paradigm fully came into its own.

222 For a lengthy comparison, see A. Arato, "Conventions, Constituent Assemblies and Round Tables" (2012) 1 *Global Constitutionalism* 1 and Chapter 3 below.

2

Constitutional Learning

I FROM BAGHDAD TO PHILADELPHIA

Constitutional politics has returned in our time in a truly dramatic way. In the last forty years, not only in the new or restored democracies of South and East Europe, Latin America, and Africa, but also in the established liberal or not so liberal democracies of Germany, Italy, Japan, Israel, New Zealand, Canada, and Great Britain, issues of constitution making, constitutional revision, and institutional design or redesign have been put on the political agenda. Even in the United States, given the new or renewed problems of our versions of presidentialism, federalism, and electoral regime, Article V of the constitution has come to be experienced as a veritable prison house, and judicial constitution making (think of Citizens United!) is often seen as much as a threat to as the protection of democratic mechanisms. And, most recently, in countries currently experiencing revolutions, whether externally imposed[1]—namely Afghanistan and Iraq—or entirely internal—such as Tunisia, Egypt, Libya, and Yemen—constitutional politics has turned out to be a central stake in the ongoing political process. We are living in an epoch in which nations seem to be slouching, or being prodded, toward "Philadelphia," and Americans, as the heirs of Madison and MacArthur, are sorely tempted to try teaching others the secrets of their country's success as a supposedly continuous 200-year-old constitutional democracy. But to be an effective teacher, it is not enough to be in the position of political-military superiority. One must first relearn to learn. And learning entails recognition that there is something new to be learned.

It is astonishing how unprepared Americans were for the job of constitutional pedagogues that the government unilaterally assumed in Iraq. After several variants of a top-down, imposed, non-consensual process of constitution making were advanced by Secretary Rumsfeld and Civilian Administrator Bremer, it was a *Fatwah* of the Ayatollah Ali al-Sistani demanding free elections to a constituent assembly that should have (but of course did not) implicitly remind Americans of Thomas Paine's well-known dictum that, "The constitution of a country is not the act of its government, but of the people constituting a government." Moreover, it was painfully obvious that most of the government's supposed

[1] See A. Arato, *Constitution Making Under Occupation* (New York: Columbia University Press, 2009).

specialists advising the Coalition Provisional Authority were quite unaware of the more recent lessons of a dramatic wave of constitution making, culminating in the new constitution of the Republic of South Africa.[2]

Yet, that something new has emerged in the world of constitution making was recognized very early. Already in the midst of the dramatic events of 1989–90, it was the German constitutional scholar Ulrich Preuss who first called our theoretical attention to the transformation of inherited paradigms of constitution making. In a series of articles and also a book[3] he insisted on the obsolescence of the revolutionary democratic model as old as the American, French, and perhaps even the English Revolutions, and the emergence in Central Europe including the old German Democratic Republic of a new model no longer based on or appealing to the *potestas absoluta* of the sovereign, unified constituent power of the people. Preuss identified a multiplicity of constitution-making events and stages, legal continuity, changes through amending the old constitution, the organizing role of round-table negotiations, and the decline of constituent assemblies as the marks of the model he saw in action, as an expert advisor of the Round Table of the German Democratic Republic. Now with many years' hindsight, especially with the full unfolding of the new paradigm in South Africa, one would certainly add the negotiation of an interim constitution, and the drafting of a final one by a freely elected assembly, to this list. More controversial perhaps would be the inclusion of a constitutional court created under the interim constitution in the process of generating the final one.

Back in the early 1990s, Ulrich Preuss gave a variety of answers to the question of justifying the new paradigm. No longer based on the authority of a pre-constitutional people, the constitution would be the very source of the meaning of the people as a legal entity and actor. But this answer would have entirely reversed the relationship between *constituant* and *constitué*, and Preuss did not seem to veer so far away from Carl Schmitt, who once greatly influenced him. Thus he gave another answer, also non-"Schmittian," but one close to my own stress on the role of civil society: that the round tables represent not the unified, monolithic people, but the multiplicity, diversity, and plurality of citizens. This argument then prepared the ground for a new conception of reflexive, self-limiting, open-ended, civil-society-based constitutionalism. As to the question of legitimate origins, the approach seemed to recover something of Hannah Arendt's claim about America, where, according to her, the constituent power was based on organized, political society or societies, rather than the people in the state of nature or the multitude. For Preuss, civil society replaced Arendt's small republics, thereby going beyond American exceptionalism.

[2] See ibid.

[3] See U. Preuss, "The Roundtable Talks in the German Democratic Republic" in J. Elster (ed.) *The Roundtable Talks and the Breakdown of Communism* (Chicago, IL: University of Chicago, 1996); U. Preuss, *Constitutional Revolution* (Atlantic Highlands, NJ: Humanities Press, 1995). His co-authored article with Elster, "Constitutional Politics in Eastern Europe" in J. Elster, C. Offe, and U. Preuss (eds), *Institutional Design in Post-Communist Societies* (Cambridge: Cambridge University Press, 1998) has given up his earlier, original perspectives.

A few years later, the argument concerning the emergence of the new was very much deepened by János Kis,[4] the leader of one of the main parties of the Hungarian National Round Table, the Alliance of Free Democrats (SZDSZ). Where I was connected to Preuss through his reliance on the concept of civil society, Kis further developed the notion of the self-limiting revolution we both inherited from the Polish Democratic Opposition. In my view, he was the first to clearly see a process of transformation fundamentally different from either reform or revolution, one based on both precise legal analysis and learning from the history of revolutions, which, even in the sympathetic treatment of Arendt, have almost always failed to establish constitutional democracies. Kis postulated a third type of change, first called regime change, later re-christened as coordinated transition, capable of accomplishing radical transformation of fundamental principles of legitimacy in the context of legal continuity. Where Preuss stressed the underlying role of civil society in the generation of new actors capable of compromise and self-limitation, Kis insisted on the process of inclusive negotiations capable of transforming mere modus vivendi into overlapping consensus concerning the principles of constitutional democracy.

For a long time, I believed that both approaches were highly important and built my own conception around them. In particular, the idea of post sovereign constituent power I derived from their parallel and complementary reconceptualization of the old notion of the *pouvoir constituant*.[5] In spite of these efforts, I have been repeatedly forced to notice that neither the new analyses nor, more importantly, the experience on which they were based were taken into sufficient account by the rapidly increasing number of scholars concentrating on constitutional politics, or, again more importantly, by the main actors and their advisors engaged in designing constitutions, including their processes of design. This was the case even before more classical revolution and constitutional reform both returned to the political scene, seeming to validate the old dichotomy, marginalizing the possibility of another form of constitutional transformation, and before there were cases of failure of post sovereign constitution making, for different reasons, in Hungary and partially in Nepal.

Undoubtedly, the failure to develop sufficient interest in the genuinely new phenomena had also to do with trends in legal theory and in political science. Most constitutional theorists in the United States, and even more in civil law countries, have had traditionally little interest in comparative politics. Thus, many of the legal advisors to recent constitution makers abroad have had little academic training in the politics of the areas where they have become involved. The rather monstrous, ineffective, and rigid Dayton formula for Bosnia was one outcome of such efforts. Moreover, the now vast comparative literature on

[4] J. Kis, "Between Reform and Revolution" (1995) 1 *Constellations* 3; J. Kis, "Between Reform and Revolution" (Spring 1998) 12 *East European Politics and Societies* 2 300–83.

[5] See A. Arato, *Civil Society, Constitution and Legitimacy* (Lanham, MD: Rowman and Littlefield, 2000) and more recently A. Arato, "Conventions, Constituent Assemblies, and Round Tables: Models, Principles and Elements of Democratic Constitution-making" (2012) 1 *Global Constitutionalism* 1.

democratic transitions has paid relatively little attention to constitution making; undoubtedly the anti-legal prejudices of contemporary political science play a role in this.[6] Without using legal categories, and uninvolved in the normative problems of the actors, even a sophisticated analyst such as Jon Elster managed to see primarily the paradoxes facing constitution makers attempting "to fix their boats in open sea" (or pulling themselves from quicksand, Münchausen-like, by their own hair) rather than the innovative dimensions of their solutions. Though rich in political detail, as well as in attempts at causal analysis, his conception is ultimately more about the aesthetics, rather than the politics, of constitution making.[7]

More deeply committed to democratic and constitutionalist outcomes, two contributions by American authors stand out as the most interesting efforts to address in a creative way the problems, successes, and failures of constitution making in the new democracies. Bruce Ackerman, relying on the preliminary results of his ongoing effort to bring together republican and liberal interpretations of constitutional democracy, addressed in particular the *legitimacy* problems of both piecemeal parliamentary constitution making and constituent assemblies dominated by former communists.[8] Above all, he was concerned that the brief window of opportunity to make liberal constitutions, "the constitutional moment," would be missed. On the other hand, Stephen Holmes was extremely critical of premature attempts to establish constitutional closure, and especially of an early emphasis on human rights jurisprudence that in his view limited the ability of political communities to learn, as well as that of governments to act, or to build new legitimacy for their actions through appeals to substantive justice.[9] In line with classical conceptions of the constituent power, whether American, French, or British, both interpreters were highly skeptical about the powerful role of constitutional courts in the constituent process, as at the time of their writing in Hungary, and by implication, later in South Africa. That role, however, was a logical component of the post sovereign paradigm, even if not exhibited equally in all cases.

In what follows, in search of a synthetic position, I try to explore the complementary strengths and weaknesses of these two approaches. I will try to show that Ackerman, under the influence of his own interpretation of the American model of constitution making, and its ability to generate legitimacy, neglected the need for a process open to learning and reflexive self-correction. Conversely,

[6] One partial exception is J. Linz and A. Stepan, *Problems of Democratic Transition and Consolidation* (Baltimore, MD: Johns Hopkins University Press, 1996).

[7] See J. Elster, "Rebuilding the Boat in the Open Sea. Constitution-making in Eastern Europe" (1993) 71 *Public Administration* 169–217.

[8] B. Ackerman, *The Future of the Liberal Revolution* (New Haven, CT: Yale University Press, 1992).

[9] S. Holmes. "Back to the Drawing Board" (Winter 1993) 2 *East European Constitutional Review* 1 21–5. The argument is almost completely incorporated in S. Holmes and C. Sunstein, "The Politics of Constitutional Revision in Eastern Europe," in S. Levinson (ed.), *Responding to Imperfection: The Theory and Practice of Constitutional Amendment* (Princeton, NJ: Princeton University Press, 1995).

I will argue that Holmes, whose model at times seemed to come close to British parliamentary sovereignty, which he apparently regarded as the best guarantee of learning, was remarkably little concerned about the requirements of a constitution's democratic legitimacy. While rightly stressing learning, he did not see the danger of losing the normative dimension when learning has no limits, in terms of either time or substance. Unfortunately, neither author saw the link between process and substance. Ackerman in particular initially recommended a presidentially led procedure that was obviously inconsistent with his reservations regarding presidential government in normal, non-constitutional politics.[10] Curiously enough, neither of the two approaches, given their American and British assumptions, discovered the great innovation of round-table constitution making in the context of real or fictional legal continuity, and its ability to simultaneously solve problems of legitimacy as well as learning. This achievement becomes fully visible only from a point of view that combines and goes beyond the two approaches.

II ASSEMBLIES AND COURTS

We have long assumed that constitutions can be made by extraordinary or ordinary powers, by the *pouvoir constituant* or by various *pouvoirs constitués*. In the latter case, according to the classical doctrine of the separation of powers, the main role will be played by legislative assemblies, or by powerful executives who can manipulate assemblies, or even bypass them through plebiscites. While especially in common law countries the courts certainly do play a major role in shaping the constitution in Kelsen's material sense,[11] constitutional courts are supposed to be irrelevant, for almost logical reasons, to the original establishment of a constitution.[12] This is so because within any plausible scheme of the modern separation of powers courts can play their constituent role only under the guise of adjudication or interpretation. When there is nothing to interpret, because the old constitution is dead and the new one has not been created, constitutional courts have nothing to do, and indeed their existence becomes temporarily questionable.

At least this is the case in a classical European theory of constitution making that emphasizes revolutionary rupture, as well as entirely new and purely democratic beginnings. What is quite astonishing therefore is the role constitutional courts actually played in the constitution-making processes of several transitions to new or renewed democracies in Central Europe (Hungary, Poland, Bulgaria), Latin America (Chile, and later Colombia and Venezuela), and South

[10] There may have been a development, however, given the time lag between his two positions on presidential powers. See B. Ackerman, "The New Separation of Powers" (2000) 113 *The Harvard Law Review* 3.

[11] H. Kelsen, *General Theory of Law and State* (Cambridge, MA: Harvard University Press, 1945) 124. Woodrow Wilson's depiction of the court as "a constituent assembly in permanent session" was a polemical way of pointing to this state of affairs during the heyday of the substantive due process of the Lochner courts.

[12] When indeed there is (unlike in Great Britain) an original moment of constitutional creation.

Africa. The common presupposition for such an original role is the characteristic legal continuity in these very different patterns that represented revolts not only against specific dictatorships, but against the very idea of dictatorship, linked by definition to the dominance of will and discretion over law.[13] Evidently, legal continuity requires enforcement, and the only plausible mode of enforcement against the political branches of power could be a court, moreover, one endowed with special institutional prestige and even charisma. Thus, when the South African Constitutional Court set up by the interim constitution sought to defend previously agreed constitutional principles against the draft of the constitutional (National) Assembly, which was dominated by the powerful African National Congress, it had the authority to enforce its decision.

The new role of constitutional courts tends to surprise not only advocates of European theory, but even Americans more used to activist jurisprudence. Both Ackerman and Holmes are very suspicious of powerful constitutional courts during the early development of new democracies, but for apparently different and even opposing reasons. According to Ackerman, given the "softness" of the legitimacy of the constitutional background in the case of elite-negotiated round tables, and the piecemeal creation of constitution by a variety of instances, a constitutional court such as the one in Hungary in the period between 1990 and 1998, which was formally one of the most powerful in the world, had weak democratic justification for its repeated exercise of counter-majoritarian review.[14] Moreover, to the extent that the constitutional background remained incomplete, an active court had to wind up assuming democratically illegitimate quasi-constituent powers. As far as Holmes was concerned, the human rights jurisprudence of such a court (which he compared, remarkably, to the unelected former Politburo[15]) was suspicious because it interfered with the freedom of action and the legitimation needs of the new and still uncertain parliamentary governments. Still, Ackerman and Holmes were obviously aware of the fact that the U.S. Supreme Court has declared only two federal statutes unconstitutional in its first seventy years: with the greatest of caution and subtlety in *Marbury v. Madison*,[16] and rashly and disastrously in the *Dred Scott*[17] decision. In Hungary, dozens of statutes or part of statutes were invalidated in a period of only seven years.

Interestingly, both Ackerman and Holmes relied on aspects of the original process of constitution making in the United States in their search for models. Ackerman focused on the spatial dualism of separating constitutional assembly

[13] See A. Arato, "Good-bye to Dictatorships?" (2000) 67 *Social Research* 925–55.

[14] Ackerman, *The Future of the Liberal Revolution* Chapter 6. The book was written before the drafting of the South African interim constitution, and it is hard to know what Ackerman would say about the role of the Constitutional Court, even more pronounced than that of Hungary.

[15] Holmes, "Back to the Drawing Board" 23; Holmes and Sunstein, "The Politics of Constitutional Revision in Eastern Europe" 300.

[16] (1802) 5 U.S. 137. See Ackerman, *The Future of the Liberal Revolution* 100.

[17] *Dred Scott v. Sandford* 60 U.S. 393 (1857).

("convention") and ordinary legislatures, and what he at one time took to be the charismatic proto-presidential leadership of the constitution-making effort. Holmes, temporarily putting aside his new-found preference for a British-type monism,[18] had in mind the temporal dualism of two constitution-making efforts: the one in 1781 that produced the Articles of Confederation, and the Philadelphia Convention of 1787 that clearly was the result of learning from the experience of six years of failed constitutional government.[19]

In spite of the American experience of two early constitutional syntheses that he notes,[20] Ackerman feared that if a new constitution did not emerge from the original revolutionary setting, the window of opportunity for legitimate constitution making may close altogether. He predicted that this would lead to either ongoing constitutional tinkering through parliamentary amendments, or the freezing of illegitimate constitutions, depending on the amendment rule in place. Holmes, who evidently supported parliamentary constitution making and considered attempts to separate constitutional and normal politics as unrealistic, and even undesirable, feared instead any early insulation of constitutional settlements from change, through difficult amendment rules or vigorous constitutional review or both, whether or not the constitutions were legitimately produced. In advocating an early version of the "hegemonic preservation" model,[21] Holmes, along with his co-author Cass Sunstein, claimed, more correctly for Romania than Bulgaria, that early settlement of a well-entrenched constitution was the aspiration and achievement of Communist elites surviving from the old regime.[22] They rightly recognized the importance of the interim constitutions in Hungary and Poland, but then, remarkably, advocated leaving these constitutions, with their monolithic parliamentary amendment rules, indefinitely in place, along with an entirely open process without time limits, as seems to be the case under British parliamentary sovereignty. I agree with Ackerman that we have seen that pattern in places inspired by the Westminster model, notably in Israel, yield very negative results.[23]

[18] I say "new-found," because of his important article "Precommitment and the Paradox of Democracy" in J. Elster and R. Slagstad (eds), *Constitutionalism and Democracy* (Cambridge: Cambridge University Press, 1988), which represents a classical American position on constitutional entrenchment.

[19] In neither case was the British type of parliamentary sovereignty operative, above all because of federalism. See Holmes, "Back to the Drawing Board" 25. It was also not quite logical in the present context to compare the second American effort of 1787 and the first French effort of 1789–91. Both first efforts produced highly inflexible constitutions. The second French effort of the National Convention, however, completely failed when the constitution of 1793 was not put into effect. In fact the French pattern in each revolutionary epoch seems to have been exactly the one Holmes proposes (1791 and 1793; 1848 and 1852; 1874; 1945 and 1958). But these repeated French efforts at constitution making, linked to many political disasters, would not inspire much confidence today, in spite of wide admiration for the institutions of the Fifth Republic.

[20] Ackerman, *The Future of the Liberal Revolution* 56–7.

[21] R. Hirschl, *Towards Juristocracy* (Cambridge, MA: Harvard University Press, 2004).

[22] Holmes and Sunstein, "The Politics of Constitutional Revision" 290; Ackerman too seems to buy this story, see Ackerman, *The Future of the Liberal Revolution* 60, which does not help his case arguing for an early constitutional moment. See my alternative in Chapter 4 of Arato, *Civil Society, Constitution and Legitimacy* 159ff.

[23] Arato, *Civil Society* 290 and elsewhere. Also Ackerman, *The Future of the Liberal Revolution*.

Both analysts were making obviously important arguments. In the name of institutionalizing a legitimate constitution that could become the reference point for a future constitutional patriotism, Ackerman recommended American lessons that allowed the U.S. constitution to become an object of public celebration already in its own time, or at the very latest after the ratification of the Bill of Rights.[24] Thus, he stressed a separate assembly in which everyday political considerations and institutional interests of already established political bodies were not present, and opportunities for public mobilization and participation in the ratification process, as well as charismatic leadership of the greatest hero of the revolution (presumably, if there was such a leader). But Holmes, who stressed constitution making as part and parcel of ordinary politics, was surely right to place emphasis on the institutionalization of constitutional learning, especially for populations (unlike the Americans) largely without the experience of any previous democratic government. For these reasons, the fact that their political recommendations were almost at opposite ends of the spectrum was disturbing. Especially striking are their very different relations to the time dimension of constitution making. Holmes proposed open-ended, purely parliamentary constitution making with little legal supervision and control, for a long period.[25] Relatively early, dualistic constitution making under presidential leadership was Ackerman's recommendation. The latter of course could not have objected to at least "preservationist" or "synthetic" exercises of counter-majoritarian review, in the context of a "harder" constitutional background of sufficient democratic legitimacy. Yet their diverging proposals seemed to suggest that there was apparently no way to combine both the virtues of institutionalized learning and legitimacy.[26]

III FROM PHILADELPHIA TO BUDAPEST

Reading these American proposals with the eyes of their addressees in recent (or future) new democracies could easily lead to a skepticism blind to their respective emphases on legitimacy and learning, emphases that should have been welcome then, and are even more welcome now, when some of their negative predictions have been unfortunately realized. But it is hard to blame the skeptics living in countries where new constitutions had to be made, in view of both historical experience and theoretical considerations.

[24] L.W. Levy, "Bill of Rights" in L.W. Levy (ed.), *Essays on the Making of the Constitution* (New York: Oxford University Press, 1969).

[25] Apparently, Holmes and Sunstein would support a somewhat more insulated constitution along with a more active judicial review at a much later stage of development.

[26] One ordinarily tries to promote both virtues through a moderately difficult amendment rule. For East Europe, Holmes and Sunstein specifically deny this option, even if the amendment rule they support would be quite consistent with it.

To begin with, Holmes' recommendations did not hold up too well from the point of view of the needs of countries in transition from long periods of arbitrary government.[27] In the countries of provisional constitutions where the processes of constitution making were left indefinitely open—namely Poland and Hungary—it has been inordinately difficult to bring the process to a legitimate conclusion despite repeated efforts, precisely because of the constant intermingling of constitutional and ordinary politics that Holmes considered harmless or even beneficial.[28] Ackerman predicted this, in part referring to the Israeli experience, where he rightly notes that the constitution-making moment was missed in 1948.[29] Meanwhile, however, the amended texts from 1989 to 1990, in part the products of non-freely elected parliaments and unelected round tables, were constantly under attack, and every parliamentary super-majority capable of constitution making was immediately denounced as a "constitutional dictatorship" in the making. And indeed, given electoral systems with huge potential disproportionality and flimsy constitutional amendment rules, a "dictatorship" that might impose a constitution of a harder or more authoritarian democracy was possible at any moment—when a new super-majority considered its supposed popular-plebiscitary support sufficient to bypass parliamentary consensus building.[30] This is what finally happened in Hungary, as we will see in Chapter 4 of this book. Holmes and Sunstein accepted rather lightly the idea that a normal parliament should be a quasi-constituent assembly, not realizing that with the open-endedness they promoted, this model could easily degenerate into either self-dealing imposition by a temporary majority, or the kind of permanent constitutional revolution that would be unable to found any system of authority, before itself winding up with an authoritarian outcome.[31]

At the same time, there was little evidence that would suggest that constitutional courts have really interfered with the freedom of governments to act in cases that really mattered, or to build political legitimacy in support of their actions. For example, projects of reprivatization and retroactive justice were in fact quite unpopular in Hungary, where the Court did, for a time at least, interfere with such attempts emanating from parliament, efforts that Holmes

[27] It is hard to know in fact what we are to make of the example of Khasbulatov's cavalier use of constitutional amendments Holmes and Sunstein bring up ("The Politics of Constitutional Revision" 281ff), since that very pattern in Russia played a crucial role in the disaster of 1993, which involved an armed clash between the president and the parliament.

[28] See the series of articles by W. Osiatinsky for Poland: "Brief History of the Constitution, A" (1997) 6 *East European Constitutional Review* 66; and "Poland's Constitutional Ordeal" (1994) 3 *East European Constitutional Review* 29. In the end the Polish effort was successful, the Hungarian one was not. For the reasons and a comparative analysis see Arato, "Refurbishing the Legitimacy of the New Regime: Constitution-making Endgame in Hungary and Poland" in *Civil Society.*

[29] Ackerman, *The Future of the Liberal Revolution* 63–4.

[30] See G. Halmai's essay "Az 1949-es alkotmány jogállamosítása" in Bozóki (ed) *A rendszerváltás forgatókönyve. Kerekasztal tárgyalások 1989-ben* vol. VII (Budapest: Uj Mandátum, 2000) who correctly predicted the outcome under the first FIDESZ government of 1998–2002.

[31] Holmes and Sunstein, "The Politics of Constitutional Revision" 283.

claimed to be potentially useful for legitimation building. As far as the freedom of action of governments is concerned, even in the Hungarian case, where the Court attempted to interfere with the economic stabilization efforts of the social liberal government in 1995, in the end the financial damage was minimal and the greater "social sensitivity" imposed on the government may have been perhaps beneficial in the middle term. The Court's decisions arguably helped to channel and reduce more extreme forms of social discontent that could have perhaps brought down the whole stabilization program.

There is a deeper objection still to an argument that so hugely privileges learning over normativity. In legal and constitutional matters, one must learn not only to learn, but also *how not to learn*, as Niklas Luhmann so often argued.[32] In order for normative structures to be taken seriously, facile change in the face of disappointment must be avoided. In this respect, the essence of a modern dictatorship, especially of the Soviet type based on the absolute priority of discretionary power,[33] was that it was unable to learn how not to learn—in other words, how not to alter norms in the face of ever-changing policy considerations. To most fundamentally break with such a regime was to learn *how not to learn* in one very crucial dimension—that of constitutionalism. Admittedly, Soviet-type regimes also had "learning disabilities" in the area of policy, where the point of economic reform was indeed learning to learn. But the political institutions capable of making this type of learning possible could emerge only if actors develop respect for normative rules, which was not possible without institutionally safeguarded structures of self-limitation. That is the point of human rights jurisprudence and judicial review from a functional point of view.[34]

The last point was well captured by Holmes' own important earlier article on pre-commitments.[35] In general, self-limitation makes government stronger, not weaker. He could undoubtedly answer that there are both disabling and enabling limits, which means precisely what I claim here: that governments must learn both how to learn and how not to. There are areas where they must be fully able to act (for example, the initiation and implementation of a determined economic reform, and the de-statization of the institutional structure), and areas where they must not be allowed to become strong, if for no other reason than to be able to concentrate their resources on essentials. But this differentiation and distinction cannot be spontaneously made by executives or even parliaments, who in general seek to extend their strength in all areas important to them, and especially by politicians who have been socialized under arrangements where

[32] N. Luhmann, *A Sociological Theory of Law* (London: Routledge, 1972) 31ff.

[33] See E. Fraenkel, *The Dual State* (Oxford: Oxford University Press, 1945) and A. Arato, "Critical Sociology and Authoritarian State Socialism" in *From Western Marxism to Democratic Theory* (Armonk, NY: M.E. Sharpe, 1993).

[34] See Luhmann, *Grundrechte als Institution* (Berlin: Duncker & Humblot, 1965); J. Elster, *Ulysses and the Sirens* (Cambridge: Cambridge University Press, 1984).

[35] S. Holmes, "Precommitment and the Paradox of Democracy" op.cit.

political power knew no formalized limitations. For the sake of a genuinely new legal identity in post Communist states what had to be learned was the rule of law, and this learning could not be delayed without grave consequences for how democracy was going to be understood. Even parliament could not be allowed to step into the shoes of the modern prince, and this could only be prevented by establishing counter-powers from the very outset. Often, it is just when parliament does claim absolute powers that the loss of its legitimacy should be feared, and not when it is forced to share power.[36] There are only two imaginable counter-powers that can accomplish the task of limiting parliament, a constitutional court and the presidency, and of these two possible "defenders of the constitution," the constitutional court is certainly the "less dangerous."[37] Only this form of the limitation of parliamentary rule could be understood within the framework of constitutionalism as an enabling limit, rather than a disabling one.

Latin America of course has traditionally had strong presidents, and weak courts. Until recently, constitutionalism in the region has been notable through its absence. This is why in a country such as Mexico, the setting up of constitutional review has been widely considered essential for all recent reform attempts. It is, I think, undeniable that the new constitutional courts of East and Central Europe (with the exception of the vastly over-politicized Russian Court of Justice under Zorkin, which became a direct player in political conflicts) have been on the whole successful in helping to turn constitutions into genuine normative limits on power. There are several spectacular cases from Hungary, Slovakia, and Bulgaria—countries where constitutional review has been active—bearing this out. But even without similarly dramatic cases in Poland, the Czech Republic, and Romania, we have reason to believe that the mere existence of even relatively weaker forms of constitutional review have had a disciplining and civilizing effect on the holders of legislative and executive power. Yet, as I argued, the case is not strong that the limits to governmental power they established were disabling limits, in terms of Holmes' own important distinction. With this said, however, the very success of constitutional courts in the face of Holmes' objections seems to expose them to Ackerman's.

Even granting that in the process of transition from dictatorships it is not parliamentary sovereignty but the rule of law that signifies the most fundamental dimension of change in political regimes, the success of constitutional courts becomes especially difficult to justify from the normative point of view in the face of soft or insufficiently legitimate constitutional backgrounds. Constitutional review by a court can be made compatible with democratic legitimacy only when the constitution itself is democratically made. The court can be a

[36] According to Arendt, too, the separation of powers enhances rather than decreases power.

[37] The Kelsen v. Schmitt debate on this point was decided in the court of history, when President Hindenburg offered the chancellorship to the Führer of the NSDAP. See C. Schmitt, *Der Hüter der Verfassung* (Berlin: Duncker & Humblot, 1969) and H. Kelsen, "Judicial Review of Legislation. A Comparative Study of the Austrian and the American Constitution" (1942) *Journal of Politics* 4.

vehicle of the rule of law only on the foundations of a constitution that is not primarily its own product. The rule of a court would be the rule of an elite, mostly unaccountable. The court itself as *the* major constituent power is a usurpation, even if clever political maneuvering—as in Hungary—disguised constituent activity by avoiding it when both public opinion and elected officials could be antagonized.[38] Such maneuvering was certainly bound to fail, indeed did fail and in turn led to a compromise of legality itself, when the court one day faced both of these supposed embodiments of the will of the majority. Even if Ackerman's warnings of the complete collapse of constitutional courts has been positively confirmed only by Russian and Albanian developments, the shift from activism to a more quiescent mode in Hungary, even before the recent FIDESZ constitutional experiment, with its ultimately successful attacks on the Court, should be considered a partial confirmation of the same thesis.[39]

But Ackerman's more accurate diagnosis of potential problems was linked with a set of solutions that were far more problematic than those of Holmes.[40] The idea of a dualistic process of constitution making, in which a special convention focuses on constitutional and only constitutional politics, has rarely been successfully tried in non-federal states.[41] In the case of a freely elected, politically powerful normal legislature that may not want to defer to another assembly, this model comes perilously close to the dangers of dual power and civil war. Such was the actual experience of Russian constitution making in 1993, with the disastrous consequences that we see today. Ackerman's second-best option, a sovereign constitutional assembly, actually (probably unavoidably) tried in Romania, has little chance of preventing a constitution imposed by a provisional government in the name of popular, revolutionary legitimacy. Thus this model risks the sovereign or revolutionary dictatorship that Carl Schmitt analyzed and Hannah Arendt desperately warned against.[42] Ackerman rightly noticed the legitimation problems of the Romanian constitution, but, in my view, wrongly ascribed these to the predominant role of ex-Communists in the process, who were seen as the liberators of the country as required by revolutionary legitimacy. As Arendt has shown in her polemic against Sieyès (and Carl Schmitt), it is the revolutionary-populist model itself that produces legitimation problems in a liberal democracy.

[38] Here I strongly disagree with Kim Scheppele, as well as Lászlo Sólyom while I fully recognize the latter's merits as president of the first Hungarian Constitutional Court. In my view the problem was not so much with the court's activism, as with the failure to complete the two-stage process of producing a permanent constitution. See their articles in S. Arjomand (ed.), *Constitutionalism and Political Reconstruction* (Leiden: Brill, 2007).

[39] See the interview with Ackerman in (2003) 2 *Fundamentum* (in Hungarian). On this see below, chapter 4.

[40] The objection also applies to my own article, A. Arato, "Dilemmas of Constitution-making in East Europe" originally in (1992) 14 *Cardozo Law Review* 661–90.

[41] Massachusetts in 1780 and New Hampshire in 1784 seem to be the only exceptions.

[42] See C. Schmitt, *Die Diktatur* 2nd edn. (first published 1923, Berlin: Duncker & Humblot, 1928) and H. Arendt *On Revolution* (London: Penguin, 1990).

IV PRESIDENTS OR ASSEMBLIES?

Finally, Ackerman's idea that a charismatic president should play the central role in mobilizing for the constitution was hardly an accurate assessment of Washington's role, nor did it show sufficient awareness of the danger that a significant role for a pre-existent presidency (Washington held no public office in 1787) may strongly prejudice the new constitution toward a presidential government. And that form of government has the built-in weaknesses and dangers so eloquently stressed by Juan Linz and his collaborators.

Let us consider Linz's argument and the debate around it, which together represent the main contribution of political science to substantive problems faced by constitution makers.[43] According to Linz, presidential government, defined by the separate popular elections of the chief executive (the head of government and state) and the legislature, both for rigid terms, suffers from two fundamental problems: dual democratic legitimacy and inflexibility when facing dysfunction and crisis.

The first problem, familiar from the analyses of Marx, Tocqueville, and Schmitt,[44] leads to fundamental and dangerous conflicts concerning the right to speak in the name of the people that the president is likely to win, but often extra-constitutionally, since there is no third democratic principle to mediate between the branches.[45] This is especially so because of the second problem, the rigidity of terms that deprives the electorate of the ability to replace dysfunctional presidents and deadlocked parliaments for potentially long periods. Upon analysis, it becomes clear that the likelihood of both a weak and an overly strong executive are implied by Linz, who unfortunately has not analyzed the relation between the two possibilities within the same structure.[46] However, there is no contradiction involved because this structure can be described as the

[43] See in particular J. Linz and A. Valenzuela, *The Failure of Presidential Democracy*, 2 vols. (Baltimore, MD: Johns Hopkins University Press, 1994); A. Lijphart (ed.), *Presidential vs Parliamentary Government* (Oxford: Oxford University Press, 1992); M.S. Shugart and J.M. Carey, *Presidents and Assemblies* (Cambridge: Cambridge University Press, 1992); M.S. Shugart and S. Mainwaring, *Presidentialism and Democracy in Latin America* (Cambridge: Cambridge University Press, 1997); and G. Sartori, *Comparative Constitutional Engineering: An Inquiry into Structures, Incentives, and Outcomes* (New York: NYU Press, 1997).

[44] Linz refers to the 18*th of Brumaire*, but see also Tocqueville, *Recollections: The French Revolution of* 1848. (Atlantic Highlands, NJ: Transaction Publishers, 1995); and C. Schmitt, *Legalität und Legitimität* (Berlin: Duncker & Humblot 1932), with the latter's evocative image of a horse race between parliamentary and plebiscitary sovereigns.

[45] Not really dealing with the United States, Linz, as well as his critics, neglects the role of a Supreme Court that does not always refuse to deal with such political questions. See Louis Fisher's fine book, *Constitutional Conflicts between President and Congress* (Kansas: University Press of Kansas, 1997).

[46] This corresponds to the dual intellectual background of the modern presidency: the doctrine of the separation of powers of Montesquieu and the royal prerogative as analyzed by Locke.

combination of constitutional weakness coupled with potential extra-constitutional strength.[47]

Linz's critics have made their most telling objections regarding the idea of weakness. Accordingly, presidencies can be strong without extra or illegal procedures because of either greater party political or greater constitutional powers than admitted by Linz. However, party political powers mean the control of the legislature by the president's party, a possibility that is not likely to have been unnoticed by Linz, who was our best comparativist. This outcome, however, can be *guaranteed* only by a one-party system, such as that existing until recently in Mexico, that is by a dictatorship or at least a semi-authoritarian regime. Even in two-party systems there is a one in two chance (if monocameral) or three in four chance (if bicameral) of a divided government that can be only partially improved if elections are held at the same time. Analogously, constitutional powers beyond those assumed by Linz can certainly reduce the problems of structural rigidity and weakness (assuming, of course, what cannot always be assumed—namely competent presidential use of these powers). Extensive powers of decree, the ability to initiate legislation, control over foreign policy, unique appointment powers, the absence of impeachment, and absolute vetoes can exist in various combinations with varying strength. But they reliably point beyond the dilemmas of constitutional weakness/plebiscitary strength, when presidents can in effect govern alone, even when they face a hostile parliament. In that case, however, we have transcended presidentialism in the direction of what Carlos Nino rightly called hyperpresidentialism, representative democracy in the direction of Philippe Schmitter's *dictablanda*, or Guillermo O'Donnell's delegative democracy.[48] We see attempts to establish such a regime in today's Turkey, which have produced a veritable constitutional crisis, whatever the outcome.[49]

Linz's critique of presidentialism thus remains as a warning to all those who would establish a regime of the U.S. type, with its particular model of a constitutionally weak plebiscitary presidency. If he can be faulted, it is for neglecting to link methods of constitution making with alternative outcomes in governmental structures. The omission has bearing on the problem of reform, since historically no directly elected presidency has ever been successfully transformed into a parliamentary executive, even after the hiatus of a dictatorship. This is so, I think, for logical reasons, and is not a mere empirical regularity. From the point of view of popular sovereignty, in contrast to the ideals of parliamentary government, directly elected presidencies have a normative surplus.[50] This appears

[47] For my views on this subject, as reconstructed by M.V. Crespo see Chapter 10 in E. Peruzzotti and M. Plot (eds) *Critical Theory and Democracy* (London: Routledge, 2013).

[48] Indeed, almost all examples of "successful" presidentialism discussed in Shugart and Mainwaring, *Presidentialism and Democracy in Latin America* are delegative hyperpresidentialist democracies.

[49] That case is a textbook demonstration of the correctness of the Linz argument. See Chapter 5 of this volume for further discussion of Turkey.

[50] See V. Crespo, *Del Rey al Presidente* (Mexico: El Colegio de Mexico, 2013).

even more pronounced in comparison to the practice of parliaments where the actual choice (and sometimes removal) of the head of state may be a function of ad hoc and opaque negotiations within or among political parties. Thus, when there was a genuine opportunity in Brazil to replace presidentialism, both during constitution making in 1988 and subsequently in the process leading up to a referendum on this matter, reformers made a mistake in fighting for parliamentarianism instead of a rationalized and improved version of French semi-presidentialism.[51]

On both occasions in Brazil the process was deformed by the role of a presidency fully in place during constitutional negotiations. Along with the case of the 1993 Yeltsin constitution in Russia, this example shows how wrong Ackerman's suggestion was to concentrate on a strong presidential leadership in democratic constitutional politics.[52] Admittedly, the link between the role of a presidential figure in constitution making and a presidentialist outcome may not be absolute.[53] By reducing the executive prerogative inherited from Britain and through the institution of the electoral college as originally intended, the American framers aimed to produce a weak presidency.[54] It was only when party politics transformed elections and the electoral college that the characteristic combination of constitutional weakness and plebiscitary strength began to emerge.[55] However, the fact that the Philadelphia Convention was not deformed by charisma was due above all to Washington's great self-restraint, his refusal to play the role attributed to him by Ackerman. He hardly spoke at the convention, and his Virginia delegation (unlike Hamilton, for example) never spoke on behalf of a strong executive. Although each historical period may have a Washington, a San Martin, a Havel, or a Mandela—capable of great self-limitation in constitutional politics or state making—there always seem to be many more Bonapartes, Bolivars, De Gaulles, Wałesas, Yeltsins, Putins, Illiescus, Menems, Fujimoris, Berishas, and Erdogans whose ideas of democracy are equivalent to the expansion of their own plebiscitary power.

[51] I agree with Giovanni Sartori as against both Linz and Stepan that semi-presidentialism can be freed of the problem of a dual executive that could produce difficulties for the French model analogous to the dual democratic legitimacy of parliamentary government.

[52] As the great work of C. Rossiter, *Constitutional Dictatorship* (Princeton, NJ: Princeton University Press, 1948) shows, the episodes Ackerman stresses as successful, presidentially led extra-Article V revisions of the U.S. Constitution, associated with the figures of Lincoln and Roosevelt, were also examples of emergency government bordering on constitutional dictatorship. Such precedents, as Justice Davis warned in *ex parte* Milligan in 1865, can become dangerous instruments in the hands of presidents and staffs less loyal to constitutional democracy.

[53] But see the evidence of T. Ginsburg, Z. Elkins, and J. Blount, "Does the Process of Constitution-making Matter?" (2009) 5 *Annual Review of Law and Social Sciences* 5 209–23, who on this issue do believe that the method of constitution making does make an apparent difference.

[54] See T.J. Lowi, *The Personal President, Power Invested, Promise Unfulfilled* (Ithaca, NY: Cornell University Press, 1986).

[55] As already noticed by J.C. Calhoun, to his great chagrin. See J.C. Calhoun, "A Discourse on the Constitution and Government of the United States" in Calhoun, *Union and Liberty* (Indianapolis, IN: Liberty Press, 1992) 259–60.

Once a presidential or semi-presidential constitutional structure is institutionalized, however, it is very difficult to reverse. Even fine-tuning such a system may be difficult if it is protected by a difficult amendment rule, even in the face of dysfunctions that may inconveniently reappear after any election that produces "divided government." A presidentially led, plebiscitary process of constitution making where constitution makers are imbued with a very strong sense of their democratic mandate and legitimacy, as in Ackerman's reading of American history and in his recommendation for new democracies, is likely to produce a difficult amendment rule such as Article V. While it is true that actors of doubtful legitimacy may also to try to freeze their "premature" constitutional syntheses for their future self-protection, a democratically mobilized society, as Ackerman well knows, would have a much better chance to protect its constitutional creation against numerically or qualitatively inferior majorities. Such an outcome seems to confirm the position of Holmes, who has insistently warned about the insufficient learning potential of a premature constitutionalism. That objection, however, cannot be countered simply by insisting on the illegitimate beginnings of the two constitutions (of Bulgaria and Romania) that were actually made according to a timetable that resembles that of Ackerman. Even an excellent constitution in Bulgaria the origins of which involved legitimation problems, [56] could not fully compensate for subsequent functional difficulties. Just as Holmes is concerned with the institutionalization of learning yet cannot deal with the problem of legitimacy or guarantee that constitutionalism would be among the things learned, Ackerman's pursuit of democratic legitimacy and constitutionalism was unable to take into account the learning problems of constitutional government.[57]

V FROM (MADRID AND) BUDAPEST TO JOHANNESBURG AND BEYOND

The call to "go back to the drawing board" after the first flush of post 89 constitution making was justified. But subsequent results depended on getting rid of the widely shared prejudice that the recent transitions to democracy were only "catch-up revolutions" that had much to learn but little to teach.[58] Hannah Arendt, who was sensitive to the originality of historical ruptures, has warned against locating the constituent power in juridical and institutional states of

[56] On Bulgaria, see my forthcoming *Adventures of the Constituent Power* (London: Cambridge University Press) Chapter 3.

[57] His neo-Jeffersonian preference for learning through constitutional revolutions may occlude the very problem of the institutionalization of learning, that was a great concern of Jefferson's friend, Condorcet.

[58] J. Habermas, *Die Nachholende Revolution* (Frankfurt: Suhrkamp, 1990). A patronizing attitude is present in the Holmes and Sunstein article as well, and is based on the fallacious thesis that the East and Central European transformations were fundamentally heteronomous and externally caused: Holmes and Sunstein, "The Politics of Constitutional Revision" 286ff.

nature.[59] But finding only the American experience on the positive side of the ledger, she could not tell us how such a state of affairs can be avoided, especially in the case of old regimes far less attractive than the American colonies, and in the face of the traditional prestige in Europe of revolutionary-democratic constitution making.[60] It was left to the Spanish, and East Central Europeans, who had already had too many revolutions, as well as South Africans, to gradually discover the answer in the midst of their radical but non-revolutionary change of regimes: round-table-led, two-stage, post sovereign constitution making presupposing legal continuity.

The great advantage of post sovereign constitution making is that it de-dramatizes conceptions of the constituent power, linked to mythological and dangerous notions of total rupture and the full embodiment of the will of the people. Instead of assimilating constitutional revision to revolutionary constitution making as Ackerman does, post sovereign constitution making allows us to do the reverse and conceive democratic, legal revision as the model for the very creation of constitutions.

We can speak of post sovereign constitution making where an assembly is the main agent of the final constitutional design, but without claiming unlimited powers. But, contrary to the claims of Holmes and Sunstein, post sovereign constitution making rejects the exclusive role of a single assembly in constitution making.[61] To avoid the sovereign aspirations of extraordinary assemblies, such as the ones advocated by Ackerman, the paradigm is at home both with ordinary parliaments playing a constituent role, and with special constitutional assemblies, if both are bound by an interim constitution or other functionally equivalent devices. In neither case is a US-type double differentiation of constituent and legislative powers necessary, though it would be in general desirable.[62] This does not mean that safeguards should not be used to avoid the conflation of ordinary and constitutional politics. In India, for example, two entirely different sets of session with different rules were used for the same constituent assembly, in its constitutional and legislative roles.[63] In such a setting, neither parliament nor the government rooted in it is provisional for the duration. Constitution making by two separate chambers is a sign, though not a necessary one, of one version of this type of process. A normal parliament whose two chambers meet together exceptionally as the "constitutional assembly," as first required in Poland and then in South Africa, is another version, reminiscent of the formation of the first constituent assembly from the three orders of the

[59] See Arendt, *On Revolution*.

[60] Just as Ackerman, whom she so greatly influenced, Arendt rehabilitated the concept of revolution on the basis of the one exceptional revolution.

[61] Holmes and Sunstein, "The Politics of Constitutional Revision" 297–8 and elsewhere.

[62] Though admittedly, during the first stage of such a process, if a round table plays the main role as against the parliament in place, an element of double differentiation is recovered.

[63] See G. Austin, *The Indian Constitution* (Delhi: Oxford University Press, 1972).

Estates General. But the Constituent Assembly of 1789–91 cut the umbilical chord to the legal order of the old regime, and claimed the plenitude of all powers, moves that do not fit into the ideal type of post sovereign constitution making developed here.[64] But we should not be misled by mere nomenclature; an ordinary parliament having constitution making among its tasks can be labeled a constituent assembly, during the process or by historians afterward. The central mark of what is called post sovereign constitution making here is operating under the constitutional amending rules of an interim constitution, or, when unavoidable, the amendment rules of an old regime whose fictional status is transformed in a constitutionalist direction.

Obviously, post sovereign constitution making presupposes legal continuity, or the absence of legal rupture between two succeeding legal orders. Legal continuity, however, is itself difficult to formulate, because there are undoubtedly instances when, especially under the threat of force, parliaments ratify changes that they cannot resist. Conversely, there can be illegalities that take place within a context of overall legality. We should speak of legal continuity only when the crucial legal rule, the amendment rule, actually constrains and limits the mutual expectations and actions of actors. An operational test for such actual legal constraint, at least as a thought experiment, consists in asking whether or not it made any difference to the outcome that an assembly engaged in constitution making, including a sitting parliament, was using an existing amendment rule rather than operating according to rules of its own choice. Generally, the latter would be simple majority decision making in the case of sovereign constituent assemblies. (Where the existing rule of change is simple majority voting, this particular test cannot be applied.) I should note, however, that using a rule that was never autonomously used before, such as the amendment rule for a previously non-operative Soviet-type constitution, satisfies, even if as a marginal case, the requirement of legal continuity—if using that rule constrained relevant parliamentary and extra-parliamentary actors (as it demonstrably did in all the East Central European cases).

So defined (and keeping in mind the ideal typical character of the model), we have had a very large number of cases with at least elements of post sovereign constitution making since the mid-1970s: Spain (but not Portugal), Brazil (but not Argentina), Poland, Hungary, Bulgaria, and South Africa. Similar efforts entirely failed in the German Democratic Republic (GDR) and in Czechoslovakia,[65] in the sense that parliaments were unable or unwilling to produce new constitutions for the units in question, both of which turned out to be unviable

[64] See J. Elster, "Arguing and Bargaining in Two Constituent Assemblies" (1991) Working Paper Number 4, Center for the Study of Constitutionalism in Eastern Europe.

[65] On these two cases see my forthcoming *Adventures of the Constituent Power*, Chapter 3.

as states.[66] But obviously not all of the cases where a working constitution was produced should be counted as "successful" in the normative sense of contributing to the emergence of a culture of "constitutionalism." Thus while post sovereign constitution making surely exists, we need to ask what can make it legitimate in light of justified criticisms of parliamentary constitution making in the processes of reform. In other words, when ordinary parliaments produce new constitutions, there is the well-grounded suspicion that this is merely a species of governmental imposition seeking incumbent advantage, capable of producing neither legitimacy nor stability. The obvious and immediate response, that this method helps us avoid other evils, the specter of dual power and constitutional dictatorship by a sovereign constituent assembly is normatively of insufficient weight.[67]

The question concerning the conditions of legitimacy hides at least three other questions: (1) Which assemblies can legitimately produce new constitutions under the post sovereign model; (2) On the foundations of which legality can and ought they to do so? And most importantly, (3) how should assemblies proceed to achieve constitutional legitimacy?

VI WHICH ASSEMBLY?

With respect to this question, there are almost always choices, some based only on legality while others also on legitimacy. In Spain, it could have been the last Franquist Cortes that did pass a Law of Reform, overwhelmingly ratified in a popular referendum, or the first democratically elected parliament that in fact produced the new constitution. In Hungary, it could have been the first democratically elected parliament as the democratic opposition wanted, or the last Kadarist parliament, as the state-party wished. In effect, the materially new constitution, one which was never was accepted as ultimate or fully legitimate, was the product of two rounds in which, speaking formally, each parliament was dominant. But here, the formal role of the last communist parliament, while materially not entirely insignificant, merely legalized the dominant role of the round-table agreements. Even the work of the latter was corrected by a popular referendum in November 1989, which determined that the regime would be parliamentary from the outset and not semi-presidential. In Poland, there were as many choices as parliaments (namely four) and three failed before the fourth succeeded. Unlike in Hungary and the GDR, here the last Communist parliament was never seriously suggested for the role of constitution making, and the first post Communist one—the "Contractual *Sejm*"—failed because it was only in part freely elected. Thus this body had insufficient legitimacy to actually vote

[66] In the Czech and Slovak case I always thought that the inadequate constitutional structure had a causal role in the dissolution of the state. This interpretation is supported in the excellent article by A.K. Stanger, "Czechoslovakia as an Unintended Consequence of the Velvet Constitutional Revolution" (1996) 5 *East European Constitutional Review* 4.

[67] See Arendt, *On Revolution*.

on the fine document its drafting committee produced. In the third, the first freely elected *Sejm* (or in the assembly of the *Sejm* and Senate together) no one had a constitution-making majority because of extreme political fragmentation.[68] Finally, in South Africa, multi-party negotiations at Kempton Park resulted in an interim constitution that was passed by the last apartheid parliament. This was identical to the Hungarian pattern, and in both cases (in contrast to Spain) the democratic forces in the transition did not succeed in restricting rule making before free elections to only the organic regulations necessary for these elections. But what makes South Africa distinctive is that here the process was so structured from the outset that the first post apartheid constitutional assembly had to replace the interim constitution with the final one.[69]

What seems to be clear from all these examples is that only a freely elected assembly has the full legitimacy to play an important creative role in constitution making. But even this condition seems insufficient in light of Serbian and Croatian experiences. When a formally free election takes place under electoral rules calculated to give the winner an enormous surplus of seats, and/or under conditions of competition (timing, media access) that give incumbents all the advantages, a parliament may not sufficiently represent all the new political forces to have its constitution fully accepted by them. Almost all authoritarian governments with sufficient real or imagined legitimacy tend to try the road of manipulated elections at one point or another in order to conserve some of their power, and perhaps freeze the process of democratization in some kind of soft dictatorship or hard democracy.[70] The Mexican case demonstrates even the long-term viability of this approach, at least under conditions of high initial regime legitimacy. But there were ultimately failed attempts of this type in Spain, Brazil, Chile, Russia, Hungary, Bulgaria and even South Africa.

The great innovation, one that pointed beyond the dominant role of undemocratic parliaments to draft new constitutions or to control the elections by which the new drafters would be chosen, was the round-table negotiation, pioneered in Poland and perfected in Hungary and South Africa.[71] Round tables resembled US-type constitutional conventions in that they were negotiating fora outside regular parliaments that continued to function as such during constitution making. At least in the case of the developed form, the concern of the round table is primarily constitutional legislation, though other issues regarding the

[68] Party fragmentation is, however, not a general condition in East Europe as Holmes and Sunstein assert; neither the first nor the second freely elected parliament in Hungary, nor the last elected in Poland could be so characterized.

[69] See the two first-rate chapters by D. Atkinson, "Brokering a Miracle: The Multi-party Negotiating Forum" and "Principle Born of Pragmatism? Central Government in the Constitution" in S. Friedman and D. Atkinson (eds), *The Small Miracle* (Pretoria: Sigma Press, 1994). Also see my forthcoming *Adventures* Chapter 3.

[70] In O'Donnell and Schmitter's vivid terminology "democradura" or "dictablanda." See G. O'Donnell and P.C. Schmitter, *Transitions from Authoritarian Rule* (Baltimore, MD: Johns Hopkins University Press, 1987).

[71] For the Hungarian case, see A. Arato and Z. Miklosi, "Constitution-making in Hungary" in L. Miller (ed.), *Framing the State* (Washington, DC: USIP, 2010) as well as Chapter 4 below.

conditions of free elections are also negotiated. (Attempts to restrict the constitutional work of round tables to a few organic rules from the point of view of elections have succeeded only for the early form in Poland and Bulgaria, but with undesirable results of significant concessions to the government in place, in terms of institutions or the timing of elections.) Unlike the Philadelphia Convention, round tables submit their product to a fully legal process of ratification by the existing parliament, that is, however, informally under the full control of one of the negotiating partners, the governing forces of the old regime. Finally, claiming no democratic legitimacy for themselves or the undemocratic parliament, round tables differ from conventions in that their product is typically only an interim set of rules. In this model, the creation of the "final" constitution is the job of a freely elected parliament or constitutional assembly.[72]

In order to work, round tables must presuppose either a relative equality of forces as in Hungary, or the assumption of the same on both sides, or an orientation to democratic consensus on the stronger side, as in the cases of Czechoslovakia and South Africa. Under such conditions, fairly strong constitutional protections, including courts, can emerge from round tables. Characteristically, round tables tend to produce proportional or mixed electoral systems enabling the presence of all relevant forces on the terrain of constitution making rather than the majoritarian voting rules preferred by the Communist parties, where they could not impose partially non-competitive rules, as in the Soviet Union in 1988, and even at the Polish Round Table of 1989 (which was exceptional because the first in the Soviet imperium). Generally, round tables reject models of presidential governments (Poland was an exception, and Hungary almost was when direct elections of the president were initially conceded). See Table 1.

Thus the pattern that can produce an assembly capable of legitimate constitution making in a previously authoritarian regime seems to be something like the following: (1) round-table-type negotiations; (2) the creation of organic rules for a free election, or an interim constitution containing such rules, by the last non-democratic parliament under the guidance of the round table; (3) a free election under proportional representation (PR) or at least mixed rules; (4) constitution making by the new assembly. This schematic conception is also a diagnostic tool (in the sense of prudential judgements, and not causal analysis, for which we have far too few cases that differ in too many dimensions) for empirical cases of constitution making. Where steps (2) and (3) cannot be satisfied, as initially in Poland, it will be difficult to produce a constitution; where (1) and (3) are violated, as in Serbia and Croatia, only a constitution of doubtful legitimacy will likely be produced. But even where only one of the conditions cannot be sustained, as in Hungary where the first freely elected parliament never even considered making a new constitution, the completion and/or the legitimacy of

[72] Efforts to have a partially democratic parliament (in Poland) to produce constitutions failed, among other things because of the problem of legitimacy. But paradoxically, a freely elected parliament may entirely disregard the constitutional product of a round table, as did the *Volkskammer* of the GDR. An interim constitution forced through an undemocratic parliament as in Hungary and South Africa is a solution for this dilemma.

Table 1 Types of Transition, Constitution Making, and Government Structure in Eastern Europe 1989–96

	Reformist		**Round-table negotiated path**			**Rupture**
Types of transition	**Hegemonic**	**Strong populist forces**	**Government + opposition –**	**Government + opposition +**	**Government – opposition +**	**Collapse or insurrection**
Country	Serbia Croatia Russia (phase I)	Spain Baltic Slovenia	Poland Bulgaria	Hungary [GDR]	Czechoslovakia	Romania Russia (phase II)
Constitution making	Russia, Ukraine: parliamentary amendment Serbia, Croatia: new parliament	Spain: parliamentary Slovenia, Lithuania: new parliament Estonia: constitutional assembly Latvia: restoration of 1922 Constitution	Poland: round table and parliamentary amendment Bulgaria: round table and constitutional assembly	Hungary: round table and parliamentary amendment [GDR: new round table]	Czechoslovakia: round table and parliamentary (failed) Czech Republic: new parliament Slovakia: new parliament	Constitutional assembly and strong informal role of presidency
Structure of government	presidential	Spain: parliamentary Lithuania: semipresidential Others: parliamentary	semipresidential	parliamentary	parliamentary	presidential
Structure of legislature	unicameral but in Russia expanded for some issues	Spain, Slovenia: assymmetrical bicameral Baltic: unicameral	Poland: bicameral Bulgaria: unicameral	unicameral	Slovakia: unicameral Czech Republic:initially unicameral, bicameral?	bicameral Russia also federal
Constitutional adjudication	Serbia, Croatia, Ukraine: weak Russia: strong (on paper)	Spain: strong Latvia: none Estonia: weak Lithuania: medium Slovenia: strong	Poland: weak Bulgaria: medium	Strong	Czechoslovakia: weak Slovakia: medium–strong Czech Republic: medium (on paper)	Romania: weak Russia: medium (on paper)
Electoral rule	Russia: partially free; Croatia: majority Serbia: initially majority	Spain, Slovenia: PR Lithuania: electoral threshold 4% Latvia, Estonia: PR & 4+5%	Poland: partially free, later PR + plurality; after 1993: 5% Bulgaria: PR	Hungary: mixed with 4 then 5%, [GDR: PR]	PR with 5% for parties, higher for coalitions Russia: mixed Romania: PR, initially no threshold, later 3%	
Constitutional revision rule	Serbia, Russia, Ukraine: qualified parliamentary majority Croatia: parliamentary presidentialism initially, possibility of referendum	Spain: two track Slovenia: 2/3 parliamentary majority, possible referendum Baltic: parliamentary generally without referendum	Poland 2/3 of combined parliament Bulgaria: partially constitutional assembly, partially parliamentary	Hungary: 2/3 of parliament; [GDR: partially unchangeable, partially 2/3 of parliament]	Czechoslovakia: 3/5 of lower house, 3/5 of each nation in upper house; Slovakia:3/5 of parliament Czech Republic: 3/5 of parliament (of each house)	Russia: many levelled, parts strongly entrenched Romania: presidential. initially; 2/3 of each house; possibility of referendum

the project will remain in doubt. As the similar South African case shows, renewed constitution making in the freely elected assembly can erase the birth defect of an interim constitution produced with insufficient democratic legitimacy. Similarly, as the Spanish and Slovenian examples demonstrate, one missing condition, such as formal round-table negotiations may not doom the effort, if compensated for by either or both informal, multiple negotiations or an orientation of power holders not to use a position of advantage to institute self-serving rules. Such orientation seems to have played a role in Spain, when Prime Minister Suarez offered to negotiate and compromise with forces he had roundly defeated in a recent popular referendum.

VII WHICH LAW?

Can we say that countries on a path where these four conditions were satisfied, will be in a good initial position to succeed? Not reliably, because other things can go wrong, as the Czechoslovak transition, despite fulfilling these conditions, indicates. János Kis, who from a juridical point of view provided an outstanding analysis of the structure of "regime change" (as distinct from both revolution and reform), points to the legitimation crisis that characterizes this type of transition.[73] I am convinced, in spite of the single possible counter-example of Spain, that as long as the authoritarian system or authoritarian leaders retain sufficient legitimacy, they will tend to prefer the top-down, manipulated electoral road of slow, evolutionary change. In spite of another single counter-example, namely Czechoslovakia—whose round table was more formal than real—where oppositional forces alone are legitimate and the ability of the government to repress crumbles, one has reason to expect that the new forces would not negotiate with holdovers from the old regime.

But in the context of a break in legitimacy, when the old forces no longer enjoy support and the new ones do not yet have a form of support that is linked to a belief in their justification to exercise power, the political situation becomes extremely unstable, with potentially great dangers for all organized forces. According to Kis, only consensually agreed rules of the game can stabilize such an unpredictably explosive situation. I believe that the most important such rule is adherence to legality. In Kis' scheme regime change (or negotiated transition) is distinguished from reform because of the break in legitimacy, and is also different from revolution precisely because of legal continuity. There can be no doubt, therefore, that the initial phases of this type of transformation must take place on the ground of the legality of the old regime, and that the new legal order must emerge from the old by using the latter's rule of change.

Thus there is no real choice regarding the second question, concerning legality. A law that does not yet exist cannot be used. The existing law must be used,

[73] J. Kis, "Between Reform and Revolution: Three Hypothesis about the Nature of Regime Change" (1995) 1 *Constellations* 3.

even if only to transform itself. However, this is a difficult point to swallow in the case of lawless regimes, in which there is no rule of law at all or even dualistic ones where political prerogative always trumps normal legality.[74] In fact, the model does not seem to be applicable to authoritarian regimes that are not hypocritical enough to establish formal written constitutions or at least have some formal appearance of parliamentary sovereignty. Certainly where there is a written constitution with a formal amendment rule, as in all Communist states, there is a loophole through which the initially essential elements of the rule of law can be introduced. It can be objected, of course, that legal continuity using such an amendment rule will be based upon a fiction, since the rule of change of the constitution in the material sense[75] of Communist regimes is the unwritten one, according to which the will of the political bureau of the central committee is the source of all changes in the legal order. Nevertheless, the fiction can immediately acquire legal force[76] as soon as power holders and their opponents agree that they implicitly adhere to the *sine qua non* of constitutional regimes: the supremacy (hierarchical superiority) of the constitution in the formal sense. With this agreement, the legal system under such regimes begins for the first time to stabilize the mutual expectations of actors in the public law domain.

But the fact that there is no choice regarding the laws used to steer non-revolutionary changes of regimes does not mean that any pre-existing laws, which include a law of change, are compatible with success. Even when an inherited amendment rule can be used to negotiate the organic rules for a democratic transition, it does not follow that such a law will also serve the purposes of post sovereign constitution making. Such a rule may involve too many concessions to authoritarian participation in democratic development, as in Chile, where the outgoing military regime forced the democratic parties to accept government under an authoritarian constitution passed in 1980, not only along with difficult amendment procedures, but also nine senators appointed by Pinochet for long terms who could block proposed amendments.[77] It may also have overly high consensus requirements among new forces. This was the case of Czechoslovakia, where constitutional amendments could be passed only with the consent of three-fifths of Czech and three-fifths of Slovak deputies in the upper chamber, giving two-fifths plus one of either nationality or one-fifth plus one of the whole chamber veto power. Of course, the Communist party could establish as well as use such a rule previously, because it controlled all the deputies in any case. Using the rule seriously, in a democratizing setting, was an entirely different matter and could be the main reason for the failure of constitution making, as in Czechoslovakia.

[74] Fraenkel, *The Dual State*.

[75] See Kelsen, *General Theory*.

[76] See H.S. Maine, *Ancient Law* (London: J. M. Dent & Sons, 1917). on the legal role of fictions.

[77] See the chapter on Chile in Linz and Stepan, *Problems of Democratic Transitions*.

Finally, rules of amendment may also be overly easy ones to use, inviting continuous democratic tinkering with supposedly finished constitutions. Ongoing constitutional learning may be a good thing, but, as already argued, in a period of quasi-revolutionary change it is equally important to give a settled structure to the institutional life of a new regime.[78] Such a step is all the more crucial when the old regime was characterized by legal nihilism on the deepest level and we wish this spirit to be replaced by the rule of law.

The answer to these difficulties seems to be that laws of change unsuitable for democratic constitution making ought themselves be changed, using the original rule of change. Whether or not this is logically possible and whether such a method is compatible with the aim of producing a new legal order, there are formidable political difficulties facing the procedure. We have reason to assume that in cases such as Chile and Czechoslovakia actors that expect to be in the weaker position under a democratic regime would oppose changing the rule of change for the same reasons that they would later use its built-in minority veto provisions. And in the context of the original revision rule, they have the means of resisting its own revision. In the context of the difficulty implied by overly flexible amendment provisions, parliaments would have a good reason to use the rule to change the rule, in this case to make it more difficult, and to protect thereby their constituent work against future parliaments. But when they do wish to do so, they run into the problem traditionally faced by British parliaments: namely, how to justify tying the hands of a future parliament by a majority significantly less qualified than that required by the future amendment rule. Let us note that parliamentary constitution makers cannot take any solace from the experience of the United Kingdom, where a constitution changeable through simple parliamentary majorities has shown remarkable stability. Given the traditionally inherited constitution in the material sense, parliament in Westminster is never in a position where it *must* assume the constituent role. Parliaments of new democracies, however, find no ready-made structures with traditional legitimacy that they must respect for political, even if not narrowly legal, reasons. In many places, easy rules of change have indeed meant a great deal of constitutional tinkering (e.g. Austria, with hundreds of amendments since 1945). In democracies where a new order of public law has to be produced, and where there is a good deal of contingency regarding the structure this order is to have, parliamentary constitution making under an easy amendment rule means that the constituent process might remain indefinitely open, as in Hungary from the 1990s until 2011.

[78] Arendt's arguments against permanent revolution remain decisive, but it should be noted that they apply to a parliament that indefinitely remains a quasi-constituent assembly and is not bound by strong constitutional conventions. On this point see A. Arato, "Revolution, Restoration and Legitimacy" in M. Kennedy (ed.), *Envisioning Eastern Europe* (Ann Arbor, MI: University of Michigan Press, 1995), and Arato, *Civil Society* Chapter 3.

VIII WHAT PROCEDURE?

Ackerman's important insight is that closing the process of constitution making itself requires enhanced democratic legitimacy. However, given the heterogeneity of social and political contexts, this enhancement cannot be simply achieved by the imposition of concrete models. Nor will flight to a high level of abstraction help, if this means that we seek to directly institutionalize an abstract normative conception such as "veil of ignorance" or "deliberative democracy." The extent to which we can err in this direction is indicated by the extremely heterogeneous list of seven points proposed by Jon Elster, hitherto the least normative of the analysts of constitutions. According to him, these desiderata belong to a design that is to "create optimal conditions for deliberation" for processes of constitution making. The character of the list on the whole is indicated by one of its points, "the principle that the constitution should not come into force until, say, twenty years after it is adopted." This idea satisfies one of the parameters of the veil of ignorance only at the cost of total political (and empirical) irrelevance.[79]

We can do better by focusing on a plurality of normative principles that can be publicly used to legitimate a given process of constitution making only if some inevitably imperfect procedures can be reasonably claimed to be oriented to them. These principles derived from post sovereign patterns of constitution making can in principle at least be adopted under other forms. Elsewhere, I have emphasized legality, publicity, the plurality of democratic channels, consensus, (partial) empirical translations of a veil of ignorance, and reflexivity as such principles.[80] These desiderata are moreover interconnected, a point that I have insufficiently stressed. Here the advantage of a multi-stage post sovereign process comes clearly into view, because different principles of legitimacy can be relied on in the different stages. While plurality, inclusion, consensus, and a veil of ignorance are most important for the first stage, publicity and electoral accountability become more important in the second.

IX WHAT PRINCIPLES?

Legality (with Publicity and Consensus)

Even if based on a fiction, legal continuity can do what it is supposed to do from a functional point of view, namely help actors coordinate their expectations. The matter is not so simple from a normative point of view, where the legality of a

[79] J. Elster, "Deliberation and Constitution-making" in Elster (ed.), *Deliberative Democracy* (Cambridge: Cambridge University Press, 1998) 33–4. I do not claim of course that all his seven points are similarly irrelevant. I myself have stressed the need to link public and non-public forms of deliberation, the use of referenda, and the importance of PR for constitution-making assemblies. (See A. Arato, "Forms of Constitution-making and Theories of Democracy" in Arato, *Civil Society* 224–7.)

[80] See Arato, "Forms of Constitution-making."

hated old regime, and even its fictional legality, cannot carry much weight except to the narrowest law and order mentality.[81] Frank Michelman has been right to stress that democratic (or "republican") politics can be fully justified only if all actors are "always under law."[82] In his view, this principle applies even to the moment of the original constitution of the democratic order. But in this latter context it is not clear to what law he is referring: to natural law, the principles of a dialogic ethics, a pre-existing legal identity, or to the fortunate juridical circumstance that Americans found themselves in even before the revolution under the common law and in part under constitutional charters? The fictional constitutional legality of an authoritarian state is both less substantial and more difficult to apply than in the case of the Americans in 1776 or 1787, and especially 1867. Yet adherence to even such a law (until it is changed) can help stabilize the identity and security of individuals in the midst of dramatic change. Moreover, even this law announces to populations that the elites who take charge of their fate are subject to rules, and cannot merely impose their arbitrary will.

But all rules, and especially the fictional legality of an authoritarian state that was not designed for use in any case, require interpretation that can of course become the veil of renewed discretion. Only processes of consensual decision making can guarantee that *one* elite is not imposing its will on the others under the cover of law, while the publicity of the proceedings of round tables, for example, is needed to avoid the agreement of self-chosen *elites* to take on the character of arbitrary imposition. It seems to me that the fiction of legal continuity can carry the burden of legal legitimacy only when the interpretation of law is consensual and is supervised in a public process.

Publicity (with Plurality of Democracies)

But, of course, publicity cannot mean full transparency, nor a purely deliberative institutional design. When an assembly is fully open to public scrutiny, its ability to deliberate can be easily impaired. In any case, as we have seen in the case of the Polish Round Table which was fully public and in the case of Spanish parliamentary constitution making, as well as during the formally public negotiations in South Africa at Kempton Park, key actors cannot be prevented from meeting and negotiating also in private.[83] The Philadelphia Convention has shown the way here, by meeting in secret and calling for what turned out to be a highly public process of ratification, in which both the cultural and political

[81] The issue is different in South Africa where the legality of the apartheid regime was considered valid from the point of view of the bulk of the white population. Even an anti-apartheid party such as the Democratic Party took this stand. Moreover, this legal system, like some but not all modern dictatorships, operated as a modern legal order, again in relationship to the dominant minority of the population.

[82] F. Michelman, "Can Constitutional Democrats be Legal Positivists? Or Why Constitutionalism?" (1996) 2 *Constellations* 3.

[83] The practice of repeated secret negotiations was called *bosberaad* in South Africa, and the settings were appropriately picturesque. See Atkinson, "Brokering a Miracle?" 24. The same practice was called *Magdalenka* in Poland after the villa where the leaders of the two sides met.

public spheres of the states could participate. Thus the Convention had to be able to justify its decisions in terms of arguments that could be publicly advocated: public-regarding arguments typified by *The Federalist Papers*, for example. Even this would not have sufficed however, if the public discussion outside could not have a palpable effect on the outcome. In the United States, such an effect was structurally difficult to guarantee, and even calls for a "second convention" as normatively justified could have become obstructionist. Fortunately, however, there was a key instance where the federalists (and the main author of *The Federalist*) were forced to back down: the passing of the Bill of Rights under Article V. From this historical example three requirements follow. First, the need to have two interrelated discussions, with different structures of publicity, one emphasizing deliberation in a unified setting even at the cost of secrecy, and the other emphasizing openness in a plurality of settings even at the cost of deliberation. In the case of parliamentary constitution making, of course, the forms of these would be quite different than in the American case. Elster rightly mentions the differentiation between the drafting committee and the parliamentary plenum. Second, discussion by the public of civil society as in America implies the need to provide enough time for a societal debate of proposals and drafts. Third, there is a need for a ratifying process that can actually make a difference to the outcome.

Plurality of Democracies (with Consensus)

Thus referenda can be used for the post sovereign paradigm, but in view of the multi-stage model they are less required as a democratic check than in sovereign constitution making dominated by one extraordinary assembly in a single stage. Moreover, it is unclear why in federal states at least ratifying conventions could not play the role of a second democratic channel, one preferable to plebiscites. Of course, either way there is the risk of failure, especially since in the case of parliamentary constitution making there may be ordinary political reasons for trying to embarrass a parliamentary majority. Here processes of prior consensus building become especially important. If major political forces must agree to a draft before it is proposed for ratification, the likelihood of failure is very much reduced. By consensus, following Lijphart, I mean procedures that favor minority participation in majority decisions.[84] Proportional representation, with a low threshold or none at all, prepares the ground for almost all forms of consensus democracy, since the minorities must be made present before they can participate.[85] Yet presence does not make much difference in the context of majoritarian decision rules. Parliamentary decision rules, on the other hand, such as in Hungary in 1995–96, or informal agreements like those in Spain earlier, requiring the agreement of a certain number of parties in the drafting committee, can

[84] A. Lijphart, *Democracies* (New Haven, CT: Yale University Press, 1984).

[85] A. Phillips, *The Politics of Present* (Oxford: Clarendon Press, 1995).

introduce significantly higher consensus requirement into a parliamentary amendment rule.

Consensus (with Reflexivity)

Consensus requirements may lead, however, to the failure of otherwise promising drafts. The problem is sometimes unavoidable, since in some cases (say where there are four parties, as in Turkey recently) the requirements would have to be set either too low to add to legitimacy (three parties would equal a simple majority as well as a three-quarters majority), or too high (anything more than a simple majority of four is unanimity), and may give a politically highly exploitable veto to possibly small minorities. In such a case, the veto potential of small opposition parties can lead to the loading of drafts with all kinds of symbolic and dysfunctional elements. Even where ruling coalitions with constitution-making majorities avoid imposing constitutions, overly heavy consensus requirements can lead to results that the majority can no longer accept. The only solution is the expansion of participation, for example by including parties that for example have not passed electoral thresholds.[86] But in general one must be careful about introducing consensus requirements that are as high as the unanimity rule recently used in Turkey for the Constitutional Reconciliation Commission, or the Canadian amendment rule, under which both the Meech Lake and Charlottetown accords failed.

In order for consensus requirements to be compatible with producing a constitution, the actors must learn to use consensus in constructive ways. And this brings us back to Holmes' stress on the institutionalization of learning, or what I have called (following Teubner and Preuss) constitutional reflexivity, meaning that a constitution contains its own constitutional means of self-correction and self-development. Of course one might say that such a learning device, such a dimension of reflexivity of constitutions is the amendment rule, which must not be too difficult if it is to allow learning nor too easy if it is to be an amendment rule at all. But as Holmes argued, during the constitution-making period one may wish for greater flexibility than under a settled constitution. His answer was that a settlement should be delayed while one relies on a relatively easy rule of change of a temporary constitution. However, this suggestion can mean that the window of opportunity for constitution making can be shut, and that it can be reopened only at the cost of unacceptable concessions to obstructionist minorities. Most importantly, the delay can mean that the initially high, symbolically based support for a new democratic regime is dissipated. Therefore, what must be learned is how to use consensus for the generation of legitimacy, and to use legitimacy to reduce consensus requirements. The two-stage process, which

[86] See a proposal of mine for Turkey, A. Arato, "Democratic Constitution Making and Unfreezing the Turkish Process" (2010) 36 *Philosophy & Social Criticism* 3–4.

very much helps with the generation of legitimacy, is also an important condition of increased reflexivity, by incorporating learning into the process, and by allowing the second stage to reflect on the lessons of the first. It allows a synthesis not only between the two different senses of time we have seen stressed by Holmes (long and open ended) and Ackerman (short and involving closure), but also between the two desiderata of learning and legitimacy.

X THE INSTITUTIONALIZATION OF LEARNING: THE SOUTH AFRICAN CASE

Obviously learning from elsewhere, and facing a political situation of great complexity, the South African constitution makers responded to the problem of consensus building and institutional learning in an original and highly instructive manner. As in Spain and Central Europe, here too the basic method followed was post sovereign constitution making within legal continuity, relying on a non-sovereign "constitutional" assembly that united the two chambers, and thus partially differentiated between normal parliament and the constitution-making body. Here too formalized negotiations (two major rounds: Codesa and the Multi-party Negotiating Forum at Kempton Park) solved the problem of having to enact rules of change through a parliament of the old regime, without the necessary political legitimacy. Using the existing amendment rule the introduction of these rules replaced the constitution of the apartheid regime by the interim constitution of a democratic one. Up to that point, the process showed an uncanny resemblance to other recent cases, in particular to Hungary.

Beyond this, however, the South African negotiators made their greatest contribution to the institutionalization of learning within the constitution-making process while avoiding the twin dangers of the excessive normalization of constitutional politics and the logic of permanent revolution. These options did have support among some of the contending parties. But the negotiators of the ANC and the National Party came up with the establishment of a two-stage process of constitution making. In it, the interim constitution and constitutional principles established in comprehensive negotiations and enacted through the last apartheid parliament provided only the legal framework within which the newly elected constitutional assembly could create the definitive post apartheid democratic constitution. The negotiators at Kempton Park not only established a rigid timetable within which the new constitution would have to be produced, but enacted a series of selective incentives and fail-safe mechanisms that made it very difficult for the new assembly to evade its constituent task. While there was a high consensus requirement in the assembly, in the case that consensus failed a draft could be taken to a referendum. Quite unusually, the new Constitutional Court (established as part of the interim constitution) was empowered to supervise compliance of the constitution makers with the principles (and indeed the penultimate draft was rejected, and sent back for revisions, before final approval by the court).

Several important things were gained in this elaborate procedure. First, the two stages allowed for a period of testing of the operation of the provisional constitution and learning from this experience. Second, the highest consensus requirements for drafting could be reserved for the abstract principles, while the final document's passage required only a parliamentary supermajority. Third, elements of consociational democracy, so important for the stabilization of the initial context of the transition, could be kept from being frozen and could be replaced in the final draft by constitutional forms of protection of minorities. Finally, the legitimation resources of the "*ruptura pactada, reforma pactada*" generated through the act of liberation from the old regime were incorporated in the constitutional principles, whose persistence in the final draft makes clear that the new basic law is the constitution of the "regime change" and is neither a document imposed by the new majority nor simply another legislation produced by parliament for ordinary political reasons. Agreeing to constitutional principles at the outset, when normal politics under the new institutions had not yet begun, indeed saved something of the idea of the veil of ignorance during the constituent process.

Of course, critics could charge that the agreement to the interim constitution and to constitutional principles amounted to the fundamental decision concerning the character of the new regime, a decision that the freely elected constitutional assembly could only refine and elaborate, but not fundamentally change.[87] Since neither the parties at the negotiations, nor the last apartheid parliament that formally enacted their work had full democratic legitimacy, defenders of a revolutionary democratic process of constitution making can easily point to the element of non-democracy at the foundations of the new constitution. But in the narrow legal sense this element of non-democracy is equally present in the case of the model of sovereign constituent assemblies, where revolutionary legitimacy is ultimately presupposed.[88]

In South Africa, too, the process could work for some of the actors only because of an element of revolutionary and even charismatic legitimacy, embodied in the ANC and Nelson Mandela. However, for other actors it was the element of legal legitimacy, that is legal continuity, that obviously mattered. The non-democratic part of the process created no legitimation problems, because the major actors and the groups behind them were able to identify with it for different reasons.[89] And while in theory it may be preferable to limit the non-democratic instances to the production of organic rules, the needs of threatened minorities (not only the old rulers) in the context of quasi-revolutionary change

[87] See Atkinson, "Brokering a Miracle?" for example at 102, who, however, is happy about this outcome, avoiding both pure majoritarianism and consociationalism.

[88] See Arato, "Forms of Constitution-making."

[89] For this reason the ambiguity about some issues, such as whether or not there was a provisional government, whether or not the drafting body ("constitutional assembly") was a constituent assembly or an ordinary parliament, was calculated and functional. See I. Sarakinsky on this point, "Rehearsing Joint Rule. The Transitional Executive Council" in Friedman and Atkinson, *The Small Miracle* 82ff, 88–9.

could not in the end be protected without comprehensive constitutional legislation. Finally, it is not true that the freely elected assembly was deprived of its autonomous ability to shape the new regime. In particular, while the interim constitution established consociational democracy, the new parliament could (but was not bound to) replace consociational institutions with constitutional forms of protection.[90]

Granted, it is all the same unusual to allow a constitutional court, a mere *pouvoir constitué*, to be a part of the *pouvoir constituant*, in other words, to play an openly defining role in constitution creation. The step was of course important in South Africa if the constitutional principles were to be taken seriously, if the two-stage process of using consensus to reduce consensus was to work. But this procedure loses its strangeness in the context of post sovereign constitution making within legal continuity. After all, the constitutional assembly too was constituted power and, as always, its being "always under law" had to be guaranteed by another instance. Thus, with their most unusual innovation, the South African constitution makers teach us that the place of the people as the *pouvoir constituant*, sovereign and unbound, must be an empty place if we are to successfully institutionalize constitutional democracy.

[90] It could of course be said that the interim constitution-cum-constitutional principles already involved a choice for constitutionalism.

3

Conventions, Constituent Assemblies, and Round Tables: The Principles of Legitimacy of Democratic Constitution Making

I INTRODUCTION

Many of us outside South Africa have been inspired by the country's paradigmatic process of constitution making during the first half of the 1990s. This process,[1] composed of two great stages with a democratic election between them, involving the making of two constitutions and with a multi-party negotiating forum or round table, constitutional assembly, and constitutional court as its three main institutional agents, was not unprecedented. It has been to various extents anticipated by constitution makers in Spain in the 1970s, and in several Central and East European countries in 1989 and 1990. However, the South African process has been the most complete and most consistent development of what I will in general refer to as the post-sovereign paradigm, and more specifically by its new institution, the round table form.[2] It is the normatively distinguished case that allows us to understand the meaning and the deficiencies of the forerunners. In this chapter, I will argue that the round table[3] is an authentic

[1] From the impressive literature I relied on: S. Friedman and D. Atkinson (eds), *The Small Miracle* (Pretoria: Sigma Press: 1994); M. Faure and J.-E. Lane, *South Africa: Designing New Political Institutions* (London: Sage Publications, 1996); H. Ebrahim, *The Soul of a Nation* (Cape Town: Oxford University Press, 1998); and P. Andrews and S. Ellman, *Post-Apartheid Constitutions* (Johannesburg: Ohio University Press, 2001).

[2] I understand that in South Africa the term round table is sometimes avoided, because there were proposals for a final constitution to be made by such a body, and perhaps because of the well-known failure of three "round table conferences" concerning India in London in the 1930s. That fact should not disguise the near identity of the type of negotiating body, involving regime and opposition forces, that worked out interim arrangements for democratic transitions in at least six countries (Poland, Hungary, Czechoslovakia, German Democratic Republic, Bulgaria, and South Africa, in that order Nepal's related process did not involve a governmental actor.). See J. Elster (ed.), *The Roundtable Talks and the Breakdown of Communism* (Cambridge: Cambridge University Press, 1996); A. Bozoki (ed.), *The Roundtable Talks of 1989. The Genesis of Hungarian Democracy* (Budapest: CEU Press, 2002).

[3] Below I will use the term round table or round table form to indicate a process or paradigm of constitution making that I elsewhere also call multi-stage post-sovereign constitution making. When speaking about the

democratic form of constitution making, to be placed side by side with the convention pioneered in the United States, and the constituent assembly made classical if not actually invented in France. I will argue that it is normatively (and not just strategically) preferable to these earlier forms. Nevertheless, I will note its path-determined aspects, and the difficulty of applying the *complete* paradigm where forces of an old order have the legitimacy to carry out full constitutional reform, or where forces of the new can succeed in carrying out a revolutionary rupture. Yet even in these cases, I will argue that the principles and some of the structural elements of the new paradigm can be the key to solving the almost inevitable *legitimacy* problems of reform and revolution.

II HISTORY OF FORMS: CONVENTION, CONSTITUENT ASSEMBLY, AND ROUND TABLE

Four forms of original, democratic constitution making can be organized around the reform and revolution polarity if we reconstruct it around two axes of legality and legitimacy, and rupture and continuity.[4] We can then map out four possibilities, to which, typologically, four types of democratic change of constitutions correspond. *Reform* (where legality and legitimacy are both continuous) would have its typical form of change according to the established rules of change or amendment rules. Sovereign power sometimes incorporated in a single organ can play a role under reform, but this is a form of sovereignty defined by constitutional rules, hence limited at least in the procedural sense. *Revolutions* (where both old legality and legitimacy are ruptured) as in Pennsylvania during the American Revolution and then in France in 1789 and 1792, classically rely on sovereign constituent assemblies. Here the sovereignty of this body retains its classical sense as discussed by Bodin and Hobbes, as *legibus solutus* without legal limitations. These two forms are fairly well known, though the concept of revolution in particular has been generally understood differently than here. The role of the popular factor has been stressed, though it is questionable whether many "revolutions" were carried out by anything more than minorities. There has also been a tendency to define it in normatively progressive terms, a temptation that I will avoid here. Thus counter-revolutions are also revolutions, as I understand them. On the other hand, while the presence of coups in revolutions has been almost an historical constant, against Hans Kelsen, I do not identify coups and revolutions. In his interpretation, this happens because he identifies legality and legitimacy and their ruptures.[5]

central institution of negotiation within this form, I refer to the round table forum or round table institution. I owe this important clarification to Julian Arato.

[4] This requires that we do not follow Kelsen in identifying legality and legitimacy, but those who differentiate between these domains. See H. Kelsen, *General Theory of State and Law* (Cambridge, MA: Harvard, 1945).

[5] Thus he can only have two major types of transition, reform and revolution. Coups in my version need not involve breaks in legitimacy. However, revolutions logically contain coups in my scheme. This is the case not only because of legal breaks, but because after ruptures a new organized force must take power if the state is

More importantly, in the scheme offered here I get two additional, equally pure types: continuous legitimacy, with legal rupture, to which the American convention form corresponds, as its only democratic subtype.[6] This form was pioneered in Massachusetts and New Hampshire in the 1780s, and relied upon by the slightly later Federal Convention. All of these conventions (as against the historically prior use of the term in England) presupposed existing republican forms of government. Ackerman rightly called this *revolutionary reform*.[7] From the point of view of sovereignty, this is a mixed form. While no organ can unambiguously be said to be the incarnation of state or popular sovereignty, in its democratic variant,[8] the actors often speak, using phrases such as "We the People," as if they had the right to fully invoke the name of the sovereign. Unfortunately, until at least 1865 in the United States, it could not be resolved whether sovereignty was supposed to belong to "the" people of the Union or the "peoples" of the states.[9] While the unitary one of these two sovereigns signified an absence, thus a negative principle, the pluralistic one referred to specific institution(s) that were supposed to incarnate the people(s), or make them fully present, namely state (ratifying) conventions.

Finally, in the context of a full break in or breakdown of legitimacy but with continuous legality we get the round table form. This is the post sovereign form par excellence, since, classically, the actors at the round-table forum represent a plurality of social interests and opinions rather than a unity, and they are more or less conscious of this fact. While occasionally there are references to popular sovereignty as the ultimate principle of the paradigm's legitimacy, these claims can only have the meaning of a sovereign that can never be embodied or be fully present. I will return to this issue, but I start with an ideal typical form of presentation of the four types of change along with the relevant models of constitution making.

Table 2 can use some commentary. First, the link between transition type and constitution-making method is strong, but not absolute. In principle, in a particular form of transition there can be ways of using any of the constitution-making methods. I myself made a suggestion to that effect with

to survive. We have seen this from the Russian to the Islamic Revolution. Alas, the recent revolution in Egypt confirms this insight. See my short piece, A. Arato, *Egypt's Transformation: Revolution, Coup, Regime Change, or All of the above?* (2011) at http://www.comparativeconstitutions.org/2011/02/andrew-arato-on-egypts-transformation.html accessed December 1, 2015.

6 The other subtype is the generally plebiscitary form in the so-called *autogolpe* or self-coups common in Latin America. I do not treat this in this chapter as a democratic form. There are cases, however, such as Russia in 1993, where the two subtypes are difficult to differentiate within the actual historical process. Here, as in Venezuela, we may speak of a process that begins as deformed versions of the convention, and end up as plebiscitary self-coups.

7 B. Ackerman, *We the People* vol. II (Cambridge, MA: Harvard University Press, 1998).

8 Under the populist authoritarian variant, invariably the president claims to be the incarnation of the people, a claim more or less plausible depending on the amount of empirical support behind the executive.

9 This was true only to a lesser extent in Massachusetts and New Hampshire where the duality of ultimate claimants to the voice of the people was between townships and the conventions.

Table 2 Major Types of Democratic Transition with Forms of Constitution Making

	Legitimacy continuous	**Legitimacy ruptured**
Legality continuous	Reform: Major amendments or new constitution within same regime. Sweden 1974 (legitimate) Hungary 2011 (illegitimate) Turkey (between 1983 and present)	Regime change with legal continuity: *Round table* with interim constitution(s): Poland 1989–97 Bulgaria 1990 Hungary 1989–96 (failure) South Africa 1993–96 Nepal 2006–15
Legality ruptured	Type 1 "revolutionary reform": (democratic legitimacy) *Convention:* Massachusetts and New Hampshire 1780s (marginal cases with continuous legality) US Federal Convention 1787 Latin American cases, e.g. Colombia 1990s (West) Germany 1948 Type 2: (self-) coup with plebiscitary legitimacy: 18th Brumaire of Napoleon Bonaparte 1799 + L. Napoleon 1853 Argentina 1949 Peru 1993 Russia 1993 Venezuela 1999	Revolution *Constituent Assemblies:* Pennsylvania France 1789–91; 1793–95; 1848; 1945–46 Weimar 1919 India 1948–50 (legal continuity from UK point of view)

respect to the Turkish reform process,[10] and argued elsewhere that in Iraq the round-table, two-stage model was grafted into a process of the revolutionary overthrow of the previous regime.[11] Usually, it is particularly serious legitimation problems with a type of transformation in a particular context that lead to such attempts at grafting, but the generation of legitimacy using a non-characteristic constitution-making model may not succeed, as the Iraqi example shows. There is at the very least an elective affinity, if not causality, between transition type and form of constitution making that is difficult to set aside.[12]

Second, there can be a process that starts one way and turns into another. Several Latin American cases, such as Argentina in 1949 and Venezuela recently, start as conventions, and wind up as plebiscitary coups or as sovereign constituent assemblies (or a combination of the two). Reform[13] can fail and turn into round

[10] A. Arato, "Democratic Constitution Making and Unfreezing the Turkish Process" (2010) 36 *Philosophy and Social Criticism* 3–4.

[11] A. Arato, *Constitution Making under Occupation* (New York: Columbia, 2009).

[12] Thus I argue that learning across types, and especially from the new type, should work on the level of principles rather than concrete method. See A. Arato, *Civil Society, Constitution, and Legitimacy* (Lanham, MD: Rowman, 2000) Chapter 7; and Chapter 2 of this volume.

[13] Pervasive authoritarian attempts at reform do not belong in my typology. Regarding them, A. Przeworski, *Democracy and Market* (Cambridge: Cambridge University Press, 1991) maintained that "liberalization," a broader category, always fails. I consider the Mexican reforms under the PRI, focusing on electoral rule change, successful for a very long period. See Arato, *Civil Society* Chapter 1.

tables, as in most cases here, but also into revolutionary constituent processes as in India and other post-colonial cases.[14]

Third, classification cannot be absolutely neat because one major element can be missing from a form that nevertheless is classified with others that are largely similar. For example, the conventions of Massachusetts and New Hampshire were legally established (there was no legal rupture) and so also were some Latin American cases, provided for by the amendment rules. (Other Latin American cases involved later ruptures, leading to the plebiscitary or revolutionary types). Conversely, there was a legal break in Nepal where the incomplete and troubled process in other respects belongs to the round table form. Interestingly, the prototypic post-sovereign case of Spain did not have a round table and its interim rules were established from above and confirmed by a referendum. Fourth, and finally: substance may be different than form; the real process may be different than the formal process. Thus, for example, Carlos Menem led a constitution-making effort in Argentina in 1993–94 that was based on the American convention (without illegality) in form, but plebiscitary in substance. The question arises whether the transition in a round-table country such as Czechoslovakia was not simply hiding what was in effect a revolutionary collapse, or even an overthrow of the old regime. The fact that the constitution-making effort through the round table failed and was replaced by processes carried out by normal parliaments assuming sovereign powers in both Slovakia and the Czech Republic sustains this hypothesis.

That outcome also indicates that a form can fail, as Table 2 notes for the Hungarian case, where the process was finally subverted in 2011. Such a failure can be argued empirically, by the fact that a process was either replaced by another one or led to political chaos or a new form of authoritarianism with or without a paper constitution. Thus the replacement of reform by round tables in Poland, Hungary (in 1989), and South Africa, the replacement of revolutionary reform by a quasi-revolutionary autogolpe as in Venezuela, or the round-table model by an illegitimate reform in Hungary in 2011, all represent failures of the previous model, if not of constitution making in general. Alternatively, failure can be ascertained by a comparison to a fully developed, normatively attractive mode. In the case of round-table-led regime change, that model in my view is that of South Africa.[15] While it is hazardous to judge in terms of this normative comparison alone, when both empirical and normative approaches converge, we are justified to speak of failure. Even then, a process can always be redeemed by a subsequent one. Whether that will be possible and likely in Hungary now is the ultimate interest of Chapter 4.

Here I will concentrate on the three *democratic* forms involving general discontinuity in one of the two domains having to do with original constitution

[14] Or it can succeed, as did the initial top-down reform in Spain, by turning into a multi-stage process with an interim constitution, the law of reform.

[15] See my two essays in (2010) 26 *South African Journal of Human Rights* 1.

making capable of producing new regimes. To an extent, I will neglect coups and self-coups because I do not regard plebiscitary legitimation as democratic at all, and will mention these only where they are results of the failure of conventions and constituent assemblies. (They can also become relevant with the failure of reform!) However, a historical-comparative analysis cannot avoid also touching on the model of reform.

As already implied, uncannily, the various forms tend to originate from one another. The convention form in its most dramatic appearance, as the American Federal Convention, grows out of a project of reform.[16] As in the case of several state conventions, the project was originally only a large-scale reform of an existing system, constitutionalized by a treaty, the Articles of Confederation. The framers, and eventually the states, violated that project and produced much more radical change within an established structure of state(s) legitimacy. The drafting Convention, one that could only recommend measures to state-ratifying conventions, was the main instrument of legal break within a generally intact legal and institutional system. This Convention was doubly differentiated from legislative and other powers: it exercised no other powers than constitution making, and no other institution had constituent powers until the moment of ratification.

While it may be an exaggeration to say that the constituent assembly grew simply out of the convention, this is more or less what directly happened in Pennsylvania in 1776, when the dual power of two assemblies, the convention and the regular legislature, could not be stabilized.[17] The result was a sovereign constituent assembly, still under the name of a convention, along with a radical democratic constitution. More importantly for the future, the American model of the Federal Convention failed in France in 1792–3, in spite of its significant influence on theory. Important authors and leaders wrote on the American constitutions, including the convention form, and the most sophisticated (Sieyès, Condorcet) repeatedly expressed their preference for "double differentiation," for electing an extraordinary convention for the sole purpose of constitution making with no other powers in the state.[18] Under the conditions in France this proved impossible: in 1789 because of the existence of a society of orders and an estates assembly based on it, and in 1792 because of a second revolution that swept away the powers of the elected Legislative Assembly. The practice produced sovereign constituent assemblies, and it is this practice that became canonical for democratic and radical theory, especially (and paradoxically) because the result in 1793 was the never-instituted democratic constitution,

[16] Of course the convention had a distinguished history before. It is reconstructed by G. Wood, *The Creation of the American Republic* 2nd edn. (Durham, NC: University of North Carolina Press, 1998); and in E. Morgan, *Inventing the People* (New York: Norton, 1998); as well as Ackerman in *We the People*.

[17] See R.R. Palmer, *The Age of Democratic Revolutions* (Princeton, NJ: Princeton University Press, 1959) and Wood, *The Creation of the American Republic*.

[18] Chapter 1 above; and A. Arato, *Adventures of the Constituent Power*, Chapters 1 and 2 (forthcoming).

whose failure remains an untestable counterfactual. But the association of the second such body, the *Convention nationale*, with the concomitant revolutionary dictatorship and the Reign of Terror, meant that others, mainly liberal democrats, continued to look back to the 1789 prototype, the *Assemblée constituante*, with its liberal, if barely successful, 1791 Constitution. Thus the name constituent assembly survived, and the most important difference between the two forerunners, whether the constituent assembly should offer its product for popular ratification, remained forever unresolved.

The round table form is generally the offspring of two parents: the reformist and revolutionary. With few exceptions,[19] in most historical contexts an old regime in power tries and yet fails to enact successful comprehensive reforms on its own. Almost everywhere there is also a revolutionary or radical democratic scenario in the wings, demanding a democratically elected constituent assembly, without making clear how the activists can answer Lenin's significant objection from 1905,[20] namely that unless they take power the old regime would still dominate such elections. (The Hungarian democratic opposition rejected calling for a constituent assembly for this very reason.) In any case, for a variety of reasons, and with the exception of Iran, revolutionary power was not available from the mid-1970s to the 1990s. Better still, it remained a mere potentiality, more feared by the old regimes than trusted by its possible agents. The latter either did not believe the power existed, or were wary of using it even if it were available. This was true in South Africa too, significantly because this country did have a powerful revolutionary movement. Yet the Convention for a Democratic South Africa (CODESA) and the Multi Party Negotiating Forum (MPNF, and even the previous "talks about talks") emerged from a similar constellation as the other round tables: the impossibility for old regime actors to save their system through mere reform (tried out in the 1980s) and the inability of oppositional, even revolutionary movements to carry out a revolution. The round table form, born of this strategic constellation, gives to the reformers a negotiated first-phase process in which they can attain the guarantees enshrined in an interim constitution. The very same form provides radical democratic forces with a freely elected constitutional assembly, which unlike the American state-ratifying conventions of 1787–88, may re-draft the constitution proposed in unelected negotiating instances.

The *strategic* reasons for moving from form to form are clear. Following the reformist process, the rules of the Articles of Confederation would not have achieved the result of a more centralized system many of the large American states wanted. They needed to break the rules, and the doubly used institution

[19] These exceptions all involve legal ruptures, as in Iraq and Nepal. Even in Iraq, a subsequent confrontation between top-down reform, led by the occupying power's Coalition Provisional Authority (CPA), and radical democratic challenge led to the type.

[20] V. Lenin, "Two Tactics of Social Democracy in the Bourgeois Revolutions" in *Selected Works* I (Moscow: Progress, 1970).

of conventions (for drafting as well as ratifying), associated with popular government, legitimated these breaks.[21] At the same time, it should be noted, anything like the revolutionary constituent assembly formula, known from the Pennsylvania prototype, would not only have been unacceptable to the majority of the delegates, but politically the Federal Convention did not have the power to accomplish such radical self-conversion. The one related proposal, to have ratification of the draft only by an elected *national* convention (by Gouverneur Morris) was not even seconded.

As for the French Constituent Assemblies, however attractive American precedents may have been to some of their protagonists, the leading revolutionaries and constitutional experts had no wish to share power with aristocratic institutions of the past, even temporarily. Even the king, left in place, was deprived of his veto over the constitution to be made. However, normative or theoretical justification was not missing in this case either. The move to an all-powerful constituent assembly was accomplished in 1789 in the name of a unitary notion of popular sovereignty embodied in a single assembly with the plenitude of power. As previously stated, in America popular sovereignty played a role, too, but in an antinomic form, with the notion of the people understood alternately in national and "federal" terms.[22] Here, the notion of sovereignty embodied in a single instance had to be and was absent.[23] As to the second French Revolution in 1792, it was the power of a popular revolution, rooted in Paris, that made moderate republicans such as Condorcet, who were otherwise committed to double differentiation, accept the destruction of the freely elected legislature, again in the name of unitary popular sovereignty but this time to be controlled by direct democracy of the referendum. The protagonists argued strongly that a genuinely democratic constitution could only be produced by an assembly whose election was fully democratic, but whose authenticity would nevertheless have to be checked by popular referendum. This hope was fulfilled by the constitution of 1793, but not by the Convention's dictatorship, exercised by its most powerful committee, that suspended it.

Finally, from 1989 to the 1990s, from Poland to South Africa, it was the combination of the old regimes' collapse of legitimacy and the insufficient power of oppositions that led to the new post sovereign formula, with its first stage negotiated at round tables. Most oppositions would have preferred not to negotiate with previous oppressors, but for strategic reasons they all had to. At the same time many, especially in Central and Eastern Europe, did not wish to adopt any version of a revolutionary perspective, given the revolutionary ideologies of the

[21] While this was said most clearly when substituting state conventions for state legislatures, Madison's *Federalist* 40 makes a clear case also for the unauthorized propositions instituted by patriotic individuals at the Federal Convention.

[22] The alternative understandings continued until the civil war.

[23] And occasionally such an idea of sovereignty was clearly rejected, such as in Madison, *Federalist* 22, where Hamilton calls the accumulation "in a single body all the most important prerogatives of sovereignty" an execrable tyranny. However, the implications of this view for the constituent process were not thought through.

old regimes. Thus the new model is linked to a post revolutionary consciousness, if not yet an ideology, centering in civil society rather than the state. While popular sovereignty in the form of majority rule still played an important role, and a greater one in South Africa than elsewhere because the nature of the earlier apartheid regime made consociational arrangements suspicious, this was no longer conceived as embodied in a single institution or agent, as in most revolutions. The majority would rule through many institutions, including the Constitutional Court. Equally, post revolutionary ideas of reconciliation between former enemies representing important parts of the population, the rule of law applied to the process, as well as the result of constitution making were all important facets.

The historical influence of all these forms is undeniable. The American form has influenced French development, but in a paradoxical manner. Unused in the practice of original French constitution making, despite use of the term *Convention nationale*, the convention formula involving double differentiation found its way into French amendment rules, which in turn were almost never used, similarly to the (national) convention in U.S. Article V. In the United States, only the states were to have constitutional conventions, doubly differentiated as the theory required, and they did so frequently under a stable federal order.[24]

That order itself, the Federal Constitution, formally speaking had only had partial—and relatively few—amendments since 1787, while the fourteen or so French Constitutions emerged through coups, revolutions, and semi-legal revisions of the revision, but never through a convention or assembly of revision formulas. With its many constitutions, Latin American history is generally similar to the French pattern. Though U.S. institutions, including at times the convention, were widely imitated, most actual processes of alteration happened through coups, self-coups, and revolutions using plebiscitary imposition, or—in name at least—sovereign assemblies. In the older case of Argentina under Perón, and the recent case of Venezuela under Chavez, the convention formula under the name constituent assembly (*constituyente*) was used, but broke down and was turned into that of sovereign constituent assemblies.[25] Yet there is a single, late success story for the convention model. Under a different name, the Parliamentary Council at Chiemsee composed of delegates of the *Länder*, which drafted the highly successful German Federal Basic Law and sent its product back to the states for ratification, came close to the American Federal Convention type of

[24] See for example C. Fritz, *American Sovereigns: The People and America's Constitutional Tradition Before the Civil War* (New York: Cambridge University Press, 2009).

[25] The case of Colombia in 1991 is an interesting mixed type. See D.T. Fox et al., "Lessons of the Colombian Constitutional Reform of 1991" in L. Miller (ed.), *Framing the State in Time of Transition. Case Studies in Constitution Making* (Washington, DC: USIP Press, 2010) 467–82; see also N. Figureoa, "Counter-Hegemonic Constitutionalism: The Case of Colombia' (2012) 19 *Constellations* 2; and J.I. Colón-Ríos, "Carl Schmitt and Constituent Power in Latin American Courts: The Cases of Venezuela and Colombia" (2011) 18 *Constellations* 3. Comparing Venezuela with Colombia see also A.R. Brewer-Carias, "The 1999 Venezuelan Constitution-Making Process as an Instrument for Framing the Development of an Authoritarian Political Regime" in Miller, *Framing the State* 505–32.

constitution making.[26] Interestingly, here history moved in the opposite direction to France in 1789–93, where convention became the sovereign constituent assembly. For German liberals and democrats, according to inherited doctrine, the constituent assembly was the type that would have been most suitable to express *the sovereignty* of the political community. In the context of occupation and division, they deemed producing a constitution by a constituent assembly as inappropriate. A non-sovereign drafting assembly was for them thus only a second best. For that reason too, the *Grundgesetz* was meant to be only a provisional constitution, a promise unredeemed in 1990.

This last example too shows that the sovereign constituent assembly formula has been hegemonic for democratic constitution making, producing notable successes such as India's constitution, failures such as Russia in 1918, but also the short-lived constitutions of the Weimar Republic and the Fourth French Republic, and many, many cases in between. Very often, as Lenin anticipated in 1905, the constituent assembly turned out to be a mere instrument for whatever force was able to convene it and here Latin America and Africa with their many constitutions are again important cases in point.

Finally, the round-table-based form has now a real history, with successes and failures. Leaving out the so-called "miracle" of Spain, which had no initial negotiations, at least formally, Poland, Bulgaria, and South Africa count as successes with workable final constitutions; the German Democratic Republic and Czechoslovakia were complete failures, and Hungary is a semi-failure (I used to say partial success![27]), the outcome of which is hopefully still in doubt. The application of the form in the externally imposed revolution of Iraq was probably a failure that looks worse and worse with the passing of time;[28] and we still do not know the outcome for Nepal, where it was applied after a legal break, but also where the first interim constitution was aggressively challenged by various nationalisms.[29] On the purely empirical level,[30] then, it would be very difficult, if not impossible, to determine the superiority of any of the three forms that seem to be always adopted for situated, strategic reasons first of all. I turn therefore to a brief set of structural and normative comparisons.

[26] By also binding the minority of states that did not ratify, the makers of the *Grundgesetz* did not even in the first instance produce a treaty, as arguably in the case of the Federal Convention. See Madison, *Federalist* 39.

[27] A. Arato, "Post Sovereign Constitution-Making in Hungary: After Success, Partial Failure and Now What?" (2010) 26 *South African Journal of Human Rights* 1.

[28] See Arato, *Constitution Making under Occupation* as well as A. Arato, Book Reviews (2014) 12 *International Journal of Constitutional Law* 3 808–16.

[29] Not only was the interim constitution thereby weakened, but an almost insoluble conflict was introduced regarding the nature of federalism, around the polarity of ethnicity versus territoriality.

[30] The largest scale empirical study by Z. Elkins, T. Ginsburg, and J. Melton, *The Endurance of Constitutions* (Cambridge: Cambridge University Press, 2009), as important and sophisticated as it is, does not make a distinction among the three forms discussed here.

III COMPARING AND DEBATING THE THREE FORMS

Analytically, it is relatively easy to depict the difference among the three great democratic types, and very schematically I would emphasize seven dimensions in which there are differences among them, as shown in Table 3.

Again commentary may be helpful on some of these points where Table 3 is not self-explanatory. I use the term double differentiation, as introduced by Claude Klein,[31] in the path of Carré de Malberg, to indicate that the (generally) earlier legislature that stays in place does not engage in constitution making, while the main assembly or assemblies involved in making the constitution assume no other power in the state, executive or legislative. There is no differentiation in this sense where normally elected parliaments engage in the making of a new constitution, as in Hungary in 2011. Differentiation is single where ordinary legislatures do not make the constitution, but the constituent assembly assumes legislative powers (often in the form of decree power) and often, through its committees, executive ones. When the process involves two main stages of drafting, differentiation can take the double form in one stage and the single or even an undifferentiated form in the other. Since in this later case generally a prior legislative assembly is undemocratically convened, it is unlikely that it will retain its powers under a freely elected constitutional assembly. This latter combination of two doubly differentiated stages was advocated in Iraq by the American CPA to be sure, but collapsed with the abandonment of a co-opted legislative body.[32]

Table 3 Forms of Democratic Constitution Making and their Elements

	Differentiation	Stages	Final stage	Elections	Rules	Constitutions	Sovereignty
Convention	Double	multiple	Passive	Middle; rule negotiated	External, partially violated	One: final	Antinomic (in 1787), not embodied
Constituent assembly	Single	One, or two (with plebiscite)	Active or passive	Beginning; rules imposed	Internal to assembly, self-imposed	One: final	Embodied organ sovereignty (one-or two-body version)
Round table	First: double Second: partial (role of Constitutional Court)	Multiple	Active	Middle, rules negotiated	External	Two: interim and final	Not embodied

[31] C. Klein, *Théorie et pratique du pouvoir constituant* (Paris: PUF, 1997).

[32] On this see my third chapter, "Sistani v. Bremer" in Arato, *Constitution Making Under Occupation*.

As to the role of the final relevant body in the process (assembly or electorate), I call it passive when it can only ratify or refuse to ratify the constitutional draft, and active when it can either modify it or produce a new one. Here levels of passivity are not the same. Referenda, though important in terms of their "shadow" on the previous process, are primarily passive. Ratifying conventions *à la americaine* are formally passive but potentially active, since they can and did suggest important amendments that the subsequent amending process can and did take very seriously. The Bill of Rights was the American result. Finally, I do not exclude some kind of combination of referenda and ratifying conventions, as suggested by Ackerman and Fishkin ("deliberation day"),[33] though these have historical examples or analogies only in the township ratification processes in revolutionary America.[34]

The place of sovereignty in the model is less a descriptive than a theoretical issue. Thus it belongs mostly to the normative differences among the models. Here I would only like to say that the concepts of sovereignty of the actors and my assignment of a type may differ. The actors may claim embodied popular sovereignty not only, and necessarily, in the revolutionary constituent assemblies, but also in the cases of the convention and the round table, and express it in preambles. In my view, both the federalist problem of duality, and the multi-stage process make such a claim problematic. At times these difficulties are recognized at least as regards *popular* sovereignty, and it is admitted that although ultimate authority is one thing, "the people spontaneously and universally moving toward their object" is quite another.[35] The admission of impossibility in the latter case bifurcates factual and legal meaning of popular sovereignty on the one side and on the other denies that the people can (or should) make constitutions in their collective or corporate, that is, embodied capacity.[36]

This exclusion of embodiment leads to significant differences among convention, constituent assembly and round table, which are difficult to evaluate, however. I will try through three two-by-two juxtapositions, leaving for later the purely normative considerations, first on a combination of legal and political levels.

Convention versus constituent assembly

The critical comparison, to my knowledge, focusing on double differentiation, has been attempted only by French writers during and after the

[33] B.A. Ackerman and J.S. Fishkin, *Deliberation Day* (New Haven, CT: Yale University Press, 2004).

[34] The Massachusetts township ratification of 1781 was very active, in that not only were amendments suggested, but the towns were able to vote on the text article by article.

[35] Madison, *Federalist* 40.

[36] *Federalist* 63 speaks of "total exclusion of the people in their collective capacity" but specifically in relationship to government. I believe that the argument, logically, applies to both constituent and constituted powers.

Revolution.[37] From the beginning, the fundamental argument in defense of conventions, based on the separation of powers, has been that the always dangerous legislative power should not be allowed to transform its own parameters and, conversely, a constituent power should not become too closely identified with legislation if it is to establish a workable separation of powers. The argument for the convention is thus based on a distinction between constituent and constituted power, but in a version ultimately derived from the ideas of Montesquieu.[38] At least this is the way the case was argued in France, notably by Sieyès. In America itself, the influence of Locke was perhaps more important, and particularly his avoidance of the term sovereignty when distinguishing the original and, by strong implication, constituent power of the people and the legislative power of government. With lots of caveats having to do with the problem of representation, the defenders of the constituent assembly see the same distinction in terms of Rousseau, who in fact did not differentiate legislative and constituent powers.[39] The key is popular sovereignty, here expressed through electoral majorities. A constituent assembly elected by a majority supposedly expresses and embodies the will of the sovereign people, and therefore cannot, like a convention, share power with an instance elected at a previous time. Legislative power is also a supreme power and, if defined in terms of sovereignty, there cannot be two supreme powers in the state.

Those who would argue for the convention model[40] could respond with a different notion of popular or national sovereignty, one that cannot be embodied in a single person (king) or institution (assembly) or group (the Parisian popular insurrection) without usurpation. From this point of view, a single-stage, single-assembly model as in France runs the danger of just such an usurpation. Thus, not only double differentiation, but also the multi-stage character of the story of the Federal Convention involving at least five instances each of which could have an influence, more potential than actual in three of their cases, on the draft (the Convention, Congress, state legislatures, the electorate of the states, and freely elected state conventions) all keep the model from usurpation. Finally, Carl Schmitt has referred to constitution making in the form practiced in France in

37 Namely by: Sieyès, Condorcet, and Lafayette criticizing Sieyès, as well as Laboulaye, Carré de Malberg, but omitted by Schmitt and those who follow him; and by B. Ackerman, *Future of the Liberal Revolution* (New Haven, CT: Yale University Press, 1992), where he pronounces the two forms more or less equivalent.

38 On this see R. Carré de Malberg, *Contribution à Théorie générale de l'État* II (1920) (Paris: Dalloz, 2004).

39 Arguably the presence of the figure of legislator in original constitution making could be such a difference in Rousseau as long as we assume, without textual support, that when the sovereign dissolves and remakes a constitution there will no longer be a need for the authority and expert advice of such an external law giver. That figure also anticipates the American notion of 1787 that the actual drafter only recommends or proposes. See Madison, *Federalist* especially 41, and John Marshall in *McCulloch v. Maryland* 17 U.S. 316 (1819).

40 I have in mind interpreters such as Carré de Malberg and Hannah Arendt, whom I follow, and who see the distinction between the two forms clearly, as both of whom focus on the issue of sovereignty. Neither the original actors nor Bruce Ackerman could make this argument, because of the antinomic presence of embodied popular sovereignty in their conceptions.

1789 and 1793 as well as Weimar as sovereign dictatorship.[41] While he meant to use this category he invented in either a neutral or positive sense, we would be well advised to treat it as a warning. Being in the state of nature, liberated from all prior constraints including the separation of powers, was central for Schmitt. While it is not entirely clear whether the dictatorship is exercised by the assemblies or by the provisional, revolutionary governments that control them, nor whether self-limitation can effectively block the road form sovereign dictatorship to what is *ordinarily* considered arbitrary dictatorial rule, the elective affinity (not identity) of revolutionary constituent assemblies to dictatorship is thereby demonstrated.[42] There is no such elective affinity for conventions that, in spite of some very specific illegality or extra-legality, operate under established rule of law systems the constitutions of which they replace, without legal rupture. Yet the specific danger of the convention is dual power, mediated by Federal structure in the United States, but which led to the defeat of one assembly, the ordinary one, by the other, the extraordinary one, under presidential leadership, for example in Russia and Venezuela.

Constituent assembly and round table

The political debate between the two models occurs in two dimensions: dictatorship versus democracy, and radicalism versus conservatism. Obviously, it cannot be denied that the revolutionary constituent assembly is capable of a more radical break with the past if one focuses on the identity of the rulers and the direct beneficiaries of rule rather than their manner of ruling. An agreement with the former rulers reduces the extent of the break. This is a serious problem from many points of view, all having to do with the "conversion," or preservation of illegitimate forms of earlier power. Nevertheless, the two-stage process does allow the constitutional assembly of the second stage to accomplish a change of regime if that has not already occurred in the negotiated phase. Given the political focus of regime change, the price of the formula will be reform rather than revolution in some important domains, mainly in the socio-economic sphere.

It is meanwhile questionable whether revolution has ever realized its social and economic goals of equality and justice, or just generated alternative systems of inequality and injustice. On a constitutional level, undoubtedly the fact that the new regime does not have to be designed together with those attached to an old form of life is in part responsible. Important population segments, some politically opposed to the old regime, some in favor, even the majority, can therefore be entirely left out of the construction of the new, which will then make no

[41] In C. Schmitt, *Die Diktatur* (Berlin: Duncker & Humblot, 1921) and less frequently but still emphatically in C. Schmitt, *Verfassungslehre* (Berlin: Duncker & Humblot, 1928).

[42] E.-W. Böckenförde, "Verfassunggebende Gewalt des Volkes – Ein Grenzbegriff des Vervassungsrechts" in *Staat, Verfassung, Demokratie* (Frankfurt: Suhrkamp, 1992).

concessions to conservative life forms. The religious in France and the peasantry in Russia are two salient examples, the protagonists of two civil wars. The result is almost always resistance and new forms of repression, often enduring long term. In the Soviet Union, the war against the peasantry ("the kulaks") and Stalinism is the final consequence of revolution, and should not be seen merely as a Thermidor.

Thus, it is in the dimension of democracy and dictatorship that the round table formula has its obvious political superiority. Given that the transition under these two forms is from authoritarian regimes, constitutional democracy represents the more fundamental break, not the establishment of a new dictatorship.[43] Revolutionary constitution making, in spite of its democratic appearance in the constituent assembly form, tends to exercise dictatorship as Marx in 1848, Lenin in 1905, and Schmitt equally maintained,[44] and, as we will see below, produces legitimacy problems that are difficult to resolve without authoritarian reversion. The round table form avoids sovereign dictatorship, and produces a variety of plausible answers in each of its stages to the problem of legitimation.

Convention and round table

It is on the question of sovereignty that the round-table model can fully complete the logic of the American convention, without the historical attachment to the concept of the unitary popular sovereign and the resulting antinomy of nationalism–federalism. Having adopted the idea of the second convention, which, formally speaking, lost in America, multi-stage constitution making here has really come into its own. In the fully developed South African case we can see an equal number of relevant actors as in 1787[45]: the round table called first CODESA and later the Multiparty Negotiating Forum (MPNF), the old parliament, the electorate, the constitutional assembly, and the Constitutional Court. More importantly, in comparison to the convention with its one formal drafting agent and relatively passive (even if potentially influential) other participants, three of these agencies play an important role in drafting and design, and none of them can claim fully sovereign or unlimited status.[46]

[43] Admittedly this is so from my normative point of view. From another point of view, the transition from a secular to a religious dictatorship (as in Iran) can be deemed equally fundamental.

[44] For Karl Marx on the Frankfurt Assembly see https://www.marxists.org/archive/marx/works/1848/11/23a.htm accessed November 16, 2015; see also V. Lenin, "Two Tactics of Social Democracy in the Bourgeois Revolution" in *Works I* (Moscow: Progress, 1970).

[45] To review: the Convention, Congress, state legislatures, state electorates, and state conventions were then the five actors. In the original version in Massachusetts there were only four: state legislature, townships, electorate, and convention, though the towns came in at two distinct moments: initiation and ratification.

[46] In the United States the ratifying states could and did, as has been most clearly articulated by J.C. Calhoun. The sovereign claim for "we the people" was necessarily more abstract, since one could not point to an organ that could speak this language.

It is important to stress the transformation of the problem of sovereignty in the round-table model. The American understanding of constitution making, as the preamble to the constitution shows, took place in the name of the sovereign people. Yet in the conflict between federal and national conceptions, it was difficult to identify the body fully representing the people, the body where their representatives met that did all the drafting, the Federal Convention, or the bodies that had the final word, the state conventions. In this sense, in spite of the possible claim that could be and was made on behalf of the peoples of the states, the sovereignty of the whole was not embodied in any instance even on the level of constitution making, and Hannah Arendt's judgement concerning the banishment of the (organ) sovereign can be partially upheld.[47] Yet the appeal to the sovereign as the author of the constitution meant that organ sovereignty could not be reliably banished from the American scene.[48] Moreover, in different historical contexts as we see from Ackerman's theory, and especially transported elsewhere to more centralized settings, the American conception allows the revival of the idea that a constitution should be the work of a unified popular sovereign, represented or unified by an organ of the state. This leads to dual power when there are two plausible claimants, or the subversion of process when one of them triumphs. The multi-stage round-table formula that divides the work of discussion, drafting, and enactment goes a step further in the direction banishing organ sovereignty, with the place of the king essentially becoming an empty place holder.[49]

The whole history of the American model of constitution making, and the difficulty of applying it elsewhere, suggests exceptionalism, a notion that by no means escapes Hannah Arendt's brilliant analysis. Condorcet already noted the problem, calling the American transition one from a free to a more free constitution, and, as he noticed for France, generally such is not the context of original constitution making.[50] In most places, well-functioning republican institutions are not available for the purposes of double differentiation. Moreover, as Carl Schmitt noted, in America the making of a new type of federation and constitution making coincided, more or less. This not only made impossible the clear decision of the constituent power about the form of the state, as Schmitt stressed, but also provided a stabilizing framework for multiple institutions that elsewhere had a tendency of reverting to a duality of power. Thus the model has always had the greatest chance of success where the relevant

[47] See H. Arendt, *On Revolution* (New York: Viking, 1965).

[48] A. Arato and J. Cohen, "Banishing the Sovereign? Internal and External Sovereignty in Arendt" (2009) 16 *Constellations* 2.

[49] C. Lefort, "Permanence du theologico-politique" in *Essais sur le politique*. (Paris: du Seuill, 1986).

[50] N. de Condorcet, *Discours sur les conventions nationales* (Paris: Didot, 1847).

individual states were embedded in larger federations,[51] or where the creation of federal institutions occurred in the context of stable unit constitutions.[52]

The round-table process of constitution making not only makes more explicit the critique of sovereignty latent in the American convention model, but also makes the achievement of overcoming organ sovereignty in constitution making less exceptional. Neither pre-existing republics nor federations of any kind are required, and there is no need to create federal states when using the model.[53] Round-table negotiations and compromise do revive the contractual form insisted on by Schmitt for federations, but transpose contractuality, the South African Constitutional Court's "solemn promise," to the interaction of political actors in general, beyond territorially definable polities.[54] Thus, at the very least it should be said that the ability to institute democratizing, and in its second stage, a democratic process of constitution making regulated by constitutional rules where there has been neither democracy nor constitutionalism before, dramatically reduces the exceptional nature of the circumstances where post organ sovereign conceptions can apply. This means that the circle of authoritarian rule and dictatorship can be broken by a method that does not itself risk a new authoritarian form.

But this is not yet the full political advantage of the round table over the convention form. That superiority I see in terms of the already-stated objection at the Federal Convention, renewed by the Anti-Federalists, that it is impermissible to give the *last* enacting instance, supposedly representing "the people" a simple yes or no choice in the case of complex packages; in other words, not to allow the elected bodies[55] to make their positive constitutional inputs.[56] Put this way, the objection presupposes the notion of embodied sovereignty, specifically in the ratifying conventions. But it can be restated in terms of learning theory, relevant to politics. Accordingly, the societal discussion in which, for example, *The Federalist Papers* was only one among many important publications should have been allowed to have an effect on the outcome beyond simply getting the assent of people in conventions who preferred more things in the document

[51] From Massachusetts and New Hampshire in the revolutionary period to many individual states later on

[52] From the Federal Constitution to the *Grundgesetz*, and potentially even the convention for the Future of Europe. It is another matter that the creation of such federations alters the constitutions of the unit states, as Schmitt noted, but only in the sense of limited reform. This can happen implicitly or through formal amendment.

[53] Elsewhere I have argued that because of its two stages, the method has also the virtue of being able to separate state formation from constitution making proper, which will no longer keep open the structure of the state. This possibility, realized in South Africa, where it was enforced by the Constitutional Court, answers Schmitt's objection that the U.S. Federal Convention conflated the two processes. See my "Conclusion" to Arato, *Constitution Making under Occupation* and A. Arato "International Role in State-Making in Ukraine: The Promise of a Two-Stage Constituent Process" (2015) 16 *German Law Journal* 3.

[54] See Schmitt, *Verfassungslehre* Chapters 29–30 on the Bund (Federation).

[55] Namely the only elected ones for this purpose in 1787, though the form does allow the election of the drafting convention. In that case the injury is not allowing an equal voice to equally legitimate, elected bodies.

[56] See my critique of Preuss in the Introduction above.

than they rejected. For this reason, the second convention idea, linked to that of an interim constitution,[57] was an important one from the point of view of democratic theory, whatever the reasons for its failure at the time. In the new model, the interim constitution and the public discussion around it and the elections for the constitutional assembly provide the context for making many new inputs into the final document. *Thus there is both learning with respect to the convention model, and the institutionalization of learning within the new model.* The constitutional assembly has a chance to make fruitful the results of the latter learning, through its own discussions, the works of its committees, the inputs of external participants, the certification process, as demonstrated uniquely but correctly in South Africa, and relevant re-drafting. All this represents tremendous democratic gains over the passive ratification in referenda, which become unnecessary for the new model.[58]

The problem of elections

Finally, I should consider a supposed normative disadvantage of the round table: the initial drafters are not elected, but co-opted. While free, competitive elections did not occur in the case of early historical prototypes of constituent assembly and conventions, these forms definitely allow and now generally entail "initial" free elections. With respect to the convention, the path-determined aspect (discussed below) of these models produces the difference that can involve two separate elections in the case of the convention but only one for the round table. Conscious of the legitimation problem involved, most protagonists of round tables try to generate compensating forms of legitimacy. It is an empirical question to what extent they succeed, but the South African case shows a high level of representation can be their combined result. With respect to the elected constituent assembly, that is also possible on the same historical path as the round table, with an authoritarian regime as the initial starting point, it is important to emphasize first that in both types there is only one election, and the question then becomes whether it is superior to have that election at the very beginning or in the middle of the process. Second, in the case of constituent assemblies (unless aspects of the negotiations characteristic of the round table are adopted) the rules of election will be imposed by either the old regime (as Lenin feared in 1905) or by the holders of revolutionary power (as he imagined, with good reasons but with a lack of success in 1917–18). This produces a legitimacy problem for the outcome, normatively and potentially empirically as well.

[57] See Chapter 1 above.

[58] Interestingly, referendum is used in the most pathological case, that of Iraq, where the constitutional assembly was indeed marginalized and not even allowed to take a final vote. In Poland, however, a referendum in 1997 was an important democratic part of the multi-stage process, all the more necessary because of the absence of many parties of the right from the drafting assembly.

The choice, then, is either co-opted representation with subsequent non-imposed electoral rules, or imposed rules with democratic representation.[59] Note again that elections in the round-table model do take place, for the second, definitive drafting body. It is thus arguable[60] that in the case of constituent assemblies, an imposed stage replaces a negotiated stage in the round table, while in both models democratic elections happen only after such an initial stage. Thus with respect to electoral legitimacy, the models are either equal from a normative point of view, or (as I believe) the round-table form is superior to the constituent assembly in this dimension as well. As to the convention, with respect to the issue of elections, it may be normatively superior to both alternatives, as well as to most versions of comprehensive parliamentary reform (two elections involve more democratic input than one), but, as I will argue below, the round table compensates for this difference by generating other forms of representation that, significantly, can be more inclusive than the results of elections. Inclusion at the earliest stage may be a value superior to having an electoral authorization.

Here one should pay attention to the constitutional context of initial constitution making. Under a republican form, with regular elections, and with fair, that is, relatively passive electoral rules, these existing rules can be used without the fear of producing incumbent advantage. If the rules are highly disproportional, however, the advantage of having an election first is reduced by the exclusionary effect. Under a dictatorship facing a revolutionary overthrow, where there are no free electoral rules in place, a convention presents the same difficulty as a constituent assembly. If the rules were imposed by either the dictatorship still in place or by revolutionary forces, the electoral advantage over the round table would be very much weakened. If a method was worked out whereby the rules for electing a convention would be negotiated, a difficult problem in a revolution, the model would have in effect grafted a key dimension of the round table into a revolutionary process. Thus the normative advantage of the convention over the round table with respect to elections, applies at best for already republican or democratic forms with fair and inclusive electoral rules.

The synthetic nature of the new model

The fact that the round table realizes the lost aspirations of some important architects of both the convention and the constituent assembly already indicates its synthetic nature. Of course the synthesis I have in mind was nowhere deliberately intended: as far as I can tell, the participants paid no attention to the

[59] We see the second option clearly operating in Egypt currently, where the military high command simply imposed the initial rules.

[60] And was argued in France by the Gaullists after 1946.

convention form, and, on the democratic side, abandoned the constituent assembly formula first and foremost for strategic reasons, given historical constraints. Thus, what follows has a reconstructive nature, focusing on structural and normative features rarely entirely clear to participants.

Yet it has been rightly remarked that the round-table forum is something like a convention, and one could equally say that the constitutional assembly paired with it resembles in some respects the constituent assembly of the classical model. As to the first point, neither round-table forum nor a convention such as that of Philadelphia "are known" to the previous constitutions.[61] Both only recommend, but do so in a way that the recommendations become more or less a constitution. The differences should be noted as well. As already argued, the round-table form does not have initial electoral legitimacy, even one with a long chain such as the Federal Convention whose members were delegated by elected state legislatures. Of course, other conventions in the states were elected. By its nature, the round-table forum cannot be an elected body, since its task is to establish for the first time the rules by which free and fair elections can take place. Its legitimacy problems are initially greater, a point easily lost in the South African case, where the charismatic ANC leadership had such great prestige among the majority of the population. And this leads to the next difference already noted: the round table's first constitution is only an interim one, and it leads to very serious legitimacy problems where it could tend to become permanent, as in Hungary. The convention produces a final constitution, one that the ratifying instances can only accept or reject.

The similarity of the constitutional and constituent assemblies is also significant. Both are democratically elected, at least after the first French prototype. Neither is doubly differentiated. It is true that the South African Constitutional Assembly was technically the two chambers of parliament meeting together, while they could meet separately as a regular legislature. But this is a very low degree of double differentiation, anticipated in part by the Indian Constituent Assembly, meeting sometimes under one set of rules as parliament, and at other times, under other rules, as the constituent assembly.[62]

Nevertheless, the already-mentioned differences are equally important. The constitutional assembly of the round-table model is not sovereign, operates under constitutional rules not under its own disposition, and is accountable for adhering to these rules (and in South Africa: to substantive principles) to another body from which it is indeed sharply differentiated: the Constitutional Court. While the latter subordination of the *constituant* to the *constitué* has been clearly practiced only in South Africa, in the case of procedural violations, at least of

[61] Gouverneur Morris at the Convention July 23, 1787, in J. Madison, *Notes of Debates in the Federal Convention of 1787*, ed. A. Koch (New York: Norton, 1987) 351; M. Farrand (ed.) *Records of the Federal Convention of 1787* (New Haven, CT: Yale, 1911) vol. II 92.

[62] G. Austin, *The Indian Constitution* (Delhi: Oxford University Press, 1966).

amendment rules, a similar logic would necessarily have come into play in most other round-table countries.[63] Thus the Constitutional Court, created by the interim constitutions of this model, becomes a functional substitute for the double differentiation that cannot be accomplished between the legislative and constituent powers.[64]

As a synthetic, multi-stage form, the round table combines many of the advantages and especially the creative aspects of conventions and constituent assemblies, but escapes the dangers of both inherent in their remaining links to organ sovereignty. It is this synthetic character that allows the form to make more radical change in regimes than the American convention form, which has never implied a socioeconomic transformation of an existing regime, and without the danger of revolutionary dictatorship inherent in constituent assemblies. Like the convention, but much more consistently, it replaces a model of sovereign constitution making with an affinity for dictatorship with another, where the imagined will of the people is expressed through a variety of instances, none of whom can claim full identity with or embodiment of the popular sovereign. But, like the constituent assembly, it culminates in a stage of democratic constitution making, where the elected instance really makes a new constitution. And all these elements are linked together by a new type of constitutional framework, enshrined in an enforceable interim constitution. But is this model itself of universal significance, or is it one simply specific to a particular set of paths?

IV PATH DETERMINACY OF ROUND-TABLE FORM

So far we have had only examples of the use of the round table form under collapsing dictatorships and uniquely under the apartheid state, which was indeed a dictatorship for the majority of the South African population. The round table involving negotiations with a party that controls the existing machinery of government would not easily find relevance in a state already in the hands of freely elected officials, or where a multiplicity of such states wish to form a new overarching constitution. Moreover, even under dictatorships, a revolutionary force that has gained all the power is not likely to enter into negotiations with the defenders or beneficiaries of the old regime.[65] So, in the case of revolution, reform, and constitutional treaty making the model does not seem to be applicable in spite of its synthetic and attractive character, and in spite of its

[63] The distorted process by which a new constitution, called a basic or fundamental law, came into being in Hungary in 2011 will be reviewed in Chapter 4 below.

[64] It can also be seen as the functional replacement of the referendum, putting the final drafting body under *ex post* control, but only a negative one.

[65] For example, currently in Libya they were certainly not likely to do so. A country in a state of collapse, brought about by civil society and a plurality of political actors, as in the case of Nepal, is another matter. In that case a plurality of actors, including conservative ones not directly tied to the old regime, can enter into a process of round-table negotiation and compromise even after a legal break.

affinities with constituent assemblies and constitution-making parliaments, as well as contractual agreements.

Let me distinguish first, as I have in the past, between the model and its principles, and this time also between the model and its parts. The nature of the round tables, born in the legitimation crises of old regimes, yet involving the presence of its actors in negotiations, raises the problem of legitimacy in particularly serious ways. In this it is significantly different than the other democratic approaches here, which, as we shall see, paradoxically do not question their own legitimacy because they are initially much more sure of possessing it.

As against all other democratic alternatives, the round-table multi-stage method begins with the depleted legitimacy reserves of failed reform.[66] The thin legality on which both regime and opposition take their stand is enough to functionally coordinate their expectations. It is not enough to legitimate deals and compromises, especially since the work of the negotiated instance was supposed to bind the work of the elected one. Neither the former old regime reformers nor the new oppositional forces strictly speaking have democratic legitimacy. This too is especially important, because it drives participants to try to solve the universal problem that a system cannot begin under its own rules, or: where there is no democracy one cannot begin democratically.[67] The actors of round tables have thus been especially creative in finding new sources of legitimacy: pluralistic inclusion as wide as possible; decision making by consensus as broad as possible; openness to public scrutiny or inputs; scrupulous adherence to the letter of agreements or to the new, emerging legality; democratic elections as soon as possible, under relatively passive rules: and attempts to operate under an empirical veil of ignorance regarding outcomes (or: the avoidance of self-serving rules by majorities!) are the main alternatives generated. When there is charismatic leadership available this helps as well, but it is relatively rare and cannot be engineered.

There is little doubt concerning the transferability of these principles. We find many precursors in American and French models, and even more, echoes and influences in all that occurs afterwards—for example, the Convention for the Future of Europe was scrupulously interested in the public character of the proceedings. By having to face the problem of legitimacy squarely, the lesson is being offered to future reformers and revolutionaries who, on the basis of past experience, should be less confident about the reach of their authority to make constitutions.

But constitutional learning can take more from the new paradigm. Starting with the recognition that it is specifically the round table institution that is path

[66] J. Kis, "Between Reform and Revolution: Three Hypotheses about the Nature of Regime Change' in (1995) 1 *Constellations* 3; J. Kis, "Between Reform and Revolution" (1998) 12 *East European Politics and Societies* 2 300–83.

[67] Arato, *Civil Society* 230–1; H. Lindahl, "Constituent Power and Reflexive Identity: Towards an Ontology of Collective Selfhood" in M. Loughlin and N. Walker (eds), *The Paradox of Constitutionalism* (Oxford: Oxford University Press, 2007) 9–25. See also Introduction and Chapter 1 above.

determined, the multi-stage character of the new process with an active but not sovereign democratic body as its final stage can have a much wider application. This is especially so regarding the pluralistic structure of the constitution-making body, which cannot be engineered in elections, but can be facilitated by adopting a passive, electoral rule based on proportional representation. If such a rule is not there in the case of reform, it can be the object of a reform before reform. A revolutionary provisional government can adopt a passive rule favorable to multi-party representation from the very beginning. As to consensual rules of decision making, since parliaments and constituent assemblies control their own rules, it is possible to adopt high consensus requirements such as qualified or even double majorities formally or at least informally. Finally, it is up to assemblies to consult with outside actors as much as they wish, and to invite public scrutiny of at least some of their proceedings.

What I would like to argue in this chapter is that none of the above will be done unless the relevant principles are first thematized and internalized, whether for strategic or properly normative reasons. Thus first and foremost, it is learning from the principles that is important.[68] Even if every single structural aspect of the new method (inclusion, interim constitution, formal role of a court, public inputs) were taken over, this would be without value if the normative standards were neglected.[69] There are always ways of interfering, even with the best electoral rule, to use illegitimate methods to achieve consensus, to intimidate a court, and to manipulate the public inputs. But two questions then arise: Do all the principles have to be accommodated, and if not how many would be sufficient and in what combination? And, secondly, do these principles rely on merely sociological meanings of legitimation, or do they also satisfy a deeper normative meaning on legitimacy? In short, adopting Rousseau's phrasing from the beginning of *Du contract social*: "The post sovereign form of constitution making exists. What can make it legitimate?"

V THE LEGITIMACY OF THE POST SOVEREIGN FORM

The normative foundations of post sovereign constitution making, already repeatedly touched upon, deserve separate and more systematic treatment. I will attempt this under the heading of legitimacy, which in my view is more appropriate in politics than the more general conception of justice. As always in

[68] Such learning can be achieved also through the examination of the principles involved in a very large number of empirical cases. It is interesting that the normative lessons drawn by Elkins, Ginsburg, and Melton in *Endurance* converge to an extent with my analysis, even though their concern is more stability than democracy. The concept of legitimation I think links these two concerns.

[69] In Chapter 5 below on Turkey I shall also try to show that paying attention to the principles may be insufficient without at least learning something from the institutional design of the new paradigm, without necessarily imitating the whole scheme. In my aforementioned forthcoming book, Arato, *Adventures of the Constituent Power* I try to make the argument for cases more difficult than the reformist process in Turkey, namely the recent revolutions of the Arab world.

politics, we can claim at best "imperfect justice," that is, legitimacy for arrangements that may always retain elements of exclusion and domination.

The meanings of legitimacy

The concept of legitimacy[70] is most generally a mediating link between norm and fact. It addresses the question whether a set of political relations "should be" and "are" considered sufficiently just. As can be seen from the difference between "should be" and "are," the mediating role is complicated by the fact that the concepts of legitimacy and legitimation themselves have both normative-philosophical and empirical-sociological senses. The mediation can work only if there is an internal relation between these two non-identical meaning levels, and I will maintain this partially following both the early and later work of Habermas.[71]

When I argue that the core gain of the round-table-led regime-change model has to do with the generation of political legitimacy, I have in mind legitimation primarily in the sociological, rather than the philosophical sense, even if the two cannot be separated entirely. Thus it is a matter of justifications of political rule empirically available, one that citizens, groups, and administrative staffs are likely to find valid under the given historical circumstances. This should not be confused with either legality or legitimacy as a normative matter from the point of view of moral philosophical reflection. By legality I mean the following of existing procedural rules, which admittedly also carries, on its own, a relatively weak sociological legitimation potential, as critics of Weber's rational legal legitimacy rightly noted. It is based on the necessity in any social arrangements, inevitably involving "double contingency," for actors to be able to coordinate their expectations.[72] In modern society, this coordination is the function of differentiated legal orders. As the very important idea of unjust law indicates, the origin and content of laws are relevant to the question of whether the law is legitimate in more than a minimal sense. But in that case, legitimacy cannot and ought not to be reduced to legality.[73]

Matters are more complex concerning the distinction of the sociological and the philosophical. While sociological legitimacy is ascertained from the observer's point of view, the philosophical attempts to fuse the horizon between the normative view of the interpreter with the articulated perspectives of participants.[74] The sociological does analyze the probable views of the participants,

[70] See also Chapter 1 above, where I deal with the contrast between legitimacy and authority.

[71] J. Habermas, *Legitimation Crisis* (Boston, MA: Beacon, 1975) and J. Habermas, *Between Facts and Norms* (Cambridge, MA: MIT, 1992).

[72] Parsons; Luhmann; Habermas. The Hobbesian monopolization of violence, adopted by Kelsen, is merely a special case of this.

[73] Kelsen, *General* Theory.

[74] H.-G. Gadamer, *Truth and Method* (New York: Seabury, 1975).

but without attempting to criticize them, except perhaps from the point of view of possible success and failure both linked to the issue of diffusion and generality. However, the normative conception is inevitably critical with respect to the legitimacy offerings of elites and their acceptance by others, however general the latter may be. Moreover, if one follows the tradition of contract theory from Hobbes to Rawls, legitimacy from a philosophical point of view can be imputed to constitutions on the bases of their content.[75] Legitimacy from the sociological point of view of a Max Weber, for example, is much more likely to depend, in significant part, on the actual process of constitution making. We have repeatedly seen that otherwise fully acceptable liberal democratic constitutions can be open to challenge based on the manner in which they were made. Thus, while the philosophical meaning of legitimacy of constitutions can perhaps be ascertained from the liberal point of view, the sociological has a deeper relationship to the democratic one. Thus we cannot simply normatively prefer the philosophical-normative to the sociological-empirical, however strange that may sound.

However, as Habermas realized,[76] an analysis focusing on sociological legitimacy (unless it is to work through unreliable surveys) cannot entirely dispense with normative-philosophical considerations.[77] For political sociology and comparative politics this move has an epistemic or hermeneutic rather than normative function, however, in helping to identify the norms in society or in a process that is meant to play and can play a legitimation role in the sociological sense. Yet the task is not to substitute the analyst's own views of what is legitimate and illegitimate for the views of relevant actors, but to use these as the basis of interpretation to discover what empirically can and cannot be made legitimate. But only the existence of social contestation concerning legitimacy can confirm that the analyst's discovery of legitimation problems is based on empirical insight rather than normative projection.

On the purely normative level, the Rousseauian question concerning the legitimacy of constitution-making forms seems to have an easy answer. It is generally assumed that the principle of legitimacy of all democratic forms of constitution making is popular sovereignty, as it is expressly declared in many constitutions. Yet even on the most abstract level, this principle is asserted with different meanings under different paradigms of constitution making. As we have seen, under the revolutionary sovereign paradigm it has been asserted that the sovereign people, as *legibus solutus*, is prior and external to the constitution. It is also legally unlimited. Since sovereignty in this conception cannot be divided, it must act through a single deliberative body. This unitary national body, an

[75] See J. Rawls, *A Theory of Justice* (Cambridge, MA: The Belknap Press of Harvard University Press, 1971) and the essays by Lindahl, "Constituent Power and Reflexive Identity," and D. Dyzenhaus, "The Politics of the Question of Constituent Power," in Loughlin and Walker, *Paradox of Constitutionalism* 129–46.

[76] Habermas, *Legitimation Crisis*, and again in *Between Facts and Norms*.

[77] I would also add that the philosophical conception should also try not to do without either the sociological perspective or the democratic dimension of the process.

elected constituent assembly, is supposed to be as free of constraint as the people itself.[78] But immediately another question of Rousseau would be (and was historically asked): How can it be known that the will of the assembly is the general will rather than merely a corporate one? Thus, even here the meaning of the people is doubled in those "two-body" versions where a ratificatory referendum is utilized (the will of all checking the authenticity of the general will). Advocates of this version, originally in France from 1792 to 1795, saw themselves as adopting the Rousseauian distinction between "legislator" and "sovereign," thus a unitary model of popular sovereignty, though in contrast to the idea of the Social Contract they assigned the real power not to the sovereign but to the legislator.[79]

Under revolutionary reform, at least when using the convention form, the popular sovereign is supposed to act under legally established though extraordinary bodies that control their own procedure. These bodies are factually plural, but on the level of theory and self-understanding they are imagined as unitary. In the American case, given the antinomic views of the actors, the people here too were collectively imagined in a two-body version, one supposed to represent a unitary national sovereign ("we the people") and the other supposed to represent each people of a plurality of state sovereigns (the peoples). Here in contrast to the two-body version of the revolutionary sovereign paradigm both bodies were conceived as having real power. For example, the states of North Carolina and Rhode Island, unlike the losing sides in national referenda, could have stayed out of the new Federation and its constitution, preserving their local power. But as already argued this doubling of power, an ever-present potentiality of the American model of the convention, came with a huge cost, as Americans were to find out in their civil war.

When it comes to comprehensive reform, the sovereign is the amending power legally provided for under previously existing procedures that it does not control, as do the constituent assembly and convention that enact their own procedures.[80] The amending power can be one body, as a parliament, thereby resembling the unitary constituent assembly, with the difference that under reform this body can be limited by the constitution that is about to be changed, until it is changed. This power can also be exercised by a combination of bodies, similarly to the convention and round-table forms, by what has been called a complex organ. But, under reform these bodies are linked to one another through a much more rigid procedural frame. Given party government, they may all be controlled by the same party.

[78] E.J. Sieyès, *What is the Third Estate?* See M. Sonnenscher (ed.), *Political Writings* (Indianapolis, IN: Hackett, 2003).

[79] K. Baker, *Inventing the French Revolution* (Cambridge: Cambridge University Press, 1990) Chapter 11.

[80] Parliaments are often given control over their procedures by constitutions. This control, however, does not extend to derogating from constitutional requirements concerning amendments, for example the size of the majority required, the need for ratification, or the requirement that two parliaments pass the same amendment act.

However, arguably, under reform, there must also be a body, generally a constitutional court, that controls adherence to the given procedures and thus becomes a secondary organ of the popular sovereign. This form of doubling under reform has existed empirically only in the very few countries where constitutional courts assumed the task of amendment review. It is radicalized under the post sovereign form, where duality becomes a true plurality. Here the popular sovereign is an absent god (*Deus absconditus*) that acts through a plurality of agencies, one of them the court, none of which can claim to embody it without usurpation. Popular sovereignty in this last model comes close to what Carré de Malberg under the Third Republic called "national sovereignty," an anticipation of Claude Lefort's concept of democracy as an empty space. We may think of this idea, as did even Carré de Malberg, as corresponding to the American practice of sovereignty as well. But Ackerman was not wrong in terms of the classical American self-understanding in restricting the notion, based on the separation of powers, to the constituted powers, while maintaining in the first version of his dualistic theory[81] an embodied notion of popular sovereignty.

Thus while the idea of popular sovereignty is foundational for all four forms of democratic constitution making, despite anticipations in revolutionary reform, the post sovereign paradigm's version of this principle is unique, as I argued in Chapter 1 following Lefort and Habermas. Its notion of the people is disembodied, rather than incorporated in an actor or an institution, or even in the two of them, as in the revolutionary reformist version. It could even be said (and indeed has been) that popular sovereignty here is only a negative principle, one that implies a built-in critique of all forms of usurpation and popular dictatorship. Lefort's own version of empty space is hard to distinguish from a minimalist version of democracy, or polyarchy. It is true that Lefort has also indicated that keeping the place empty would always be an ongoing struggle with claimants who would usurp the "place" of the people, and alone seek to speak in its name. But even that idea would identify democracy, implausibly, if not merely negatively then at least as a perpetual struggle. This may be true in revolutionary contexts, but it cannot describe even the aim of democratic revolutions that, as Arendt rightly claimed, do not seek to remain permanent. Beyond the view of the empty place, with the help of Habermas, I have tried to articulate the institutions required to keep the place empty, which in fact allows the transition from the philosophical concept of democratic legitimacy to the sociological one.

Here there is admittedly an overlap among all the four forms of democratic constitution making. This is the case because the idea of popular sovereignty has one thing in common in all its versions, namely the claim that ultimately it is

[81] In Ackerman, *We the People* I. This is the case even though his description of constitutional moments always involves a plurality of actors, none of whom could be said to be "the" American sovereign.

those subjected to the law who should also be its authors.[82] I have treated this notion throughout this book as a fiction, but more positively, it could be said to be a counter-factual norm, the plausibility of which depends on sociologically reconstructible *empirical* practices that bring the fiction closer to reality.[83] Such practices are, for example, the election of drafting assemblies, the public nature of their deliberation, and the ratification of their products by elected bodies or the electorate as a whole. Yet neither electoral legitimacy nor public involvement can be sustained even minimally if elections and referenda are not themselves regarded as "free and fair," if public communication is not sustained by and enforced by the relevant rights of communication. Thus law must play a role in the legitimation of the constituent assembly and convention, even when these meet after the initial rupture of legality.[84] Together, electoral and legal legitimacy along with publicity are the sociologically relevant principles that bring the normative idea of popular sovereignty closer to reality. As we know, however, elections, legality, and public discussion can all be feigned and manipulated. Thus, conversely, as already argued, only with the help of the normative critical philosophical analysis can we determine the actual meaning of electoral, legal, and public institutions and practices of a society in a constituent process. We must know how these ought to be functioning if we are to be able to judge their actual relevance during constitution making. In other words, elections must be judged in terms of the free and fair criteria, legality should be seen as enforceable even against the holders of power, and publicity must be understood to be open and relatively unconstrained. Yet even here philosophy cannot separate itself from sociology. Once we know what the normative criteria are, we must still examine whether the actors in a society do view them as important and do consider them institutionalized, practiced, and enforced.

It would be a mistake, however, to interpret the relation between philosophical and sociological legitimacy as the higher being diffused to the lower. Forms of empirical legitimacy, specific to each society but often categorizable under ideal types, do emerge from below. Thus the types of legitimacy in the sense of Max Weber are not exhausted in cases of revolution, revolutionary reform, and comprehensive reform by plausible translations of the normative principles derived from popular sovereignty. Admittedly, traditional legitimacy can play only a moderate role in radical forms of change, although the acceptance of some actors as playing a crucial role could be on traditional grounds, such as in the case of the army in Egypt. More importantly by far, political charisma, derived from roles in liberation struggles as well as the personal qualities, of

[82] It is over the counterfactual nature of this notion the versions disagree, or rather they disagree over the meaning of the counterfactual.

[83] See Morgan, *Inventing the People*. It will not do to translate the "fiction" as "myth": see Margaret Canovan, *The People* (London: Polity, 2005).

[84] Of course in revolutions political power can abrogate "revolutionary legality" as happened in 1793 in France and in 1918 in Russia. However, these acts produced in both cases the deepest crises of legitimacy, namely civil war.

leaders often plays an important role. This will be the case even under the post sovereign model, as the example of Nelson Mandela well demonstrates. But as a warning to designers of constituent process: charisma (unlike the institutions of elections, legality, and publics) cannot be planned or manufactured, and hence it would be hazardous to rely on it to any great extent.

The need to move from the normative concept of legitimacy to the sociological one is somewhat differently and more completely solved in the post sovereign model, as we shall see. In order to understand this better I shall first focus on the legitimation problems of the sovereign options that exist in spite of the fact that in principle popular sovereignty and its sociological translation is supposed to supply what is missing. This very often does not happen because of difficulties inherent in the models of change that underlie the options, reform and revolution, and even revolutionary reform.

Legitimation problems of reform, revolution, and revolutionary reform

I have defined revolution by the rupture of both legality and legitimacy, and regime change by the break in legitimacy in the context of legal continuity. According to the logic of the four-part scheme, revolution and regime change by definition involve breaks in legitimacy and thus, it might seem, have problems of legitimation to solve. To the extent, however, that a new constitution is to be made, all the forms have significant legitimation problems even if the protagonists of round tables during changes of regime seem to be the only ones fully aware of these. Actors within the other schemes imagine that the appeal to popular sovereignty deals with such problems automatically. But they are wrong, both because of the difficulties involved in translating popular sovereignty in empirically relevant terms and because of the logic of at least reform and revolution.

In the case of reform, a simple mechanical constitutional amendment by a legally established, freely elected legislature, using the existing revision rule, admittedly should have few legitimation problems. Here mere legal legitimacy seems to be sufficient. However, when that rule is used to replace a whole constitution (and that can be done even by single amendments, simple in form), and especially where such an option was not explicitly provided for, important normative questions are raised among participants. Written constitutions and the distinction between constituent and constituted powers have been historically introduced to limit "self-dealing," the ability of incumbent governing authorities to change the fundamental rules of the game to their advantage, and a reform that does so is prima facie problematic. This was the great insight of the Indian judges of the basic structure doctrine fame, who did not even have codified eternity rules to rely on.[85] The problem is made worse when the ease of replacement is facilitated by highly disproportional electoral outcomes and an

[85] G. Austin, *Working a Democratic Constitution* (Delhi: Oxford, 2000).

easy, one-dimensional, purely parliamentary amendment rule, as in Hungary recently. This can be seen in the most famous majoritarian polity, where there is no differentiation between constitutional and ordinary laws, and between the constituent and legislative power, namely the United Kingdom. There the law of the constitution permits any form of constitutional change by simple majority, except, it has been repeatedly claimed, the enactment of forms of entrenchment.[86] Yet the conventions of the constitution imply that a sitting parliament cannot introduce a new type of regime on the basis of the mere will of its simple majority.[87] Thus it has been generally recognized that any significant constitutional reform requires a new mandate from the electorate, and thereby the agreement of the voters with the decision of two parliaments. Paradoxically, this reticence, which indicates a genuine problem of legitimacy, could be explained precisely by the fact that the United Kingdom has no formal amendment rule, and by the conventional fear therefore of the temptation to continually alter the material constitution.

Parliaments under a formal constitution with a regular amendment rule, even if this rule is assigned to a single organ, may not have this fear. As a result, the legitimation problem is exacerbated when governments insist on their legal right to fundamentally change and even replace the constitution, as long as they have the votes, and therefore the power to do without the participation of minorities and the inputs of a wider public. Here the idea of legal legitimacy shows its relative weakness. Yet governments are likely to imagine its sufficiency, especially if they take a legalistic attitude to a single-level amendment rule that is confused with the "constituent power." A multi-level amendment rule as currently in Spain, Bulgaria, and South Africa may help, but in those cases governments must accept the right of the constitutional court to police the separation of the tracks. They may be reluctant to concede this, unless under one of the very few constitutions that mandates amendment review. But when governments go ahead and try to change the constitution as a whole using merely the legal amendment rule and excluding the opposition, as in Hungary and recently in Turkey, not only the battles with the constitutional court but the veritable constitutional crises indicate the high relevance of the legitimation problem.

In the case of revolutions, to be sure new revolutionary legitimacy is generated, linked to the processes of liberation, by an often charismatic elite or leadership. Here the high-level involvement of masses (never "the people" as a whole) in the overthrow of an old regime can establish a kind of identity between liberating elites and large population sectors. For a time it is possible that most population segments are united around the liberators. Nevertheless, in

[86] This limitation has been heavily contested by H.L.A. Hart, and I think with justice. But he has reduced the problem to a logical paradox of omnipotence, and has not considered the basic structure issue. If parliamentary sovereignty is (lamentably) the basic structure of the constitution, then amending it may be ultra vires.

[87] In Schmitt, *Verfassungslehre*, confirmed by I. Jennings, *The Law and the Constitution* 5th edn. (London: University of London, 1966).

a complex society, there may be large-scale agreement concerning what should be replaced but not likely concerning what should be put in its place. This is why in the period of construction, Arendt's "constitution" in the sense of a process, legitimacy problems and consequently repressive substitutes for legitimacy develop: the consensus of liberation is not easy to retain through a program of new construction, especially when a revolutionary elite imposes it. As a result, the friend-enemy relations quickly alter in the midst of revolution. When an elite imagines that its earlier credits earn it the right to dominate the constituent process and to impose a constitution through either minority will or even a narrow majority there is likely to be broad opposition to these efforts. Yet this is exactly what revolutionary elites tend to imagine. As a result the sociological preconditions of popular sovereignty are tampered with: elections are manipulated or falsified or not held at all, legality is violated, and the public sphere is invaded by governmental power.

The constituent assembly form relied upon in many revolutions as the organ of popular sovereignty is supposed to be the main solution of the legitimacy problem of constitution making in revolutions. But similarly to the case under reform, constituent assemblies can claim to embody the people only if they are elected. And elections, as Lenin was to find out in 1918, are a risky business for even powerful revolutionary governments. Unlike Lenin, most revolutionary governments hope to solve the problem in advance, by choosing electoral rules protecting or favoring the new governmental incumbents. But the fact that revolutionary governments impose such rules, often with visible distributional consequences, raises significant legitimacy problems anew. Moreover, even when the rules are imposed, they may turn out to have unexpected consequences. Thus the law of the revolutionary regime itself is violated, as when the Committee of Public Safety refused to fully enact the constitution of 1793 after it was ratified, or when Lenin dissolved the constituent assembly in 1918 after he lost the elections for this body. Finally, when the law is violated and elections are disempowered the public sphere becomes the greatest danger. While revolutions do tend to begin with an explosion of public freedom and free communication as Arendt noted, they more often than not turn against these principles that originally nourished them.[88] Thus, for all these reasons, revolutions not only start in civil war but can also lead to new ones, as in France in the 1790s and Russia after the dissolution of the constituent assembly in 1918. This is a sign of a contest around legitimacy, and the repressive nature of many post-revolutionary regimes is a tacit admission of a fundamental legitimation problem, of the need to replace hegemony by domination, using Gramsci's terms, or reliance on a single sociological principle, namely revolutionary or leadership charisma.

With the exception of the American cases and West Germany, it is variously systemic and normative problems that undermine legitimacy for revolutionary

[88] Arendt, *On Revolution*; K. Marx, *18th Brumaire of Louis Bonaparte* (New York: International Publishers, 2004). The latter, alas, imagined the problem to exist only in the case of bourgeois revolutions.

reforms. This form of change I defined in terms of a legal rupture in the context of continuity of legitimacy, if not of a whole system then at least one or more of its key institutions. It has two versions, a republican mode characteristic of the United States and a much more common plebiscitary-populist mode. The latter shares its normative problems with revolution. While an institution such as the presidency or the military command may have general support when dismantling an old regime, the construction of the new here too can lead to new divisions. Moreover, given the instability of plebiscitary democratic support, resting on momentary states of will, and the weakness of its representative capacity, the model is likely to suffer from an aggrieved version of the problem of dual democratic legitimacy analyzed by Juan Linz in the case of presidential regimes. Even when democratic legislatures are suspended, many citizens are likely to find alternative and more plausible instances of representation in civil society, often religious elites. The repressive nature of such politics is again the likely testimony to this. But even the republican option centering on constitutional conventions has a serious difficulty when legal rules are ruptured, as it was clear around the time of the adoption of the U.S. Federal Constitution. Moreover, unless there is great normative and even sociological homogeneity among the republican institutions, as in that one case, the alternative claims of popular sovereignty by competing institutions, the normal legislature and the constitutional convention on the one hand, and the union and the states on the other, can easily lead to dual power, new ruptures of legality and serious challenges to the legitimacy of the body or bodies that win this struggle. Not surprisingly, these conflicts have been managed historically either by overarching (or underlying) federal arrangements or, as in West Germany, by an external occupation. Elsewhere, the outcome can easily be dual power followed by a constitution without legitimacy as in Russia after 1993, or one where legitimacy is constantly challenged. Finally, federalist stabilization works only if there is broad agreement about the nature of the division of powers. When developments or governmental projects seem to threaten a fundamental alteration of these arrangements, as in the Federalist period in the United States, this regime too can have a legitimacy crisis linked to an authoritarian phase.[89] The compromises of the constitution-making period avoided such a crisis only narrowly, and temporarily.

My general argument so far should be summarized. Popular sovereignty in its various forms provides the foundation of normative legitimacy under most efforts of democratic constitution making. Claims based on popular sovereignty are convincing only where there are plausible empirical translations in the form of elections, public discussion, popular referenda, and legality. Both reformist and revolutionary process tend to undermine several of these forms of translation, the former by weakening the differentiation of constituent and constituted power, thus raising the issue of incumbent self-dealing, and the latter by undermining the legality that is required for elections and public discussion to remain

[89] See S. Elkins and E. McKitrick, *Age of Federalism* (Oxford: Oxford University Press, 1993).

free, fair, and open. In both cases the exclusion of oppositions leading to an absence of new negotiations concerning the rules of transition also play an important role. Admittedly, revolutionary reform, in its republican version at least can protect legality, and allow the generation of new rules under the supervision of public discussion. But the danger of this form is dual power, which can be stabilized by federal structures only exceptionally. The popular sovereignty claimed here is more plausible than under reform or revolution, but unfortunately competing sources can claim it in principle, equally plausibly. If the legitimation problems of reform and revolution have to do with insufficiency, in the case of revolutionary reform the problem may be antinomic abundance.

Empirical forms of legitimacy under the round-table paradigm

Finally, to repeat the key claim made above, in the case of regime change and the round-table paradigm, the actors themselves are generally much more aware of their legitimation problems than under other democratic forms. This is a great advantage, and leads, paradoxically, to the normative superiority of this model, admittedly from an external point of view. The problems are easy to point out. Negotiating with old regime actors who have lost their legitimacy, including new ones in agreement with the old, excluding others, making agreements the quid pro quo character of which can be justified only in terms a strategic modus vivendi are all problematic from the point of view of democratic legitimacy, and the main actors recognize them as such. This is why, at its best this model turns out to be a factory of legitimation, introducing elements like *public* openness, *inclusion* of new participants, fully *consensual* decision rules, as well as treating the fictional *legality* of old regimes as actual, as if they could be made elements of the rule of law. And even this is not enough. To defend themselves from the charge of usurping the constituent power, the participants also tend to affirm the merely provisional nature of their constitutional product, and to admit to not having the right to completely replace free elections and the making of the final constitution by those elected under new rules. These steps, free elections and final constitution making by an elected assembly, add the missing democratic component to the legitimation framework of the paradigm. While it is not only unproblematic but necessary to establish an independent body enforcing the initial agreement, it is equally important to make these agreements in such a way that the final process retains its open and democratic quality. Thus in general, the enforcement is limited only to procedural aspects.[90]

All of the empirical principles of legitimation that are used in the post sovereign paradigm are compatible with the democratic idea behind the notion of popular sovereignty. On the sociological level, the new paradigm does not take away the principles of election, legality, and the public sphere, but seeks to both

[90] Thus, however understandable the enactment of thirty-four constitutional principles was in South Africa, it would have been perhaps better to restrict these to procedural aspects. Yet it could be argued that they were necessary under the circumstances of extreme societal division.

reinforce them and add to them. One main purpose of round-table negotiations is to make sure that elections will be free and fair, the public sphere will be opened, pluralized and remain open and plural, and legality be enforced. Since there is little trust on the political sides, typically new institutions are immediately established to guard elections, to supervise the free communication of ideas, and to enforce the law.[91]

That law itself, enacted as the interim constitution, is supposed to be worthy of enforcement. Thus it must already contain fundamental rights, separation of powers, and an independent judiciary. How is that substantive result to be guaranteed? The round-table model guarantees it through two features of sociological legitimation that are more or less unique to it: (relatively wide) inclusion and (relatively) consensual decision making. Here the distinction with reform and revolution is again salient. Under reform a dominant party assumes the legal legitimacy to enact constitutional change alone, as long as it can, given the parliamentary arithmetic and the amendment rule in place. While wider inclusion could be the source of legitimacy here too, it may also compromise the project of the government. Thus either before consensus is even tried, or after it fails, the project of reform can easily turn majoritarian.[92]

Similarly, in revolutions, the victorious party can rely on prior legitimacy, the one achieved in the process of liberation, rather than the legality that was broken. Such a party always has a project that it seeks to realize. Revolutions, unlike typical parliamentary politics have strong friend-enemy relations, and all those seeking to interfere with that project are seen as enemies rather than mere opponents. (Admittedly this can happen in reform projects too, if the stakes are high enough as currently in Turkey.) It would have been certainly possible for the Jacobins to make a deal with the Gironde in the Convention Nationale, but being centralizers they did not wish to make any concessions to supposed federalists. It would have been very possible for Lenin to even dominate the constituent assembly given the Bolshevik possession of executive power, but obviously he wished to make no concessions at all to the right Social Revolutionaries or the Mensheviks whom he treated as enemies, rather than partner revolutionary actors.

It is important to stress that elections under revolutionary and reformist scenarios do not automatically produce inclusion and consensual decision making. This is especially the case with the majoritarian electoral rules that revolutionary agents prefer. But as we have seen in contexts of comprehensive reform attempts in Turkey and Hungary, it is generally on the basis of highly disproportionate electoral rules that dominant parties undertake comprehensive reform attempts. When they do concede consensual process, as the AKP government did in Turkey in 2011, they may very well find their

[91] Classically in South Africa: a transitional executive commission, a new electoral commission, a media commission, and a new constitutional court. See Chapters 2, 3, and 6 of Friedman and Atkinson, *Small Miracle*.

[92] This happened recently in Turkey where the AKP government sought to move toward an executive presidency, but where the consensual process agreed upon defeated the initial effort in 2012–13. See Chapter 5 below.

dominant constitutional views too difficult to enact and thus they themselves may in the end deadlock the process. Such subversion is all the more possible, because reform presupposes that there is already some kind of working constitution already in place. There is no "constitution-making compulsion," many of the government lawyers will say, and in some contexts they may be right. In others they may be terribly wrong, however.[93]

Finally, the round table as an ideal type has several factors favoring inclusion and consensus. First and foremost, given an authoritarian or paper constitution as the fall-back position, it is agreed on all sides that a new constitution must be created, even if there is strong disagreement concerning many of its contents. Since no one side can impose it, it is also assumed that the constitution must be a negotiated product. Second, the governing party and the oppositions do start out as enemies, and the round table is possible and necessary only when neither can destroy the other. Thus, destruction of the enemy has become impossible, and there is a mutual need to convert, if reluctantly, the friend-enemy relation into one of opponents. But this alters also the status of other actors, whom either side may have also seen as an irreconcilable antagonist. Third, neither of the main forces has the democratic legitimacy of a freely elected party, nor the charisma gained from a successful struggle for liberation. Even Solidarity and the ANC failed to overthrow the previous regimes, though in their case it would not be wrong to postulate a charisma of liberation playing a secondary role. Thus, it is difficult for either side to exclude third, fourth, or other actors that also claim to be part of the negotiating process. These would then either become separate members, as in the former German Democratic Republic and South Africa, or become included in umbrella groups as in Czechoslovakia and Bulgaria, or a combination of these two forms as in Hungary. It is true, if neither of the main sides wishes to include an actor, it is not likely to be included. But when one side wishes to include an additional member (FIDESZ and the so-called third side in Hungary; Inkatha in South Africa) the other side cannot exclude that potential participant. Empirically, this is reflected in the number of participants at the main negotiating fora, which tends to increase through time.

Fourth, formal inclusion would be without value if rules of consensual decision making are not agreed upon. Such rules of the actual round tables generally did not yield veto rights for small parties, but did guarantee significant input for many of them. Of this there were two consequences: unpredictability and something like a veil of ignorance. Packages concerning the power structure had to be agreed upon the results of which could not be easily predicted, and thus no one could tell who would benefit from them, old or new forces, large or small parties. In such a situation old and new as well as large and small tended to become interested in the guarantees of constitutionalism. Table 1 in Chapter 2 indicates,

[93] As it turned out, they were very wrong to make this claim in Hungary. I have always hated this phrase that was quite inappropriate under an interim constitution, at that time within the post sovereign paradigm.

if in a preliminary way, that this is exactly what the round tables produced whenever they were successfully concluded. Yes, we could also ascribe the very same outcome to international influence, acting through external advisors, proposals in the international public sphere, as well as the pressure of organizations, regional and global, that new democracies have sought to join. But this type of influence generally manifested itself in the tables of rights that are surprisingly uniform in the period from the mid-1970s to the 1990s. In addition to rights, only the round tables tended to produce the full institutional scaffolding to make them real, ranging from a separation of powers relying more on the courts than on executives, to electoral rules that preserve the kind of vetoes that are in the way of those seeking to introduce authoritarian institutions. This role of the round table can be confirmed by empirical-theoretical considerations, to which I now turn.

VI HEGEMONIC PRESERVATION OR INSURANCE?

There are certainly many ways a primarily normative analysis as above can go seriously wrong. One of these is to disregard the path-dependent nature of all ideal typical paradigms. This issue I have already addressed. Another way, equally important, would be to assume that normative principles could be adopted without paying attention to interest and motivation. This issue requires separate consideration.

In order to fully present my approach, I would like to set it off against two social science theories, "hegemonic preservation" and "insurance." These theories are complementary to mine to the extent that they focus on empirical origins or conditions of possibility, as well as quality and endurance of the results.[94] These issues are important for me as well, and I would like to bring them into my normative-historical presentation so far. This will allow me also to test approaches contradicting mine, in whole or in part. Conversely, social scientific theories, having long as well as lamentably cast off the huge shadow of Max Weber, can easily assume that by satisfying the empirical conditions of origins and survival the problem of legitimation can be dispensed with. In the last part of this section I will try to address that error, and reintroduce the theory of post sovereign constitution making to deal with it.

The first of these social scientific theories is the deservedly well-known conception of Ran Hirschl. It has the advantage that it focuses on a relatively small group of seriously examined cases in part distinct from the ones I have studied. It also has the virtue or defect, we shall see which, of offering a diametrically opposed type of explanation to mine in terms of models. For Hirschl, constitutionalism is the result of a type of imposition. I, however, consider constitutionalism, though not constitutions in general, as more often than not the product

[94] As Elkins, Ginsburg, and Melton, in their book *Endurance* recognize, endurance is not in itself a value.

of negotiations, which my post sovereign model insists on.[95] The other current pertinent social scientific theory is the work of Tom Ginsburg and his collaborators, originally involving another group of distinct cases, but extended to the study of constitution making and preserving the largest possible data set of countries. This work has the advantage[96] of having an implicit normative scheme that can serve as a bridge back to my own conception. However, the problem is that the Hirschl and Ginsburg approaches overlap to an important extent, not only in their rational choice methods, but also some of their conclusions regarding cases. I will make an attempt to separate them around three polarities: concepts of *conversion of power* versus *guarantee against power*; the idea of *monistic* versus *pluralistic constitution making*; and *non-legitimacy* versus *legitimacy*.

Hirschl has polemically titled his conception "juristocracy" and more helpfully as "hegemonic preservation." As regards his cases, four common-law heritage countries,[97] namely Israel, Canada, New Zealand, and South Africa (and elsewhere Turkey and the European Union[98]), the first term is a vast exaggeration. In none of the cases can it be remotely said that judges rule.[99] Hegemonic preservation is a much more interesting and defensible concept. The idea is basically that constitutionalism in the sense of limits on majority power emerges where previous power holders pessimistic about the future seek to guard important advantages against future majorities and/or try to give their future policy choices judicial cover. Hirschl speaks of three elites in this context: political, economic, and legal. But only the first elite, namely political power holders, matters for the explanation because he pretty much postulates that capitalist interests as well as lawyers and judges in general and almost everywhere support at least economic constitutionalism based on the defense of property. The key thesis thus concerns the hegemonic political elite in each setting, having a clear

[95] From the outset I want to indicate that on a formal level I accept Weber's argument that imposition and agreement are both always present. This notion is repeated by interpreters such as Przeworski and Elkins et al., claiming that constitutions are always the result of negotiations. It is useful, however, to consider imposition and negotiations as ideal types that can be approximated to a greater or lesser degree, but never completely realized. This was Weber's initial point. With that said, the statement that constitutions are always the result of negotiation and renegotiation is misleading.

[96] I do not consider the large data set to be an advantage because of two interrelated problems: First, Elkins et al. chose to focus only on constitutions in the formal sense and they treat constitutional and non-constitutional constitutions as parts of the same set. Second, new constitutions produced by amendments are treated as the enduring old ones. Thus, for example, the nationalist myth that Hungary's 1989–90 constitution is still the Stalinist one of 1949 is repeated. Such formalism is striking in authors who otherwise reject the formalist approach to constitutions and constitutional jurisprudence. See, for example, T. Ginsburg, *Judicial Review in New Democracies: Constitutional Courts in Asian Cases* (Cambridge: Cambridge University Press, 2003) 69ff.

[97] R. Hirschl, *Towards Juristocracy* (Cambridge, MA: Harvard, 2004).

[98] R. Hirschl, "Constitutional Courts vs. Religious Fundamentalism: Three Middle Eastern Tales" (2004) 82 *Texas Law Review* 1819; "Hegemonic Preservation in Action? Assessing the Political Origins of the EU Constitution" in Weiler and Eisgruber (eds), Altneuland: The EU Constitution in a Contextual Perspective, Jean Monnet Working Paper 5/04 (2004).

[99] E. Lambert, *Le gouvernement des juges* (1921 edn.) (Paris: Dalloz, 2005).

understanding of an adverse future, willing and able to impose a constitution to shape it. Even his depiction of the obviously negotiated South African case appears as mostly the work of the previous, hegemonic white Afrikaaner elite, with the parties of the black majority effectively neutralized.[100]

Hirschl tends to define constitutional democracy in terms of entrenchment (moderate to difficult rules of amendment), fundamental rights, and their judicial enforcement. In this we largely agree. But while he did not try to make this argument entirely general, it is his distinct implication that such a system is more likely to emerge from imposition by power holders than any other process as long as their power positions come under serious and fully anticipated threat.[101]

Whatever we think of Hirschl's actual analysis of cases, the hegemonic preservation argument is logically coherent and significant. And the logic is seemingly re-enforced by many historical cases he does not treat. While it is certainly highly plausible that the heavy entrenchment of the U.S. Constitution in Article V is to be chalked up to Federalism as Dicey has already maintained, there is a potential argument even here that its high level was meant as a protection against possible national majorities at a time when it was the number of states rather than people that mattered. The introduction of judicial review fifteen years later could also be interpreted as a rearguard defense of the Federalist minority already eclipsed politically.[102] Closer to our time, as in a once-famous Stein Rokkan thesis,[103] the introduction of proportional representation by the bourgeois parties of Northern Europe can be very well interpreted as a shift to an electoral system more capable of preserving the status of old parties than the first-past-the-post majoritarian schemes under which they prospered before universal suffrage. Finally, in 1980, under the leadership of General Pinochet, the

[100] I consider this last depiction as seriously mistaken historically, representing less the work of social science than a disappointed revolutionary political position Hirschl adopts from others. "However the ANC did not sell out a revolutionary position because the revolution never materialized. Instead there was a negotiated settlement designed in no small part to head off the possibility of revolution": Hirschl, *Juristocracy* 96.

[101] Again, to be more accurate, he speaks of the alliance of three power holders: political, economic, and judicial elites. But he considers the position of the second two to be constant, and always for constitutionalism. Thus it is the shift of political elites that is alone causal as typified by the evolution from Ben Gurion to the Ashkenazi elite of the 1990s, or more dramatically P.E. Trudeau's shift on the charter, and the National Party's reversal on a Bill of Rights. In any case, while he does not make this clear, it is the anticipation of threat that is important in his argument. In Israel, for example, no majority outside the old elite ever materialized, nor in my view could materialize. But this may not have been the view of the relevant actors.

[102] See Ginsburg, who neglects the issue of the initial entrenchment, without which the Federalist "hegemonic preservation" would not have been possible. Indeed an early decision of the Supreme Court was trumped by the Eleventh Amendment even under the very difficult Article V. Ginsburg calls the American introduction of judicial review a textbook case of his insurance theory, but in this case at least he could have also said hegemonic preservation. Ginsburg, unlike Hirschl, does not consider the establishment of judicial review a single-stage strategy, and stresses not only the initial framing but also the activity of courts themselves, which requires clever strategy given shifts in political power.

[103] S. Rokkan,. *Citizens, Elections, Parties. Approaches to the Comparative Study of the Processes of Development* (Colchester, UK: ECPR Press, 2009).

Chilean dictator, political institutions, among them a very strong constitutional court, were put into an imposed constitution to help preserve over time some of the powers and advantages of the rulers and beneficiaries of the dictatorship.[104] Similar concessions were imposed by military leaders elsewhere, most explicitly by General Evren, the leader of the coup of 1980 in Turkey. Thus, something very much like hegemonic imposition does seem to exist, whether or not Hirschl's own cases support this conception. Let me focus on cases that *seem to* support it.

Even here there are problems. I believe that these very cases too either contradict the full thesis of hegemonic preservation because they do not lead to constitutionalism, at least in the beginning, or lead to solutions compatible with constitutionalism only because of important considerations Hirschl has neglected. What they do not sustain is the idea of the authoritarian origins and undemocratic nature of the package of entrenchment, constitutional courts, and their enforcement of fundamental rights.

I think it can be shown that what seems to be hegemonic preservation has a constitutionalist outcome in the context of political support and pressure by forces other than a hegemonic elite, on normative or empirical grounds, and not when these are both absent. Of these, normative grounds are moreover superior, because they can appeal to forces and interests that are originally not main partners in constitutional bargains. The U.S. Constitution was a highly negotiated product that was thoroughly discussed and debated in the public spheres of the states. Article V may have already been seen by some as a very high threshold for democratic constitutional politics, but during the first Congress it was used to make ten amendments to the constitution, in line with the demands of its opponents. It was the amendment rule not as entrenchment but as tool of revision that allowed a constitution-making stage demanded by the Anti-Federalists to be added to the process. In 1793, the same rule was even used to trump a decision of the Supreme Court (*Chisholm v. Georgia*).[105] Instead of being seen as undemocratic, Article V was first experienced as a democratic opening and a method of improvement *especially* in the context of a previous rule change of the Articles of Confederation that required unanimity rather than the support of three-quarters of the states. Finally, while the resistance of judges in the 1800s was indeed to democratic politics that could leave the older system behind, it was the minimalism of Marshall and his colleagues that allowed them to succeed as against an early failure following *Chisholm*.[106] Moreover, while

[104] For a fairly full list see Przeworski, *Democracy and Market*, whose judgement that the list would hold indefinitely turned out to be largely wrong. It makes little sense therefore to say as Elkins et al., *Endurance* 60 that Chile is still under Pinochet's 1980 Constitution. Even more egregiously they imply the same for Hungary after 1989–90. For Ginsburg's earlier discussion of the Chilean case, ibid. 83–4.

[105] 2 US 419, 1793.

[106] This problem, the role of political strategy, is well explored by Ginsburg not only in the well-known American case, but in a convincing general, comparative analysis.

Madison along with Jefferson could and did oppose what they regarded as judicial over-reach, he could not very well go against the constitution, namely his own work. The establishment of the system of the early nineteenth century, hardly juristocracy or even *gouvernement des juges*,[107] was the work of both political sides, as the alliance of the Federalist Marshall and the Republican Story was to show.

Analogously, but differently, the introduction of proportional representation in Northern Europe was highly strategic and self-interested on the part of bourgeois parties threatened with disappearance, but *it could be made legitimate* easily enough. This was because the socialist parties that would potentially lose a big advantage were themselves strongly committed historically to proportional representation. On normative grounds too, this system had much to recommend it against its disproportional predecessor that was the graveyard of small parties, and thus much representation.

The contrast with efforts like Pinochet's and Evren's is fairly clear. Here there was no question of opposition support or a general one on empirical or normative grounds. As a great deal of comparative politics research stresses, both generals, imposing semi-authoritarian constitutions, sought and gained preserves of power that allowed old power holders linked to the military or the armed forces themselves to retain under new constitutions undemocratic powers and privilege gained during emergency rule. It is here that one can strictly speaking use the term hegemonic preservation, but the result aimed at and in the short term sustained had little to do with constitutionalism.[108]

As I argued over ten years ago,[109] there is an enormous difference in principle (if not in terms of every possible device) between *conversion* of power and seeking *guarantees* against power. *Conversion* (in Chile: "authoritarian preserves"; in Turkey "tutelage institutions") is an attempt to transform an older form of power under authoritarian conditions that can preserve an element of authoritarianism in a democracy, making it either a soft dictatorship or a strong democracy. It is a zero-sum relationship in which the power preserved by one side does not benefit another. *Guarantees* against power are on the contrary positive sum, and yield something not only for actors and interests other than the initiators alone, and indeed for actors who are not part of any initial bargain. Guarantees are universal as against forms of conversion, which are particular. Guarantees are compatible with democracy, but push it toward its liberal interpretation.

[107] A term coined by Lambert, during the Lochner era.

[108] This is so even if some of the initially less important institutions used elsewhere, not linked to authoritarian preserves through the structure of appointments, could play a role in achieving and consolidating constitutionalism.

[109] In Arato, *Civil Society* 20ff.

Arguably (this is my position[110]), they make democracy under modern conditions more rather than less democratic.

The first important conversion of which I am aware was carried out by the Convention of 1795, which created a unique two-thirds rule for the next elections: two-thirds of the members of the new legislature had to come from the convention itself. Such electoral conversions reappeared in the partially unfree elections of the Soviet Union in 1989 and even in Poland later in the same year. But the more typical forms of conversion today concern the organization and supports of executive power, which have had many forms. Some *openly* provide reserves for authoritarian power such as military-dominated national security councils, military courts, and special military prerogatives dealing with emergencies. Others have a "bionic" structure responsible for appointments, often lifetime appointments to important constitutional bodies such as courts, upper chambers, and councils of state. There are also apparently neutral institutions such as the presidency that provide a hold over power only in a given context. Based on electoral surveys and the availability of a specific popular candidate, their intent is to strongly influence *the immediate period after* a transition.[111] Finally, as already noticed by O'Donnell and Schmitter[112] there are even devices that work negatively by depriving enemies of the right to participate, as in the case of Evren's law on parties and even the very high 10-percent threshold for participation his junta and its advisors established.

This is an admittedly heterogenous list, but what ties it together are *agency, object, calculation*, and *origins*. As to the first, conversion of power is the work of Hirschl's hegemonic, unitary *agency* that can retain the upper hand in some negotiations not only because of the reserve power of the military over violence, but as in Poland, the real or imagined role of external powers.[113] The *object* of a conversion as against a guarantee is always particular. It will benefit only one particular group or elite, usually its original agent. In the case of conversion the relation of means and ends must be highly determined. Not only is the goal a particular one, it is only this particular goal that can be achieved, barring an unlikely volte face by the very same actors.[114] The actors who seek to convert their power calculate that such a turn of events will not occur.

[110] See Habermas, *Between Facts and Norms* and also C. Lefort "Politics and Human Rights" in Lefort, *The Political Forms of Modern Society* (Minneapolis, MN: University of Minnesota Press, 1986); A. Arato and J. Cohen, *Civil Society and Political Theory* (Cambridge, MA: MIT, 1992) firmly supports this position.

[111] In Turkey in 1983 there was not even an electoral choice involved: Evren's presidency was directly imposed.

[112] G. O'Donnell and P.C. Schmitter, *Transitions from Authoritarian Rule* (Baltimore, MD: Johns Hopkins University Press, 1986) vol. 4, 9–10, where they speak of two tiers, positive and negative, of what I call conversion.

[113] Przeworski treats Poland in 1989 as a military regime. At the very least the timing of this first Communist transition should have been seen as the source of reservations that never actually worked as the miscalculation concerning Soviet tolerance at that particular time became clear.

[114] I admit that there are some forms of conversion, usually revealed by their more universalistic structure, that can change their function with the passing of time, and become power reserves for someone else (e.g. the presidency in Poland and Turkey).

As for *origins*, whether conversion of power or guarantees will be sought and, if so, what type depends on the types of actor involved; and whether conversion will be at all possible depends on the power constellation as a whole. Military juntas, whether in Chile, Turkey, or now in Egypt have many advantages gained under unjust authoritarian regimes. Since they are not political parties nor other legitimate democratic actors, during the transitions to democracy they will be in a poor position to protect their advantages and (given past crimes) generally their persons too unless their earlier power is converted into those of institutions that are likely to remain loyal to them. Even amnesties and property rights are of no value to them unless strong institutions can enforce them. Thus we see the military reservations and the bionic institutions affirmed and achieved in the context of top-down and even some negotiated transitions where such forces still have the upper hand.

However, what is crucial is that the needs of liberal or potentially democratic actors can be served in other ways than through conversion of power in the forms just described.[115] The bourgeois parties of Northern Europe had no need to establish undemocratic reservations to protect their interests. They could do so as long as the political rules of the game were changed, admittedly in their favor. Again, I call these alternative forms *guarantees*.[116] Without exception the devices involve the protection of minorities and the restriction of the power of majorities, whoever will have majority power. The typical forms are proportional representation, extensive tables of fundamental rights, entrenchment with at least medium-strong amendment rules, judicial or constitutional review, and bicameralism with different electoral rules, but without overly long-term appointments. The last two items indicate a possible overlap: unelected senators and judges chosen for life and indeed the inclusion of military judges in constitutional courts move these forms from guarantees to conversions.

Finally, entrenchment and strong review powers of a court, logically connected, call for a special comment. It is these features that Hirschl stresses in his four countries and also in Turkey. Yet they represent conversion only where they protect elements of conversion for a period, as both in Chile and Turkey. Where they protect fundamental rights, on the other hand, or proportional representation they must themselves count as guarantees. Thus it is a serious matter that Hirschl's treatment neglects the distinction between conversion and guarantees as he goes through cases. He does not even note that in the four common-law countries entrenchment and strong review powers protect fundamental rights

[115] In 2000 I put Communist Parties under whatever name between the two poles of military juntas and bourgeois parties. This turned out to be right in terms of their self-conception (initially many even sought guaranteed seats for themselves, a practice as old as the constitution of 1795 with its two-thirds rule favoring members of the Convention) but wrong for several such parties in terms of their actual electoral potential revealed later.

[116] Even here it is important that the guarantees are established legitimately.

above all, while in Turkey[117] initially the protection of conditions was paramount, all of which allowed the violation of rights by executive and military agencies.[118]

Without seeing the contrast I insist on, Hirschl cannot explain what it is that makes these cases, where constitutionalism is the result, actually work. In the eyes of new political forces, for example the clearly anticipated majority in South Africa, the constitutional revolutions he treats would have been illegitimate if they represented conversion, rather than (mainly) liberal democratic guarantees. This is shown by the fate of consociationalism in the South African case, once enthusiastically recommended by Arend Lijphart.[119] Admittedly, this form, when based on genuine agreement of political forces, can sometimes be seen as a guarantee.[120] In South Africa in the 1980s and early 1990s, however, consociationalism would have implied the conversion of white power, only achievable by imposition. It could not be made legitimate, except as an entirely transitional partial device. It is important that the National Party's first choice was consociationalism if apartheid were to be given up, and Hirschl should not have neglected this fact, often admitted by important actors like Roelf Meyer.[121] The move from power sharing to constitutionalism, achieved under the pressure of democratic forces rather than based on anticipation and conversion, thus represents a key feature of the South African process of constitution making. Most of the National Party had to be dragged to constitutionalism in spite of its resistance, even if retrospectively it benefited from it. For the ANC, as Justice Sachs shows,[122] majoritarianism was replaced by constitutionalism as the first best by 1990. For the National Party, on the other hand, while majoritarianism did of course become the worst option, constitutionalism remained only a third- or second-best option, depending on a given leader or faction.[123]

[117] Hirschl, "Constitutional Courts vs. Religious Fundamentalism."

[118] It is another matter that a form of conversion may change its meaning over time. In Chile, for example, the junta's hand-picked court enabled the referendum to be free and fair in 1988. See R. Barros, *Constitutionalism and Dictatorship* (Cambridge: Cambridge University Press, 2002). On Turkey, see Chapter 5 below.

[119] A. Lijphart, *Power Sharing in South Africa* (Berkeley, CA: Institute of International Studies, University of California, 1985).

[120] The distinction between conversion and guarantee cannot be seen in terms of putting specific institutions on each side. Constitutional review is a guarantee, but it is conversion of power when judges are appointed for life by the old regime. Yet even when intended as conversion, it can turn out to be a guarantee if judges establish an independent posture. For this institution, as Ginsburg stresses, the initial institutional design is only one source of the institutional practice; the other is (and was already in America) the Court's own activity. I think the Israeli case bears this out, weakening thereby the Hirschl thesis.

[121] R. Meyer, "From Parliamentary Sovereignty to Constitutionality" in *Post Apartheid Constitutions* (Athens, OH: Ohio University Press, 2001).

[122] A. Sachs, *The Politics of Accommodation: Constitution Making in South Africa* (Luanda: NDI, 1998).

[123] It is also a serious matter that Hirschl de-emphasizes the problem of legitimacy. While there may not be a one-to-one relation, legitimacy in the normative sense is generally a potent symbol of the difference between the guarantee and conversion.

My conclusion to this section, then, is the following: Hegemonic preservation is possible, and with sufficient power it is sustainable. But it has legitimacy problems, since structurally it represents the conversion of power, even when coupled with some genuine guarantees. An outcome has a much better chance of being carried out and stabilized if it is democratically legitimated, but then the question is whether we should treat it merely as elite hegemonic preservation. If dependence on normatively based acceptance by others (Anti-Federalists in America, socialists in Northern Europe[124]) is fundamental, have we not stepped over the threshold from imposition to implicit or explicit negotiation? And in that case will negotiation not be the more general method by which a constitutionalist outcome can be achieved?[125]

The second conception I wish to treat, the insurance model, implicitly takes a step from a single-actor model and imposition to negotiation and interaction.[126] According to Tom Ginsburg, where "there are no parties that will be confident in their ability to win, all parties will prefer to limit the majority, and therefore will value minoritarian institutions such as judicial review."[127] Unlike the earlier analysis of Adam Przeworski, Ginsburg rightly, if again implicitly, includes party equality at the moment of negotiations as equivalent to electoral uncertainty afterwards. He is especially right to do so where no previous democratic elections have tested the supposed equality of the forces.[128] But, unlike Przeworski, he has not made the difference between imposition and agreement clear enough. While the discussion refers to negotiations and insists on the difference between a setting with party pluralism and another with a dominant party, it is easy to see how even the latter could conceivably be included as a *special case* of insurance. This would seem plausible where a dominant party is pessimistic about its future chances, as against the other possibility, said to be likely here,

[124] The situation is different with proportional representation where the analogy with Northern European bourgeois parties was almost complete. The National Party clearly abandoned the first-past-the-post system as its long-time first choice, and the ANC supported proportional representation because of its long-held ideological opposition to the Westminster model. One could surmise, as in the case of Havel, that its leaders did not want to win a total victory making one-party government inevitable. But their rejection of one-party government itself had already occurred, in exile, as they witnessed the experience of their African supporters abroad.

[125] This question cannot even be raised if we treat all constitution making as negotiation, as do Elkins et al. and Przeworski.

[126] This is partially disguised by the rational choice methodology common to insurance and hegemonic preservation theories that makes the latter appear as a special case of the former in spite of what I will argue concerning their huge normative difference.

[127] Elkins et al., *Endurance* 25. This analysis, which implicitly assumes guarantees rather than conversion, was anticipated in 1991 by Przeworski, *Democracy and Market* 82–7, who has distinguished between three contexts of constitutional "negotiations": one where a dominant party can impose, another where the strengths of parties are equal and imposition is impossible, and a third where the future strengths of all parties and electoral outcomes are uncertain.

[128] Of course what matters is belief, here the belief in equality. While the equality of many actors would still likely function as uncertainty, the equality of a few, or especially two major ones can lead to the exclusionary corporatist or consociationalist bargains stressed by O'Donnell and Schmitter, *Transitions from Authoritarian Rule* in their chapter on pacts.

that they anticipate future success. A pessimistic dominant party will accordingly choose insurance, but I would add only if it is not strong enough to opt for conversion as defined here. Ginsburg thus has no difficulty in citing an early version of Hirschl's theory in supporting the idea of insurance.

To distinguish between hegemonic preservation and insurance theories[129] the already introduced contrast between conversion and guarantee should be kept in mind. It can be historically shown that ruling parties or elites, whether in Chile, Hungary, or South Africa prefer conversion, and this is always the main element of "insurance" in their first constitutional proposals. In Hungary and South Africa, they were forced to abandon such schemes only under pressure: the impossibility to legitimate a scheme to important actors in the country or outside, and/or the unwillingness of new forces to accept them. When on the contrary we see "insurance" presented in terms of guarantees as in Israel and Canada among Hirschl's cases, and Hungary and South Africa in both Hirschl and Ginsburg, we are right to suspect a plurality of negotiating actors behind the scheme. Conversely, a plurality of roughly equal actors could not produce conversion of the powers of one previously dominant elite, because of the veto powers inherent in such a setting procedurally or implicitly. Admittedly, a very few dominant actors in the exclusionary types of pact stressed by O'Donnell and Schmitter[130] may produce multiple conversion in terms of corporatist or narrowly consociationalist bargains. But these they rightly depict as taking place before the *upsurge of civil society*. After that upsurge, which may take place before any negotiations as in Central Europe and South Africa, or during them,[131] such bargains are either not possible, or they do not tend to hold, as the same analysis shows for the Spanish case. Hegemonic preservation is real and possible, but only where a dominant actor or actors can impose elements of exclusionary power conversion. This is already a principled difference between hegemonic preservation and insurance.

But a deeper difference is even more important. Any reader of Przeworski's early version and Ginsburg's current one will recognize the shadow of John Rawls' veil of ignorance behind insurance theory.[132] As a matter of fact, in many cases, since the actual motives of the actors are often unknown, we may sometimes be dealing with just the type of imputation from results that Rawls

[129] Ginsburg does recognize the important difference the different types of actor make for insurance. See Elkins et al., *Endurance* 82. In the Chilean context he rightly treats the establishment of the constitutional court as serving the departing autocracy, that is, as conversion, not the new democracy.

[130] O'Donnell and Schmitter, *Transitions from Authoritarian Rule*.

[131] Unfortunately there is also the possibility of the upsurge occurring after them, as in the case of Nepal where the effect was very harmful for the legitimacy and the coherence of the process. This is one reason among many why inclusion should be very wide during the first stage.

[132] This is explicitly recognized by Przeworski, who adopts the veil of ignorance idea as an empirical one.

himself practiced.[133] But this imputation is generally plausible given the inclusion of a plurality of actors and the use of consensual decision rules. Thus the veil of ignorance in the normative sense may depend on empirical veils of ignorance, however partial. Accordingly, the actors act because they are (or *as if* they were) unable to anticipate what their future advantage might be, and are therefore able (or willing) to rely only on principled arguments to support their positions. While specific future minorities may indeed need protection under constitutionalism, the main actors will argue that *all* minorities will have the same need. This is a valid argument. Whatever the motive, and it is important enough *though rarely actually known*, the validity of the argument and its consequences cannot be reduced to it. Plausibly reconstructible as the veil of ignorance, the insurance theory has normative as well as empirical foundations.

Where there is hegemonic preservation, characterized by conversion of power, *Realpolitik* replaces normative argumentation. We establish these future reserves of power because we need to and want to, and because we can. Given relative certainty about the future as depicted by Hirschl, incumbent advantage is used to block the consequences of that future. Born of certainty rather than uncertainty, hegemonic preservation seeks to make part of the future different but even more certain, to the advantage of self-serving incumbents. Insurance, on the other hand, even when linked to relative certainty about the future, as in the case of the Indian Congress in 1948, is established by actors who act as if there was uncertainty, and in such a way as to help to make the future less certain. After all, that is what fair electoral systems do. No one can predict with any certainty that a dominant party itself may not split, as happened in the Indian case and may yet happen in South Africa. Similarly, the protection of enforceable rights can benefit minorities and individuals who have not yet appeared on the scene. Conversion as already argued involves no universal perspectives, and is less conducive to a shift and transformation in the objects served by the relevant institutions. Given dictatorship as the starting point, conversion helps to produce a semi-authoritarian or semi-democratic system. Only sheer traditionalism can support it ideologically, or perhaps a national security rationale. Democratic or liberal ideologies cannot justify *the naming* of bionic officials for a given purpose or *the establishment* of institutional preserves for unaccountable and uncontrollable bodies. As Przeworski indicates, solutions born as functions only of a given power constellation, in effect Rawls' modus vivendi, tend to last only as long as that constellation remains secure. But I would add that this is so, unless an *overlapping consensus* emerges, and that is not possible in the case of conversion, but only for guarantees.

Of course nothing would stop a currently hegemonic party turning liberal democratic and making the same arguments as those seeking insurance, honestly or not. We disregard democratic motivation in the name of some kind of

[133] This is also true for Hirschl's hegemonic maintenance. Neither he nor Ginsburg can tell, for example, to what extent the actors are motivated by democratic norms and values. It would be foolish to exclude this for Nehru, Suarez, Michnik, Kis, Mandela, Havel, and so on.

rational choice *Denkökonomie* only at our intellectual peril. But in all cases where the outcome is constitutionalist we are right to suspect some pluralism behind a monolithic appearance, whether in India, the constitution-making process of which is so well explored by Granville Austin, or even Israel, where Hirschl mentioned in passing that behind the old Ashkenazim elite on which he insists were the very contrasting political forces of Likud, Labor, and Meretz. In negotiating settings pluralism thus turns out to be more important even than uncertainty about the future. After all, when there are many actors they all may be uncertain about a predictable future, or be certain and in error concerning an unpredictable one. In both cases they can present themselves to have acted under uncertainty. Pluralism contributes to the production and the appearance of uncertainty and indeed to future uncertainty. It is true that in India in 1948 future short-term electoral outcomes were predictable, if not entirely certain, yet the result was the attainment of guarantees. This shows that the insurance theory is best understood as a combination of a real need for insurance and an ideal commitment to an order where there are guarantees. Which of the two is more important in a given context, motive or principle, is itself an empirical question. Weber's ideals and interests are always present but in different combinations and proportions. As Ginsburg and Przeworski both periodically recognize, without noting the inconsistency with their method relying on a version of Occam's razor, the international importance and dissemination of the principles and institutions of constitutionalism since the 1990s, stressed by an interpreter like H. Klug, itself can have motive-forming power in national settings.[134]

Thus the insurance theory as relinked to Rawls' theory of legitimacy represents the best hope for constitutionalism as an outcome. What is its relation to legal models or paradigms of constitution making? Ginsburg and his co-authors when examining such methods come up with very scant, skeptical, and I think quite misleading conclusions that I briefly discussed in the introduction.[135] They do not even consider separately the two-stage method perfected in South Africa, which along with the American forerunner were earlier pronounced by Ginsburg as textbook cases of insurance.[136] Neither the doubly differentiated American Convention is distinguished from constituent assemblies of the sovereign type, nor is the round table treated as distinct from constitution making through normal legislatures. With distinctions not made, the question is not asked, and thus the right answer cannot follow. The gap between abstract theory and cases, description and recommendation has not been filled.

[134] H. Klug, *Constituting Democracy* (New York and Cambridge: Cambridge University Press, 2000) *passim*; Przeworski, *Democracy and Market* 99; Elkins et al., *Endurance* 6–11.

[135] T. Ginsburg, Z. Elkins, and J. Blount, "Does the Process of Constitution Making Matter?" (2009) 5 *Annual Review of Law and Society* 209–23. They consider only two normatively relevant issues: public participation and institutional self-dealing that is a version of hegemonic preservation. They then argue that while public participation makes a minor difference to the quality of the immediate outcome of constitution making, institutional self-dealing is supposed to have made no difference at all.

[136] Ibid. 55ff.

I have no great confidence that such a gap can be filled along with a definitive test for the insurance theory by a study relying on large samples, even a better chosen and more differentiated one. What I think *can* be shown is the internal relations of process and result, demonstrated by thoroughly considered comparative cases. In this sense the insurance theory expanded by the stress on inclusion and participation as well, but as separate categories, can be linked to process, serving as a link in the argument concerning outcome and stability. As a preliminary step, I would like to already admit that given this theory's abstractness even when expanded with concepts of legitimacy, different types of constitution making can satisfy its demands. But I do want to argue that with the paradigm of constitution making presented here as the multi-stage post sovereign round table one has the best chances of satisfying the conditions of insurance and legitimacy.

First, and this is not insignificant, leaving aside Rawls, whose construction was purely hypothetical, the insurance theory emerged historically in the midst of the series of mostly post revolutionary changes of regime in Southern Europe, Latin America, and finally Central Europe. Its first traces are in Przeworski's definition of democracy as uncertainty, and in O'Donnell and Schmitter's rehabilitation of pacts as methods of democratic transition.[137] As already noted, the developed conception is in Przeworski's 1991 *Democracy and the Market*, which was most directly influenced by events and outcomes surrounding the Polish Round Table of 1989. Interestingly this context produced some steps backward: where O'Donnell and Schmitter considered negotiated pacts to be a much more likely road to democracy than the *via revolutionaria*, Przeworski stressed the likelihood of what I called conversion in pacts of "extrication."[138] Today, after Hungary, Bulgaria, and South Africa we can see that what has been called extrication need not be highly exclusionary nor involve conversion of power. The guarantees posited by Przeworski for a route he linked to authoritarian collapse, and thus negotiations only among new actors, can be attained in negotiations with the forces of the old regime. Indeed, aside from military power holders, it certainly seems to be possible to negotiate full constitutionalism with incumbents and beneficiaries of old regimes. The paradoxical result, already glimpsed by O'Donnell and Schmitter, that it is better for democracy to negotiate with old regime actors when it is at all possible, than to fully overthrow them, is thereby confirmed. The revolutionary elimination of old actors may be unavoidable, but then the danger is also very present that we may very well replace one imposition by another.

[137] Both in O'Donnell and Schmitter, *Transitions from Authoritarian Rule* v. IV.

[138] This was linked to O'Donnell's and Schmitter's depiction of initial pacts, thinking mostly of military-led authoritarian regimes as likely to have a corporatist or consociationalist character.

Next, what the expanded insurance theory tells us is that not just any negotiations will do.[139] First, they have to be inclusive. Second, their inevitably elitist character needs to be diminished. Third, full democratic legitimacy can only be attained if the final outcome is made dependent on elections. All this leads to a two- or multi-stage process preoccupied with the problem of legitimacy. Why the first, negotiated stage? Assuming even that an entirely neutral electoral formula could be achieved, inclusivity may not be the result of elections, especially where a great movement like Solidarity or the ANC has long incorporated popular aspirations. Constitutionalist constitutions in the narrow insurance model could admittedly be the work of two great forces, each uncertain about the future. In the expanded insurance model stressing inclusion for the sake of legitimacy, they should be the work of all those representing a significant segment of opinion and interest. Only a constructed rather than elected framework of negotiations can accomplish this, at least reliably, since even radical proportional representation could sometimes have an exclusionary result. But when constructing a negotiating round table the criterion of inclusion becomes even more important. While an election may legitimately deny representation to some, a construction does not have that advantage. Starting with an old ruling party or elite, there would be a great advantage for this actor in having only one partner or, if that is impossible, to exclude the most radical or disruptive elements of the opposition (e.g. FIDESZ in Hungary in 1989, Inkatha and the white extreme Right in South Africa). While the exclusion of radicals is more likely than not disadvantageous to the opposition side, such efforts cannot be made legitimate. Whether in Hungary or South Africa, assuming the existence of multiple organizations, the logic of greater inclusion is difficult to resist. It may be true that all constitution making involves some plurality and some negotiation, as Przeworski and Elkins et al. stress. The paradigm proposed here, however, implies *inclusive* negotiations that may have been confirmed, even in the problematic survey model of Elkins et al., as conducive to stability.[140]

But construction of a negotiating framework implies still an elite-driven process, even if greater inclusion diminishes this aspect. Moreover, inclusion cannot be perfect given the emergence of new actors in a democratizing context. Negotiated solutions are inevitably, always with some justice, denounced as exclusionary. The gap between the empirical and ideal veil of ignorance furthermore is always real. Even when parties do not know what would really benefit them, they choose what is likely to be advantageous only to them, and those outside, practicing *the hermeneutics of suspicion*, always notice or suspect that this is the

[139] This is the position of Elkins et al., and it converts to a distinction between negotiation and imposition if we restate it as inclusive versus exclusionary negotiation. I prefer my own approach, because theirs can be reduced to thinking about the issue as a mere matter of degree.

[140] This is their stated result, only we do not know the weight in it of real inclusion of as many parties as possible, because of the confusion of real and illusory, and inclusion with participation forms such as the referendum.

case. Both the veil of ignorance and exclusion produce gaps that need to be further diminished, and an opening up to the public sphere and its inputs is a help here. Jon Elster is right: when compared to the French between 1789 and 1791, the American framers may have been helped by the secrecy of their proceedings to make needed compromises. The Polish Magdalenka, and the South African bosperaaden partially confirm this claim, as does the absence of publicity from all but a few plenary sessions in Hungary. In the last case, however, the exclusion of the public linked to a secret deal about the presidency, tended to delegitimate the round table agreements until a referendum confirmed and corrected this gap. Thus, the linking of what may inevitably be secret to public sessions and information, and possibly popular participation in the result may still be very important in imposing public regard arguments on the participants, and increasing the weight of principle as against motive and interest in the proceedings.

While democratic elections should not be held at the beginning of this process, they are nevertheless indispensible.[141] The public sphere does not normally exert power but only influence, and the referendum is a blunt instrument easily challenged, as the Hungarian case referred to shows.[142] The final constitutional product should not be made by a combination of old regime actors along with co-opted and self-selected representatives, even with the help of a referendum. Thus democratic elections for a constitution-making assembly are mandatory midway in the process. The first problem, then, is how such elections are to be organized, and the second how the two or more stages are to be interlinked. A negotiated interim constitution is the solution to both problems. It can provide for all the fair conditions of democratic elections and specify how much of the negotiated solutions must be preserved in the final constitution or altered only under restrictive and enforceable conditions. Thus an interim constitution can and should establish rules for final constitution making, limiting the sovereignty of the decisive constitution-making body as well as incentives and penalties motivating its members to finish the job.

Finally, as we have seen in Iraq and Nepal, full legal continuity with an old regime—though potentially important for producing security and predictability for the process—is not an absolutely necessary condition for this paradigm. But legality and its enforcement are all the more important for the process once it has begun. The interim constitution will be useless, along with the previous agreements, if they are not enforced. Thus the Hungarian and South African examples of establishing strong constitutional courts already in the interim constitution are necessarily part of the developed model. From a legitimation point of view

[141] Kis, "Between Reform and Revolution."

[142] It was immediately charged by supporters of direct election of the president that the narrow majority of the parliamentary option came to be only because the relevant question was linked to others (the famous four yeses) that prejudiced the voters against all proposals of the Hungarian Socialists. Actually, the voters could have voted on each question separately (unlike in Turkey in 2010) but did not. Even this did not help.

this lends the process as well its result a *constitutionalist* character. As the Hungarian Constitutional Court stated, the rule of law can only be created through the rule of law.

Beginning with the veil of ignorance and the insurance model, adding inclusion, publicity, democracy, and legality may seem to be simply adding arbitrary legitimation principles to the model. While additional symbolic resources like charisma may be very useful for the success of negotiations and the stability of the result, the principles stressed here are logically interconnected rather than arbitrary. As a legitimating framework the veil of ignorance is not reducible to some actors' ignorance or sense of uncertainty. Empirical ignorance is only relative ignorance. And even a relatively inclusive bargain is exclusive; there is always imposition as well, as Weber stressed. How can this imposition be legitimated? By bringing in more actors? Such an inclusionary process on the level of political society has its limits. Thus the only ways of including many others actually and potentially are through the influence of civil society and the accountability of elections. The negotiating actors must know, and this is what publicity does, that they may have to face popular protests and mobilization if their constitutional projects are too incumbent protecting, or in other ways misguided. And they must know that the sanction of elections is available if the interim constitution does not provide for an increasingly legitimate process. Initial constitution making can fail, but most actors involved would like to make it succeed. While the long-term success may or may not be linked to initial legitimacy, short term one certainly depends on it. To attain it, the process must rely on more legitimating principles than just the uncertainty and ignorance of the makers. Among these, publicity, elections, and legality are the most essential as well as attractive.

PART II

TWO CASE STUDIES

4

The Hungarian Paradox

I INTRODUCTION

Hungary is the first state where round-table negotiations led to the enactment of a complete, materially new, constitutionalist constitution.[1] It is also the first and thus far only round-table country that has experienced a reversion to a hard or "illiberal" democracy—or: a soft, electorally based authoritarian form of rule. This development seems paradoxical, and raises significant doubts about the validity of the conception of this book, which strongly implies that the round-table model is a preferable rival to other democratic forms of constitution making. At the very least, preferable should mean resulting in a more stable democratic outcome, or what has been called a consolidated democracy. The Hungarian liberal democratic outcome has not been consolidated, nor proved stable.

One way of dealing with this paradox would be to argue that the authoritarian turn in Hungary could be fully explained by factors completely outside of institutional developments, and that, counterfactually, no method of constitution making and no constitution could have prevented it. This assessment would be an easy way out for the theory I propose here, but would come at the high cost of implying that constitution-making methods and results do not matter much for the stability of democracy. I continue to believe the contrary, and also that political actors assume such irrelevance only at their own peril. Another way of diminishing the paradox is to claim that the current outcome in Hungary, as undesirable as it is, can be explained in part by the flaws of a deficient version of the multi-stage process that yielded too little legitimacy for a constitution that contained some very serious structural flaws.[2] That is the task and thesis of the current chapter.

The Hungarian transition is blessed with excellent analysts and interpreters. Many of them, however, only sharpen the paradox, and without intending to do so imply the irrelevance of the constitutional dimension for democratic stability. Some maintain that the round table and within it the democratic opposition

[1] See A. Arato and Z. Miklósi, "Constitution Making and Transitional Politics in Hungary" in L. Miller (ed.), *Framing the State in Times of Transition* (Washington, DC: USIP, 2010).

[2] See ibid. and A. Arato, *Civil Society, Constitution, and Legitimacy* (Baltimore, MD: Rowman and Littlefield, 2000).

were not only highly successful in achieving a constitutional democracy with no undemocratic forms of the conversion of old power, but indicate a superior process even when compared to Poland and South Africa.[3] Others go so far as to argue that the initial Hungarian process represented the exercise of the democratic constituent power that generated a high level of legitimacy.[4] I will try to show that neither of these claims can be sustained, and the error is ultimately the same. Hungary's constitutional transition can be seen as preferable to or more legitimate than those of South Africa or Poland or even Bulgaria only if we disregard the multi-stage requirement of the round-table-led process, the need for a second or final stage of completion, rooted in democratic elections. While Poland's and Bulgaria's round tables did produce initial results that were deficient when compared to Hungary's, the South African Multiparty Negotiating Forum (MPNF) produced an interim constitution in no respects inferior to the Hungarian one. Indeed, I would maintain that its explicit provisions for the second stage of constitution making alone represent a significantly superior accomplishment. Moreover, the MPNF's and ANC's concessions to power sharing, stressed by critical interpreters,[5] were no greater than those negotiators agreed on in Budapest on September 18, 1989, at the conclusion of the National Round Table (or Nemzeti Kerekasztal (NKA)). What is more important was that in Bulgaria, South Africa, and Poland, a final stage of constitution making based on the democratic elections of non-sovereign assemblies was completed. In all these countries as well as in Hungary the results of the round-table negotiations had serious legitimation problems, all having to do with *unelected* elites bargaining with representatives of *authoritarian* governments. As I will show, this weakness of legitimacy is both re-constructible from a normative point of view, and can be empirically discovered in the contentious politics of a given country. The link between the two interpretations that I reject is rooted in this very legitimation problem, one that necessitated the round-table process to be linked with multi-stage projects of completion. Such completion did not occur in Hungary. When the process was recently brought to an end by the FIDESZ government, the procedures of the making of the so-called Fundamental Law directly contradicted both the experience of the Hungarian Round Table, but also the way the completion of the process was organized elsewhere.

To make my position clear, I do not claim the illegitimacy or the total lack of legitimacy of the initial round tables in either the normative or the empirical sense. Such illegitimacy was always the claim of right-wing, would-be revolutionaries (in South Africa left-wing), and has been occasionally revived by interpreters close to the now governing FIDESZ, an important participant in the

[3] J.W. Schiemann, *The Politics of Pact-Making: Hungary's Negotiated Transition to Democracy in Comparative Perspective* (London: Palgrave Macmillan, 2005).

[4] K. Scheppele, "Unconstitutional Constituent Power" manuscript, to be published in R. Smith and R. Beeman (eds), *Constitution Making* (Philadelphia, PA: University of Pennsylvania Press, 2015).

[5] Schiemann, *The Politics of Pact Making* 35, 139–46. He relies on Jung and Shapiro, who themselves wrote before the making of the final constitution when the consociational elements were removed.

Round Table.[6] As indefensible as their totalizing claims may have been, these in themselves contributed to legitimacy problems including the lukewarm attitude or indifference of the population at large to its own constitution. Nevertheless, as I have always maintained, to different extents, the various round tables responded to the legitimacy problem by combining the norms of inclusion, consensus, publicity, and legality. In two cases, Poland and South Africa, the process could assume historical merits in the struggle for liberation, and the related charisma of political leadership. Yet in all these cases, and especially in Hungary, which lacked such recent experience or leadership, it was the actors of the opposition who maintained, at least initially, that unelected round tables have the right to negotiate only the rules of the game required for free elections, not complete constitutions. This is what happened in Poland and Bulgaria, though inconsistently in the first case because a very strong presidency was conceded to the old regime and the elections agreed to were only partially free. These concessions, however understandable at that time, exacerbated the legitimacy problem so often unrecognized by interpreters, but relied upon by right-wing revolutionaries, who at least in Poland have so far failed.[7] In Bulgaria, a functionally equivalent concession of calling for very early elections that the Communists would be able to dominate led to even greater conflicts around legitimacy. These were to an extent solved by new negotiations at the (constitutional) Grand National Assembly, and by the relatively high quality of the resulting constitution.[8]

In spite of the intentions of the radical oppositions in Hungary and South Africa the inherited authoritarian constitutions were fully replaced by the round tables. To deal with the legitimacy problem, at least in part, both new constitutions were designated as interim.[9] However, the implicit promise to produce a final constitution continuous with the interim document was kept only in South Africa. In Hungary as well the consociational dimension was greatly reduced—not, however, through a new constitutionalist constitution made by an assembly elected for that purpose, but by a new round of elite agreement in 1990. The result here, of a liberal democratic constitution that gave accountable governments genuine power to act, was important. Indeed, it confirms some of the judgements of those who argue that Hungary was the first Central European country to achieve a constitution without authoritarian residues. But the process that led to this result was not only deficient from the normative point of

[6] In the case of FIDESZ this leads to the contradiction in interpreting their own turn at constitution making in 2010 and after, as a revolution on the one hand and a completion of the round-table-led process on the other. On this, see below.

[7] See the excellent chapter by W. Osiatynski, "The Roundtable Talks in Poland" in J. Elster (ed.), *The Round Table Talks and the Breakdown of Communism* (Chicago, IL: University of Chicago Press, 1996) 40–1.

[8] R. Kolarova and D. Dimitrov, "Round Table Talks in Bulgaria" in Elster, *Round Table Talks*; R. Peeva "A bolgár kerekasztal tárgyalások összehasonlító szempontból" in A. Bozóki et al., *A rendszerváltás forgatókönyve* (Budapest: Új Mandátum, 2000).

[9] In Hungary, that designation was made by the old parliament, within a new preamble added on the motion of an individual deputy. Yet the designation factually corresponded to the intentions of the opposition at the round table.

view, but immediately denounced by many actors excluded from the new bargain, including FIDESZ, who abstained in the voting process.[10]

This chapter reconstructs in detail the link between the deficient Hungarian constituent process and the authoritarian reversion led by FIDESZ, the governmental party after 2010. A full explanation of this development would have to take into account the process and the costs of economic system change, the emerging system of social stratification and welfare, the development of the party political structure, as well as contingent political and policy choices of governments in power. None of that can be my task here. I do strongly believe, however, that structural and symbolic weaknesses in Hungary's constitution and constitutional development were significant factors in and presented important opportunities for the authoritarian reversion that, most visibly at least, began in the domain of constitution making. I certainly will not maintain that constitutional failure was in itself *sufficient* cause for the authoritarian reversion, but only that it was a *necessary* one if the reversion was to take place through legal continuity rather than a revolutionary break. In spite of speaking about a "revolution of the voting booths" FIDESZ did not carry out a revolution in the legal sense, and did not have the power or the authority to do so in this deeply divided society located within the European Union.

In analyzing the Hungarian case, I will try to also highlight the strengths and weaknesses of the round-table model. I will proceed in several steps. I will first argue that the authoritarian turn was not inevitable, and the round-table-led constitution-making effort diminished rather than exacerbated this threat. Here I will reintroduce and further refine the distinction between conversion and guarantee developed in Chapter 3 above. Second, I will examine the legitimation problems of the Hungarian National Round Table and argue that the clear differentiation between conversion and guarantee cannot be easily accomplished in a single-stage, round-table-led transition process. The illusion of one-sided conversion can survive even when only guarantees are mutually conceded. Third, I will reconstruct the main structural flaw of the constitution of 1989–90: the combination of a highly disproportional electoral, and weakly entrenched parliamentary amendment rules that allowed a legal alteration of its basic structure. Paradoxically, I will maintain that a very powerful Constitutional Court within the same structure exacerbated an antinomy between parliamentary sovereignty and constitutionalism, one that could be resolved or at least diminished only through projects of completion. Fourth, I will consider three completion projects aiming to redress both structural problems and the weakness of constitutional legitimacy: the pact of 1990, the failed constitution making or completion effort of 1994–97, and the interpretive activism of the Constitutional Court, an activism that stopped short of the genuinely constituent step of assuming amendment review. Fifth, I will consider the FIDESZ constitution-making effort

[10] In particular FIDESZ abstained on voting on the amendment package, even though some of its amendments offered from the floor were accommodated. See C. Tordai, "A Harmadik Köztársaság alkotmányának születése" in Bozóki et al. (eds), *A rendszerváltás forgatókönyve*.

of 2011 to 2014, and try to show why it was not a completion of the round-table-led paradigm, but instead its violation—in spite of observing legal continuity. Sixth, I will consider the horse race between constitutional court and government under the FIDESZ Fundamental Law, comparable to other similar competitions in India and Turkey that were resolved differently, and argue that the consensual heritage of the round table allowed even the packed Constitutional Court, for a time at least, to resist a new form of electorally based absolutism.

II WAS THE AUTHORITARIAN TURN INEVITABLE?

Let me start with openly confronting two pessimistic theses, according to which the reversion or survival of some kind of authoritarian outcome was inevitable in the Hungarian case, or at least extremely likely. If this were so, the constitutional domain would merely belong to a superstructural "stage" where deeper developments would play out. That is not my view of the place of constitutions in social and political systems. But the idea that the Central European countries would have great difficulty in managing a double (Elster) or triple (Offe) transition to new regimes, economies, and states was plausible even if seeing "the tunnel at the end of the light"[11] was rather premature. Nevertheless, I have repeatedly argued against this deterministic thesis, and note that its advocates themselves were forced to moderate it in light of developments in the region dominated by the round-table countries.[12] In comparison to post Communist regimes further to the east, it is hard to escape the conclusion that processes of regime change within legal continuity, associated mostly if not universally with round-table negotiations, played an important role in the fact that twenty years after the transitions political democracy appears to be consolidated in five countries out of six. Although there have also been serious conflicts between economic liberalization, including privatization, price reform, dismantling of unproductive industries, trade liberalization, and redistributive, welfare-oriented pressures from below that have sometimes culminated in populist mobilizations, the new democratic political systems have so far withstood and even helped to manage these conflicts.[13] If this is the case, then the arrangements negotiated at the round tables would have played an important role in the stabilization of constitutional democracy.

However, a second pessimistic thesis based on the older literature on democratic transitions would contest the positive role of round-table negotiations. Adam Przeworski, who links his doubts about negotiated transitions to his own version of the pessimistic double transition analysis, raised serious doubts as to

[11] C. Offe, *Der Tunnel am Ende des Lichts* (Frankfurt: Campus Verlag, 1994). Unless of course we interpret liberal democracy as tunnel rather than light. Then I would have no problem with this imagery.

[12] Arato, *Civil Society* Chapter 1; J. Casanova, "A spanyolországi demokratikus átalakulás tanulságai" in Bozóki et al., *A rendszerváltás forgatókönyve.*

[13] Arato, *Civil Society* 32; also J. Elster, C. Offe, and U. Preuss, *Institutional Design in Post-Communist Societies* (Cambridge: Cambridge University Press, 1998) Chapter 8.

whether a process negotiated with old regime power holders could deal with emerging problems. Accordingly, he predicted that the economic transitions everywhere would lead at worst to poor capitalist countries, and at best involve long transitional periods of economic weakness characterized by unemployment, rising prices, increasing inequality, and weakening public and welfare services.[14] He further argued that the new political institutions would not be able to manage the crises, because of their own haphazard nature and instability, and would therefore open the door to Latin American types of populism and authoritarian options. Both of the institutional defects were supposedly the result of different aspects of the "extrication" process, namely transitions negotiated between old and new elites. According to Przeworski extrication inevitably leaves guarantees interpreted as undemocratic institutional traces. This claim on the whole corresponds to the judgement dominant in the transition literature, with some notable exceptions.[15] As a result of the outcome of extrication, he goes on to argue, after initial agreements democratic forces will engage in a struggle to remove the authoritarian traces. They can generally do so only gradually, thus the incremental constitutional development through amendments experienced early in Poland and Hungary is programmed into the very process. Instability, incoherence, and the removal of the veil of ignorance are the results.[16]

I have elsewhere tried to show that a negative comparative judgement of negotiated agreements is based on the experience of dictatorships dominated by military elites, and does not apply to civilian-controlled authoritarian polities, whether they are of the right or the Communist left.[17] Thus Spain with its civilian ruling elite turns out to be a model rather than a miracle (as argued by Linz and Stepan, and Jose Casanova showed against Przeworski). Paradoxically, a recent version of this pessimistic thesis seems to claim that Hungary was also a kind of miracle, or at least an important exception to the general rule. According to John Schiemann's detailed book on the transition, negotiated transitions leave authoritarian institutional traces logically as well as empirically. According to him, Hungary, exceptionally, has been able to avoid the negative logic of two-sided negotiations with representatives of the old regime because of its unusual combination of "dominant risk takers within the democratic opposition" and "dominant risk averse regime actors."[18] While the analysis of the attitudes of the actors is partially correct, by insisting on risk-taking courage it neglects the fact that the very risk takers such as János Kis (along with the editors of Beszélő the founders of the "radical" Alliance of Free Democrats (SZDSZ)) were at one time

[14] A. Przeworski, *Democracy and the Market* (Cambridge: Cambridge University Press, 1991) 189.

[15] See Schiemann's citations in *The Politics of Pact Making*; the exception, however, is J. Linz and A. Stepan, *Problems of Democratic Transition and Consolidation* (Baltimore, MD: Johns Hopkins University Press, 1996).

[16] Przeworski, *Democracy and the Market* 78–9.

[17] Arato, *Civil Society* Chapter 1.

[18] Schiemann, *Politics of Pact Making*; Przeworski seems to anticipate this when saying that aside from Poland and Bulgaria the other countries were "less affected by elements of extrication," *Democracy and the Market* 67.

the first to suggest compromise and semi-democratic solutions to help initiate a process of "extrication" from the old regime. They were no more willing to take risks on behalf of the population than their moderate competitors in the Hungarian Democratic Forum (MDF). The risk takers became irreconcilably opposed to such concessions on cognitive grounds, namely when they rightly realized after the Polish Round Table, quickly followed by the elections and government formation, that the former risks of Soviet intervention were greatly diminished.[19] There was little difference between them and the Polish democratic opposition, except time and sequence. The Polish opposition had little time or willingness to take risks, because Poland's was the first in a series of transitions the limits of which could not yet be known. These limits were greatly expanded by the very outcome of the Polish negotiations, elections, and the formation of a Solidarity-led government, which were willingly accepted by the Gorbachev government in the Soviet Union. The consciousness of time—the ability to outwait the government—mattered in Hungary, but based on primarily cognitive assumptions. Moreover, the Hungarian opposition rightly saw itself as much weaker than the historically much more important Polish movement led by Solidarity. According to an important thesis introduced by János Kis, the Hungarian opposition that gathered around the Round Table of the Opposition (EKA) could not accept Polish-style concessions to the representatives of the old regime because it did not have the confidence of the social groups, old and new, potentially mobilized, who would be inclined to denounce an elite bargain. In their eyes, only a fully liberal-democratic constitutional product could retroactively legitimate agreements between the old power and new elites with weak representational status. I agree with this judgement, even as I will argue that imputed legitimation through the result was still quite insufficient. But in any case, their own weakness did move the more radical opposition to a less compromising position, while the rightly understood weakness of their governmental opponents allowed them to do so.[20]

Equally importantly, by stressing the Hungarian round table's supposedly exceptional nature, the logic of round-table negotiations that favor precisely such attitudes is missed. How do I see that logic? In short, during such negotiations even civilian regime actors, whether in Spain, Hungary, or South Africa, generally do start out with projects seeking to convert their power. Nevertheless, as all these cases show, they are all able to accept forms of guarantee instead.[21] Indeed, they ambiguously and even incoherently seek both guarantees and forms of conversion. The first government proposals concerning the

[19] J. Kis, "Between Reform and Revolution: Three Hypotheses about the Nature of Regime Change" (1995) 1 *Constellations* 3; and J. Kis, "Between Reform and Revolution" (Spring 1998) in 12 *East European Politics and Societies* 2 300–83.

[20] L. Bruszt and D. Stark, "A politikai játéktér újraformálása" in Bozóki et al., *A rendszerváltás forgatókönyve*, following the diagnosis of Kis and the SZDSZ argument for the weakness of both sides.

[21] The distinction between conversion and guarantees was first made in Arato, Civil Society, Constitution and Legitimacy 20ff, and is further developed in Chapter 3 above.

setting up of a constitutional court in Hungary reflect this ambiguity.[22] While the proposals contained elements of power conversion, such as a top-down appointment structure at a time when the government could still control the process, coupled with very long judicial terms, they also included guarantees, such as a very extensive jurisdiction for the court. And while the proposals included the limited possibility of the invalidation of laws that would be available against any parliament, they also included a parliamentary override that assumed the preservation of their own dominant position. Of course, these differences reflected uncertainties concerning who was likely to win democratic elections and by what means. It is likely that different regime actors wound up combining elements of conversion and guarantee, because of their different preferences and judgements concerning the overall situation in which their party found itself. Moreover, there was a time lag that favored elements that preferred guarantees. When it looked likely that the MSZMP could win, its leaders preferred strategies that could help convert their power, in the case of the constitutional court a scheme that contained parliamentary override of court decisions. When, after three Hungarian by-elections, and the Polish elections, it looked more likely that the opposition would win, the strategies and the constitutional proposals associated with them shifted, and they no longer felt the need to insist on parliamentary override.[23] Moreover, a similar dynamic was likely within the type of guarantees accepted and even sought. While regime negotiators initially preferred consociational forms of power sharing as the form of guarantee closest to outright forms of conversion, they could accept constitutionalism as well, meaning a form of guarantee that would allow their full participation in political life and provide personal security of their members.[24] Both in Hungary and South Africa a similar shift was noticeable, even within guarantees involving no formal power sharing. With respect to elections, Communist parties everywhere initially preferred first-past-the-post elections that could turn pluralities into a huge majorities, but readily accepted, as did the South African National Party, much more proportional rules when their electoral weakness became apparent.

With respect to electoral rules, the various parties of the disunited Hungarian opposition were no different than the ruling party: each party sought, almost always mistakenly,[25] the rules that seemed most favorable to it. Yet, having no

[22] Tordai, "A Harmadik Köztársaság alkotmányának születése"; G. Halmai, "Az 1949es alkotmány jogállamositása" in Bozóki et al., *A rendszerváltás forgatókönyve*; Schiemann, *Politics of Pact Making*.

[23] Schiemann, *Politics of Pact Making*; and Tordai, "A Harmadik Köztársaság alkotmányának születése."

[24] See Arato and Miklósi, "Constitution Making and Transitional Politics"; and Tordai, "A Harmadik Köztársaság alkotmányának születése."

[25] The SZDSZ (the liberal Alliance of Free Democrats) sought a large number of single member districts, which turned out to favor its competitor, the MDF (the populist, and at that time more moderate Hungarian Democratic Forum), which wanted more proportional seats initially. The historical parties were right to seek proportional representation, but quite wrong to press for a few provincial member lists rather than a large, national one.

authoritarian past to defend, the opposition preferences were simpler and did not need to shift as much with the passing of time. Most importantly, actors of the opposition could accept forms of conversion of power only when the threat of violence from above remained very serious, as under military-dominated old regimes undefeated by war. In Central Europe this acceptance continued as long as the tolerance of the imperial occupying power was not tested. For similar reasons, opposition actors were able to accept even consociational guarantees only to a very limited extent, and then only temporarily when they judged (or misjudged) the external danger to be still relevant. On the other hand, whatever their previous ideology, they were all likely to favor constitutional guarantees, both because of their beliefs and because the electoral power of the old ruling parties in free and fair elections was untested. At the time the negotiations ended, no party, neither the government nor the various oppositions, could be certain regarding the outcome of free elections. For all these reasons the roundtable models with civilian participants converged in the insurance model rather than in the hegemonic preservation model.[26]

It is right to emphasize the element of time required to allow the transformation of the priorities of regime actors. Wishing to hold on to their original positions these actors tended to want to accelerate the time of negotiations, as well as the time leading to free elections. In some instances, as in Bulgaria, they succeeded—but the constitutional outcome even in that country indicates that the successes tended to be short-lived. However, the interest of oppositional actors was to extend time, not only the time of negotiations and the time leading to free elections, but of the transition process as a whole. When they succeeded, the insurance model had fully come into its own.

Still, the insurance model based on the idea of a "veil of ignorance" does not in itself yield the two-stage constitution-making paradigm. Nor is it correct for most countries to restrict it to the stage of constitution making as distinguished from extrication. Przeworski seems to have Poland and perhaps Bulgaria in mind when he makes a distinction between "extrication" and "constitution,"[27] indicating either that there were no extrication-type problems in a country such as Hungary, which is false, or that extrication and constitution could be accomplished in the same act, which is true. This second interpretation is confirmed by Przeworski's own introduction of the veil of ignorance in the empirical sense, meaning that a constitution is produced before the actors can know their respective strengths, in other words, before free elections. This insight leads to the important recommendation that constitution should come first, before elections.[28] Under these circumstances, it is likely the parties who do not know the outcome will seek to insure themselves against electoral uncertainty and negotiate a constitution with constitutionalist protections that will be more stable than constitutions imposed by a single actor or even a collusion of a few actors.

[26] See Chapter 3 above and references there to the competing positions of Ran Hirschl and Tom Ginsburg.

[27] Przeworski, *Democracy and the Market* 66–7, 67ff, 79ff. [28] Ibid. 87–8.

Unfortunately, however, as the democratic oppositions everywhere maintained (most successfully in German Democratic Republic (GDR) Round Table[29]), that a constitution that is agreed to before elections will have important legitimation problems because it can be enacted only by the old Communist-dominated parliament, subverting the rights of the first freely elected body.[30] Structurally suitable for democratic politics, such a constitution will remain politically vulnerable. An *interim* constitution enacted by the deficient parliament under the guidance of the round table seems to have been the optimal solution to the difficulty. It allowed *a* constitution to be made both before free elections and after them, as long as a permanent constitution was made within the terms of the same overall process. But even an interim constitution would have serious legitimation problems if the making of a permanent constitution was subsequently subverted—in other words, if the interim constitution itself tended to become permanent. This is what happened in Hungary. Unfortunately, the doubtful legitimacy of the interim constitution was only one of the legitimation problems of the Hungarian transition regime. To these problems I now turn.

III LEGITIMATION PROBLEMS

As already seen, in Hungary the problem of the legitimacy of round-table agreements had been raised from the outset. It was fundamental for all spokesmen of the democratic opposition gathered around the Opposition Round Table (EKA) that the old Communist-dominated parliament, created in unfree and mostly uncompetitive elections, did not have the right to enact a new constitution from above. At the time, this was the aim even of the reformists of the regime led by the Justice Ministry. Moreover, most of the EKA participants initially believed that they themselves lacked the electoral legitimacy to enact a constitution together with representatives of the old regime. When their initial position (not to draft a new constitution through comprehensive amendments) had to be abandoned, the claims of insufficient legitimacy were not subsequently abandoned nor even revised. Indeed, given the absence of publicity from most of the real negotiations, and the unclear conditions under which part of the opposition agreed to the MSZMP project of electing the presidency early in a popular election, doubts about legitimacy became even more serious. As one interpreter, András Sajó, rightly maintained, since the presidency was tailor-made for one particular individual, Imre Pozsgay, to use a popular election to enhance his powers the veil of ignorance that covered a very crucial part of the agreements

[29] U. Preuss, "The Round Table Talks in the German Democratic Republic" in Elster, *The Round Table Talks*. The GDR actors, however, were to find out what others elsewhere knew in advance, when the freely elected first *Volkskammer* refused to even discuss their constitutional draft.

[30] In Poland the same realization was made in the context of the so-called contractual Sejm, which was elected in only partially free elections.

was removed.[31] Thus, Sajó goes on to argue, the process undermined the legitimacy of the constitution that emerged from it. To be sure some interpreters, and I was among them, argued that the referendum of November 1989 provided some democratic legitimacy for the overall outcome. This referendum of the "four yeses" returned the scheduling of the election of the president to after that of parliament, and initially to its indirect, parliamentary modality. It was indeed the only moment in the Hungarian constituent process involving popular participation and consultation.[32] However, others stress that the campaign threw a negative light on the previous agreements as a whole, helping to discredit one of its important architects, the reformist forces of the MSZ(M)P[33] led by Pozsgay.[34] This ambivalence greatly continued to exacerbate conflict within the opposition once united in the EKA. One possible conclusion from this is drawn by András Körösényi[35] who very rightly criticizes the questionable substantive role of the old parliament in enacting the new amendments, and, mostly wrongly in my view, the absence of consensus at the conclusion of the Round Table. He does not seem to understand that there was a high level of consensus regarding most of the public law package and especially on the goals of the process. Nevertheless, he may be right to the extent that the referendum campaign that very much corrected the outcome also created the unfortunate impression that there was no consensus to begin with. Here the normative and empirical meanings of legitimacy, which Körösényi confuses, part company.

In my view, the contrast between perspectives on legitimacy reflects not only the actual ambivalence of the Hungarian situation, but the contrast between normative and sociological meanings of legitimacy as well. There was a serious argument from a normative point of view that the constitution of 1989–90 was a fully liberal democratic one. In liberal normative conceptions such a result in itself allows the imputation of legitimacy to the process, whatever its empirical heterogeneity. Accordingly, while the empirical veil of ignorance was often

[31] A. Sajó, "The Round Table Talks in Hungary" in Elster, *The Round Table Talks*, 93–4. According to János Kis in "Between Reform and Revolution" this version of the presidency was more dangerous than the one conceded in Poland precisely because of its plebiscitary character.

[32] See Tordai, "A Harmadik Köztársaság alkotmányának születése" 493; as well as A. Bozóki, "A kerekasztal tárgyalások és a rendszerváltozás" in Bozóki et al., *A rendszerváltás forgatókönyve* 46–7; and A. Arato, "Post Sovereign Constitution-making in Hungary: After Success, Partial Failure, and Now What?" (2010) 26 *South African Journal of Human Rights* 1 19–44.

[33] By the time of the referendum the old MSZMP (Hungarian Socialist Workers Party) was dissolved and a new MSZP (Hungarian Socialist Party) took its place.

[34] As Zoltán Ripp very well puts it, after applauding the combined strategy of the opposition: "the agreement bore the imprint of a separate deal, whilst the referendum bore the marks of the violation of the agreement." Z. Ripp, "Unity and Division: The Opposition Round Table and its Relationship to the Communist Party" in A. Bozóki (ed.), *The Round Table Talks of 1989. The Genesis of Hungarian Democracy* (Budapest: CEU Press, 2002). In Arato and Miklósi, "Constitution Making and Transitional Politics" we too expressed some doubts, along with a positive evaluation of the popular element.

[35] A. Körösényi, "Mozgékony patthelyzet. Reform és változatlanság között a politikai és alkotmányos alapszerkezet változásai, 1990–2005" (2006) 15 *Politikatudományi Szemle* 32, especially 61–2.

punctured in the actual process, the result was such that it could have been produced under the ideal veil of ignorance. Nevertheless, the legitimacy of the same outcome remained in doubt from a different normative perspective, a more strongly democratic one rejecting mere imputation and focusing on the actual process, one seen as insufficient from the procedural point of view.

This second normative perspective is closer in spirit to the view that played a role in the emergence of empirical legitimation problems. Indeed, both non-participants and important actors within the process have subjected the agreements and the outcome to withering criticism. And the critics could rely on one important normative consideration—the new constitution was only very partially the product of a freely elected assembly, and even that part was, as we shall see, achieved by a manufactured majority of two parties, relying on less than 50 percent of the votes, who thus imposed their agreed amendments on the rest of the first freely elected parliament. While the charges of the critics never did yield a legitimation crisis as deep as that of the old, Communist regime, that outcome was avoided only by the indifference of most sectors of the population with respect to the new constitution. And that meant the following: while no significant movement could be mobilized *against* the constitution, no such movement was ready to *defend* it when a new, manufactured, constitution-amending majority moved to replace it.

In order to understand how this happened, how the conflict within normative meanings of legitimacy, as well as between normative and empirical evaluations, became acute, not just in theory but also in practice too, a differentiated analysis of the legitimacy problems of the round-table constitution-making process is necessary. János Kis offers such an analysis, not without some ambivalence of his own. His key concept is the tension between consensus and compromise in the history of the Round Table.[36] According to him, no such negotiating process is possible without consensus between and among "partners" concerning the ultimate goal, in this case liberal democracy. Contrary to Körösényi, Kis argues that this consensus regarding the ultimate goal survived the whole process despite appearances and was incorporated in the constitution of 1989–90. But he stresses that the very nature of the process requires compromise among "parties" who had different worldviews and, more significantly, strongly divergent interests. In any given case, the structure of the compromise depends on the relation of forces, but a compromise to an extent in conflict with norms underlying the consensual goal cannot be entirely avoided. While in my own view this need not mean acceptance of elements of conversion or even power sharing, the creation of specific democratic rules too has distributional consequences. To be sure, the parties can be quite wrong about the relationship of their interests and elements of the institutional design, but they will bargain as if they have been able to pierce the veil of ignorance. As some win and others lose they acquire different relationships to the outcome. Even if the veil can be

[36] Kis, "Between Reform and Revolution" 307, 322.

imputed from a philosophical point of view and has some empirical reality on the level of beliefs, the illusion of self-serving bargains cannot be removed in a purely negotiated process where the actors have only a tenuous relationship to representation. In such a context even constitutionalist guarantees could be portrayed as forms of conversion.[37]

According to Kis, the tension between consensus and compromise could have been reduced if the pact at the end of the National Round Table had been fully consensual, or if a new constitution had been successfully made by greater consensus in 1994–96, thereby bridging the legitimation void in either case.[38] Neither happened in Hungary. Even the referendum in Kis' conception could not save or replace the missing consensus at the end of the National Round Table.[39] Thus at least in the first version of his argument, Kis tended to suggest that it was merely rules of the game that were substituted for normative legitimacy.[40] However, with some ambivalence in the second version he seems to argue that consensual rules of the game help produce deliberation and the rule of law, both of which contribute to legitimacy at least in the normative sense.[41] Again it may seem that differences in perspectives, particularly between those of participant and observer, lead to different results. While the normative, philosophical view, one appropriate for participants in the societal debates leads to at least a partial diagnosis of legitimacy, doubts on the sociological level of the external observer remain. This second perspective remains more important if we recognize along with Kis that it is first of all in the sociological-empirical sense dealing with empirical beliefs that crises of legitimation affect politics.[42]

While almost all interpreters have expressed at least some doubt concerning the legitimacy of the interim constitution, it is certainly possible to maintain the contrary. It is hard to know whether it is the empirical or the normative meaning that Kim Scheppele has in mind when she asserts the full legitimacy of what she calls "the constituent power" during the process of round-table constitution making. She does this to provide not only a strong contrast to the effort of FIDESZ after 2010, but to reaffirm a perspective common in the milieu of the Sólyom-led Constitutional Court. László Sólyom himself, as an important Round Table participant, has admitted the absence of legitimation in the original process, as well as for all the sides that negotiated. Yet he nevertheless

[37] Indeed that imputation of conversion to guarantees is reinforced by the survival of economic powers in the hands of beneficiaries of the old regime, whether in Poland, Hungary, or South Africa, as E. Hankiss and J. Staniszkis were the first to argue, and Žižek more recently.

[38] Kis, "Between Reform and Revolution: Three Hypotheses" 410; Kis, "Between Reform and Revolution" 368.

[39] Kis, "Between Reform and Revolution" 369, 376.

[40] Kis, "Between Reform and Revolution: Three Hypotheses" 407.

[41] Kis, "Between Reform and Revolution" 370.

[42] Kis, "Between Reform and Revolution: Three Hypotheses" 405; Kis, "Between Reform and Revolution" 314. Interestingly, he has taken the sociological or external observer's perspective when analyzing the crisis of the surrogate or negative legitimacy of the old regime that philosophically he considered entirely illegitimate.

described the Round Table, in the same text, as "the real legislator and the constituent power," here either simply contradicting himself or assuming that the constituent power can do without constituent authority or even legitimacy.[43] Elsewhere, however, he went on to claim that a genuine constituent power was in operation because of his certainty "that the people agreed that it wanted regime change, in content based on multi-party democracy and the actualization of human rights." Undoubtedly seeking to legitimate the later constituent activity of his Court (which he repeatedly affirmed without hesitation), this admirer of Kelsen was even willing to implicitly mobilize a form of populist mythology of origins derived from Carl Schmitt.[44] Luckily, he was not consistent on the subject. He elsewhere admitted that the process "did not originate among the people. The change of regimes ... was neither a real revolution, nor popular upheaval."[45]

While following Sólyom, there are however some unique features of Scheppele's recent argument. I have in mind more than the indefensible and counterproductive claim that the "Hungarian Constitutional Court, through the 1990s, practically ran Hungary ... a courtocracy."[46] On a theoretical level, in her very understandable and convincing attempt to fully discredit the FIDESZ constitution-making project, she seeks to explicitly mobilize the Sieyès-Schmittian conception of the constituent power as the basis of the contrast between 1989 and 2014. This concept, which Sólyom also flirted with, is in any case inappropriate for any stage of the multi-actor Hungarian constitution-making process. The most significant problem with this interpretive effort, however, is that it winds up disguising the roots of the authoritarian reversion that process made possible.

Scheppele's methodology is difficult to understand. While in many respects following Kis and one of my co-authored articles, she stubbornly refuses our theses of general legitimation problems, which as we have seen even Sólyom at times admits to. Even more seriously, she misses the problem with the MDF-SZDSZ pact, one that reduced rather than increased the consensual character of parliamentary government, and was widely and rightly seen as exclusionary rather than an act of a united and consensual Hungarian *pouvoir constituant*.[47] Behind the

[43] L. Sólyom, "The Role of Constitutional Courts in the Transition to Democracy. With Special Reference to Hungary" in S. Arjomand (ed.), *Constitutionalism and Political Reconstruction* (Leiden: Brill, 2007).

[44] Author's translation. From L. Sólyom, "A jogállami forradalomtól az EU csatakozásig. Az alkotmányfejlődés keretei" in L. Majtényi and Z. Miklósi (eds), *És mi lesz az alkotmánnyal* (Budapest: Eötvös Károly Intézet, 2004) 15–16.

[45] Sólyom, "The Role of Constitutional Courts" 287. In view of this admission, it remains really mysterious how he can claim "revolutionary legitimacy" for the Constitutional Court even in quotation marks, which he often neglected to use.

[46] K. Scheppele, "Constitutional Negotiations. Political Contexts of Judicial Activism in Post-Soviet Europe" in S.A. Arjomand (ed.), *Constitutionalism and Political Reconstruction* (Leiden: Brill 2007) 318.

[47] She also misses the reason why a constituent assembly, required by the normative model she adopted, was not in fact called in Hungary. By then, it probably had nothing to do with Moscow's tolerance, but rather with

whole argument lies a metaphysical reference to the general will of the population, a will that is ultimately tested only by the very real replacement of the old through a new constitution, one that indeed had a largely liberal democratic character.[48]

The constitutional result itself had its own ambivalence. Sólyom eventually denounced the very notion of an interim constitution even against the text itself, the words of which on this score he attributed to an (illegitimate) intervention by the old parliament into the work of the Round Table. On the contrary, Scheppele accepts that the constitution of 1989–90 announced its own transitional character. This she attributes to a desire to keep learning open (which makes sense but cannot be documented), rather than to the widely perceived legitimation problem, which can be and has been noted by many analysts.[49] Nevertheless, although she seems to accept my idea of a multi-stage constitution-making process, in the face of the factual failure of a consensual second stage in 1994–96, she argues against me that in Hungary the process was actually completed, and by the Constitutional Court, in her view the body that through the 1990s "ran Hungary"! I will return shortly to this view of the Constitutional Court as a quasi-constituent power, based on the views of Sólyom.

To make matters clear, I wish to argue that legitimation problems have been the main (though not the only) reason why a new constitutional synthesis was necessary, replacing the interim constitution but preserving the public law structure of the new regime of 1989–90. Yet, from a comparative sociological framework, I have viewed the legitimation outcome of the Round Table more positively than some interpreters, while at the same time insisting on the legitimation problems, coupled with structural weaknesses within the interim constitutional structure.[50] For a long time, I considered these two problems when taken together as especially dangerous for constitutional democracy. Within that broad comparative investigation, I have found that the issue of their legitimacy comes up at almost all round tables directly or indirectly, as expressed by either the reluctance to make full constitutions (Poland, Czechoslovakia, Bulgaria), the making of only interim constitutions (Hungary, South Africa), or the failure to have a constitutional product taken seriously, however excellent this may have been in content (GDR). Negotiating with old regime actors who have lost their legitimacy, including new actors in agreement with the old, excluding others, making agreements whose quid pro quo character can be justified only in terms of a strategic modus vivendi, are all problematic from the point of view

the problem of timing early elections. Moreover, the Hungarian actors at the time consciously rejected a revolutionary break with the old regime. Scheppele, "Unconstitutional Constituent Power" op.cit.

48 Admittedly, both Sólyom and Scheppele think that subsequent democratic elections legitimated the rules under which they occurred.

49 In response to Sólyom, "A jogállami forradalomtól az EU csatakozásig," see J. Kis, "Az alkotmány véglegesítése" in Majtényi and Miklósi, *És mi lesz az alkotmánnyal.*

50 From a slightly different point of view this was the position of A. Bragyova, *Az új alkotmány egy koncepciója* (Budapest: MTA, 1995) 18.

of democratic legitimacy, and the main actors recognize it as such one way or another. Paradoxically, contrary to models of revolution and reform, this is why, as already argued, at its best this model of radical change turns out to be a factory of legitimation, introducing elements like *public openness, inclusion* of new participants, fully *consensual* decision rules, as well as treating the fictional *legality* of old regimes as actual, as if they could be made elements of the rule of law. Moreover, to defend themselves from the charge of usurping the constituent power, the participants also tend to affirm the merely provisional nature of their institutional solutions; to admit to their not having the right to completely substitute for free elections; and for the making of the final constitution by those elected under these rules. Free elections and final constitution making by an elected assembly, add the missing democratic component to the legitimation framework of the paradigm.[51]

The Hungarian pattern, as many participants of the Round Table realized, had all the legitimation difficulties of this model in general, adding some Hungarian specificities. None of the participants were democratically elected. The old ruling party played an important role. The new participants, though they established their credentials in the Oppositional Round Table, were formally present at the invitation of the ruling party, except for FIDESZ, which was brought in against the will of that party. Others, like the radical Hungarian October Party, were excluded and demonstrated against this exclusion. Public visibility and accountability were weak, especially due to the wishes of the old ruling party but readily conceded by some oppositional actors, mostly the moderate opposition and the legal experts. The presence of the old parliament in the process was too active, repeatedly modifying some of the agreements. It changed the electoral rule, added to the laws that could only be enacted with qualified majorities, and altered the mode of presidential elections according to the positions of the then still ruling communist party. There were well-founded rumors of private deals between leaders of the old ruling party and new party leaders that violated the consensual nature of the agreements. The process subsequently allowed a relatively large-scale conversion (in Hungarian: *átmentés*) of previous political to new economic powers. While a program of retributive justice was rightly excluded, nothing like a truth and reconciliation process was provided for. Most seriously, while the new constitution was formally pronounced as provisional, no procedures were enacted concerning the making of the final constitution. Thus the illusion was created that in a non-democratic, only partially legitimated instance, the Round Table created Hungary's permanent constitution.

[51] The thirty-four substantive constitutional principles, agreed upon at the Multi Party Negotiating Forum in South Africa apparently contradict this last claim. They were necessary under the circumstances of extreme societal division, and possible in my view, because of the charismatic nature of the ANC and its leadership.

At the same time, leaving the single chamber amendment rule of the 1949 constitution in place, the expectation was created that governments in power would continue to repeatedly modify the new constitution according to their shifting interests as incumbents, thereby obliterating the two-track structure distinguishing between constitutional and normal politics. This idea was confirmed by the pact of 1990 of two opposing parties with less than 50 percent of the popular vote, but over two-thirds of the seats, that modified the constitution substantially, without however producing a new one. FIDESZ, I should admit, was at that time rightly critical of the pact between the Alliance of Free Democrats (SZDSZ) and the Hungarian Democratic Forum (MDF), not so much of the substance of the agreements as of its exclusionary form.

I do not say that the process was therefore not legitimated at all. The Hungarian version of the Round Table, the NKA, has realized some but not all of the desiderata that has helped to legitimate other broadly similar processes, above all the one in South Africa. There was a wide inclusion of nine very different participants in that Round Table. The plenary sessions at least were public, though the more important actual negotiating sessions were not. The rule of law was rigorously maintained. Or in the terminology of Kis, all negotiating parties adhered to the rules of the game, until the old Communist parliament explicitly violated the Round Table agreements and the fundamental assumption underlying them by amending the new constitution to allow for the direct election of the president. That move was unfortunately supported by one of the very first decisions of the Constitutional Court, whose very wording allowed the old parliament to be a "constituent power" after all. Yet before this happened the referendum of 1989 managed to overcome the seemingly corrupt bargain concerning the election of the president of the republic, even if it unfortunately brought even more attention to it. The referendum was the only moment of popular participation in the process, important for that very reason. But to produce the full political legitimacy associated with the model, its completion was in my view necessary. This could have been done even without the initial enactment of the necessary rules, by using the existing amendment rule to produce new rules. However, it was important in this process to avoid even the appearance that a new constitution would be expressing merely incumbent advantage and the desire for political preservation of power. This was increasingly difficult, when several elections and their results fully punctured the veil of ignorance.

To sum up, because of their consciousness of their own legitimacy problems the round-table-led constitution-making paradigm represents potentially workshops of legitimation. I have in particular insisted on the likelihood of martialing pluralist inclusion, consensual decision making, publicity, and legality during all stages of the process and democratic elections during the second stage.[52] To me all these desiderata, and especially their combination, allow for normative

[52] Arato, "Post Sovereign Constitution-making in Hungary" and A. Arato, "Regime Change, Revolution and Legitimacy" in G.A. Tóth (ed.), *Constitution for a Disunited Nation* (Budapest: CEU Press, 2012).

justification,[53] and can play a role in promoting empirical beliefs in legitimacy. All of them were realized in South Africa, but in Hungary consensus was only fostered regarding the ultimate goal, publicity was largely excluded, and democratic elections failed to play the required role. These omissions are best seen within a comparative framework, since, under what was likely the best constitution in Hungarian history, constitutional substance helped to disguise the problems. Because of that substance it is impossible to speak of a legitimation crisis as under the old regime in 1988–89, only legitimation problems. These problems led to the crisis of the constitution of 1989–90 only in the context of serious structural flaws in the constitutional design, to which I now turn.

IV STRUCTURAL PROBLEMS

If an interim constitution does not provide for procedures for making the final one, along with the necessary incentives to follow these, it seems to take serious structural problems within the multi-stage model to produce a final constitution. There were such problems in Poland, where struggles between parliament and the state president produced a great deal of confusion and instability.[54] It was generally assumed that Hungary's interim constitution had no analogous structural flaw, thus there was no "compulsion to make a constitution" (*alkotmányozási kényszer*). I have always hated that expression, and disagreed with the diagnosis. But I was unfortunately more or less alone, Cassandra-like, in understanding that the combination of a highly disproportionate electoral rule and an easy, parliamentary single chamber amendment rule without any limitation functioned as a kind of sword of Damocles hanging over the constitution.[55] After FIDESZ's use of these rules between 2010 and 2014, no one should have doubts in this matter.[56]

The origins of these two rules were quite different. While the electoral rule emerged from a process of deliberate compromise[57] in which government and the opposition parties, both relatively strong as well as relatively weak, had a chance to make significant inputs.[58] Almost all parties misunderstood their coming electoral interests, contributing to an empirical veil of ignorance over the

[53] Indeed their discovery requires a normative perspective, as I have learned from Habermas. See J. Habermas, *Legitimation Crisis* (Boston, MA: Beacon, 1975).

[54] Arato, *Civil Society* Chapter 6.

[55] In Hungarian see *Civil társadalom, forradalom és alkotmány* (Budapest: Uj mandátum, 1999) 245–71; in English see for example A. Arato, "Election, coalition and constitution in Hungary" (1994) 35 *The Hungarian Quarterly* 3; B. Kiraly, *Lawful Revolution in Hungary* 1989–1994 (New Jersey: Atlantic Highlands, 1995); and Arato, "Post Sovereign Constitution-making in Hungary."

[56] I think the politicians of FIDESZ got the point during the MDF-SZDSZ Pact in 1990 that excluded them, when 46 percent of the votes yielded over two-thirds of the seats.

[57] For the discussion within the EKA see Bozóki et al., *A rendszerváltás forgatókönyve* v. III 90–135.

[58] Schiemann, "A választási törvény megalkotása" in Elster, *The Round Table Talks*; also his book, *Politics of Pact Making*.

process. The rule is a mixed, two-ballot, two-round rule, that appears fair in the sense that it incorporated all perspectives, even after it was amended (on the mistaken interests of individually elected deputies) by the last Communist parliament. Within the projected 386-member parliament it contained 176 single member seats, to be elected in two rounds, up to 152 seats elected in proportional competition with county lists, a 4 percent national cut-off threshold, and a small national compensational list of at least 58 seats. As is now well known, the ruling party and its parliamentary deputies both originally preferred single member constituencies, but so did the liberal SZDSZ, both mistakenly as it turned out. The three historical parties rightly preferred proportional representation, but wrongly pushed for more disproportional county lists, and, even more wrongly, accepted the 4 percent threshold.[59] The National Round Table participants may have mistakenly thought that the overall scheme resembled the mostly proportional two-ballot German system, with a cut-off. In their defense, we can admit that no one knew how disproportional this complex system would be in practice.[60] Later interpreters were more at fault in not noticing or stressing this disproportionality or considering it acceptable because of the needs of governability and stability of governments.[61] They were even more wrong in not understanding that such high disproportionality, even an exclusionary threshold that dramatically reduces the number of parties,[62] is inappropriate when electing constitution-making assemblies, as three out of six parliamentary assemblies elected under this rule turned out to be. They can be partially excused for these mistakes, because in three elections, from 1998 to 2006, disproportionality indeed decreased, empirically.[63] However, this did not diminish the theoretical reasons why it could significantly rise again.[64]

In the Hungarian case the difference between the votes and seats of parties that benefit from the count was indeed very high, and as opposed to British and Americans versions also highly visible because of the importance of the national vote count. It was 21 percent in 1990; almost 24 in 1994, 12.5 in 1998; 11 in 2006, 6.5 in 2006, and 16 percent in 2010.[65] This meant that the constitution-making majority that played that role or attempted to do so would most likely be one manufactured by the electoral rule, whether this happened for a minority as in 1990 or slim majorities in 1994 and 2010. The reason why the Hungarian electoral rule

[59] Bozóki et al., *A rendszerváltás forgatókönyve* III. 110, 116.

[60] G. Szoboszlai, "Választási rendszer, választójog" (2006) *Fundamentum* 3, who argues that some like József Antall assumed, on a mistaken German analogy, that the proposed mixed system would be proportional.

[61] M. Dezső, "Választási rendszer, választójog" (2006) *Fundamentum* 3.

[62] See G. Wiener, "Választási rendszer, választójog" (2006) *Fundamentum* 3.

[63] Dezső, "Választási rendszer, választójog"; Szoboszlai, "Választási rendszer, választójog."

[64] As I warned repeatedly—see interview with me in the same issue of (2006) *Fundamentum* 3. The distinction between party structure (responsible for the temporary drop in D, or the index of disproportionality) and the electoral rules is made by Wiener, "Választási rendszer, választójog" 72, 73, thus affirming the structural disproportionality, in spite of the then still empirical trend.

[65] For a slightly different but analogous calculation see Wiener, "Választási rendszer, választójog" 71, 72.

has been so disproportional is complex and has misled some interpreters. For example, F. Rueb has claimed that around 50 percent of the votes, while earning a surplus of seats, could nevertheless not yield a constitution-amending majority of two-thirds.[66] Not only has he been factually as well as theoretically wrong to make such a claim in light of the 1990 and 1994 elections, when two parties, each time, could convert a minority or bare majority of votes into the amending number of two-thirds of the seats, but as 2010 was to show, even a single party, FIDESZ, could make the very same conversion of votes into seats.

For comparative purposes it is worthwhile to look at the disproportionality in other round-table countries in the constitution-making period. In Bulgaria, the GDR, and South Africa, only one election in each was relevant, and the respective figures were: 6 percent, 0 percent and 0.35 percent. In Poland, more similar to Hungary's fragmented process, two elections should count (1991, 1993, with a disproportionality of 5.5 percent in 1991—but to the benefit of five parties with a 1 percent gain each—and over 29 percent in 1993). Note, however, that the second result came about not because of a Hungarian-type disproportionality of the rule, but was in large part caused by the strategies of parties, in light of a new 5 percent threshold. In any case, the result created serious legitimation problems, with President Walesa initially claiming, with some effect, that he must represent the excluded parties and voters.[67] The crisis of constitution making that was the initial result was temporarily resolved with important concessions to the participation of excluded parties and groups, and more definitely with Walesa's loss in the ensuing presidential election.[68] Similarly, in Bulgaria the relatively small disproportionality in the elections of the constitution-making Grand National Assembly in 1990 contributed to a very divisive process, though here the speed of rushing to elections was a more important factor.

What is the theoretical point in all this? Different genuinely competitive electoral rules can be justified, depending on the purpose of the assembly that is being elected. As for disproportional rules, their defenders justify partial misrepresentation through the criterion of governability. The problem is, however, that when the purpose is electing a constitution-making body, the inclusion of all those politically active is a high desideratum. Admittedly, a highly fragmented assembly produced by very proportional rules can lead to decision problems, as it did in Poland between 1991 and 1993. Putting parties with manufactured amending majorities in the position where they are able to impose constitutional settlements on minorities cannot be justified, as Osiatinsky rightly

[66] In Elster, Offe, and Preuss, *Institutional Design* 124, 142.

[67] Arato, *Civil Society* Chapter 6; W. Osiatynski, "Poland's Constitutional Ordeal" (1994) 3 *East European Constitutional Review* 2 29; W. Osiatynski, "A Brief History of the Constitution" (1997) 6 *East European Constitutional Review* 3 66.

[68] See the excellent article by L. Garlicki and Z.A. Garlicka, "Constitution Making, Peace Building and National Reconciliation: The Experience of Poland" in Miller, *Framing the State* for the details and the interaction of electoral rules and constitution making in Poland. I have presented the process, with a similar interpretation in *Civil Society* Chapter 6.

stressed for Poland in light of its temporary constitutional impasse after the elections of 1993.[69] This distinction, between governability and representation, is an additional reason for (doubly) differentiating between legislative and constitution-making assemblies, as in American convention models after 1781, in addition to the important criterion of inhibiting self-serving and self-aggrandizing behavior by legislatures. When such a differentiation is not possible, as it was not in Hungary or Poland, the other rules, the electoral rule and the constitution-making or amending rule take on the same public-regarding functions as double differentiation. That the electoral rule can make a huge difference in helping to avoid both majoritarian imposition as well as bias for the legislative branch has been shown by the recent examples of Colombia (1991) and Tunisia (1994) in contrast to countries where the rules were (Venezuela, 1999) or appeared to be much more disproportional (Egypt in 2012). One great advantage of the multi-stage process is that this lesson can be learned mid-stream, after democratic elections. This is what happened in Poland. But as the history of elections between 1990 and 2010 in Hungary have shown, the lesson there was not learned. Indeed the one important change to the electoral rules, during the parliamentary session of 1990–94, made them even more disproportional by raising the threshold from 4 to 5 percent. A very promising attempt to keep a mixed system, but to change it into one resembling the German "personalized proportional system" failed during the parliamentary session of 2006–10.[70] By then the writing was on the wall, but, as usual, too late.

Of course, if well constructed a constitution-making rule could diminish the importance and dangers of the electoral rule, even if it is disproportional.[71] Not only can the consensus requirement be made more effective than using simply a higher percentage of votes required, but referenda, and even organized public discussion can play a role in policing authoritarian tendencies. So can the requirement that two parliaments with an election in between enact the required changes. Many Hungarian analysts have habitually disregarded this relationship. Unfortunately, it could be said that, contrary to the electoral rule, the constitution-amending rule, and the omission of new rules of constitution making all emerged in a fit of absent-mindedness, probably favored by two dimensions of Hungarian history: the Anglophile tradition of the absence of a written constitution and the old Marxist opposition to the separation of powers. Both led to a paper constitution in 1949 in which parliamentary sovereignty became what orthodoxy has been described in Israel—the synagogue to which one did not go to. It was this rule, the inherited constitutional amending rule,

[69] Osiatynski, "Poland's Constitutional Ordeal."

[70] For the details, see Wiener, "Választási rendszer, választójog" 75. I have already recommended adopting the more or less proportional German system in 1994, and it seemed for a while that the center left coalition wished to move in that direction. See Arato, "Election, Coalition and Constitution in Hungary" 126–7.

[71] Dezső, "Választási rendszer, választójog," who defends the disproportional rules in Hungary on behalf of governability, and thinks these rules satisfy modern European requirements, to her credit makes the suggestion of changing the amendment rule.

two-thirds of the absolute number of a single chamber parliament (art. 14-3, 1949; art. 23-3 until 2010; art. S-1 and S-2, 2012), which does not in any way distinguish between amendment and replacement, survives the demise of two constitutions. Thus given the high importance of amending rules it has never been true that, according to an old adage, "the only thing left of the Stalinist Constitution of 1949 was that the capital of Hungary is Budapest." This joke, which expresses the position of most of the serious literature, disregards the very major matter of the amendment rule.[72]

The tradition of parliamentary sovereignty[73] has been renewed by the formal dimension of round-table constitution making, according to which in 1989 it was the regular parliament that enacted the interim constitution in the form of normal amendments. This formality was coupled with the legitimation problems of extra-legal unelected round tables that did not try nor wish to justify their own work by trying to legalize their own extraordinary status, or seriously entrench the compromises made. The effect was exacerbated by the fact that the enacting parliament came into being as a result of tightly controlled Communist elections, only very partially competitive. Thus it was generally doubted that an ordinary parliament, especially a highly tainted one, could tie the hands of subsequent parliaments, especially ones freely elected, by "casting in cement" as the Hungarian saying goes, its constitutional product. The argument survived in all freely elected parliaments as well, down to the constitution-making one dominated by FIDESZ, which, in spite of early plans, left the amendment rule as it had been ever since 1949. Undoubtedly political interests of dominant parties, wishing to keep a free hand in altering the constitution whenever they pleased, played a role. In the case of the Round Table constitution, dubbed interim, this desire was more legitimate, though as the South African parliament demonstrated, a negotiated settlement could contain detailed rules of constitution making binding all parties. For that to happen, however, the parties have to understand the symbolic force of the solemn promise they make to one another.

That only happened in South Africa. Here new rules of constitution making were enacted in the interim constitution, distinguished from the amendment rule of the latter.[74] The rules for the making of the new constitution, produced by MPNF negotiations, involved both the joint seating of two chambers, a two-thirds vote of the "constitutional assembly," fail-safe rules that if the body did not succeed in two years a referendum would potentially be held, as well as rules

[72] There are important exceptions, however. Sajó's early essay "Round Table Talks in Hungary" was one; along with his *Az önkorlátozó hatalom* (Budapest 1995) 54ff and a few attacks by J. Sólyom from the very logical perspective of the Constitutional Court. See *Az alkotmánybíráskodás kezdetei Magyarországon* (Budapest: Osiris, 2001) 155. Most developed is the critique of Bragyova, *Az új alkotmány egy koncepciója* especially Chapter 7, who distinguishes between a merely legislative amendment rule like the Hungarian, and a constituent one, that he seems to prefer, before recommending their multi-leveled combination.

[73] See Bragyova, *Az új alkotmány egy koncepciója* 271.

[74] Interim Constitution of South Africa 62 (amendment rule of the interim document itself) and 68–74 (rules of the making of the new constitution) http://www.constitutionalcourt.org.za/site/constitution/english-web/interim/ch5.html accessed December 2, 2015.

for certification and if need be, recertification by the new Constitutional Court. In Central Europe, no round table assumed it had the legitimacy to require difficult constituent rules to be followed by freely elected assemblies. In Bulgaria, nevertheless, the first of the latter, the Grand National Assembly, was to accomplish this very task in producing a two-level, differentiated revision rule, which made fundamental changes to the constitution much more difficult, involving the popular election of a new Grand National Assembly in the process.[75] Again, Poland was closest to Hungary, because here even the first freely elected parliament was not able to produce a permanent constitution. Yet in Poland, that body did produce both detailed rules for the making of a new constitution,[76] along with an interim "small constitution" that unlike the Hungarian document of 1989–90 incorporated these rules.[77] The rules involved the two chambers, Sejm and Senate, producing a joint drafting committee as well as meeting together, and voting by a two-thirds majority to enact the new constitution, which then had to be confirmed in a popular referendum.[78] Importantly, the combined rules distinguished between amending rules, which remained in the hands of two-thirds of the lower chamber,[79] and the making of the new constitution by the national assembly cum referendum formula. The amendment resembled the one in Hungary, but the two rules together were closer to the earlier Bulgarian rules in form if not in contents. While the Constitutional Tribunal's role in policing the distinction was theoretically weakened by an override clause[80] absent in Bulgaria as well as Hungary, the Polish "national assembly" rules for constitution making did yield a new constitution in 1997, even if after a very long third-stage process, delayed by first parliamentary fragmentation and later by extra-parliamentary strategies led by the President of the republic, Lech Walesa.[81] Thus Hungary remained exceptional with its one-chamber, two-thirds amendment rule, involving no formal differentiation between amending and making or replacing.[82]

[75] Constitution of Bulgaria, Arts. 153–63. The Grand National Assembly has important restrictions here. It can act only on revision proposals for which it was elected, and must decide by two-thirds of all the members. The first Grand National Assembly was elected under the only restriction of having to vote by the qualified majority of two-thirds. Peeva, "A bolgár kerekasztal tárgyalások összehasonlító szempontból." The point was moot, since in spite of a partial boycott, 309 members out of 400 accepted the draft.

[76] Constitutional Law, April 23, 1992.

[77] Constitutional Law, October 17, 1992, Art. 27.

[78] See Garlicki and Garlicka, "Constitution Making, Peace Building and National Reconciliation"; Osiatinsky, "Poland's Constitutional Ordeal"; as well as Arato, *Civil Society* Chapter 6.

[79] Constitutional Law, October 17, 1992, Art. 106.

[80] The rules for the Constitutional Tribunal in the Small Constitution simply preserved the rules, including the override provision, from the inherited Communist Constitution that established the Tribunal in 1982.

[81] Garlicki and Garlicka, "Constitution Making, Peace Building and National Reconciliation."

[82] Until, as I will show below, the "parentheses" of 1994–98, which in this respect was badly conceived and failed.

Unsurprisingly, the most serious objections to the existing amendment rule in Hungary came from the one institution clearly incompatible with parliamentary sovereignty, the Constitutional Court.[83] It was not a surprise, because the amendment rule as it stands represents a tacit override clause. I have already mentioned that the project of the old Hungarian Ministry of Justice in 1988 and early 1989 for a constitutional court involved an override clause, however inconsistent that was within the conception with its mixed attempts at conversion and seeking guarantees. This clause started out as one requiring only the absolute majority of parliament to reverse a decision of invalidation.[84] With the retreat of the MSZMP from seeking conversion to seeking guarantees by way of consociational forms, the majority required to override the Constitutional Court was increased to two-thirds of members present, as in the case of the so-called two-thirds laws.[85] At this point the proposal resembled the Polish rule in effect until 1997. Finally, in the Round Table agreement the feature of a parliamentary override was eliminated.[86] Few have noticed, however, that the parliamentary constitutional amendment rule, requiring the vote of two-thirds of all the members, is only marginally different than the last MSZMP proposal, and was itself potentially an override clause. It was repeatedly used as such from 1990 to the present, with the recent cases, in which the FIDESZ government was involved, drawing the objection of the Venice Commission of the Council of Europe.[87]

When objecting to the amendment rule, it is this feature of an implicit override provision that members of the Constitutional Court undoubtedly hated the most. In particular Sólyom strongly objected to this rule and especially its repeated use, mostly for purposes of ordinary, daily politics. His view of the post 1989 use of the amending power has always been very negative, starting with the Pécs conference where I first met him, during the amendment round following the MDF-SZDSZ pact in 1990. He considered the amendments to the constitution, according to him numbering thirty or so, insignificant for constitutional development, with the exception of three or four provisions.[88] While much in this attitude can be supported, nevertheless it reveals the contempt of the lawyer for mere politicians, lamenting in effect that "the hour of the lawyers" had passed. What is behind the argument, however, is the belief that under any traditional conception of the constituent power, there cannot be two such competing powers in the state.

While there have been many activist courts in history, it would be hard to find another major jurist who so explicitly affirms the power and authority of a court

[83] Sólyom, *Az alkotmánybiráskodás kezdetei.*

[84] Schiemann, *The Politics of Pact-Making* 117. [85] Ibid. 122.

[86] For the debate that settled this, see Bozóki et al., *A rendszerváltás forgatókönyve* vol. IV, 410–13.

[87] Venice Commission on the Fourth Amendment to the Fundamental Law.

[88] Sólyom, "A jogállami forradalomtól az EU csatakozásig" 9; "The Role of Constitutional Courts in the Transition to Democracy" 286.

to freely interpret the law of the constitution.[89] Sólyom wrongly imagines that given what has been called the new constitutionalism, the charge of *un gouvernement des juges* is merely a matter from over a hundred years ago when Lambert coined the phrase. He has been misinformed, as the great success of the juristocracy thesis has shown.[90] Nevertheless, he is factually right concerning the emergence of judicial activism in Hungary—only he should not have exaggerated it, and made such a great virtue of it rather than recognizing it as a reluctant necessity (one that, as I shall try to show, could not in the end succeed).[91]

According to Sólyom, the very situation in which the new regime was inaugurated by amendments and a patchwork constitution rather than an entirely and formally new one, was favorable for a constitutional court. That body could thus develop "unwritten constitutional principles, substitute rules and creative interpretations." And, it could fill in the many gaps, as well as satisfy "the symbolic needs of the people" neglected in the original process.[92] But could such activism itself be made legitimate? To make that argument, Sólyom has elsewhere had to claim that the round-table constitution was a final one, having exactly the same status as all other liberal democratic constitutions, and that the self-affirmation of the document as interim was either a mistake, or worse an addition by the illegitimate parliament contrary to the views of the round table. In other words, he neglects the deep doubts of the participants, himself among them originally, to produce a new constitution through the old parliament, or even by the unelected round table behind it. Thus the addition of the preamble by the parliament, containing a reference to an interim status, expressed the views of the opposition at the Round Table rather than the government, which was much more interested in fully constitutionalizing the negotiated agreements.[93]

However, if we consider the round-table constitution as fully valid as Sólyom does, it was wrong to deny its own textual claim regarding the interim status, even if no rules or timetables were provided to produce a final, definitive document. In spite of his flirtation with Schmittian mythology, here the jurist turns fully positivist and Kelsenian—if unenforceable, apparently, a preamble has no

[89] One should not, however, confuse Sólyom's highly activist views with the actual practice of the Constitutional Court, which was certainly less aggressive. External interpreters who know Sólyom better than the case law such as Ackerman, Scheppele and myself, are prone to make this mistake, as G.A. Tóth kindly pointed out to me in personal correspondence. For his own view of the activism problem see G.A. Tóth, *Túl a szövegen. Értekezés a magyar alkotmányról* (Budapest: Osiris, 2009).

[90] See both R. Hirschl, *Towards Juristocracy* (Cambridge, MA: Harvard, 2004) and J. Waldron, *The Dignity of Legislation* (Cambridge: Cambridge University Press, 1999).

[91] On activism and the Hungarian debates around it, see Tóth, *Túl a szövegen*.

[92] Sólyom, "The Role of Constitutional Courts in the Transition to Democracy" 305.

[93] That view of the government was strongly contested by many jurists, including A. Bragyova, himself a constitutional judge between 2005 and 2014. Bragyova, *Az új alkotmány egy koncepciója* 17.

normative validity. Hence there was no need to complete the project of constitution making at all or, if it was to be completed, that was the job of the Constitutional Court and that Court alone, as Scheppele too maintained even after the FIDESZ constitution making of 2010–11. This was Sólyom's version of the absence of a "compulsion to make a constitution" (*alkotmányozási kényszer*). Perhaps one element of completion was nevertheless needed, namely the resolution of the potential conflict between two quasi-constituent powers, the Court and the amending power. In principle this could happen either through the act of amending power, or the Constitutional Court. The first would require a new procedurally and substantively legitimate constitution preserving the public law structure of the regime change, but one better entrenched against purely majoritarian alteration. The second would have required, even according to Sólyom, "a fundamental re-interpretation of the status of constitutional adjudication."[94] In Hungary, as I will now try to show, both were tried and both failed, opening the door to a "revolution of the voting booth."

V TWO PARLIAMENTARY ATTEMPTS TO COMPLETE THE LIBERAL DEMOCRATIC CONSTITUTION

By completion of the constitution-making process, I mean both the generation of a significantly higher level of legitimacy for the constitution than for ordinary laws enacted under it, and the creation of a rule of change that can entrench the higher law against ordinary legislative and executive attempts to alter and especially to replace it. Concerning only the second dimension, the entrenchment, a mere "revision of the revision" could technically attain it, in other words the use of the inherited amendment rule to create a new, and better one. While no longer deemed illogical, as by Alf Ross or even prima facie illegitimate, as by Carl Schmitt, such a revision of the revision has long been considered problematic in the tradition of parliamentary government. In the British context, for example, the right of a parliament to tie the hands of another parliament was never recognized—although, as H.L.A. Hart has shown, both options of denying entrenchment and affirming its possibility could equally follow from the supposed omnipotence of parliament. In the American tradition, it has been historically assumed since Jefferson that only the authority of a body drawing on greater legitimacy, in particular popular sovereignty and generally a process involving a constitutional convention, could entrench the constitution against the acts of ordinary legislatures.

Undoubtedly, even at the time when the circles around the new Hungarian Constitutional Court were highly skeptical concerning the making of a new constitution, a process that would likely produce a worse constitution in their view, they would have been happy with a revision of the revision. This alone would have partially freed the Court of the competition of a rival power to make

[94] Interview with G.A. Tóth (1997) *Fundamentum* 1.

or change the constitution. But given assumptions about parliamentary government, no one seriously proposed it, although there was a discussion of alternative amendment rules among jurists.[95] Undoubtedly, realistic expectations regarding political parties also played a role. While constitutional amending majorities were available in only three parliamentary sessions out of six, it was highly unlikely that parties in power would confine themselves to revising only the amendment rule if they had no substantive changes in mind. Early in their governmental period, the parties would not likely do it because it would mean tying their own hands and enhancing the power of the Court. Late during that period, they were open to the weighty charge of wishing to limit their successor after having themselves had the freedom to act. Earlier, they would not have had the motivation while later, legitimacy would be deficient. The only way that new rules for constitution making and amending would likely be produced was during a constitution-making project at the beginning of a parliamentary session in which all the parties mutually agreed to bind one another. Given such an agreement, a party to it would lose the claim to object to entrenchment when it was later in the dominant position. Among the four constitution-making episodes in Hungary this happened only once, and even then without success.

The first such episode was the already discussed round-table-led process, which as we have seen had severe legitimacy problems. At that time the idea of changing the 1949 amendment rule or producing new rules for constitution making never seemed to come up at all. It was then assumed by many that the first free elections would yield a constitution-making parliament as in Spain earlier. There were similar expectations even with respect to the first, only partially democratic Polish Sejm, though these too were disappointed.[96] The first freely elected Hungarian parliament did not do as well as the "contractual Sejm" with respect to the production of a constitution, even though it possessed greater legitimacy. To deal with the many serious problems of the Round Table constitution, the approach that emerged was a pact between the two biggest parties, the MDF and the SZDSZ, one governmental and the other in opposition.[97] This was in a sense a consensual effort, but hardly an inclusive one, especially when compared to the composition of the EKA and the NKA.[98] The partners and allies of the two parties were not consulted, nor was the MSZP, which retained some significant representation in parliament. No public discussion was organized,

[95] In his unpublished constitutional draft of 1989 Sajó suggested the use of a special second chamber for the purpose; others, such as M. Dezső and G. Halmai, discussed the role of referenda, the use of two parliamentary sessions, the expansion of the parliamentary committee with outside participants, as well as the use of a second chamber elected only for that purpose. Bragyova, *Az új alkotmány egy koncepciója* 272–5 came out for a multi-leveled structure, close to my preference, though I would have preferred a highest, but still amendable, track as in South Africa, while he supported eternity clauses.

[96] Garlicki and Garlicka, "Constitution Making, Peace Building and National Reconciliation"; Osiatinsky, "Poland's Constitutional Ordeal."

[97] For the history and the procedural aspects, see Arato and Miklósi, "Constitution Making and Transitional Politics"; for the contents, see Tordai, "A Harmadik Köztársaság alkotmányának születése."

[98] Halmai, "Az 1949es alkotmány jogállamositása" 185.

nor was the pact publicized until the short deliberation in parliament. Probably the ideal moment for constitution making, for closing and legitimating the round-table-led process was missed, at a time when the three most important new parties supporting the regime change and its emerging public law model, the MDF as led by Prime Minister Antall, SZDSZ and FIDESZ together were in a dominant position.

I do not know if the negotiators of the SZDSZ and the MDF considered or raised the question of making a new constitution rather than agreeing only to a limited and exclusionary bargain. It is almost unthinkable that they were entirely unaware of such an option. I must therefore assume that they rejected it. As it turned out afterwards, both the worldview and relationship to Hungarian history of the two contracting parties was very different, even though they shared the preference of their leaders for a more or less pure as well as strong parliamentary government, balanced only by a strong constitutional court. Thus they may not have thought that they were capable of an agreement beyond the points included in the pact, which hardly amounted to a full constitution. If this was the reason, it was a mistaken one, because the kind of differences in worldview that existed between them could have been compromised. The symbolic affirmations of identity about which they disagreed could have been kept to a minimum. Polarization between MDF and SZDSZ seemed to prove the thesis of a lack of trust, but precisely that polarization could have been reduced by a constitution-making effort, especially since that would have weakened the second revolutionaries within the MDF, the main agents behind the increasing antagonism of the two largest parties. Thus, in earlier essays I have suggested that the perceived problem was with the other partners, who had to be brought into a fully consensual, inclusive process.[99] For the MDF, the main governmental party, seeking a strong and stable government, the continued insistence of two parties, FIDESZ and MSZP on keeping elements of consensus if not consociational democracy was unacceptable. For the SZDSZ, on the other hand, the presidentialist and corporatist ideas of both the MSZP and the historical parties allied with the MDF, the FKGP (the Small Holders) and KDNP (the Christian Democrats) were even more so. It was assumed, probably rightly, that a consensual and inclusive process would have to mean that some of the ideas rejected by the two eventually contracting parties would find their way into the constitution. This is what I mean by a result orientation: in search of the best possible constitutional contents, the actual process of making it was sacrificed. This might have happened at small cost if the method of constitution making did not matter, but in Hungary it turned out that it very much does.

[99] See Arato, *Civil Society* 210–11; Arato and Miklósi, "Constitution Making and Transitional Politics" 367. There is also relevant material in Halmai, "Az 1949es alkotmány jogállamositása," but in relation to the next attempt at formal constitution making, after 1994; and also Tordai, "A Harmadik Köztársaság alkotmányának születése," but only in relation to the vote on the agreed upon amendments, explaining the negative vote of the MSZP and the abstention of FIDESZ.

In retrospect, I find the likely fears behind the reticence to generate a new constitution in 1990 exaggerated, and that the dangers could have been reduced with proper organization of the consensual process. Even with each party receiving an equal role, the power of the largest two in the end could have counteracted outcomes that tilted too far in undesirable directions. The organization of public discussion, in which newspapers and the academic communities played a role, might have had the desired effect of eliminating absurd suggestions such as the revival of the purely symbolic Holy Crown doctrine, for some incomprehensible reason attractive to the Small Holders. Moreover, some of the preferences of the excluded parties were probably less strong at the time than they may have seemed. While the MSZP still kept reintroducing the idea of a directly elected president, in 1990, with only 10 percent of the vote, they had little practical interest in the matter. They could thereby no longer hope to influence parliamentary elections, or to elect their own candidate.

It is true that some undesirable elements, probably mostly symbolic ones, might have found their way into a fully consensual constitution. This happened even in Poland, where the Church's viewpoints had to be accommodated by an almost entirely secular drafting assembly.[100] In Hungary such outcomes, and such accommodation, were excluded by the result orientation of the two contracting parties. Improvements to the constitutional contents were very real. Most important for governability was the reduction of the number of two-thirds laws and the elimination of the plastic category of constitutional laws that the court already used to require two-thirds support for all laws affecting rights. The introduction of the constructive vote of no confidence was also potentially important for governmental stability, even though there is some disagreement on this score.[101] The return to the parliamentary election of the president with the support of the early Constitutional Court, which reaffirmed the terms of the Round Table agreement violated by the old parliament, was also symbolically important, though the significance of the matter was no longer what it was initially. Finally, it was a good idea to strengthen the status of fundamental rights, and to include a habeas corpus provision, though the latter was accomplished as a result of an amendment offered by FIDESZ from the floor.

It is notable, however, that despite some contributions of its own, FIDESZ joined the MSZP in not voting for the package as a whole, by its own abstention. It is a striking fact that the two parties that were to become the leading forces in Hungary from 1994 up to the present day did not vote for the pact that was to complete the effort of the Round Table by increasing its purely parliamentary character and reducing its consensual dimensions. This if anything indicates the legitimation problems of the exercise. Despite its achievements on the level of results, the legitimation consequences were the opposite of what the two main

[100] Garlicki and Garlicka, "Constitution Making, Peace Building and National Reconciliation."

[101] Tordai, "A Harmadik Köztársaság alkotmányának születés" 496–7. Such stability was the result of the disproportional electoral rule, he argues, gliding by the very negative consequences of that arrangement.

actors may have expected. The country saw the pact as a whole as yet another elite agreement, serving elite interests rather than the public's. From the point of view of the excluded parties it was deemed even worse, as essentially an exclusionary pact. These reactions were in a sense unfair, perhaps, because the agreements had many features indeed important for the country as a whole. They helped to create a government that could act and that was relatively stable. Yet the public perception highlighted one genuine problem, namely the relative hostility of liberal and conservative elites to democratic participation. Similarly, the excluded parties rightly understood that the leading idea behind the pact was majoritarian, purely parliamentary democracy. On the level of legitimation, then, the costs were much higher than the benefits. Yet, in spite of the negative reaction, including that of many right-wing politicians and publicists even in the camp of the MDF, the result orientation survived, and was especially supported among those liberals and conservatives close to the Constitutional Court.[102]

The politicians of all parties were apparently chastened by the experience of the pact, and most of all by its negative or at best neutral reception. In 1994 all the parties included the project of constitution making, differently understood, in their electoral platforms. Such political claims at election time could have been disregarded, accept for the fact that the parties that formed the new governmental coalition achieved, with over 50% of the votes, a constitution-making/amending majority of over 70 percent of the seats. The SZDSZ, its allegiance not needed for governability, joined the coalition in part because of its desire to at least redraft and relegitimate the constitution. But the MSZP, having such a coalitional power behind it, could also not evade the task. Thus the coalition agreement contained the project of the making of a new consensual and conservative constitution. It was to be conservative, because, as expressed in an influential opinion by Kis in the daily *Népszabadság*, the goal was to preserve and relegitimate the public law arrangements of the Round Table constitution.[103] It was to be highly consensual, because there was a need to follow the inclusive logic of the round tables, as well as learn from the previous mistake of the making of the pact. Many have noticed that the electoral campaigns on the right focused their attacks on the SZDSZ in order to deprive a possible coalition of a

[102] Even as the coalition, elected in 1994, announced its plans to make a new constitution (see the coalition agreement, which I cite in Arato, "Elections, Coalition, Constitution") many near the Constitutional Court criticized the very idea, claimed that the constitution was already fine as it was, and that a new project could only make it worse. See not only the articles of Sólyom already cited, but essays of Majtényi and Halmai from 1994, cited by Halmai, "Az 1949es alkotmány jogállamositása" 199. The latter was to subsequently criticize his position. Ibid. 197–8. By 2004 he was even willing to accept my judgement that "the time bomb was ticking": See G. Halmai, "Régi kérdések – új válaszok?" in *"És mi lesz az alkotmánnyal"* (Budapest: Eötvös Károly Intézet, 2004) 6061. In 1999 he still hoped to defuse the bomb by protecting the 1989–90 constitution with all its legitimation problems. G. Halmai, "Az 1949es alkotmány jogállamositása" in Bozóki et al., *A rendszerváltás forgatókönyve*. By 2004 he suggested instead the creation of an amendment rule in a new constitution as a guarantee needed by all sides at the time.

[103] For a detailed justification of this position, implying the need for new "constitutional laws" (or Kelsen's formal constitution), but not a new constitution in the material sense, see Bragyova, *Az új alkotmány egy koncepciója* 11, 20, 23–4.

constitution-making majority. The right and principled response to this was to insist that the constitution would have to be made by including all the parties. In light of the old MSZMP's efforts even before the Round Table began to deliberate and its threats during the process to impose a constitution from above, the fears articulated in 1994, especially by FIDESZ, concerning the possibility of a "constitutional dictatorship" were by no means absurd or irrelevant. To counter such fears, the coalition therefore had to proceed and did emphatically proceed on the path of consensual constitution making.

With the rules of constitution making generated in 1994, the Hungarian transition process for a moment rejoined its Polish and South African analogs, where such rules were agreed upon in 1992 and 1993 respectively. The first step in this process was a partial revision of the amendment rule. Up until this point Article 23(3) of the constitution was both the amendment rule and the replacement rule. As to replacement, the new rule, Article 23(5) required that four-fifths of the parliament as a whole must agree to the rules for the making of the constitution. This stipulation was in addition, however, to the final approval rule, which remained the old Article 23(3), the parliamentary two-thirds rule. This old rule also remained in place for ordinary amendments, producing a three-track structure.[104] But in contrast to the rather undesirable Polish dualistic arrangement between 1992 and 1997, the new coalition announced a moratorium on amendments during the duration of the making of the new constitution. Unfortunately, however, the new constitution-making rule was not self-entrenched by the same four-fifths rule, and in one interpretation could have been at any time altered by the use of the ordinary amendment rule. The moratorium on ordinary amendments temporarily excluded that possibility. Even worse, incomprehensibly, the coalition that enacted the new rule sought to link it to a sunset provision the end point of which would come at the conclusion of the then current parliamentary session, most likely 1998. Thus, illogically, parliament enacted a form of self-binding that bound only itself, but not its successor, the reverse of what rational choice theory would admit as rational.[105] Curiously, however, the sunset clause was included only in the explanation of the amendment, not the norm-text itself, and was also explicitly included in the consensual

[104] A. Arato, "Multi Track Constitutionalism Beyond Carl Schmitt," (2011) 18 *Constellations* 3 324–51.

[105] Following Elster's distinction between binding the self and binding the other (J. Elster, *Ulysses Unbound* (Cambridge: Cambridge University Press, 2000)), I would rank, from the point of view of "rationality," the possibilities of binding parliaments in the following order:

1. (most plausible) binding only the next parliament, not itself
2. binding neither
3. binding both
4. (least plausible) binding itself, not the successor.

In Poland option 3 was realized in 1993, and in Hungary, option 4. Admittedly, ranking from the point of view of "legitimacy" may be 4–2/3–1. Binding both would have been, I think, both sufficiently legitimate and more rational than the option chosen.

rules produced by the use of the new replacement rule.[106] To this point I shall return.

The new detailed rules of constitution making enacted by the parliamentary four-fifths rule were very imaginative and conciliatory. They provided for a constitution drafting committee of twenty-four members with equal representation for each of the six parliamentary parties.[107] According to the voting rules, which were too restrictive as it turned out, not only did at least five parties have to vote by majority, but, almost superfluously, two-thirds of the twenty-four members had to vote in order for a new clause to be adopted. To protect the plan from such an onerous requirement, it was agreed that where no five-party agreement was possible, the relevant clause of the 1989–90 constitution would remain in effect. This provision also implicitly required a moratorium on amendments, so the coalition would be blocked from the subterfuge of the amendment rule to avoid complying with the new replacement rules. But it also represented the interests of conservative constitution making, stressed by Kis, resembling in function the South African thirty-four constitutional principles that tied the new constitution's main contents to the interim one. As in South Africa, the road in Hungary was apparently open to consensual constitution making based on the public law structure of the Round Table constitution.

However, the road soon closed. The story of how this happened is fairly well known, and I have told it more than once.[108] While the parliamentary drafting committee and its socialist chair consensually agreed on a draft of guidelines, which was really the first draft of a new constitution with a few elements missing, they did not receive the required two-thirds parliamentary support because of the negative votes of MSZP ministers led by Prime Minister Horn and Justice Minister Vastagh, who were allied with a number of hard right deputies in opposition, hardly in positive program, but whose negative attitude to the draft was not shared by the large majority of their own socialist caucus. The ministers could behave this way because the fall-back position of the continued survival of the 1989 Constitution was available. The fears of the democratic opposition at the Round Table, concerning the making of a complete constitution, even an interim one, were thus fulfilled. After this event no draft ever received the required committee and parliamentary support.

Here I am concerned with the reasons behind what happened, rather than with the astonishing events themselves, or the unfortunately mediocre draft

[106] Arato, "Post Sovereign Constitution-making in Hungary."

[107] When one of these, the MDF, split into conservative and radical wings, the surviving MDF repeatedly vetoed the inclusion of the new MDNP.

[108] From the actual period see M. Haraszti's witty, polemical but mostly to the point "Horn Gyula kicsi puccsa" (the little Putsch of Gyula Horn), *Népszabadság*, July 11, 1996. Halmai, "Az 1949es alkotmány jogállamositása" 185–91; Arato, *Civil society* 218–19; Arato and Miklósi, "Constitution Making and Transitional Politics in Hungary" 370–2.

itself.[109] A careful reconstruction of the positions of the main party representatives tells an important part of the story.[110] The socialist party leaders were interested in using the adjective "social" in defining the republic, in a strong catalogue of social rights, in institutionalizing a corporatist social partnership, possibly (but probably not too seriously) in a corporate second chamber, and still perhaps in the direct election of the president of the republic. Formally, Horn and his ministers referred only to the absence of the first three of these desiderata. On the other hand, the right-wing parties, including an MDF shorn of its moderate members, were much more serious about forging a stronger, directly elected presidency and a corporate upper chamber. They were also excessively interested in symbolic issues, such as the inclusion in the constitution of references to the Holy Crown, which supposedly embodied Hungarian statehood, and the historical constitution the contents of which by then were completely indeterminate.[111] More seriously, many of the main figures of the three right-wing parties sought to eliminate or dramatically reduce the powers of the Constitutional Court, whose past decisions on retroactive justice and the reprivatization of property they resented. One proposal, from a former (MDF) minister of justice and today a Constitutional Court judge, was the replacement of the constitutional guardianship of the Court by that of a new upper chamber.

These proposals and projects are at the basis of the argument that there was no sufficient consensus either to preserve or to replace the constitution of 1989. Accordingly, the process failed. As we have seen, according to János Kis, the constitution of a political community cannot be produced on the basis of mere compromise, and a fundamental consensus on the aims was needed. In his view this existed in 1989, but not in 1996, as this catalog of alternative views purports to show. In my view, however, the catalog is only part of the story. The other part is that at least five parties, or the majority of three of their representatives in the drafting committee, managed to agree to a draft, which unexciting as it was, was a workable constitution capable of preserving and continuing the public law structure of the regime change. The socialist caucus itself strongly supported the same draft. All that was needed was to get a few socialist ministers and allies

[109] Aside from an overall bureaucratic and conventional tone, when compared to a constitution such as the final one adopted in South Africa, the draft did not even address the main structural problems of the inherited constitution, namely the amendment rule and the electoral system. Admittedly this involves a personal disappointment, because I submitted proposals to parliament on the first issue, more or less using the Spanish and Bulgarian rules as two alternative models. So did Bragyova, insisting also on eternity clauses in his own multi-leveled conception, Bragyova, *Az új alkotmány egy koncepciója* 272–5. While the guidelines in their first, consensual version chose not to address the issue that would have left the old two-thirds rule in place, a later version added a referendum that was not needed to approve but if initiated could reject a constitutional proposal.

[110] Halmai, "Az 1949es alkotmány jogállamositása" 185–90. Kis too has repeatedly returned to many of these proposals, obviously incompatible with the public law of 1989–90, but with one another as well. See J. Kis, "Introduction. From the 1989 Constitution to the 2011 Fundamental Law" in G.A. Tóth (ed.), *Constitution for a Disunited Nation* (Budapest: CEU Press, 2012).

[111] S. Radnóti, "A Sacred Symbol in a Secular Country: the Holy Crown" in Tóth, *Constitution for a Disunited Nation* 85–110.

to support it as well. It is too easily forgotten that they had more power than anyone else in the consensual process. To oppose them required both power, persuasion, and flexibility on the part of their opponents, especially in the SZDSZ, which went into the coalition in part at least for constitution-making reasons, or so many of us thought. As for power, it could have been made clear that the SZDSZ would leave the coalition if the sabotage continued. If it had been joined by some members of the Socialist caucus (and why not, there had been party splits before) that could have brought down the government, and would in any case weaken it by taking away the amending power and the power to enact two-thirds laws. Instead of using the weapon of ending the moratorium against the other parties, two of whom supported the draft (FIDESZ and the new MDNP), another threat, that of leaving the coalition should have been used against the MSZP leadership.

As for persuasion, this would have presupposed greater public and press involvement. From the outset it would have been possible to organize popular forms of soft participation, but in both the MSZP and the SZDSZ legal opinion was hostile to such involvement by laymen.[112] Perhaps it was not too late to organize and mobilize when the parliamentary fiasco occurred. Finally and most importantly, it was doctrinaire attitude on the part of the SZDSZ primarily that would not concede at least some of what the Socialist leaders believed was missing. Many of these demands belonged not to the world of the older state socialism, as Halmai, for example, implies,[113] but to the worlds of European Social Democracy. Whatever one thinks of these demands, and I personally have no problem with some of them, they were relatively easy to grant: the concession of the adjective "social" somewhere defining the new political community was entirely inexpensive. The acceptance of judicially enforceable social rights could have been compromised, by making only some judiciable on the constitutional level. Finally, while the ideas of social partnership are nowhere constitutionalized, this form of the capital–labor relationship has been institutionalized all over Europe, surviving even the neo-liberal epoch. Creative formulas could have been generated allowing and perhaps supporting but not requiring collective bargaining in all industries, union shops to avoid free-rider problems, and even—*horribile dictu*—forms of co-determination. It was only because of the conservative, rather doctrinaire, inflexible economic liberalism prevalent in the liberal parties (at that time FIDESZ as well) that made such possible concessions to the socialists impossible. But the cost to liberalism was to be very great indeed.

Finally, although Kis' argument for the need for consensus as well as compromise is correct, his application of it to this situation is more problematic. The

[112] As Bragyova put it, drafting as against approval is a rational, rather than democratic exercise. See for example Bragyova, *Az új alkotmány egy koncepciója* 11. He is right with respect to the actual drafting, but neglects the possibility of democratic inputs much too much. In 2005 Bragyova became a judge in the Consitutional Court, nominated by the liberal SZDSZ.

[113] In Halmai, "Az 1949es alkotmány jogállamositása."

question is whether consensus must be prior to compromise, or whether it can be its result. In Rawls' *Political Liberalism*, for example, a modus vivendi logically predates the overlapping consensus, because of the apparent incompatibility of contending views of the world. But once socialized by their interaction, the parties involved can develop elements of the overlap, as long as their worldviews are sufficiently rational. Kis could undoubtedly argue in response that the constitutional arrangements of 1989–90 represented such a modus vivendi, and yet instead of overlapping consensus the parties have become even more antagonistic. Here the Rawlsian argument must be supplemented, but not simply by postulating a prior substantive consensus. In my view, inspired by Habermas, a strong procedural consensus can reinforce the socializing power of the necessity to live together even under rules that initially have been formed purely under compromise. This means that we must agree on the procedures of constitution making before all else and then follow through with the compromises we are able to make, showing that we actually respect one another's positions even when we disagree. These compromises, however, must be fair, under some kind of veil of ignorance, producing procedural legitimacy. Only thus is it subsequently possible to generate elements of the overlap of normative principles.

There was amazing procedural agreement in Hungary twice, during the setting up of the EKA and the NKA in 1989, and in 1994 when generating new rules for constitution making. The first time, through the attempts of the MSZMP and its secret partners, the veil was punctured, a compromise was made but it was unfair. The resulting struggle created many of the strong divisions that interfered with subsequent, cooperative, and consensual constitution making. However, in 1994, rather than conversion attempts bringing the experiment down, it was the rigidity on all sides. Unfortunately an appearance was generated that a new constitution could be made only from a position of power. FIDESZ in particular, mostly loyal to the effort, could easily conclude that MSZP-SZDSZ failed because they did not use the coalition's majoritarian power. They were not going to make the same mistake.

VI JUDICIAL COMPLETION?

For the Constitutional Court, which temporarily benefited from the parliamentary amendment moratorium that was eventually renounced, the whole episode of 1994–96 must have represented a big scare. If the existence of a majority capable of replacing the constitution happened once, it could happen again. In the eyes of most jurists who happened to notice it, the new rule for constitution making requiring four-fifths to consensually commence meant that the process lived only a limbo existence. It was technically in the constitution, but neither entrenched nor considered alive after the sun had supposedly set on it. The frightening reality of being overridden by amendments and losing many of the Court's powers was palpably a danger. One response was quiescence, which some (e.g. Scheppele[114]) attribute merely to new membership. However, there was another possible response, one that could have been established or at least initiated by the earlier, more activist Court. This response in my view[115] would have been the review and possible invalidation of constitutional amendments, a functional and potentially legitimate equivalent of producing or defending a new level of entrenchment of the constitution. This was the third possible approach that would have completed the constituent process of the Round Table, opening the door to the long-term primarily judicial legitimation of the constitution. Unlike the first two approaches, it was never really tried before the FIDESZ constitution-making episode, only hinted at.

The activism of the first Hungarian Constitutional Court is undeniable, even if not as extreme as some claimed. That it has exercised a veritable constituent power to fill in gaps in the Round Table constitution could be formally contested, but in my view the claim could be sustained at least in the case of several important decisions. What cannot be maintained, however, is that it has effectively served as the second and final stage of the round-table-led process, successfully replacing the act of legislating a final constitution as happened in Bulgaria, Poland, and South Africa.[116] However creative, the decisions of the Court were able to focus only on elements of the constitution, not the whole. In the race between two constituent powers, here lay the advantage of the amendment power.

Even László Sólyom, the aforementioned Round Table participant who represents one pole of interpreting the activism of the court, does not go so far as to claim to have completed the constitutional process. In his own view, the Court did not have to do this in any case, since the 1989–90 constitution was already a new constitution as well as a final one, whatever its preamble may have stated. A second new constitution would have been needed only if the actors wanted to produce a new constitutional identity, which in his view could only be inferior to that established in 1989–90, in a liberal democratic parliamentary republic. As to the activism of his own Court, not only was he proud of it, he also believed it was entirely analogous to constitutional and supreme courts elsewhere engaged in promoting rights revolutions.

That is a view that was energetically and I think rightly contested by Bruce Ackerman, who occupied the other pole of interpretation concerning the activism of the Hungarian Court.[117] Impressed by the unusual volume of counter-majoritarian decisions in Hungary in the early 1990s, and although agreeing with most of the substantive results, he felt nevertheless compelled to ask whether such an activism could be sustained in the longer term. Based on his own theory of popular sovereign constitution making in America, and his preservationist

114 Scheppele, "Constitutional Negotiations."

115 Arato, "Post Sovereign Constitution-making in Hungary"; "After Success" published in Hungarian in 2009.

116 As Scheppele argues in "Unconstitutional Constituent Power."

117 B. Ackerman, *The Future of Liberal Revolution* (New Haven, CT: Yale University Press, 1992).

conception of judicial review, he argued that on the soft constitutional foundations of negotiations and piecemeal amendments an activism such as Hungary's was untenable and could not be continued. Instead he called for the making of a new constitution based on popular sovereignty before the window of the constitutional moment closed.

In my view Ackerman underestimated the potential legitimating force of the round-table-led process in several countries. Moreover, his call for presidentially led popular (populist?) constitution making would have led to disaster. In Poland this almost happened with Walesa as president, and we are able to assess the disastrous results of this process in Yeltsin's Russia in and after 1993. Yet, when interpreted in the sense of the need for a second stage of legitimate constitution making, as happened in South Africa subsequent to Ackerman's essay, the argument made sense. If so reformulated, its prediction turned out to be astonishingly accurate, and it would be futile to blame the significant drop in activism merely on personalities. As I shall show in the last section of this chapter, even a packed Court was capable of acting boldly in the face of openly authoritarian threats.

What is undeniable is that after the failure of the making of a new constitution in 1996, the Hungarian Constitutional Court became much more cautious. Politically, this could be explained by the number of enemies on different sides of the spectrum, expressed also in the academic literature.[118] While parties on the right remained hostile because of earlier decisions interfering with retroactive justice and land reprivatization, the liberal party remained unhappy about the Court helping Prime Minister Antall renege on part of his agreement on the role of the presidency (vigorously asserted by President Göncz) concerning appointments of media leaders.[119] While the socialists should have been the most happy when the Court defended acquired welfare rights as a form of property, they were outraged by this very decision because it invalidated part of their own austerity package, the Bokros program.[120]

Most of these decisions, and especially the last may have been generally popular, but as a whole they alienated the political class. And it was the political class and not the population that elections with manufactured majorities of seats potentially put in the position to exercise the constituent power, in coalition or as it turned out even alone. Using the power of amendment and the ability to enact the so-called two-thirds laws, a parliamentary super-majority was potentially in the position to dramatically diminish the powers of the Court. As we know from U.S. history as well as subsequent developments in India, Israel, and

[118] This too was predicted by Ackerman: ibid. 110; and confirmed by O. Lembcke and C. Boulanger, "Between Revolution and Constitution: The Roles of the Hungarian Constitutional Court" in Tóth, *Constitution for a Disunited Nation* 269–300.

[119] See my piece, A. Arato, "Az alkotmánybiróság a média háborúban" in *Világosság* reprinted in my Hungarian volume *Civil társdalom forradalom és alkotmány* (Budapest: Új mandátum, 1999).

[120] See Halmai, "Az 1949es alkotmány jogállamositása"; unlike Halmai I agree with the contents of that decision.

Turkey, court packing, removal of jurisdiction, and the establishment of parliamentary forms of override could accomplish such a weakening.

The only answer to these potential dangers would have been to turn the very real popular support for the institution[121] into a new power, the power of amendment review. By pre-emptively defending itself, the Court could have helped to bring the process to a close. This was possible, because it was the old amendment rule, surviving several constitutions, which kept the process indefinitely open. If some amendments would be barred under it, the intended changes either would not be made at all, or, preferably, could be made only within a new constitution as indicated by Article 23(5). Reviewing amendments thus implicitly meant defending a higher rule of change.

The possibility did not escape the members of the Constitutional Court. Sólyom, president of the first Constitutional Court, and later of the Republic, once raised the question of constitutional review of amendments that are neither permitted nor forbidden by the current text as follows:

> [We, the Court] recognize the constitution above us as an absolute standard, the creation of which is in the hands of parliament. This is one kind of self-limitation and consciousness of the fact that we do not stand above parliament, but are a part of the constitutional system. *The majority of the Constitutional Court does not aspire to review the constitutionality of constitutional amendments, although theoretically it could be justified. Of course not by a positivistic method: in our constitution there are no elevated, so-called eternal rules as in Germany, by which we could evaluate the amendment*. In the case of unacceptable constitutional amendment moral critique remains: one resigns. [My translation; my emphasis][122]

The ambivalence of this statement (theoretical belief in the possibility of review of amending power versus subordination of the Court to parliament) reflects the unresolved tension in Hungary between constitutionalism and parliamentary sovereignty. But it also reflects the actual trend of the Court's relevant jurisprudence at the time. A series of binding decisions between 1994 and 2004 excluded amendment review more and more vociferously.[123]

Nevertheless, the case for the reviewability of amendments in Hungary could have drawn on a combination of arguments advanced by other courts, as well as the theoretical literature. Sólyom himself may have contemplated his own concept of an "invisible constitution" as a possible foundation for amendment review. Central to this idea is an immanent coherence hypothesis, resembling

[121] Confirmed by Lembcke and Boulanger, "Between Revolution and Constitution" 275.

[122] J. Sólyom, "A nehéz eseteknél á biró erkölcsi felfogása jut szerephez. Sólyom Lászlóval, az Alkotmánybirósag elnökével Tóth Gábor Attila beszélget" in G. Halmai, *A megtalált alkotmány/The Constitution Found? The First Nine Years of the Hungarian Constitutional Review of Fundamental Rights* (Budapest: Indok, 2000) 389.

[123] When no longer working in the Court, in a major book of 2001, Sólyom went further in the direction of amendment review than ever before. He affirmed the need for procedural review especially clearly, and even more importantly, the possibility of invalidating enabling legislation, which would have the effect of cancelling some amendments at least. See Sólyom, *Az alkotmánybiráskodás kezdetei* 276–81.

but not identical to the Indian Basic Structure doctrine.[124] According to Sólyom, "the constitution as a whole" is a coherent system of principles that is not immediately apparent from the actual paragraphs and basic sentences (*tőmondatok*). The Court must make the invisible structure visible in its opinions and precedents. Sólyom focused this "structural interpretation" primarily in the area of basic rights,[125] but logically it surely also applies, as Indian jurisprudence shows, to the framework of government stipulated by the rest of the constitution. Sólyom even applied this principle once, when he and the Court invalidated a provision of the MDF-SZDSZ agreement that slightly extended the powers of the presidency, on the basis of nothing other than the supposed structure of parliamentary government as such.

The notion of uncovering the invisible constitution when engaging in active and often counter-majoritarian review is relevant for Sólyom's assessment of the respective roles of court and parliament in what he calls "constitutional development." The first fifteen years' development, he maintains, was mainly the achievement of the Court. Apart from three exceptions,[126] he describes the thirty-odd amendments since 1990 as "minor" and "technical" changes. I take this to be a characteristic exaggeration. Be this as it may, the Court's work is seen here as making the basic structure visible, whereas the amendments are regarded as mere tinkering that neither uncovered nor endangered that structure.

Sólyom's description nevertheless rightly implies that the amending power has up to that point, for whatever reason, remained loyal to the Round Table constitution (as indeed has the court). This loyalty was tested in 1990 and 1994–96, and not only did it survive, but it also secured the Round Table constitution's fundamental principle of consensus. Instead of emphasizing the principle of consensus, Sólyom, however, came closer to the approach of Schmitt when he stressed the revolutionary legitimacy of the Court and the transformational principle of the original regime change that informs the coherence of the constitution.[127] But what is the meaning of that principle, really?

Sólyom repeatedly speaks of *jogállami forradalom*, of lawful or rule of law revolution. He has in mind here the adherence to legal continuity even in the midst of revolutionary system change. The idea combines the two principles of legality and legitimacy in one phrase. As I also have repeatedly argued, legality or legal continuity is indeed a central principle of the new model of

[124] The views of A. Bragyova, with respect to what he calls the legislative form of the amending power, resembles the basic structure doctrine, although he adopted a literalist argument as well, according to which amend means to change or expand, but not to replace. See Bragyova, *Az új alkotmány egy koncepciója* 272ff.

[125] J. Kis, "Az első magyar Alkotmánybíróság értelmezési gyakorlata" in Halmai, *The Constitution Found? The First Nine Years*.

[126] Two from 1990 (constructive vote of no confidence, and abolition of the category of laws of constitutional force) and one from 2002 (LXI. Törvény) concerning the entry of Hungary into the EU.

[127] Sólyom, "A nehéz eseteknél a biró erkölcsi felfogása jut szerephez" 384–7.

constitutional change, but not the only one.[128] Resting as it did in Hungary on an unlimited amendment rule, this principle was powerless against this rule. In other words it was powerless against the very rule it relied on and reproduced. Thus, the principle of legal continuity alone could not have stopped and could not stop a "legal revolution" in the opposite direction.

However, Sólyom's phrase missed the specific nature of the Hungarian regime change. At issue in this change was not revolutionary legitimacy, however much Sólyom wished to highlight how the radical powers of his Court were originally established, and was not derived through evolutionary practice and precedent as in U.S. constitutional history. The South African Constitutional Court (obviously more familiar with revolutionaries and the meaning of revolution than Hungarian judges!) was on much firmer ground in this regard when it justified its initial declaration of the unconstitutionality of the Constitutional Assembly's first draft on the basis of "the solemn promise" the parties in the negotiations had made to each other, expressed in the thirty-four constitutional principles.[129] Whereas revolution is the principle of the one-sided imposition of someone's first preference, the solemn promise was that of two or many-sided mutuality and coming to an agreement about the second best.

Thus, instead of stressing revolutionary legitimacy à la Schmitt, or even legal continuity, Sólyom would have done better to focus on the second major principle of the Hungarian transition, namely, the principle of consensual decision making in constitutional matters that governed the round tables. It is this principle that kept the amending power on a track consistent with the public law of the regime change, producing amendments that Sólyom derided as mostly technical, serving daily political interests only. More importantly, it was this idea, beginning to harden into a convention, that led the MSZP-SZDSZ coalition in 1994 to produce the already described highly consensual method of making a new constitution.

The Court in fact had a chance to pronounce its assent to the consensual method. In a decision that came close to amendment review, the judges upheld the new constitution-making formula of 1995 in the House Rules made on the basis of Article 23(5) in a significant, though hardly surprising decision. The litigants sued because of the absence of guarantees of popular participation in the drafting and of referenda in the ratification of the new constitution. That decision, while denying the existence of unchangeable provisions of any kind in the Hungarian Constitution, affirmed the purpose of the effort to perfect the guarantees of the realization of human rights and the goal of preserving the foundations of the existing public law order.[130] I personally sympathize with the

[128] See especially Arato, *Civil Society* Chapter 5.

[129] C. Rickard, "The Certification of the Constitution of South Africa" in P. Andrews and S. Ellmann (eds), *Post Apartheid Constitutions* (Johannesburg: Witwatersrand University Press Publications, 2001) 228, 263, 270. Rickard points out the link to the basic structure doctrine and illustrates the role of the judges in producing a multi-track constitutional structure with the ordinary amending powers undergoing some limitation.

[130] Constitutional Court Decision 39/1996 (IX. 25).

litigants who were certainly right and even prescient politically in demanding wider participation and publicity, outside of parliament, as in Poland and South Africa. Legally, however, the Court was surely also right in not requiring this in general or in any specific modality. I think the matter with referenda is a little different. It is true that the constitution does not require referenda in the case of the ratification of a new constitution, but the statute, 1989 XVII does. Even if the constitution or a new law could derogate from this, they have not, and a mere House Rule change could not do so because of the principle of *lex superior* outweighing that of *lex posterior*. It is also true that a referendum was intended by most of the makers of the drafts submitted toward a new constitution between 1994 and 1996.

Equally important, as the Court noted, was the fact that at that time parliament linked the creation of the new constitution, through a constitutional delegation, to an especially high consensus, namely four-fifths of all its votes.[131] The Court considered this procedure to be an adequate expression of popular sovereignty, with or without referendum. Implicitly, this argument involved reviewing the constitutional amendment that established Article 23(5) even while upholding it. The question is whether the same standard could have been applied if parliament returned to the method of *new* constitution-making through the amendment rule alone, one that requires only two thirds of the votes. The Court's own precedents suggested that it could and might.

János Kis[132] is right: The Court in the very beginning was willing to critically challenge amendments and even parts of the constitution through its review. But this phrasing already points to the problem: given the constitution-making approach used in 1989 and 1990 and the possible illusion of its entirely parliamentary nature, there was no distinction between constitution and amendments. Most of the valid text could be regarded as two major series of amendments supplemented by further ones. Nevertheless, the point of Kis and the relevant problems can be illustrated in terms of the very first case before the Court (Decision 1/1990 II.12), which dealt with a challenge to what is known as the "Lex Király" amendment, named after the non Communist deputy who proposed it. Lex Király amended the constitution to allow direct election of the president of the republic in spite of the decision of the Round Table as corrected by the referendum of November 1989. The case took the form of a prior interpretation of the constitution (under the Law of the Constitutional Court 1989 XXXII 1g) and thus it could claim, very superficially, to involve no ruling on an amendment. That superficial argument was later used by the Court to decline amendment review, claiming equally superficially that amendments already made supposedly formed part of the constitution, and the constitution itself could not be

[131] The Court noted, with no comment, the high consensus requirements for the Constitution Preparatory Committee: Five out of six parties and two-thirds of all the members had to agree for a proposal to be adopted.

[132] Kis, "Az első magyar Alkotmánybiróság értelmezési gyakorlata."

reviewed.[133] Nevertheless, in 1990 at least while the Court upheld the (temporary) restoration of direct presidential elections in Lex Király, a constitutional amendment, it claimed at the same time that an amendment that would have put that election before parliament's in spite of (the non-constitutional!) referendum would have been invalidated. Note that in this process the Court itself violated the Round Table agreements, upholding the unfortunate fiction that the old parliament was the constituent power, and thus its later amendment could derogate from the earlier one. It thus further contributed to undermining the legitimacy of the Round Table. At the same time, there was also an attempt soon after by the now expanded Court (Decision 894/B/1990) to affirm the need to ratify a new constitution in a referendum, claiming that the creation of a whole constitution is not the competence of parliament alone.

In spite of such ambivalent beginnings, it is difficult from a narrow legal point of view to simply dismiss the Court's jurisprudence on amendments, however little theoretical grounding has been provided for it and however pernicious the potential consequences could be.[134] Only the convention of significant consensus between opposing parties that emerged from the practices of the Round Tables presented a clear limitation on ordinary two-thirds majority amendments, and this was already disregarded by the 1990 Court decision. Moreover, the convention regarding consensus has not hardened yet. Add to this the conflation of parliamentarianism with parliamentary sovereignty common in the Hungarian tradition and it becomes clear that some textual foothold in the constitution would have been very helpful for this convention to become a significant jurisprudential foundation. That seemed to have been the position of a Court minority in 1998. Three judges[135] joined a concurrent opinion that identified such a textual foothold in "the defense of legal security and fundamental rights, as well as other constitutional institutions." These textual footholds could and had to be invoked, they argued, not directly against the amendments, but as Sólyom was to confirm in 2005,[136] at least against the enabling legislation that formed part of the amendment. Yet, even this minority of the Court postulated that to actually carry out amendment review, the Court needed direct authorization by the constitution, which of course was not there. However, the Court's

[133] Sólyom even made the argument in his 2001 book that the idea of something already part of the constitution could not apply to procedurally incorrect amendments. *Az alkotmánybiráskodás kezdetei* 276–81. Eventually, the Court too came to the conclusion that procedurally incorrect amendments were never part of the constitution. K. Kovács, "Using the Amendment Rule to Change the Constitutional Identity," unpublished paper delivered May 25, 2015 at conference in Trento.

[134] In two decisions in 1994, one in 1998, and two decisions in 2004 (23/1994 (IV.6); 293/B/1994; 1260/B/1997; 816 and 14/2003 (IV.9) and 903/2003) the Constitutional Court affirmed its lack of competence in the case of amendments. True in the already referred to 1997 decision focusing on the enabling legislation, the Court in effect reviewed and upheld an amendment. However, this was negated by the arguments used in the other cases.

[135] A. Holló, Parallel Argumentation AB 1260/B/1997 joined by A. Ádám, G. Kilényi, and A. Szabó.

[136] Sólyom, *Az alkotmánybiráskodás kezdetei* 276–81.

refusal to review amendments in 1997 implied the suspension of the amendment moratorium, still within the time frame of the 1994–98 constitution-making project, and underlined the collapse of this project as a whole.[137]

Ironically, at the time that these separate and concurrent opinions were written, a textual foothold still existed in the now defunct Article 24(5). Article 24(5) required a four-fifths majority for constitutional changes that effectively created a new constitution. It read as and only as follows: "For the acceptance of the parliamentary resolution concerning the detailed rules of the preparation of the new constitution, four fifths of the votes of the members of parliament are required." At the time of FIDESZ returning to power in 2010 this rule was still included in most texts of the constitution.[138] As already argued, together with Article 24(3), the amendment rule, Article 24(5) provided for a three-track constitution in terms of which the amendment and the making of the new constitution belonged to different procedural tracks. The constitution had already distinguished between the creation (*megalkotás*) of the new constitution and amending or changing (*megváltoztatás*) the existing one, but up to 1995 when Article 24(5) was written there was no procedural distinction between them. Even the radical constitutional innovations of 1989, although enacted mostly consensually, which were for all practical purposes a matter of real constitution making, were formally enacted by the *amendment rule* contained in Article 15(3), the predecessor of the current Article 24(3). With Article 24(5) there was now such a distinction, and the Court could and should have relied upon it, or at least affirmed that it would if the need arose.

It is true that Article 24(5) spoke of a new constitution, rather than amendments. Nevertheless, it would have allowed the judicial review not only of a process of new constitution making that violated it, but the review of all significant amendments implying a change of identity.[139] Even Article 24(5) had identity implications, since it entrenched *consensual constitutionalism* on the most fundamental level and, logically, only a *majoritarian* project would lead one to eliminate it by the mere use of the two-thirds rule. It would have made no sense to interpret "new constitution" in the narrow sense of a whole new document, detailed, formal, and named as such. Furthermore, in contrast to India, where the basic structure doctrine sufficed, the Hungarian Court would not just have had to rely on constitutional interpretation or the need to pronounce some or other constitutional clause totally unchangeable or "eternal."[140] In the case of any change the Constitutional Court deemed fundamental, it could have simply demanded that the path for *making* a new constitution stipulated under Article

[137] On the renunciation of that moratorium see Halmai, "*Az 1949es alkotmány jogállamositása.*"

[138] In 2009 this included the text on the websites of the Constitutional Court and Parliament, but not all the other available texts indicating the "legally valid" version.

[139] This relationship, between constitutional review and a multi-leveled amendment structure, seems to have been grasped only by A. Bragyova, both before and after becoming a justice of the Court.

[140] Under the constitution, in line with AB határozat 39/1996. (IX. 25).

24(5) be followed, even for some verbally brief but structurally decisive amendments, and not the amending procedure under Article 24(3). This is also indicated by the difference between the language of Article 19(3a) referring to creation[141] and that of Article 24(3) that refers to alteration.[142]

In my mind there is little question that between 1995 and 1998, when Article 24(5) had indisputably full legal effect, the Constitutional Court could and should have invalidated any structurally important amendment made under Article 24(3) violating the moratorium, however informal. At the very least the Court should have asserted its power and authority to do so. It would have been possible to refer to it in the several decisions of the Court dealing with amendment review. They could have affirmed the function, even as upholding relevant amendments, the common jurisdictional approach of courts from *Marbury* to *Kesavananda*.[143] Moreover, the narrow textual argument could have been reinforced by other principles, whether based on other text, natural law, conventions, or, most likely, basic structure. This was not done. Thus the ground for making Article 24(5) an important basis of constitutional judgments was not in any way prepared.

When the issue of the four-fifths rule became obviously salient, FIDESZ preempted any move by the Court or litigants by abolishing Article 24(5) by the two-thirds majority required by Artcle 24(3). Arguably Article 24(5) was not a whole constitution (though it potentially was) and its replacement required only an amendment and not replacement. To the formal argument that use of a two-thirds majority cannot replace a four-fifths rule the answer of even some liberals would have been that Article 24(5) was not itself entrenched to the higher level, as the highest level rules are in South Africa, for example. That argument could have been countered (as by Peter Suber[144]) by insisting on implicit entrenchment, but it was difficult to find a method by which the issue would be brought to the court.[145] Moreover, it was hardly noticed that the deepest new principle of Hungarian constitution making was at stake. But when the consensus-requiring constitution-making rule was removed, the possibility of the completion of the 1989 constitutional process by the Constitutional Court was over. The way was open to another means of bringing the history of the 1989–90 Round Table Constitution to an end.

141 "Megalkotja a Magyar Köztársaság Alkotmányát" [creates the constitution of the Hungarian Republic].

142 I assume that Article 19(3)'s *"megalkotás"* [creation] and Article 24(5)'s *"előkészités"* [preparation] mean the same, though the former may refer to the total process of constitution creation, including ratification, while the latter to the first, highly consensual part.

143 *Marbury v. Madison* (1802) 5 US 137; *Kesavananda Bharati v. State of Kerala* (1973) 4 SCC 225.

144 Suber, P., *The Paradox of Self-amendment* (New York: Peter Lang, 1990).

145 It would have been awkward to try to use the *actio popularis* with its almost universal standing that was itself abolished by the Fundamental Law, and no case was generated when FIDESZ abolished the four-fifths rule.

VII THE TURN OF FIDESZ

In my interpretation, the sociological legitimacy of the constitution of 1989 was not satisfied by either an appeal to legality or to fundamental liberal and democratic norms incorporated in the document. I am pretty confident that the survey literature from its twenty-year existence, dealing with constitutional values and their acceptance, would sustain this judgment. What I have focused on instead from the early 1990s[146] is the challenge from the right. I considered this challenge in part unjustified because of the misconstruing of the facts and achievements of the round-table-led process, but also partially justified, and increasingly so, to the extent that the defenders of the new regime did not satisfy their initial promise, explicit in constitutional text as well as implicit in their very procedures in both 1989 and 1995–96. This promise was to replace the bargained constitution by a democratic as well as consensual one. Such was the heart of the sociological legitimacy problem, and it opened the door to István Csurka's critique in the 1990s[147] as well as Viktor Orbán's in 2010. Thus the so-called "revolution of the voting booth" was the true inheritor of the earlier demand for a second revolution. The existence of the highly disproportional electoral rule, along with the old amendment rule of the constitution implying parliamentary sovereignty only made the job of the new "revolutionaries" easier.[148]

Let us look at the process in which the new FIDESZ-led government in 2011 engaged while making the Fundamental Law.[149] I will use my earlier typology from Chapter 3, not to make a fetish of classification, but in order to pinpoint the legitimation problems of the making of the Fundamental Law. While some will argue or imply[150] that this process represents the missing completion of the round-table paradigm,[151] I very strongly disagree with this, and wish to provide the interpretive grounds for the disagreement based on comparative and theoretical considerations.[152] I believe that it is essential for the constitution-making method linked to the new paradigm of transition to be *post organ sovereign* in all

[146] See Arato, *Civil Society* Chapter 3. [147] Ibid.

[148] I tried in vain to call attention to this in my many articles in the Hungarian press that pointed out the dangers, some of them collected in the volume published as *Civil társadalom, forradalom és alkotmány*.

[149] For its general critique, both in terms of process and result, see the three-part article of J. Kis "Alkotmányozas—mi végre?" I–III. *Élet és Irodalom* (2011 / 12) vol. LV 12, 13 and 14; as well as A. Arato, J. Kis, and G. Halmai (eds), "Opinion on the Fundamental Law in Hungary," Hungarian original in (2011) *Fundamentum* 1.

[150] This was explicitly claimed in the original explanation appended to the Fundamental Law, when first sent to parliament.

[151] For example: L. Sólyom, "Az alkotmányozás őszintesége," HVG, 42, October 23, 2010, 23–8) written by a major participant who earlier did not even think the process needed to be completed by a new final constitution, admittedly before the publication of the draft of the new Fundamental Law.

[152] See J. Kis, "Introduction: From the 1989 Constitution to the 2011 Fundamental Law" in Tóth, *Constitution for a Disunited Nation* 4, who also makes this point, and calls the FIDESZ Fundamental Law a negation, rather than the second stage or completion of the previous process.

of its stages and also as a whole. This means that none of the protagonists of the several stages—the Round Table, the normal parliament and the Constitutional Court—should be able to claim to fully embody the will of the sovereign people.[153] No organ of state or government is supposed to be sovereign, without limitations. In the making of the FIDESZ Fundamental Law one organ, parliament, did explicitly claim to fully embody the sovereign constituent power of the Hungarian people.[154] While not elected as such, nor given any kind of mandate to produce a new constitution, parliament became and even titled itself a sovereign constituent assembly on the basis of slightly more than 50 percent of the votes for what became well over two-thirds of the seats.[155] Consistently with that conception, the rule established in 1995–96, the four-fifths rule requiring consensus among some parties beyond the government alone, was not only disregarded but was explicitly repealed by two-thirds of the vote, using the amending power.[156] That move would have been unconstitutional, but most likely not really vulnerable to invalidation because of the previous, and in my view mistaken, declarations of the Constitutional Court rejecting amendment review. In any case, the FIDESZ government made its litigation seem unpromising through changing the rules of standing and by the packing of the Constitutional Court with seven and eventually nine new members.[157] Along with a new majoritarian appointment scheme which sought to neutralize the main check of parliamentary sovereignty in the Hungarian system, the Court's jurisdiction had already been curtailed by amendment earlier in the year. Comparison with the 1995 process that remained under the jurisdiction of the Court is again instructive.

Even though it did not complete the earlier regime change, was the making of the Fundamental Law a process that re-enacted its logic? The use of the old amendment rule and the challenge to the existing constitution's legitimacy in the Preamble of the new Fundamental Law, as inconsistent as they were, point in the direction of a legal continuity/legitimation break. With respect to the constitution-making procedure, however, unlike the one begun in 1989, this

[153] I try to clarify this concept in my articles in *Fundamentum* and Arato, "Post Sovereign Constitution-making in Hungary."

[154] For the return of the sovereignty problem with the new FIDESZ government see the important theoretical article by Lembcke and Boulanger, "Between Revolution and Constitution: the Roles of the Hungarian Constitutional Court" especially 271.

[155] This was explicitly asserted when the regular parliament converted itself into a National Constituent Assembly by a mere declaration that was disregarded by all accept the FIDESZ parliamentarians. It was, however, a correct statement of what they had actually done, without any legal provision supporting the step.

[156] See Kovács, "Using the Amendment Rule to Change Constitutional Identity."

[157] For the details see G. Halmai et al., "Opinion on the Fundamental Law in Hungary" in Tóth, *Constitution for a Disunited Nation*; K. Kovács and G.A. Tóth, "Hungary's Constitutional Transformation" *European Constitutional Law Review* 7; and Kovács, "Using the Amendment Rule." This is also a reason perhaps why when the new Fundamental Law was challenged under the 1989–90 Constitution at the Constitutional Court, the two-thirds and four-fifths problem was neglected. Perhaps the litigant (A. Hanák) did not wish to legalize the procedure by an adverse Court decision. For that challenge see the text in Tóth, *Constitution for a Disunited Nation.*

FIDESZ-led process had only one major agent. Consensual process was avoided, and the time of the exercise was impermissibly accelerated, not only compared to multi-stage efforts but even with respect to parliamentary precedents elsewhere. And, as already said, organ sovereignty was asserted. Thus not just one but many features of the new paradigm were absent, and we cannot even speak of a marginally similar case here.

Neither can there be a question in this case of recourse to two other transition types, the options of revolutionary reform or revolution. Both require ruptures in legality and I do not think that the limited illegalities involved can be interpreted as a legal rupture. As already said, unfortunately, the amendment of the four-fifths constitution-making rule by a mere two-thirds majority was never litigated, and, as I admitted earlier, that there were serious formal arguments on both sides of this question.[158] Revolution also requires ruptures of legitimacy, which was indeed claimed here, but with foundations only in the symbolic definitions and declarations of the Fundamental Law and often at variance with its structural provisions. For example, even as something like an ethnocracy[159] was declared by the Preamble, which seemed to exclude from the body of the people citizens of non-Hungarian ethnicity, no measures of citizen disenfranchisement were linked to the declaration.[160] Moreover, on the structural level no other form of sovereignty was posited other than that of parliament, and this (alas) was already established in the 1989–90 regime, even if inconsistently given the creation of such a strong Constitutional Court. Unfortunately, the Constitutional Court's passive early practice with respect to amendment review confirmed the model of parliamentary sovereignty. Accordingly, after pronouncing in its Preamble the invalidity of its predecessor, in its final provisions the new Fundamental Law claimed authority for its makers on the basis of the very amendment rule in place since 1949, something that was not even done in 1989 when the rule was used without such claims. The Round Table did not claim its authority to recommend from any provision of the 1949 Constitution, to which it was "unknown" as an institution.

It is true that as in 1989, this very same amendment rule was used to produce a completely new constitutional text, but in 2011 there were fewer structural changes than in 1989, even if those made were still very significant. Moreover, if we understand the 1989–90 Constitution as providing checks on majoritarianism

[158] The argument I have repeatedly made was formal, and it could be countered by an even more excessive formalism, based on the literal text that was not entrenched by self-reference.

[159] O. Yiftachel, "'Ethnocracy': the Politics of Judaizing Israel/Palestine" (1999) 6 *Constellations: International Journal of Critical and Democratic Theory* 3 364–90.

[160] Extending voting rights to ethnic Hungarians living abroad, and citizens of other countries admittedly moves in the direction of an ethnocracy, but as the case of Israel shows, one can speak of an ethnocracy only if there is a loss of rights by citizens of other ethnicities, de jure or at least de facto.

through a combination of consensus requiring mechanisms[161] and a strong constitutional court, the results of the Fundamental Law were ambivalent. While consensus requirements for many appointments, in particular for the Constitutional Court, were reduced, the number of two-thirds or cardinal laws was vastly increased. While the latter did not affect the FIDESZ government, which had its required two-thirds majority and planned to re-achieve it by altering the electoral law, it was nevertheless a consensus-requiring device.[162] It not only kept the dead hand of the past active in the future, when the two-thirds majority was lost, but in that case also would allow minorities to participate in the making or changing of many laws.

Of course, just as the MSZMP in 1989, FIDESZ pursued seemingly contradictory strategies. On the one hand it sought guarantees against future electoral winners in the form of consociational rules of legislation and bionic appointments, and on the other it kept the two-thirds majority amending rule that could have endangered even these achievements. The new electoral rule instituted in 2013 was the attempted solution of the apparent contradiction. Reducing the size of parliament from 386 to 199, the FIDESZ government: increased the percentage of single constituency seats from 45 percent to 53 percent of all seats, to 106 seats; reduced the percentage of proportional representation seats from 55 percent to 47 percent; unified the proportional lists in a single, national list, removing the compensational function of the older national list; and abolished the second round of elections for single constituency seats. Notably, these steps did not all point in the same direction. Whereas the first three steps meant greater disproportionality, the fourth could imply the opposite.[163] In addition, given the very aggressive redistricting that was part of the new law, the first trend (toward greater disproportionality) greatly triumphed in the 2014 elections. The 25 percent disproportion in that vote was the largest in Hungarian elections since 1990, and yet within the order of magnitude of the results of the 1990, 1994, and even 2010 elections. Nevertheless, even this electoral change continued the original double system of round-table agreements, as against the model of the German system often proposed as the much more proportional alternative. Thus despite its clearly self-serving qualities, even the electoral procedure cannot be regarded as a revolutionary rupture with what came before.[164] What can be said is that with the disappearance of the second round, the requirement to form party coalitions in advance became more evident than in the system before. If that

[161] Halmai, "Az 1949es alkotmány jogállamositása"; G. Halmai, M. Bánkúti, and K.L. Scheppele, "From Separation of Powers to Government without Checks: Hungary's Old and New Constitution" in Tóth, *Constitution for a Disunited Nation.*

[162] Kriszta Kovács rightly claims in "Using the Amendment Rule" that while in 1989–90 the two-thirds amendment rule was assumed to be a consensus promoting device, after 2010 it was used in a majoritarian way.

[163] Though this last step could contribute to reducing the number of parties.

[164] Perhaps the overall structure, one that resembled early MSZMP and governmental plans from 1988 and 1989, could be regarded as restorationist. But even these early plans were radically reformist with respect to the old regime, and became one possibility within the various plans considered by the Round Table.

became a general and less contentious practice than in 2013–14, no outcome nor even level of disproportionality could be fully guaranteed or predicted in advance, especially in elections to come.

As to the Constitutional Court, in my view the main target of the FIDESZ constitutional projects from its 2010–11 amendments to the 1989–90 Constitution, to the Fundamental Law itself, and two of its later amendments, it suffered not only the creation of a more political form of appointment, but a significant diminution of jurisdiction and restriction of standing through the abolition of the *actio popularis* that made standing universal. Yet it also gained, through the extension of the institution of "constitutional complaint" by giving standing to persons whose rights were affected by courts applying a law that was in itself not unconstitutional.[165] In the short term the gains were cancelled out by a very large and successful attempt at Court packing that raised the membership from eleven to fifteen, allowing FIDESZ to name seven new judges during the first half of its government, now "bionic," expanded to twelve-year terms. This move, accomplished by an amendment to the 1989–90 Constitution, one that eliminated the role of party parity, was potentially the most important of all, because as Halmai, Bánkúti, and Scheppele rightly stress, it "made it highly unlikely that any important element of the new constitutional program would be derailed."[166]

Yet self-serving changes in electoral rules and court packing, as obnoxious as they indeed are, do not make a revolution. If 1989 did not herald a revolution, and it did not, neither did 2011. It was not even a *counter*-revolution despite the presence of a genuine counter-revolutionary force, Jobbik in parliament, a party that did not support the new draft. At most it was a *contrary* revolution in the sense of Joseph de Maistre, that is reversing revolutionary results by methods other than a revolution.[167] Other possible criteria of revolutions[168] (a complete replacement of regime, revolutionary experience, and hermeneutic appeals to a revolutionary tradition) were also absent. Thus far there has not been any serious or comprehensive attempt to establish revolutionary retroactive justice, though eventually successful repeal of statutes of limitation and abolition of

165 Halmai et al., "From Separation of Powers" provide the overall picture, but are reluctant to admit its ambivalence. The presentation of the changes affecting the Court is more balanced in Lembcke and Boulanger, "Between Revolution and Constitution." They rightly see the return and I think intensification of the battle between Court and political branches. On that see G. Halmai, "Unconstitutional Constitutional Amendments: Constitutional Courts as Guardians of the Constitution?" (2012) 19 *Constellations* 2 182–203; M. Steinbeis, "The Return of the Hungarian Constitutional Court" *Verfblog*, January 15, 2013 http //www.verfassungsblog.de/en/the-return-of-the-hungarian-constitutional-court-2; and Kovács, "Using the Amendment Rule."

166 Halmai et al., "From Separation of Powers" 254–5.

167 See my discussion with Gábor Halmai in (2011) *Fundamentum* 1 where I did not manage to consistently use de Maistre's terminology that I had used at a previous New York conference. Of course it is gratifying to denounce FIDESZ as counter-revolutionaries, even if the terminology is not accurate. See also my entry in Verfassungsblog: "Orbán's (Counter-)Revolution of the Voting Booth and How it was Made Possible," *Verfblog*, April 16, 2011 http://www.verfassungsblog.de/orbans-counter-revolution-voting-booth, accessed December 5, 2015.

168 Arato, *Civil Society* 86–103.

pensions for old regime beneficiaries made a move in that direction. In Europe hopefully the institutionalization of a system of revolutionary justice would be quite unthinkable. Only the process of radical purges in many institutions that indeed did take place recalls a revolutionary logic. But purges of key institutions alone do not make a revolution, as the nineteenth-century U.S. spoils system indicates. The "revolution of the voting booth" remains what it always was, a slogan, justifying majoritarian imposition, along with the enactment of many authoritarian measures, which alas can take place under normal parliamentary forms.[169]

Reform is left as the main possibility. Accordingly, I first interpreted the Fundamental Law as a particularly large amendment package, similar to one enacted in Turkey in the previous year that also involved court packing. But the Fundamental Law also seriously threatened many aspects of the rule of law state, and thus potentially involved the replacement of regimes. This would be incompatible with reform. But I add: only with single stage, legitimate reforms. A series of reiterated reforms can go so far as to change a system's identity. It is true that under the basic structure doctrine ordinary amendments that threaten fundamental components and therefore the identity of the constitution are indeed illegitimate. In India they are also illegal, or have been made illegal by a long tradition of court precedents even without explicit textual guidance, as by the eternity clauses of the *Grundgesetz* and the Turkish constitution of 1983. The problem in Hungary is that there is neither a relevant set of court precedents, nor appropriate codification entrenching parts or principles of the constitution on a higher level than the rest.[170] What remains to be said, then, is that the Fundamental Law and its enactment were legal but illegitimate, or in a peculiar British usage: unconstitutional but legal.[171]

In this context, interpreters have stressed the identity change involved in the constitutional efforts of the FIDESZ government.[172] In light of the preamble of the Fundamental Law, and other provisions emphasizing the ethno-national and Christian character of the state this would be a difficult claim to deny. However, as we have just seen, reiterated reforms too can alter identity. Even if the great symbolic change occurred in one constitutional act, enacting the Fundamental Law, it is only subsequent legislative and court decisions, none in themselves

[169] Thus I disagree with Lembcke and Boulanger, "Between Revolution and Constitution" 277–9, who, focusing on the change of symbolic identity, speak of counter-revolution or national counter-revolution. Also see ibid. 291–2.

[170] Again, the only exception was arguably the implicit self-entrenchment of Article 24(5), the four-fifths rule, repealed unconstitutionally by FIDESZ, using the two-thirds rule, Article 24(3).

[171] In the United Kingdom this possibility is inherent in the constitution, having important conventions that have not been legally codified. A court, as in Canada in 1982, or a constitutional amendment such as the twenty-third in the United States, can legalize such conventions, but unless and before that is done the violations of convention remain legal. Thus Franklin Roosevelt's election to third and fourth terms, violating existing conventions, was legal.

[172] Lembcke and Boulanger, "Between Revolution and Constitution"; Kovács, "Using the Amendment Rule."

revolutionary, that could complete the transformation of a constitutional republic into a Christian ethnocracy. This has not happened yet, but the danger is admittedly very real. Moreover, within the concept of identity it is necessary to distinguish between symbolic and structural meanings, partially corresponding to actors' and observers' points of view.

Seeing itself as a revolutionary actor, FIDESZ evidently wished to signal the creation of a new identity. Others, deeply committed to the secular and universalist republic, are deeply fearful that this has already happened. Thus for some, though not all, actors, a change of symbolic identity has indeed taken place. Yet we must examine the matter also from the structural point of view, as I have just done, although I am otherwise not a neutral observer. From the observer's perspective, whether we focus on the sovereignty of parliament, the existence of consensual elements, the status of the Constitutional Court, the reform of the electoral rule, or, as I will argue, the structural tensions of the system, there are also very significant elements of continuity, along with important changes. And that very mix is a characteristic of reform, if in this case illegitimate reform.

Thus the process FIDESZ pushed through was on the whole formally legal, using the old amendment rule under the authority of the constitution of 1989. That is why I call it reform. More exactly, we can say today that it was a series of reiterated reforms, under an existing amendment rule, starting with amendments before the Fundamental Law, then the Fundamental Law itself, continuing with so-called Transitional Provisions eight months later, and then with a surprising number of five amendments still under the government that enacted the Fundamental Law. But again, the reform at the very foundation of this reiterated process was not legitimate, in part because of its claims rejecting the legitimacy of its own ground,[173] and in part because of how it was done. The legitimacy problems of this process have to do with how it was done—in other words, what was done could have been done legitimately only through a different process than the one used. Of course, this "better" process would certainly not have produced the same result, and it was thus avoided.

It is not only from my external point of view that the process had serious legitimacy problems. All other political actors continually pointed out the fact that it was non-consensually adopted and without even the use of a referendum. The contrasts with 1994–96, as well as with the positions of FIDESZ at that time, were obvious. The inconsistencies of many new elements adopted with the basic structure of constitutionalism were obvious. To these belong the attacks on the constitutional and other courts: the removal of jurisdiction, the court packing, and the forcible retirement of ordinary judges. At the same time, many of the reforms were also inconsistent with the logic of parliamentary government. These include first and foremost the establishment of long-term offices and tenures, and the great multiplication of organic or cardinal (*sarkalatos*) laws,

[173] This curious state of affairs was commented on by the Venice Commission, "Opinion." See Tóth, *Constitution for a Disunited Nation* 501.

both restricting the policy options of future freely elected governments. The first set of changes makes the protection of rule of law more difficult. The second makes democratic government weaker and less accountable. The electoral law that was created, as already argued, served the interests of FIDESZ incumbents and was even more disproportional than the previous one, in the short run correctly calculating that FIDESZ would gain the same number of seats even with far fewer votes in 2014. This was an incumbent protection measure incompatible with both the essence of written democratic constitutions, and parliamentary representation, which seek to protect the polity and the citizens against the self-aggrandizement of incumbents.

Again, all these normative qualms were constantly articulated empirically in Hungarian and even European political forums. With the exception of the governmental party, to those who care, inside and outside Hungary, the legitimacy of the enterprise has been seriously damaged. Constitutional reforms that usurped radical constituent powers could perhaps be made legitimate if only its procedural origins were at issue. Then, with the passing of time, and serious constitutional jurisprudence by a court, a secondary level of legitimacy could emerge. But here it was also a matter of content, the illegitimacy of which was to become clearer and clearer as the new provisions came into effect.

On the other hand, the ambivalence of the changes enacted by FIDESZ could lead to surprising results. As argued already, the fundamental tension of the regime of 1989 was between the strong Constitutional Court and parliament, the latter's majority being greatly enhanced by the electoral rule and armed with the amendment rule. FIDESZ tried to reduce the tension by weakening the Court and strengthening their majority by an even more disproportional rule. But even that electoral rule could barely preserve the amending majority in 2014, with some decline in support. More importantly for the initial period of the Fundamental Law, 2010 to 2013, the Court remained sufficiently strong to resist if it wished to do so. It is in this light that we should interpret FIDESZ continuing its 2010–11 practice of repeated amendments under the 1989 Constitution (fifteen in all), also under its very own Fundamental Law (five so far, which have modified large parts of the constitution). Two of these amendments pointed to an even more surprising development: the refusal off a packed and intimidated Constitutional Court to entirely surrender its earlier role of protecting fundamental rights, which forced the government to use constitutional amendments to trump judicial invalidation.[174] The return of the battle between Court and amending power, including the assertion of new claims by the Court to review amendments, support my thesis of reiterated reform as opposed to new regime change or revolution. It was that very battle, enabled by internal tensions of the constitution of 1989–90, that best reflected the public law structure established by the Round Table and the MDF-SZDSZ Pact. Its mere survival meant that, for

[174] See Kovács, "Using the Amendment Rule."

a brief time perhaps, and on the structural level at least, there has been no full replacement of identity.

VIII THE HORSE RACE BETWEEN THE COURT AND THE AMENDING POWER

In one respect FIDESZ itself may have implicitly recognized the legitimacy problems of what it had done. Contrary to an early idea of adopting the Spanish-Dutch type of amendment rule in the Fundamental Law, which would have required the assent of two parliaments, in different sessions, each voting by two-thirds, it has preserved the old parliamentary single-chamber, single-session, two-thirds absolute majority rule for the future. This was under the influence of criticisms that claimed (rightly in the given case, wrongly in the abstract) that such a new rule would "cast" the Fundamental Law "in cement," depriving future parliaments of the very same power that FIDESZ had used. Such argument belongs to the tradition of parliamentary sovereignty, in one particular interpretation (refuted by H.L.A. Hart, for example) that one parliament cannot bind another parliament exactly of the same type—the powers of one, accordingly, belong among the powers of the other. This argument is inconsistent with written constitutions and their entrenchment, thus with what Kelsen called a constitution in the formal sense. In practice the contradiction is overcome not with the other possibility inherent in the idea of omnipotence (namely that God is so powerful he can create a stone that even he cannot lift) but with the possibility of constituent and constitutional assemblies generating a higher legitimacy than that available to ordinary parliaments. In the United States, for example, this was accomplished by involving ratification through special assemblies, which was not a requirement in the case of ordinary law making. There are other ways of accomplishing the same surplus of legitimacy, like the "solemn promise" in South Africa, in the making of the interim constitution. My point is, however, that FIDESZ did not avail itself of any of these options, though many called for a referendum on the text. Thus it was particularly vulnerable to the charge that it did not have the right to bind future parliaments to a greater extent than the present one was bound. Nevertheless, it did not wish to expose its product to ratification either by a referendum or by a two-thirds majority of the next parliament. Instead, FIDESZ backed down and left the existing amendment rule in place.

Of course, a cynic could maintain that legitimation problems and vocal public opposition did not interest FIDESZ in the least. They kept the two-thirds amendment rule, as did all governments before, to potentially avail themselves of the possibility of easy amendments that could be used to trump constitutional court decisions. In FIDESZ's case, as no other before, that possibility was subsequently actualized in two of the first five amendments to the Fundamental Law. Yet functionally speaking they could have introduced the new amendment rule so that it would take effect only after the next elections, namely 2014.[175] However, they could not do this without exposing themselves to the charge of not applying to themselves a rule they argued was desirable. This in itself is the legitimation problem I have in mind. If legitimation problems did not matter at all, I would predict that close to the end of its second term, with the prospect looming of no longer being able to hold on to the two-thirds, FIDESZ would indeed seek to enact a new, more difficult, less purely parliamentary amendment rule.[176] Since I believe the legitimation problems do matter, I predict that this will not happen. Interest alone is not sufficient, even in the eyes of FIDESZ, to enact such momentous change. Still, of course, self-interest did continue to play a role, and to make sure that its interests would be served FIDESZ proceeded to significantly change the electoral rule in the direction of greater disproportionality. Since they needed or wanted to leave the amendment rule as it was, they preferred to be in a position to be able to exercise it and attain the necessary two-thirds of the seats.

These facts are highly significant for future developments. If the constitution-making process was left open in 1989–90, and was open in 2010–11, it remains open in exactly the same way now. But the kind of Court established by the Fundamental Law means the possible continuation of battles between the two main actors in the admittedly weakened new system of the separation of powers.[177]

In a famous battle with Kelsen, Carl Schmitt describes a potential *Wettkampf* (literally meaning a betting competition, and hence I translate it as horse race) between an apex court and parliament, which in the end the court must lose. Eager to refute Kelsen's case for constitutional review, Schmitt stressed that at issue in such a conflict would be sovereignty, and only a political branch, parliament, or president can act as sovereign.[178] There is no doubt that a government such as that of Viktor Orbán, or T.R. Erdogan for that matter, sees the matter in just this way, whereas for a court only the defense of constitutionalism and even constitutional democracy is at issue, whatever the judges may think. It is possible to interpret the whole "revolution of the voting booth" as a struggle initiated on

[175] This would have meant choosing the first most plausible or rational possibility as under note 104 above, much more rational than the choice of the coalition of 1994–98, which created the four-fifths rule to bind itself, but in terms of its intentions not the next parliaments.

[176] Given the narrow loss of a two-thirds majority in 2015 this would require one or two deputies of the various oppositions to agree. But any small party would have an interest in such a change of the amendment rule, which it could not hope to control in the future.

[177] I wish to avoid the impression, however, that the Court after 2010 was braver in defense of constitutionalism than its predecessor, a certainly wrong impression that can emerge with a focus purely on jurisprudence concerning amendments. While more restrained in this area, the pre 2010 Court did not face the same kind of threats, to constitutionalism and its own jurisdiction. The eventually failed attempts of the post 2011 court in the area of amendments were defensive, in the face of dangers that were by then obvious.

[178] C. Schmitt, *Hüter der Verfassung* (Berlin: Duncker & Humblot, 1928); Lembcke and Boulanger, "Between Revolution and Constitution" seem to be influenced by this description, even as they are on what was Kelsen's side in the dispute.

behalf of unlimited governmental sovereignty.[179] As with other forms of populism, this attempt takes the name of the sovereign people in vain, and in reality tries to destroy other independent institutions that democratic citizens can use for their self-expression and self-defense. While FIDESZ was never the most determined enemy of the Constitutional Court, in achieving its political success it inherited the mantle and the claims of all the right-wing parties that were. Its choice of constitutional judges indicates this new interest—some of the harshest critics of the Court such as Béla Pokol and István Balsai have now been lifted among its ranks. Still, whatever the makeup of its membership, as an institution the Constitutional Court could not simply run away from the challenge.[180] Given the two-thirds power of FIDESZ and its ability and readiness to pass ordinary laws as constitutional amendments, the struggle could only be fought by a Court that returned to the question of amendment review, in spite of its early and unfortunate precedents. As a result the power to review amendments was expanded, if in the end only with very limited success.

Other scholars and even commissions now effectively tell the interesting story of this struggle,[181] and I need only briefly summarize it here. Even before the Fundamental Law was enacted, the Constitutional Court, then with only two new members, reviewed some of the legislative acts of FIDESZ, declaring several unconstitutional. For FIDESZ, I presume, after its heady electoral victory, this was a declaration of war. In particular, a law declaring retroactive taxation of pensions of public officials was declared unconstitutional in spite of the fact that previously FIDESZ had established the possibility of such ex post facto act by constitutional amendment. This was the beginning of a type of amendment review that targeted the enabling legislation rather than the amendment directly. FIDESZ responded by passing an amendment depriving the Court of its power to review matters that affected the state budget, a very serious form of jurisdiction removal. Yet, even though part of the invalidated legislation was passed again as an amendment, the Court proceeded nevertheless to invalidate subsequent enabling legislation by using the loophole concerning matters of human dignity. That was probably put in "an amendment to the (earlier) amendment" because of international criticism. Thus the Court won round one of the race while still under the 1989 Constitution, despite the addition of new members.

[179] Lembcke and Boulanger, "Between Revolution and Constitution."

[180] Obviously, the institutional interest was also that of the individual judges, who achieved entirely new status by virtue of their being on a well-respected court.

[181] Halmai, "Unconstitutional Constitutional Amendments"; Lembcke and Boulanger, "Between Revolution and Constitution"; Steinbeis, "The Return of the Hungarian Constitutional Court"; Kovács and Tóth, "Hungary's Constitutional Transformation"; Kovács, "Using the Amendment Rule"; see also the following highly informative official documents: Halmai et al., Amicus Brief for the Venice Commission on the Fourth Amendment to the Fundamental Law of Hungary: http://halmaigabor.hu/dok/437_Amicus_Brief_on_the_Fourth_Amendment4.pdf, accessed December 5, 2015; as well as "Opinion on the Fourth Amendment to the Fundamental Law of Hungary" adopted by the Venice Commission at its 95th Plenary Session (Venice, June 14–15, 2013): http://www.venice.coe.int/webforms/documents/default.aspx?pdffile=CDL-AD(2013)012-e

It subsequently went on to successfully invalidate other statutes dealing with religious status, the media, and trial procedures.[182]

Round two turned out differently. After the promulgation of the Fundamental Law, one feature of it came to Court, through an earlier challenge concerning the constitutionality of an amendment that curtailed the jurisdiction of the Court itself. If the Court would have ruled in favor of the litigants, it would have thrown doubt on the legitimacy of the same arrangement incorporated in the Fundamental Law, though of course not invalidating it in that new form. This confusion perhaps also made it difficult for the Court to rule for the litigants—along with an additional problem, one that also came up in Turkey in 2010, that the judges were being asked to rule in favor of their own institutional interest.[183] Moreover, I should note that by this time the Court was fully packed,[184] with seven new judges having been appointed by FIDESZ. The purpose of that expansion was precisely to make unlikely adverse rulings in cases like this one. In my view, in making the earlier amendment the litigants relied on arguments having to do with speed and a lack of consensus and due deliberation, rather than the potentially stronger argument, one that would have challenged the Fundamental Law itself in which the provision was incorporated, having to do with the illegal removal and the violation of Article 24(5). But I admit, either way, the challenge was likely to lose. In any case, the Court now seemed to return to its earlier view that it had no competence to judge the substance of an amendment or for that matter, by implication, that of a new constitution.[185]

The rejection of the arguments of the litigants could have been limited to their merits alone, with an emphasis on the lack of jurisdiction conceded by the revolutionary claim of FIDESZ in the making of the Fundamental Law, belied formally by its use of the old amendment rule. However, the Court did for the first time definitively assume its competence in judging the procedural adequacy of amendments, now said to be parts of the constitution only if enacted in the correct manner.[186] This was a statement of the tautologically obvious, even if only dissenters of the Hungarian Court had previously gone so

[182] Lembcke and Boulanger, "Between Revolution and Constitution" 289.

[183] M. Steinbeis, cited by Halmai in "Unconstitutional Constitutional Amendment." Halmai's invocation of *Marbury* against Steinbeis is not accurate. While the case did affirm the jurisdiction John Marshall sought for the court, the substantive case was not at all about that. That was just the trick. The Hungarian case discussed here, however, was directly about the Court's jurisdiction.

[184] I leave aside that because of retirements FIDESZ was subsequently able to appoint five more justices. These appointments did not yet play a role in the three rounds I describe here.

[185] Decision 61/2011 (VII. 13).

[186] Contradicting the interpretation of Boulanger and Lembcke, "Between Revolution and Constitution" 289 f.n.; Halmai, "Unconstitutional Constitutional Amendments"; and Kovács, "Using the Amendment Rule," who cites the relevant passage.

far.[187] Since the Court went on to judge the plaintiffs' case for inadequate or unconstitutional procedure without sufficient merit, after noting many procedural problems, we can say that this round was won by the FIDESZ government, if barely. Arguably, the Court too had taken a hesitant step forward, toward amendment review. As the following cases were to show, when procedural competence is asserted, as I argued for the Turkish case, there is inevitably an opening to judgments on substance.[188]

The next round of the race was the most interesting one. The Court renewed the conflict in December 2012[189] when it declared as unconstitutional, by a remarkable 10:5 decision, a large part of the Transitional Provisions not originally part of the Fundamental Law but added to it later. These were in effect amendments to the Fundamental Law containing a great deal of political vitriol. Moreover, to anticipate judicial action following a complaint by the Parliamentary Ombudsman (of fundamental rights), a formal amendment, the First, incorporated the Transitional Provisions in the Fundamental Law just before the Court's decision. Nevertheless, the Court found large parts of the Transitional Provisions unconstitutional, for mainly procedural reasons, but at the same time opened the door to possible substantive review of amendments based on a postulated inner hierarchy of the constitution (that implied a basic structure doctrine), and the requirement of complying with the *ius cogens* dimensions of international law, as well as Hungary's treaty obligations.[190] As the Venice Commission noted, for the first time the Constitutional Court raised the possibility of amendment review on substantive grounds.[191]

It is important to note that the Court's decision did have a problematic aspect, one that opened the door to a different future than an evolving trend toward amendment review. The majority very much clung to the view that the Transitional Provisions, although passed according to the required absolute two-thirds majority, were neither part of the constitution, nor amendments to it. This excruciatingly formal argument was both implausible and potentially unfortunate. But it was connected to the history of the Court's rejection of amendment review based on the idea (rightly and repeatedly contested by Justice Bragyova) that parliament has the constituent power, without any substantive limits, and in a form that did not differentiate between amending and constituting.[192] This

187 And indeed two judges who were soon to distinguish themselves on the other side of the divide—Péter Paczolay and István Stumpf—recommended denying both procedural and substantive review. Halmai, "Unconstitutional Constitutional Amendments."

188 See A. Arato, "Democratic Constitution Making and Unfreezing the Turkish Process" (2010) 36 *Philosophy and Social Criticism* 3–4 473–87 and Chapter 5 below; Halmai, "Unconstitutional Constitutional Amendments"; Kovács, "Using the Amendment Rule," for two different views.

189 Decision 45/2012 (XII. 29).

190 Kovács, "Using the Amendment Rule."

191 Venice Commission on the Fourth Amendment to the Fundamental Law of Hungary.

192 Paradoxically, it is mostly the older judges, in this respect still in the majority, who wished to continue to use the old precedents, against the newer appointees who mostly took their stand on parliamentary sovereignty. Steinbeis, "The Return of the Hungarian Constitutional Court."

assessment was even inconsistent with the internal hierarchization of the constitution, now postulated. The Court's decision was thus characterized by ambivalence. The evolution of its precedents pointed to stronger amendment review, and yet the totality of these precedents led to the false and misleading conclusion that what was being reviewed was not an amendment.

Of course when introducing a new form of constitutional jurisdiction caution is warranted. Such restraint famously characterized *Marbury* as well as *Kesavananda*, both of which asserted a new jurisdiction while yielding the case to the government. Even the German Constitutional Court,[193] which affirmed its amendment review competence based on the eternity rules of the *Grundgesetz* but no other textual support, never actually invalidated an amendment on the merits. The Hungarian Court did something more complex in the Transitional Provisions case. It affirmed the abstract possibility of amendment review, and reviewed amendments pretending that they were not amendments at all. And it decided against the government, implying a highly embarrassing defeat for FIDESZ, on some important matters, much more important than Marbury getting his job or losing it, or even Swami Kesavananda keeping his property or not.

It is not easy to disentangle the strands of the Court's decision. Not only were important new justifications for a jurisdiction over amendments affirmed, but transitional provisions already incorporated by amendment have also been invalidated on procedural grounds. Obviously aiming both at the Transitional Provisions and the First Amendment, the Court objected to the continuation of the practice of repeated amendment making during the last year of the 1989 Constitution. According to the judgment, the lifting of ordinary laws to constitutional status after judicial invalidation thereby decreased the authority of the constitution and made judicial review irrelevant. The repeated practice of passing constitutional amendments, mostly in an accelerated procedure, threatened to undermine constitutional government and legal certainty. Thus on procedural grounds the Court was finally ready to defend its own jurisdiction. Touching on substance, the Court attacked the incorporation of the Transitional Provisions because this would create uncertainty regarding the identity of the constitution. Moreover, it attacked the lifting of heterogeneous, clearly not constitutional political elements (most amazingly: attacks on the MSZP, the largest party of the opposition) into the constitution, thereby most obviously compromising the Fundamental Law's constitutional character. As for the parts of the Transitional Provisions specifically challenged by the Ombudsman in charge of rights protection,[194] the Court decided that most of these were to be invalidated. The strikingly heterogeneous list included requiring voters to newly

[193] Halmai, "Unconstitutional Constitutional Amendments" 183–6.

[194] According to the Court, as a result of the First Amendment incorporating the Transitional Provisions, they could be challenged only in specific parts, not as a whole. This, however, contradicted the denial that the Transitional Provisions had neither constitutional nor amendment status.

include themselves in an electoral registry,[195] but also local election rules, passages on church recognition, as well as ideological passages attacking the MSZP because of its links to the old regime, the removal of statutes of limitation for crimes under Communism, and the denial of pension rights to old Communist officials. The Court also invalidated the attempt to further extend the limitation of constitutional review in Article 37(4) of the Fundamental Law, attached to a reduction of Hungary's state debt to lower than half of gross domestic product, if the law in question was passed before the threshold was met. Even more importantly, it invalidated an act with obvious propagandistic intent that allowed the government to tax whenever an adverse judicial decision—of the Constitutional Court or a European court—had adverse budgetary implications, as long as the state debt was more than half of gross domestic product. For the moment these statements and rules were to be struck from the Fundamental Law, though the First Amendment that remained there previously incorporated them, referring to nothing, or hardly anything.

In response, on March 25, 2013, through a new constitutional amendment FIDESZ renewed both the practice of incorporating invalidated acts directly within the constitution, and of constraining the Court's jurisdiction. This was done on the false pretense that the Court invited such incorporation, although it specifically denied the same for the First Amendment. Thus, the very extensive Fourth Amendment of the Fundamental Law[196] in itself did what the Court already objected to, with the support of the Venice Commission, namely raising invalidated acts of a non-constitutional nature to a constitutional status. Moreover, it formally sought to limit amendment review to only procedural review based on the Fundamental Law, and thus not on more abstract considerations of democratic or constitutionalist procedure. This move was backed up with the spurious claim that parliament was extending the powers of the Court, when at best it could have claimed that the amendment was codifying only what the Court itself affirmed. More accurately and worse still, as the Venice Commission noted, the new amendment was trying to eliminate the possibility of what the Court was in the process of affirming, on several grounds, namely substantive review.[197] The same amendment formally proceeded to eliminate all decisions of the Court prior to 2011 as precedents. It is hard to avoid the impression that the government was aiming particularly at the decisions of 2011–12, during which time the Court gradually moved to establish not only procedural but also substantive amendment review. While the attack on old precedents could not directly apply to the Court decision on the Transitional Provisions based on the Fundamental Law, even in this context there could have been the intention to

[195] Steinbeis, "The Return of the Hungarian Constitutional Court."

[196] See the Opinion of the Venice Commission, whose earlier report on the Fundamental Law was less critical in spirit. See points V: A – D http://www.venice.coe.int/webforms/documents/default.aspx?pdffile=CDL-AD(2013)012-e

[197] See ibid., criticizing the complete neglect of the new views on amendment review in Decision 45/2012 (XII.29).

remove some of the ground under the reasoning of many of the judges.[198] In the process an earlier warning of the Venice Commission[199] was disregarded, according to which the elimination of precedents possibly implied by the repudiation of the 1989 Constitution could lead to serious legal uncertainty.

Yet the Court was going to have yet one more chance in this round to consider the constitutionality of the Fourth Amendment, relying on principles recently established.[200] That there was ample substantive ground to establish unconstitutionality is shown by the subsequent Venice Commission Opinion, which cited not only the dissenters, but quoted its earlier recent judgment back to the Court.[201] When the Court made its decision on the Fourth Amendment, with the addition of two new members after retirements, there were altogether nine FIDESZ appointed new judges. Discounting István Stumpf, who played a key role in the previous decisions strengthening a potential amendment review, there was now an ample government-supporting majority. This split was not reflected in the part of the decision that was formally unanimous on the merits. But more importantly, there was an 11 to 4 vote denying the possibility of substantive review of amendments that was cautiously affirmed by the previous decision of the Court by a contrary 10 to 5 vote. In doing so, the Court, along with its president, neglected its own very important precedent of merely five months before. Stumpf again made a strong argument to uphold that precedent established when already under the Fundamental Law, but all other FIDESZ-appointed justices either maintained or reversed their previous positions to support the government. Three of these justices even disagreed with the one positive feature of the decision, maintaining as it did the previous precedent that constitutional amendments had to conform to international law and Hungary's treaty obligations. One of them, Béla Pokol, correctly recognized that the requirement that "the constituent power" conform to international law opened up the possibility "for a later constitutional court body to vindicate for itself the right of invalidation of the Fundamental Law itself, or its specific parts."[202]

It was with this decision, then, that Gábor Halmai's earlier argument about the Court's surrender ending judicial review seemed to become true. In my view as well, the government won the third and so far final round of the horserace. But I would nevertheless argue that the entirely negative judgment on the Court disregards several considerations. First and foremost, dissenting opinions do

[198] Paradoxically, this move would have invalidated also the decisions that rejected amendment review, leaving in place only the important decision under the Fundamental Law that strongly moved in the direction of such review, even on substantive grounds. But this road was meant to be blocked by the specific permission of only procedural review, relying on the amendment rule of the Fundamental Law.

[199] Venice Commission Opinion on the Fourth Amendment to the Fundamental Law of Hungary.

[200] Decision 12/2013 (V.24). [201] "Opinion on the Fourth Amendment."

[202] Separate Opinion of Béla Pokol to Decision 12/2013: "egy későbbi, aktivista többségű alkotmánybírói testület számára, hogy vindikálja magának az Alaptörvény, vagy egyes részei feletti megsemmisítési jogot." Of course, as the quotation indicates, Pokol had no short-term fear of this sort for the current Court, whose (then nine, now eleven) new members have been appointed for twelve years.

matter—they have a way of sometimes becoming majority opinions. In this case, international opinion has been strongly influenced by the minority, as it is clear from reading the Venice Commission report together with the dissents. Moreover, even the majority opinion, as the three government-supporting parallel opinions charged, accepted the possibility that the Court would be able to review matters of amendment substance, based on international law that includes European treaty obligations. While this possibility does not cover abuses like repeatedly passing amendments in accelerated procedure, or lifting invalidated laws into the constitution by amendment, nevertheless when the original statute violates international law, using the amendment rule as a parliamentary override clause may very well substantively expose the FIDESZ government or its successor to amendment review. Finally, as the still lone example of István Stumpf indicates, court packing cannot reliably ensure the reliability of judges. Changes in public opinion have a way of influencing the development of judges, and so can exposure to international criticism as in the Venice Commission Opinion.

With all these reservations, Carl Schmitt's prediction regarding the horse race has proven correct. In the struggle between government and court, the former is the stronger. But here I must add an "unless": unless the Court is supported by strong public opinion, and especially an electoral verdict. In the Indian case, Mrs. Gandhi's attack on the Court in the 1970s, during the emergency, would have succeeded in spite of *Kesavananda*, if the electorate had not chased her from office in 1977. By the time of her re-election in 1980, she was sufficiently chastened not to try another declaration of emergency nor oppose the important Supreme Court decision of *Minerva Mills* of 1980 that consolidated the basic structure doctrine.

In Hungary this has not happened yet, because of the weakness of the opposition, though FIDESZ, even with the more disproportional electoral rules it enacted, barely won the 2014 election and subsequently narrowly lost its two-thirds parliamentary majority. Paradoxically, a much-weakened Court in terms of personnel now is not likely to face the possibility of parliamentary override except in cases where FIDESZ and the hard right Jobbik, the Movement for a Better Hungary, are capable of acting together. This too indicates choices for the FIDESZ government, because nothing could be more likely to invite European pressure and even retaliation than cooperation with an openly right radical party.

Even absent a clear popular repudiation of the new course in Hungary, the Constitutional Court could try to remain or again become a real court if it so chooses. What would facilitate such a transformation is the heritage of the constitution of 1989, along with a European consensus that only a genuine constitutional democracy can remain a legitimate part of the two federations, the EU and the Council of Europe. Moreover, subsequent electoral outcomes in Hungary, given the increased number of two-thirds laws, a heritage of the original 1989 Round Table, may make government by consensus again unavoidable for the sake of governability. Granted, the new "bionic" appointments, including twelve-year terms for constitutional judges, and the large number of two-thirds laws already made, may also allow a FIDESZ government to govern from its grave. Whom all these arrangements will restrict is today unclear, except perhaps with respect to the Constitutional Court that may choose to be permissive with FIDESZ and counter-majoritarian if another government does come to power. The question is whether the judges themselves, as their long term continues, would be willing to transform themselves into something more than a form of power conversion. That would lead to the moral death of the institution. Politically, whether such conversion would be possible will, as always, depend on public opinion including initiative from below.

There is no question in my mind that the embarrassing FIDESZ Fundamental Law ought to be replaced in a new, consensual process that would represent the genuine ending of the journey begun in 1989 by the Round Table. This may not happen for a long time because of public disinterest and oppositional party weakness. Thus we cannot exclude the possibility of "normal" development, even for this abnormal constitution, as long as constitutional review survives or recovers. One thing is for certain: whether by amendment, replacement, or judgment, the Fundamental Law will change. We cannot yet know in what direction.

5

Turkey: Authoritarian Constitution Making, Reform, and the Crisis of Constitutionalism

The recent constitutional history of Turkey is best interpreted in terms of long-reiterated reform attempts. In the crucial period between 1995 and 2004 the reform process involved learning from the slightly earlier models of regime change in Central Europe and South Africa, but also independent discovery and application of their most important principle: consensual constitution making. The abandonment of this principle in favor of a majoritarian effort from 2007 onwards plunged the political order of this country into an extended constitutional crisis. The result of this crisis is still unclear. It could be a new form of populist presidential authoritarianism, legitimated by elections, but also the consensual completion of the process of democratization begun over twenty years ago. Paradoxically, barring a coup, or more likely a presidential *autogolpe,* it depends on the Turkish electorate and political parties to determine which of these two outcomes is more likely realized.

I THE AUTHORITARIAN CONSTITUTION OF 1982

According to converging legal positivist and post-structuralist claims as old as Machiavelli,[1] all constitutional beginnings are illegitimate and most likely violent. Therefore, the argument goes, the success of a constitution will depend only on its contents, and the specific nature of the constitutional beginning does not matter. As this study has repeatedly argued, that argument can and should be refuted on both empirical-comparative as well as theoretical grounds, even if some questionable beginnings have later led to serviceable democratic constitutions. The Turkish constitutional experience from 1982 to 2015 stands as a single case refuting the thesis that it does not matter how one organizes original constitution making, how one begins in the beginning. The making of the constitution of 1982 *was* severely pathological; it *did* have important consequences for the constitutional result; and all this *matters* down to this day, despite a series of impressive procedural and substantive attempts to improve on that result. And the pathological beginning matters because, despite all the changes, important non-democratic elements remain over thirty years later and above all because of

[1] N. Machiavelli, *Discourses* (London: Penguin, 1970) Chapter 8: "When the act accuses, the result excuses."

the survival of what I will describe as the problem of constitutional dualism, which leaves part of the state outside the constitution. It also matters because Turkey's European partners have long regarded the continued existence of the "non-civilian" or "authoritarian" constitution made in 1982 a major reason against admitting Turkey into the Union. Further, that beginning matters because it has helped to weaken the legitimacy of Constitutional Court decisions seeking to defend the basic structure of the constitution against majoritarian fiat. Finally, the beginning matters because institutions that were established then make it difficult to legitimately replace the inherited constitution by a new and consensual one, even thirty years later.

Why was the process that established the Turkish Constitution of 1982 severely pathological from a democratic point of view?[2] The agent of the coup of 1980 that overthrew the constitution of 1961, originally an organ of that Constitution, namely, the National Security Council (NSC) composed primarily of the heads of services led by Gen. Kenan Evren, chose not to elect a Constituent Assembly, or a Grand National Assembly acting as one, as already the tradition in Turkey (1921, 1924, and partially even in 1961[3]). Instead it chose to exercise constituent power (it cannot very well be called constituent *authority*!) itself. A selected 160-member Consultative Assembly was called into being, and a smaller 15-member Constitutional Commission within this body, under the close supervision of the NSC itself, drew up the final text. In typical Bonapartist fashion, this text was then supposedly authorized in a popular referendum that was itself highly constrained: discussion was forbidden, only the *yes* side had media access, non-participation was fined and most importantly, it was clear that a shift to any kind of electoral politics could follow only in the case of a *yes* vote. A military authoritarian emergency regime was the only default option: if the referendum failed direct military rule would continue indefinitely, and whenever the next constitution was offered it could be even worse. Moreover, the choice of the most important office was not entrusted to subsequent elections: again, in classical Napoleonic fashion, the constitution referred implicitly to an office-holder (the Chair of the NSC) if not literally by name, and thus a yes vote on the text entailed the election of General Evren as state president for seven years.[4]

[2] See M.F. Bilgin, "Constitution, Legitimacy and Democracy in Turkey" in S. Arjomand (ed.), *Constitutional Politics in the Middle East* (Portland, OH: Hart, 2007) 132 ff. For a different, less convincing interpretation see the otherwise very informative essay by K.K. Karpat, "Military Interventions: Army-Civilian Relations in Turkey Before and After 1980" in M. Heper and A. Evin (eds), *State, Democracy and the Military. Turkey in the 1980s* (Berlin and New York: De Gruyter, 1988) 153–4. Also see in the essays in the same volume by B. Toprak. "The State, Politics, and Religion in Turkey" 126; and W. Hale, "Transition to Civilian Governments in Turkey: The Military Perspective" (169-170) for more critical early views.

[3] I say partially, because it was a two-chamber constituent assembly, one of which was the NSC that organized the coup of 1960. See E. Özbudun and E.F. Gençkaya, *Democratization and the Politics of Constitution Making in Turkey* (Budapest: CEU, 2009).

[4] Provisional Art. 1. For the details, see Özbudun and Gençkaya, *Democratization and the Politics of Constitution Making in Turkey* 19–23.

The 1982 Constitution was thus an imposed charter, a *constitution octroyée*, one imposed by an *internal* dictatorship, and as such established structural features that could never have been enacted in an even partially democratic process. The literature fully details these elements of the constitution in the areas of civil and political rights, ethnic and religious discrimination, due process and rule of law, as well as military reservations. Admittedly, many of these features were subsequently reformed,[5] but I shall focus only on a structural point that serves to combine all of them and could not be easily altered.

The 1982 Constitution established a state within a state, or a dualistic state. But two meanings of state are involved: the state in the sense of the apparatus of violence and state as the unity of population, governmental organs, and territory. More exactly, the apparatus of violence and administration along with its own legal system was established as a state within the state as a whole, without being submitted to constitutional controls. This happens in all cases of internally imposed constitutions, from the *Charte* of 1815 and the Bismarck Constitution of the German Empire, to the Pinochet Constitution of 1980—all of which typically chose to constitutionalize (which does not mean democratize!) significant parts of state operations, but leaving other, even more important parts outside the rule of the constitution.[6] While the 1961 Constitution in Turkey intended to balance the powers of government through constitutionalist *guarantees*, the 1982 structure sought to institutionalize the powers of those who made the coup through forms of *conversion*. Their goal was "to check the powers of elected agencies and to narrow down the space for civilian politics."[7] In Chile, in roughly the same period, these forms were referred to as authoritarian enclaves.[8] In Turkey the institutions of conversion were generally called "tutelary institutions." They were centered in the NSC, the presidency, and their common political foundations, the hierarchical officer corps of the military. The NSC, whose majority was to be uniformed officers, was given the power to influence and even dominate the agenda of the cabinet. The president was given important appointment powers including the Constitutional Court, where he could pick three justices directly, and eight on recommendation from other courts. The uniformed military received a judicial role and exemptions from the control of

[5] E. Özbudun and S. Yazici, *Democratization Reforms in Turkey (1993–2004)* (Tesev Publications, 2004); L. Gönenc, "The 2001 Amendments to the 1982 Constitution of Turkey" *Ankara Law Review* 1 (2004) 1; S. Benhabib and T. Isiksel, "Ancient Battles, New Prejudices, and Future Perspectives: Turkey and the EU" in (2006) 13 *Constellations* 2; as well as Bilgin, "Constitution, Legitimacy and Democracy in Turkey."

[6] This point is most clearly seen by M. Heper, "State and Society in Turkish Political experience" in Heper and Evin, *State, Democracy and the Military* 5–6. His concept is that of a mixed constitution. Similarly, in the same volume A. Evin, "Changing Patterns of Cleavages after 1980" 208, speaks of the supremacy of the state over politics, indicating the dualism I have in mind.

[7] Özbudun and Gençkaya, *Democratization and the Politics of Constitution Making in Turkey*.

[8] See K. Siavelis and P. Sehnbruch (eds), *Democratic Chile: The Politics and Policies of a Historic Coalition, 1990–2010* (Boulder, CO: Lynne Rienner Publishers, Inc., 2014).

governmental agencies. Its hierarchical command retained internal control over all military appointments.[9]

Nevertheless, because of the predilections of the same military and the influence of Turkey's allies, it was not a purely authoritarian constitution that was established in 1982, but a dualistic one, in which (at least initially) the authoritarian elements clearly predominated.[10] Very roughly, this dualism is reflected in what the Turks describe as that of state and government, and implies constitutionalist guarantees along with forms of conversion. It would be a huge exaggeration to say that while the "state" remained authoritarian, the "government" was designed as democratic. It was not—the NSC, under the leadership of the president, and with the help also of the Constitutional Court whose membership state organs were to control, was to retain its influence over who could participate in political competition and how that competition would be organized.[11] In short, the laws relating to parties, associations, and political rights were also undemocratic to important extents, regulating their memberships and activities, and open to arbitrary interventions by undemocratic, unaccountable organs of the state. This was indeed part of the most important aim of the coup of 1980: to radically change the nature of party competition, and it is a remarkable fact that despite all the restrictive provisions, this aim only partially succeeded. What was achieved, however, was one institution, the presidency, both as the head of the state and part of the governmental executive power that would be the fulcrum around which all state powers would be organized. It was the president who was to chair the top state institution, the veritable "locus of the state," namely the NSC, a small collegial body dominated by the uniformed military chiefs.[12]

Because it was a dualistic rather than a purely authoritarian constitution, there were to be partially free elections under it. Here too authoritarian elements predominated, since initially all the traditional parties were banned, and

[9] Özbudun and Gençkaya, *Democratization and the Politics of Constitution Making in Turkey* 22–3.

[10] For the formative essay on this type of state, see E. Fraenkel, *Dual State* (Oxford: Oxford University Press, 1945). In its initial form in Turkey, as in Fraenkel's Nationalist Socialist paradigm, the prerogative state was dominant over the normative one. As the model developed in Turkey, a conflictual, but more balanced relationship emerged between the two parts of the "state," closer to Fraenkel's "dualistic" than his "dual."

[11] This is well documented by Ü. Ergüder and R. Hofferbert, "The 1983 General Elections in Turkey" and B. Toprak, "The State, Politics and Religion in Turkey" both in Heper and Evin, *State, Democracy and the Military*; and H. Shambayati "The Guardian of the Regime: The Turkish Constitutional Court in Comparative Perspective" in Arjomand, *Constitutional Politics in the Middle East*.

[12] E. Özbudun, "The Status of the President of the Republic under the Turkish Constitution of 1982: Presidentialism or Parliamentarism" in Heper and Evin, *State, Democracy and the Military*. M. Heper too was certainly right to object: "(the fact) that as compared to France the regime in Turkey under the 1982 constitution is closer to parliamentarism rather than a presidential system ... may be explained by the fact that the state elites in Turkey, when necessary, 'act' not through the executive, but the National Security Council." As the dominant figure of the NSC, the president, as holder of more than narrowly conceived "executive" powers, became "the locus of the state" in this conception. M. Heper, "Conclusion" in ibid. 253.

only newly permitted parties were initially allowed to participate. Even the formally democratic part, the supposedly proportional electoral rule, had an extremely high 10 percent threshold, which made the actual system highly disproportional and unrepresentative. Even in this form, however, the fact that there were to be partially free elections was important. Indeed, the first one in 1983 yielded a surprising result (a majority for T. Özal's Motherland Party), surprising because it was contrary to the recommendation and open pressure of the NSC and President Evren.

The dualistic nature of the constitution was even more significantly expressed by the document's amendment structure. According to the original Article 175,[13] the constitution could be amended if two-thirds of the deputies of the monocameral Turkish Grand National Assembly (TGNA) so voted, with the president's approval, or against his suspensive veto by passing it again by the same majority and, if the president still wished, gaining confirmation in a referendum (originally with two-thirds of the support of the population). Despite the president's participation this was a purely governmental process. However, here too the authoritarian dimension was present, if transitionally—under Provisional Article 9, for a duration of six years the president could require that an amendment be repassed by three-quarters of the TGNA. Thus he had the option (never used in fact) of showing the strongest possible disagreement with a constitutional revision proposal. Technically, however, even the possibility of veto override by three-quarters represented a constitutional limit on the presidency's competence to control amendments.

Thus it can be said that while *politically*, the constitution of 1982 did not fully bring the state under the constitution, *legally* it created mechanisms by which that could be achieved in the future, at least in significant part. Parliament, together with the electorate, had legal *Kompetenz-Kompetenz* as the Germans would say, though the military through the state retained what could be called political *Kompetenz-Kompetenz*. Which would dominate? In Carl Schmitt's sense, the constitution of 1982 was not only dualistic but was also a decisionless one and left a large opening (sunset provisions of the so-called provisional articles, and even more: elections and amendments) that could be utilized in a democratic direction, allowing a further process of the constitutionalization of the state than intended by the framers. At the same time, the political *Kompetenz-Kompetenz* of state power holders (or sovereignty if you prefer Schmitt)[14] retained significant parts of the informal constituent power (but again not

[13] The original 1982 text is very hard to find. For help with research and translations I am very grateful to my former student Dr. Aysel Madra.

[14] Some refer to the system as that of dual sovereignty, which in my view is a contradiction in terms: M. H. Yavuz, "Introduction" in Yavuz (ed.), *The Emergence of a New Turkey. Democracy and the AK Party* (Salt Lake City, UT: University of Utah Press, 2006) 16. Parallel governments also referred to by Yakuz seem unobjectionable.

constituent *authority*) in the form of vetoes[15] over the formal process of constitutional revision.[16] It is a peculiarity of the constitution of 1982, reflecting its decisionless quality, that this political control over constitutional change could be and has been exercised mainly by the Constitutional Court, itself a dualistic institution. In other words, the Court could act either in a generally narrowly interpreted purely legal capacity, or in an incredibly broadly interpreted political capacity.[17] Structurally, it could be either a guardian of the constitution, or of state power.[18] The first of these possibilities was expressed by the ability to invalidate statutes,[19] and at first only by implication even constitutional amendments, and the second by the power to close political parties, which was inherited from the Court of the 1961 Constitution and from the makers of the constitution of 1982.[20]

[15] Well documented in the case of negotiations over the 2001 amendment package: see Ö.F. Gençkaya, "Politics of Constitutional Amendment in Turkey 1987–2002" in G.H. Flanz (ed.), *Constitutions of the Countries of the World. Turkey* (Dobbs Ferry, NY: Oceana, 2003).

[16] Again, because of this "decisionless" quality I would not qualify the Turkey of the Constitution of 1982 simply as a "dual state" in Ernst Fraenkel's sense (*The Dual State*) where there is always a clear priority of the "prerogative" state over the "normative" one. That may have been the intention of the framers of the constitution, but succeeded only initially. A "dual state" is still a dictatorship; Turkey was not.

[17] There are of course those who interpret the Court of 1982 (and even that of 1961) as nothing but the guardian of the authoritarian, military-dominated state. They consider the conflicts of the Court with the military as nothing more than "freedom jargon" and feel no need to explain why the military under both constitutions repeatedly sought to limit the powers of review. See O. Can "The Turkish Constitutional Court as Defender of *Raison d'État*" in R. Grote and T. Röder (eds), *Constitutionalism in Islamic Countries* (Oxford: Oxford University Press, 2012) 264–7. More understandably because on focusing on party closings, Shambayati comes to a parallel conclusion in "The Guardian of the Regime: The Turkish Constitutional Court in Comparative Perspective." The close analogy to the Iranian Council of Guardians, however, is untenable.

[18] Interpreters who stress the role of the Constitutional Court as merely a tutelary or guardianship institution tend to forget the continuity of its forms dating back to the more constitutionalist 1961 Constitution. They need to explain why, if the Court was regarded as merely a tutelary institution, the acts of the NSC regime of 1980–83 were formally exempted from review of constitutionality by the Constitutional Court. And why were there repeated attempts to limit the amendment jurisdiction of the Court by military-controlled governments in 1971 and 1982? These facts are mentioned but not explained in Özbudun and Gençkaya, *Democratization and the Politics of Constitution Making in Turkey* 23; or in L. Köker, "Turkey's Political Constitutional Crisis: An Assessment of the Role of the Constitutional Court" in (2010) 17 *Constellations* 2 328–44.

[19] The power of constitutional review was formally speaking a form of guarantee, as against conversion, in terms of the distinction established in Chapter 3. Nevertheless, since the constitution contained forms of conversion, protecting these amounted to the instrumentalization of guarantees. The Turkish Constitutional Court, however, wound up using the power of amendment review, as argued below, both under the 1961 and 1982 Constitutions as forms of guarantee against both authoritarian measures (1970s) and majoritarian imposition (2000s).

[20] Köker, "Turkey's Political Constitutional Crisis" 336 explicitly notes the dualism by distinguishing between constitutional (review powers) and criminal law powers (party closings) of the Court, between protecting rights and liberties and guarding the state against the parties. But then he goes on to treat the Court as merely a guardianship institution, from the political (as against legal) point of view. In my view, the same dualism penetrated both the legal status and the politics of the Court.

II REITERATED INCREMENTAL REFORMS: FROM 1987 TO 2004

Constitutional amendments have played a major role in Turkey's long-attempted transition from the dualistic system. They have taken three basic forms: consensual in procedure and partial in content; consensual and broad; and antagonistic and partial. From 2003 at the earliest, a project of producing an entirely new civilian constitution also emerged. There was a built-in conflict whether this would be done in a consensual or antagonistic form. Behind these three forms were three sequential but partially overlapping political projects, all of which survive to this day, involving three related but distinct, sometimes complementary, but sometimes conflictual politics:

1. the politics of democratic transition that put Turkey in company with democratic oppositions under dictatorships of the 1970s and 80s, and was initially compatible with incremental constitutional amendments;
2. the politics of entering the European Union, that led to a broadening and acceleration of transition strategies, and eventually to the project of producing an entirely new constitution; and
3. the politics of redefining Turkey's identity and the meaning of its secularism, which has led to a more antagonistic, majoritarian process of constitution making.

Each strategy presupposed the need for democracy, though not necessarily defined the same way and with the same radicality. Each had elements not necessarily shared with the others. But each had to rely for some time on structural reform, specifically one similar to those in several authoritarian regimes of the time where the authoritarians holding state power retained some significant support (e.g.: close to 50 percent for the authoritarian side in a referendum on Provisional Article 4 in 1987). Originally, to the extent that each of the three politics was present, they were difficult to distinguish. At later stages, however, the parties advocating them became distinct and could enter into conflicts about their goals or at least their priorities.

It is worth discussing how the process of democratization began, because there are people who identify the dramatic acceleration process under EU pressure after 2000 (mistakenly labeled a "refolution" by Benhabib) with the whole Turkish transition.[21] While the transition should not be dated too early,[22] it is

[21] Benhabib and Isiksel, "Ancient Battles, New Prejudices, and Future Perspectives" 224; and Bilgin, "Constitution, Legitimacy and Democracy in Turkey" 143 are on one side of this, though the latter gives a fair evaluation of the 1987 and 1995 amendments; while S. Sayin in his Introduction to Özbudun and Yazici, *Democratization Reforms in Turkey* as well as the authors who begin their study in 1993, are on the other side, stressing autonomous Turkish roots of democratization.

[22] Putting the transition too early would identify with the so-called "restoration of democracy" and the enactment of the constitution of 1982 with the establishment of a democratic order. It is a mistake, however, to argue that the framers intended and or even inadvertently achieved a democratic constitution as, for example,

true that from the beginning the 1982 Constitution was confronted with reform projects, coming more from its opponents rather than its framers (who did, however, include some sunset clauses in their authoritarian design)—even if it was as yet unclear whether the goal was a democratic one or only an increasingly democratized constitution. Open articulation of the more complete program, and the idea of a new constitution would have meant exclusion from the political process for a long time. Thus *democratization* of government (meaning more democracy, more individual rights, less state in the governmental process) and *constitutionalization* of the state (meaning less of the state, fewer and fewer of its spheres and operations outside the constitution) initially remained the only passable road for political reasons. Unsurprisingly, the three political projects, not identical but originally allied, and not always clearly distinguished even among their partisans, availed themselves of the same path.

As in several countries undergoing democratic transitions, initially a series of structural and not particularly far-reaching amendments were the constitutional instruments for change, starting with a 1987 amendment package that changed the amendment rule itself. At the time, abolition of Provisional Article 4 that banned leading political figures from participation was more contentious, and it was only because of this issue that Prime Minister Özal, who did not wish the old politicians to be reinstated, called a referendum, one that he lost very narrowly.[23] In two respects amendments were made easier: in case the majority behind a popular amendment was too narrow under the old rule, the two-thirds requirement was reduced to three-fifths, plus a ratificatory referendum in which the majority needed was reduced from two-thirds to a simple majority. However, this new path of passing amendments was not usable without a president allied with the parliamentary majority. Likely more important was that the government was laying down the markers: a road of amendments could be followed to democratize the Turkish government and to constitutionalize the state. Large amendment packages in 1995 (i.e. before the massive application of European pressure, but during negotiations for a customs union with the EU) and in 2001, were to do just that. It was very important that these amendment packages were negotiated among all the parliamentary parties before being brought to a vote, ostensibly to avoid presidential vetoes and referenda.[24] While the politics of entering Europe now made an appearance, this initially only led

I. Dagi, "Democratic Transition in Turkey 1980–1983: The Impact of European Diplomacy" in S. Kedourie (ed.) *Turkey. Identity, Democracy, Politics* (London: Cass, 1996). The framers intended a dualistic constitution, with the non-democratic and not fully constitutionalized state penetrating democratic governmental mechanisms.

[23] Ö.F. Gençkaya, "Politics of Constitutional Amendment in Turkey 1987–2002"; E.J. Zürcher, *Turkey. A Modern History* (London: Tauris, 2005) 284–5.

[24] Özbudun and Yazici, *Democratization Reforms in Turkey* 14 mention this, but in my view somewhat underestimating the difference between the type of consensus characteristic of the 1995/2001 amendments and the ones after. Good descriptions of the role of the All-party Accord Commission (first called the Inter-Party Commission) in the 1995 and 2001 amendments are in Gençkaya, "Politics of Constitutional Amendment in Turkey 1987–2002" xv, xxiv–xxv; and in Gönenc, "The 2001 Amendments to the 1982 Constitution" 95.

to a change in the format of how the structural amendments were produced. Instead of a process steered by the government in power, as in the case of 1987, in 1995, and even more in 2001, the emphasis shifted to parliamentary parties and their consensus-producing process. The emergence of a new informal institution of compromise, the All Party Accord Commission in 2001[25] in effect reproduced a key dimension of the contemporary round-table paradigm of constitution making through legal continuity and consensus. Thus, while first resembling long incremental transitions in countries such as Brazil, Chile, and Mexico, especially between 1995 and 2001, the Turkish transition came to adopt features of the negotiated transitions as well, characteristic of the faster round-table models of Poland, Hungary, and South Africa. But for a long time, and until very recently, the model remained that of reform or amendment packages rather than the negotiation of an entirely new democratic constitution.

There is little question that the amendment packages accomplished a great deal in democratizing and constitutionalizing the dualistic regime, even if they did not eliminate it altogether. Aside from symbolic changes striking a positive reference to the coup of 1980, the amendments removed many of its results, such as the restrictions on forming trade unions, associations, and public organizations and their relationships to political parties. Many limits on political activity were eliminated. Most importantly, perhaps, in the biggest package of 1995, the grounds for prohibiting parties were made more difficult.[26] In 2001 amendments went even further in restricting these grounds, and added that henceforth it would require three-fifths of the Constitutional Court to rule a party illegal. The option of fining parties, also potentially ameliorating the problem, was now added.[27] The same 2001 amendments tried to strengthen the status of rights, in particular eliminating or limiting administrative interference with meetings and demonstrations, they improved the status of the Kurdish language, hitherto banned, and strengthened citizenship rights. The time of possible pre-trial detention time was reduced. There were also attempts to weaken tutelary institutions, if not to entirely eliminate them. An amendment increased the civilian members of the NSC to a majority. While this body survived all the amendments as an outpost of state power in the government, its role with respect to the cabinet was slightly weakened. The Constitutional Court was now empowered to review the laws of the early NSC regime.

Before the question of an entirely new constitution-making episode arose, two other political projects became much more visible. By 1995 there was already some European influence on the broadening and accelerating of the model of democratic transition. But the politics of renegotiating Turkey's secular identity came first, and when it came to the forefront, it first helped to slow

[25] Gençkaya, "Politics of Constitutional Amendment in Turkey 1987–2002" xv, xxiv; Özbudun and Yazici, *Democratization Reforms in Turkey* 14.

[26] Özbudun and Gençkaya, *Democratization and the Politics of Constitution Making in Turkey* 36–40.

[27] Ibid. 58.

down the initial transition model that reached its culmination with the amendments of 1995. While this amendment package in the end could still be passed in a reduced form, in spite of the difficulties presented by the Islamist Welfare (or Refah) Party insisting on its own particular issues,[28] the subsequent coming of that party to governmental leadership, followed by the last major military intervention into Turkish politics in 1997 (the soft or post modern coup), and the banning of the Welfare Party (WP) led to an impasse, if not yet the end of what was the first phase of the transition, dominated by incremental reform. We should note, however, that during its first appearance the third politics helped to short circuit rather than develop the process of democratic transition—even if this was not the aim of its practitioners.[29]

The opposite was the case during the intensification of the role of European-oriented politics. Following a low point in EU and Turkish relations, after the European Court of Human rights (ECHR) decision on the WP case,[30] the European Union became more involved in Turkish Affairs.[31] Influenced by this party ban, Turkish politicians focused on amendments narrowing the scope and meaning of banning parties, but it was also perhaps because of European involvement that Islamic successor parties increasingly reconstructed themselves based on models that would be acceptable on European legal criteria. This external role should not be underestimated, both in the midst of the discussion of the 2001 amendments, and especially in formal statements by the Constitutional Court and informal pressure by the military and its allies that actually halted the process for a period. It was then that European pressure and Turkey's intention declared by the TGNA on March 19, 2001 to make reforms in accordance with the so-called Accession Partnership Agreement that secured the passing of a very large and important package of thirty-four amendments, if not as large and radical as the originally proposed fifty-one negotiated by the All-party Accord Commission. Finally, the 2004 amendment package abolishing the death penalty as well as state security courts, asserting the equal rights of women, and establishing the constitutional precedence of international agreements in the

[28] Gençkaya, "Politics of Constitutional Amendment in Turkey 1987–2002" xv–xviii. These issues were focused on Art. 24 of the constitution having to do with freedom of religion and conscience. The WP held up changes in other articles unless it could have its way on Art. 24.

[29] For a full discussion, see Özbudun and Gençkaya, *Democratization and the Politics of Constitution Making in Turkey* 36–8. As late as 2004 this kind of blockage remained possible. At that time the Justice and Development Party (AKP) successfully opposed the inclusion of affirmative action for women in a general statement of the equality of rights.

[30] The ban against the WP was unfortunately upheld by the ECHR on February 13, 2001, probably encouraging the banning of the Virtue Party, in spite of warnings by the European Parliament. See http://hudoc.echr.coe.int/eng?i=001-60936 accessed December 3, 2015.

[31] The rapporteur Alain Lamassoure took cognizance of the ECHR refusal to rule against the banning of the Welfare Party, but expressed his displeasure concerning ongoing moves against the Virtue Party. EU Parliament Draft Report August 30, 2001, http://www.europarl.europa.eu/meetdocs/committees/afet/20011008/444737EN.pdf accessed December 3, 2015.

areas of fundamental rights and liberties, clearly responded to European pressure.[32]

By the time of the amendment package of 2004, however, Turkey's European interlocutors, now very active, were no longer satisfied with mere amendment packages.[33] One can see the change in the various European documents addressed to Turkey, which always acknowledge the changes made so far, and yet nevertheless seem to suggest that Turkey is not really getting much closer to the desired goal. At least this is the tendency of the 2001 and 2003 statements written by Lamassoure (before the final passing of the 2001 amendments, and presumably helping to nail down the result) and Oostlander,[34] and I am not forgetting the internal European reasons at play each time behind the tough and sometimes unfortunate rhetoric. But note that the second of these statements, the much tougher one, came *after* Turkey adopted extensive new constitutional amendments and legal packages addressing previous demands of the EU articulated in the Copenhagen Principles (1992) and various declarations of the EU parliament and Commission. On the one hand, the better Turkey performed the more fearful many Europeans seemed to get.[35] On the other hand, the European argument on constitutional matters was becoming more radical and detailed, eventually targeting not only the constitution of 1982 but also the reform process itself.

The 2001 Lamassoure report, after attacking the constitution of 1982, still spoke of only "thorough constitutional reform," certainly compatible with serial amendment packages even if the author stressed that "the reforms under way were still encumbered" by too many political and legal decisions that held progress back. Thus the operative phrase here was still only the end-goal of providing Turkey with a modern constitution.[36] The 2003 Oostlander report, aside from its gratuitous attacks on Kemalism, went much further on the question of method and procedure. The constitution of 1982 was now entirely rejected as the appropriate basis to guarantee the rule of law and fundamental freedoms, because of the "deepest structures of the state and style of Government." The

32 Özbudun and Gençkaya, *Democratization and the Politics of Constitution Making in Turkey* 66–7.

33 The stress here is on *very active*. Europe has been involved since the days of the military government of 1980–82 (see Dagi, "Democratic Transition in Turkey 1980–1983: The Impact of European Diplomacy") and the framing of various agreements with Turkey in the 1990s. But there was significant acceleration around 2000, as well as a new hands-on attitude regarding constitutional and legal reform: see C. Dodd, "Democracy and the EU" in B.B. Beeley, *Turkish Transformation* (Tallahassee, FL: The Eothen Press, 2002); and Benhabib and Isiksel, "Ancient Battles, New Prejudices, and Future Perspectives.

34 A. Oostlander, rapporteur, EU Parliament Draft Report March 12, 2003. http://www.europarl.europa.eu/meetdocs/committees/afet/20030428/484772EN.pdf accessed December 3, 2015.

35 See the brilliant article by N. Göle, "Europe's Encounter With Islam: What Future" in (2006) 13 *Constellations* 2.

36 EU Parliament Draft Report, August 30, 2001 points G, H, and L.

changes involved "are so fundamental" only a new constitution based on European values, or on European democratic foundations, "with the rights of individuals and minorities balanced against collective rights" would be acceptable.[37] According to Oostlander, moreover, and this is what is really new, "the current constitution was drawn up in 1982. It bears the clear hallmarks of the military. Accordingly, it does not lend itself to radical amendment in order to comply with the above requirement."[38]

What is striking is the different assumptions that seem to lie behind the European demand for changes, first expressed hesitantly in 2001 and then aggressively by 2003, and in the way that Turkish political forces addressed these demands. While the operative fiction of the Turkish changes seemed to have been that the 1982 Constitution was some kind of democratic constitution although a deficient one, a foundation that serious structural reforms could perfect, the assumption of EU statements from 2001 to 2003 was that it was entirely the wrong constitution that needed to be not improved but *replaced* by a new civil or civilian one. Of course the dualistic original construct allowed both of these wrong interpretations. But what was right about the sometimes too nasty and impatient European charges was that serial amendment processes tend to be open ended, that they may likely involve too many compromises with de facto powers, and that in fact after several waves it was only a part (even if now a significant part) of the authoritarian heritage that was removed. The most important authoritarian institution, the NSC, in fact survived, and the Constitutional Court and other judicial bodies remained in part outposts of state power, allowing ultimately both formal and not completely formal undemocratic procedures to influence some of the most important political processes. At most some of the changes shifted the proportion between formal and informal ways of using state influence.[39] Thus constitutional dualism survived, and with it the original constitutional identity. The various European spokesmen formally addressing Turkey finally came to the conclusion that the open-ended sequential amendment process was never going to be enough—the teleology of constitutional amendments must culminate in the making of an entirely new constitution, which evidently could include much that had been attained along the way.[40]

At the same time, the new European demand that only the making of an entirely new constitution would suffice was not entirely right either as a theoretical and as a political matter. As a theoretical matter, a road of sequential amendments could in the end change everything, except for three highly abstract unchangeable articles of the constitution, even if in Turkey this did not

[37] EU Parliament Draft Report, March 12, 2003 points E, F and 11.

[38] Ibid. "Explanatory statement" reform program.

[39] Ibid. Both Lamassoure (point 7: monitor the NSC for the transition period) and more radically Oostlander (point 8,9: in the long term abolish the NSC; remove military from all civilian organs) focus on this crucial dimension.

[40] It does not much matter if the European critics were right. In fact a sequential amendment process could in principle eliminate the old dualism; while a new constitution could contain it.

happen. More importantly, politically, while the EU undoubtedly had the right to regulate its own membership, and to that extent intervene in the internal developments of countries seeking to become members, it was still a question of how much internal risk and instability external interference had a right to cause, especially if there were functionally equivalent solutions to the same problems. It was certainly a delicate line, but it may be that a statement like Lamassoure's in 2001 was able to honor it, while Oostlander's in 2002, especially after Turkey had just made some important changes following the road of amendments, overstepped it in an undesirable way.

In any case the Turkish government responded to the new demands positively. When in the new Justice and Development Party (AKP) governmental program of 2006 the project of adopting a "new and civilian constitution" was announced, the EU Parliament emphatically welcomed this, and called "on all parties to support an open and consensual constitutional process."[41] Note that both parts of this statement were important: a new constitution and an open and consensual process. Paradoxically, however, while the Turks now announced their desire to achieve the first desideratum, an entirely new constitution, it was in an earlier phase, the phase of more partial amendments that they seemed to better fulfill the second. How this happened can only be explained by turning back to the third politics, the renegotiation of the national identity.

III THE END OF THE CONSENSUAL PROCESS

The goals of democratic Islamic parties or their successors converged with other democratic forces for some time, obviously so, because many of the undemocratic features of the 1982 Constitution and how it operated came to be directed against the Islamic party in its several incarnations. Among the internal transformations of the AKP with respect to its predecessors, several interpreters stress the change regarding European standards and European accession as fundamental. While there is no reason to consider the changes as insincere, it is also possible to see them as highly useful for a party that needed not only allies, but also a more universal ("public regarding") language or discourse to articulate its own particular interests and demands. Finally, it was the AKP, after its electoral victory in late 2002 through 2004–5 that managed to secure some highly desirable reform packages along with important constitutional amendments as well, thereby continuing both the program of the democratic transition and supposedly satisfying European demands. Some interpreters call this paradoxical[42] but the paradox diminishes if one looks at the dating. The really dramatic changes began in 1995 and reached their culmination in 2001 (as Benhabib and Isiksel also

[41] European Parliament, "On EU-Turkey Relations" October 24, 2007, point 5, http://www.europarl.europa.eu/sides/getDoc.do?pubRef=-//EP//TEXT+TA+P6-TA-2007-0472+0+DOC+XML+V0//EN&language=EN accessed November 19, 2015.

[42] Benhabib and Isiksel, "Ancient Battles, New Prejudices, and Future Perspectives" 228; J. Casanova, "The Long, Difficult and Tortuous Journey of Turkey into Europe" (2006) 13 *Constellations* 2 240.

accidentally note[43]) and not after 2002, and while Islamic deputies participated before and after the dissolution of the Virtue Party, two out of three of the biggest amendment packages to the constitution of 1982 were produced *before* the AKP's victory. Thus the AKP was at best an inheritor and continuator and not an initiator of the process that in the end it was to seriously disrupt.

Moreover we should note that the All Party Accord format stressed by Gençkaya and Özbudun disappeared after 2002. We must be careful here not to confuse two things: (i) the new parliamentary arithmetic; and (ii) the AKP switching to a more antagonistic, majoritarian political strategy. As to the first, even after its big electoral victory in 2002 (or its even bigger one in 2007, which produced fewer seats), the AKP could not hope to gain either the democratic reforms it preferred or elements of its own narrower constitutional goals without both allies and a friendly or at least neutral incumbent in the presidency[44] if it did not want to risk referenda. Having three-fifths of the seats to make amendments (but not quite two-thirds after 2002), the AKP had to have partners or had to be able to neutralize the role of the presidency.[45] Only the latter could fully close the road to referenda. Nevertheless, initially the first path, political cooperation, was chosen. After the election of 2002 this meant only one possible partner, however, the secular opposition CHP (Popular Republican Party), since the electoral rule with its 10 percent threshold eliminated representation for over ten parties (including two or three sizable ones) and basically produced a two-party parliament.

It is important to stress that until early 2007, partnership in the amending process with the CHP could be maintained even in the face of vetoes by President Sezer, himself a staunch secularist. A case in point: the CHP voted with the AKP to overcome, through constitutional amendment benefiting one single person, a political ban against the leader of the AKP, Mr. T.R. Erdoğan himself. Equally important here is the 2004 amendment package negotiated and enacted consensually with the CHP, dealing with the death penalty (basically abolishing it), the priority of international human rights obligations over domestic law, the abolition of State Security Courts and some other minor military privileges.

Then in 2007 came the crisis over the presidency. With the end of President Sezer's term, the AKP wanted to elect one of its top leaders, foreign minister Abdullah Gül. Without going over the complicated history involving the two parties and the Constitutional Court, it is enough to say that in the first instance the AKP failed in the face of a well-organized boycott of the CHP and a relevant

[43] Benhabib and Isiksel, "Ancient Battles, New Prejudices, and Future Perspectives" 224.

[44] See Article 175 of the 1982 Constitution.

[45] The situation was different after 2007 with more parties represented. Though with more votes, the AKP dropped way below the three-fifths figure, but had more parties to ally with potentially. The votes of the National People's Party (MHP) would put the majority well beyond the two-thirds. Yet the presidency was still needed to avoid uncertain and divisive referenda.

Court decision, whether mistaken or not.[46] Then, in a second phase in a new and slightly more representative parliament, with the support of some independents and the third party, the MHP, as well as a bare majority of the Court, the AKP succeeded in passing, by the narrowest possible majority, a package of constitutional amendments relating to the presidency, to quorums, and to parliamentary elections, amendments that after a veto by the president were confirmed in a popular referendum.[47] Attention was directed at the struggle over the presidency, in the end attained through a new parliamentary majority of the AKP, rather than the eventually highly significant direct elections achieved by the amendment. Most relevant in the present context, however, is the shift of the AKP to a majoritarian constitution-making strategy, whether constrained or voluntary. Thus, during the 2007 elections when the AKP announced its intention to produce a new "civilian" constitution, it was already practicing an antagonistic constitution-making method significantly different than the consensual one used before.

The struggle of the opposition against AKP obtaining the presidency could be seen in two equally relevant ways: as the desire of authoritarian forces based in state institutions to retain control over this important governmental position; and as the desire to stop one party (at that time having 34 percent of the votes) from being able to monopolize all important governmental positions. The presidency had important appointment powers, and as already noted participated in the constitutional amending process. The answer to the dilemma could have been a choice of a distinguished figure in no way identified either with state institutions or with the AKP. The forcing through of the presidency of A. Gül led to a dramatic worsening of relations with the CHP, with which it had been possible for the AKP to cooperate, whatever was later said to the contrary. In retrospect, one can both well understand yet still criticize AKP's choice concerning the presidency. It was undoubtedly important to link the presidency, from 1982 the agent of the state, to the government instead, and this meant also to the parties. But linking him too closely to a party that, along with its president (when it could rely on a referendum) would have a constitution-making three-fifths majority in parliament, and along with the president's important appointment powers that could also influence the judicial system—meant that this gave simply too much political power to a force that electorally represented far less than its parliamentary weight (34 percent in 2002, 47 percent in 2007).

[46] See Köker, "Turkey's Political Constitutional Crisis" for an unusually balanced view of two sides on this quorum decision, from what he considers different "positivist" perspectives. Beyond these, it could be said that the Court was defending against the silent text both the consensual principles behind the regulation of voting for the presidency and the interests of the state bureaucracy.

[47] Those who attack the Court's role in the conflict over the presidency usually forget that the same Court allowed the referendum on direct elections to take place, at that time taking a narrow position on its power to review amendments. Özbudun and Gençkaya, *Democratization and the Politics of Constitution Making in Turkey* 109, mention this decision, but only in a different context when criticizing the later, more activist position with respect to amendments.

Once the election of A. Gül was secured, a consensual path of constitution making could have nevertheless been attempted. As we have seen, since the making of the previous great amendment package, Turkey's European partners had come to strongly insist that only a completely new, civilian constitution could satisfy their requirements. The step from partial amendment packages to the project of a new constitution was perhaps unavoidable. But the appointment of a governmental "extra-party" commission by the AKP alone to draft such a document was probably a mistake in a country where the responsibility was previously and rightly understood as that of parliament and not the executive. The illogical passing[48] of (the so-called headscarf) amendments to Articles 10 and 42 of the old constitution at a time when one intended to replace it entirely, on the basis of an alliance between the nationalist MHP and the AKP, was an even greater error. With President Gül on its side, the government, having over two-thirds of votes behind it, did not have to go to a referendum, although the probable victory in such a process may have strengthened its hand vis-à-vis the Constitutional Court. In any case, the CHP now had the motivation, and with over 110 deputies the legal standing, to appeal to that Court asking it not only to rule against the amendment but in effect to freeze the entire process of non-consensual constitution making. This move represented an important challenge to the attempt to weaken or redefine secularism, and to the majoritarian project.

IV THE HORSE RACE BETWEEN GOVERNMENT AND CONSTITUTIONAL COURT

In 2007 the Constitutional Court made two decisions regarding the presidential ambitions of the AKP, one supporting each side in the controversy. For this reason, I would date the real beginning of the horse race between government and Court later, to 2008. That year, in June, the Constitutional Court judged the two constitutional amendments seeking to legalize the wearing of headscarves at universities as unconstitutional. To say the least, this decision was highly significant and very controversial. What is interesting here is the conflict involved, as well as the outcome for constitutional politics. The normative claim of the outraged parliamentary majority, firmly in the hands of the AKP government, was reduced to a fairly classical mixture of elements of legality and legitimacy. The legal claim can be summed up by the phrase "Turkish public law does not distinguish between a constituent and an ordinary parliament or Grand National Assembly." It seems to be sustained by the constitutional texts of 1960 and 1983, which indeed make no such distinction. Accordingly, the amending power under Article 175 of the 1982 Constitution was seen as the full constituent or

[48] Professors Köker and Özbudun were both members of the expert Commission. The former calls the introduction of amendments as a betrayal: Köker, "Turkey's Political Constitutional Crisis" 328. Özbudun and Gençkaja, *Democratization and the Politics of Constitution Making in Turkey* 105, speak only of the "silent shelving" of the expert draft.

constitution-making power that could entirely replace as well as partially alter the Turkish Constitution. While the argument seemed to reduce legitimacy to narrow, textually based legality, there was an independent legitimacy claim here as well, though it should in my view be rejected. And in the Turkish case, the legality claim was itself highly contestable, if not entirely fallacious.

I start with the legitimacy claim, which would be the superior of the two claims, if it were valid. It is based on the notion of popular sovereignty. The parliamentary majority, accordingly, has been elected by and therefore expresses the will of the majority of the Turkish people, who have the right to give themselves any constitution they please. There were four things wrong with this claim. First, the Turkish amendment rule was differentiated into purely parliamentary and more complex paths involving referenda.[49] There was a presumption, though not a requirement, that some important amendments should be ratified in referenda. The president could after all use his powers, even when he agreed with an amendment, to force popular ratification just because he considered the change so significant. This was not done in the case of the 2008 amendments, even though the Court showed some deference to the amending track using referenda in 2007 (and would again in 2010). Second, and equally importantly, the AKP majorities of both 2002 and 2007 were artefacts of the very exclusionary electoral law with a 10 percent threshold that eliminated many otherwise viable parties from parliament. In one case 34 percent and in the other 47 percent of the votes were turned into nearly two-thirds and then over three-fifths of the seats, though admittedly in the second case the MHP deputies supplied the missing part of the two-thirds.

Third, and philosophically this is what is crucial, in terms of the best interpretation of democratic theory, from the American Revolution and the French Declaration of Rights to the present, no body, institution, or person should be able to claim to fully embody the sovereign people, whose place must remain "an empty place."[50] The two multi-stage models of constitution making (the American and the South African) structurally favor this best, anti-usurpation interpretation of popular sovereignty. But were these two path-dependent roads open to Turkey? As the previous reconstruction shows, one dimension of these processes has been available: the search for consensus. Here the fourth objection to the legitimacy claims of the parliamentary majority comes into play: in Turkey parliament has not acted from 1983 to 2004 as if its legitimacy claims underwriting the power to make the constitution could be reduced to merely its legal powers, or even as if this power could be exercised by a single force in a single-stage process. The important constitutional changes of this period were generated in several important stages of negotiation and drafting. And at each important stage very high, generally all-party, consensus requirements were strictly

[49] This distinction between legislative and constituent amendment rules was developed by A. Bragyova, *Az új alkotmány egy koncepciója* (Budapest: MTA, 1995). On multi-track constitutional amendment rules, see Chapter 6 below.

[50] C. Lefort, *Democracy and Political Theory* (London: Polity, 1999).

observed.[51] In my view one can speak, in terms of criteria developed by Sir Ivor Jennings, of an emerging convention of the constitution, requiring high-level party consensus for the all-important acts of constitution making.[52] This convention was admittedly not a matter of law, but one of constitutional legitimacy.[53]

Turning now to legality, the theoretical idea that no organ of government can fully embody the sovereign will of the people is in fact expressed by Turkish public law, too, if not necessarily in the most desirable manner. The Turkish Grand National Assembly is not legally speaking a constituent assembly because the constitution of 1982 (like its predecessor of 1961) contained unchangeable provisions (Articles 1–3, entrenched by Article 4) that were off limits to the amendment rule, Article 175, and, as I would argue, despite appearances, constituted a differentiated third track of change. Such absolute entrenchment was of course hardly unique. Most famously, the French Third Republic with its republican government clause (Article 2 of the Constitutional Law of August 14, 1884) is Turkey's predecessor, but an even more important forerunner is the *Grundgesetz*, with its whole list of unchangeable provisions (according to Article 79(3): Articles 1 and 20; and the principles of federalism). In Turkey the eternity clauses, including secularism, were further strengthened by the provision that their amendment could not even be proposed.

Thus the argument of the government and of the parliamentary majority from a perspective of legality was very much weakened by the existence of eternity clauses in the constitution. Nevertheless, their position could be reformulated as a question of jurisdiction, or rather the Constitutional Court's supposed lack thereof.[54] The argument was supported by Article 148 of the constitution, which restricted amendment review to "only … their form" (as distinguished in the same article from substance) and restricted questions of form to numerical procedural requirements.[55] Thus even if there were legal limits to the amending

[51] These were the important votes: in 1987, 315 to 56; in 1995, 360 to 32; in 2001, 474 to 16; in 2002, 440 to 18 and 455 to 48; see Gençkaya, "Politics of Constitutional Amendment in Turkey."

[52] I. Jennings, *The Law and the Constitution*, 5th edn. (London: University of London, 1959) Chapter III, especially 133–6, superseding A.V. Dicey's famous and still interesting treatment in *The Law of the Constitution* (Indianapolis, IN: Liberty Fund, 1982) Chapter XIV.

[53] See the Patriation Reference and the Quebec Veto Reference, which best noted this difference. For the best single treatment see P.H. Russell, *Constitutional Odyssey* (Toronto: University of Toronto Press, 2004).

[54] That this is what they are doing is not clearly seen by those who use a most literalist interpretation of the constitution that excludes substantive review, and does not explicitly give the Court powers to defend the eternity clauses. See Özbudun and Gençkaya, *Democratization and the Politics of Constitution Making in Turkey* 106–9; Özbudun, "Secularism in Islamic Countries. Turkey as a Model" in G. Rainer and T. Roder (eds.), *Constitutionalism in Islamic Countries: Between Upheaval and Continuity* (Oxford: Oxford University Press, 2011) 143. A comparative knowledge of constitutional courts, and not only the U.S. Supreme Court, would have helped to avoid this particular method of interpretation.

[55] See Köker, "Turkey's Political Constitutional Crisis" 334–5 for a fair statement of this position and the debate between perspectives. For a more polemical and more one-sided version see Özbudun and Gençkaya, *Democratization and the Politics of Constitution Making in Turkey* 106–9, and Özbudun, "Secularism in Islamic Countries" 143, who repeatedly but untenably speak of "juristocracy" in the context of this one decision! Their point

power, the Court's jurisdiction to enforce them was supposedly even more limited. This line of argument leads to the following results: there are limits, but they are unenforceable. The article of the constitution, Article 4, that enacted the ban on the revision of Articles 1, 2, and 3, like "the divine and natural law" under European absolutism, could be enforced only by the self-enforcement of the parliamentary sovereign.

As the German reference shows, and as a group of important Indian cases demonstrates even more emphatically, today the defense of the differentiation of three tiers of constitutionalism (constitution making, amending, legislation) advocated by Carl Schmitt in the 1920s, where it is defended at all, pace Schmitt, can only be by Constitutional Court. The Turkish Court, unlike the Indian one, even has eternity provisions to rely on. This is also true in the German case, but in the *Grundgesetz* the potential but assumed enforcement by the Court, the *Bundesverfassungsgericht*, is without explicit authorization. Unlike in Turkey, not even procedural review is formally authorized. Thus amendment review in Turkey is potentially on stronger foundations than either in India or Germany. Nevertheless, in India the struggle ended, after the initial defeat of the Supreme Court in Mrs. Gandhi's authoritarian emergency, with the victory of that Court that could not even rely on unchangeable articles in the constitution of 1950 (the case of *Minerva Mills* 1980).[56] We have seen the contrary result in Hungary in the previous chapter.

In Turkey, however, there are special problems with this jurisdiction not shared with the constitutional structures of Germany or India. Only in Turkey, as now in Hungary's amended Fundamental Law, does Article 148 of the Turkish Constitution dealing with the powers of the Constitutional Court explicitly ban amendments on substantive grounds.[57] Permission (of procedural review) is formulated as a limitation. Moreover, it was only in Turkey that an openly authoritarian government enacted the constitution, the unamendable provisions or basic structure of which were at stake. Preservationist acts on the part of the Constitutional Court can thus be represented as guarding the work of authoritarians against democratic majorities.

It is characteristic of the dualistic constitutional identity of Turkey, as well as the dual nature of the Constitutional Court, that only one of these two serious problems was addressed effectively by that Court, the *legal* limitation to procedural review, and not its ultimate foundations, its *legitimacy*.

The legal argument of the Court involves turning the question of substance into that of procedure. As already said, the case begins with the existence of the three unchangeable articles, whose revision cannot even be proposed according to the fourth article of the constitution. Thus no procedure that amends them

is that the Court had acquired, very briefly as it turned out, if at all, a veto over constitutional change, which in my view would be quite short of the rule of judges.

[56] For the whole great story see G. Austin, *Working a Democratic Constitution: The Indian Experience* (New Delhi and Oxford: Oxford University Press, 1999), 8, 10, 11, 15, 17, 19, and 24.

[57] Art. 148: "Constitutional amendments shall be examined and verified only with regard to their form."

or even proposes such an amendment can be valid. This step is uncontroversial. Moreover, no procedure to alter any other part of the constitution that would derogate from Articles 1–3 could be valid either. Thus if changes to Articles 10 or 42 or any other article actually attacked secularism or the republican nature of the state, the procedures used would be unconstitutional. Otherwise an Islamic state and a monarchy could be established in some other part of the constitution, derogating from Articles 1 and 2. Finally, and admittedly this is a point I did not fully anticipate earlier,[58] the Court very cleverly has noted that the only way to decide whether the right procedure was used is to see if the substance of the amendment in question attacked the substance of Articles 1–3. So substance could not be off limits, in an epistemological sense, in the case of amendments that have relevance to the unchangeable provisions. In such cases, one can only decide whether the procedures were unsatisfactory by looking at substance.[59] This is what turning substance into procedure means. Even now, many people in Turkey will not like hearing this, but I think the argument so far is very strong, even foolproof.

It is another matter whether the Court really found the substance of amendments to Articles 10 and 42 at variance with Article 2 of the constitution (in a somewhat tenuous argumentation), or, even if it did, whether it would not have been wiser to have followed the *Marbury, Kesavananda*, and the German Maastricht court judges in firmly asserting the jurisdiction, but allowing the amendments "as long as" certain conditions of legal protections were set (*Solange I* and *II* is the popular term of reference to another famous pair of decisions by the German Court). The Court itself used the absence of legal protections for secular minority women in a Muslim majority country, and the improbability of the parliamentary majority later generating these even in the face of repression and abuse.[60] Thus it could have used its power to guide legislation in the desired direction, instead of invalidating it altogether.

More relevant for the moment is the validity of the Court's legitimacy claims, and their relation to the freezing of the constitutional process. In a democracy, when a Constitutional Court enforces either a two- or a three-tier constitutionalism, it is of course fully conscious of invalidating the acts of freely elected representatives, who often make legitimacy claims, as in Turkey. One would have to be very stupid not to anticipate the counter-argument that the Court is putting itself in the place of the constituent power, and indeed in the case of amendments the description by Kelsen (and others) of constitutional review as merely

[58] What I argued in a Milliyet interview and elsewhere, was that even 100 percent of the vote would be procedurally invalid in the case of eternity clauses. The Court's focus on banning even the proposal of amendments here amounts to the same thing, and it has better textual basis. For the interview, see http://www.milliyet.com.tr/Siyaset/HaberDetay.aspx?aType=HaberDetay&Kategori=siyaset&ArticleID=982363&Date=25.08.2008&b=AKP accessed December 3, 2015.

[59] E. 2008/16, K. 2008/116 (June 5 2008; date of publication in the Official Gazette: October 22, 2008, gazette no.: 27032). I thank my students Aysel Madra and Ertug Tombus for translating major parts of this text.

[60] Ibid.

negative legislation is not really tenable. From John Marshall to the Turkish Constitutional Court the response of the judges themselves is often based on a preservationist argument:[61] we are acting not on our own behalf, but to preserve the work of the original constituent power (the Court speaks of the "primary constituent power") against mere legislation, or here even the amending power, in both cases against the acts of mere *constitué* (constituted) powers. The problem in Turkey is that the defended past here seems to be that of the authoritarian Bonapartist constitution makers who produced the 1982 Constitution—in particular its unchangeable articles, being enforced against the democratically elected representatives in the current parliament. The work of the founding fathers of the Indian Republic and even the consensual actors at Chiemsee who enacted the *Grundgesetz* were worthy of protection. The work of General Evren's junta is not.

It is here, however, that the argument of the Court failed the country and is untenable in terms of the current state of constitutional theory. On the one side, their references to the "primary constituent power" and to the unchangeable articles as incorporating its "fundamental choice ... regarding the political order," recalling the theory of Carl Schmitt, were radically underdetermined procedurally. Even worse, the Court's stressing revolutionary breaks, "ruptures of political regimes" in the operation of the constituent power "outside the legal framework," even closer to the spirit of Schmitt, yields the decided impression that implicitly the model of the past is used also to provide concrete standards for the future. To oppose one form of usurpation, by parliament, the Court seemed to be raising another to a standard, that of the Bonapartist junta of 1980–3 (or perhaps the two juntas, of 1960 as well as 1980), speaking in the name of the people, using a constrained referendum. Or, to be fairer, if the Turkish people wished to fundamentally change or renegotiate their constitution and the state definitions inherent in the first three articles, they seemed to be given the choice of either undergoing a coup or making a complete political revolution. A bad choice, obviously, when the citizens of the country could have been offered the path of enhanced legitimacy already embarked upon, but for the moment disrupted. Unfortunately, the implication was that if the citizens of Turkey desired neither coup nor revolution, they would have to put up with a frozen constitution as long as the Court was its guardian.[62] And, with the future closed, this would amount to a form of legitimation in terms of a particular past that indeed cannot trump a more democratic present, even when imperfectly represented by parliament.

This critique is based on the text of the Constitutional Court decision, but in the form just stated it is not entirely right. If we are to debate about original intent at all, there is also an argument to be made that the Court in developing

[61] B. Ackerman, *We the People. Transformations* vol. I (Cambridge, MA: Harvard University Press, 1998).

[62] This is the point that many opponents of the Court's amendment review stress, the prospect of a frozen constitution. See Can, "The Turkish Constitutional Court as Defender of *Raison d'État*" 276; Özbudun and Gençkaya, *Democratization and the Politics of Constitution Making in Turkey* 109.

activist review was in fact acting against the intentions of the Evren junta, turning constitutional meaning against that original intent. Professor Özbudun inadvertently brings attention to this fact when he relies on the intent, and the narrow text, of the authoritarian framers, who, as he is in a good position to know, wanted to block the road to the type of constitutional review used in the previous period. That review indeed involved the invalidation of several constitutional amendments, at least in part. If he is right, the question was (as in the case of electoral rule): to whom did the junta of 1980–3 want to give a free hand vis-à-vis the Court;[63] and why did the AKP and its defenders wish to rely on that very empowerment?

Ceren Belge, in a highly influential article very critical of the Constitutional Court, argued that the September 1971 amendment first mentioning review restricted to form had an attack on judicial independence as its goal. She admits that the amendment was a product of a military-imposed cabinet.[64] This amendment was bypassed in 1976 and 1977 by the Court when invalidating parts of other amendments based on Article 9 (that played the same role as the current Article 4 vis-à-vis the republican character of the state), actions that were perhaps behind the much more detailed and restrictive formulation of Article 148 in 1982. Belge documents that in fact the invalidation of the key amendment in question (and, referring to Article 9, all amendments supposedly challenging the structure of the regime) occurred in a period when the Court was unusually solicitous of civil rights, according to her because of a temporary left and Republican alliance. Thus the important precedents for the Court's 2008 action come from its most progressive period.[65]

Moreover, as opposed to a group of provisional articles now gone from the 1982 Constitution that expressed the will and interests of the junta of 1980–3, the unchangeable three articles of the 1982 Constitution only reaffirmed the common project of Turkish state makers from the 1920s. Among these was the aggressive secularism to which Özbudun rightly calls critical attention.[66] Equally burdensome was the assumption of the unitary, homogenous nature of the state. These provisions should be open to renegotiation of course both on normative grounds and in today's changing circumstances; but it makes some sense that their transformation cannot in law, and ought not in legitimacy, be a matter of simple constitutional amendments. Nevertheless, the preservationist

[63] While Can, "The Turkish Constitutional Court" 271, mentions these restrictions of the Court by the military junta, he does not ask himself why they were made, and instead seems resentful that the Court "itself eliminated" the limitations from the 1990s. He does not seem to understand that this happened in the context of a long-term reform process, seeking to constitutionalize the constitution.

[64] C. Belge, "Friends of the Court: The Republican Alliance and Selective Activism of the Constitutional Court of Turkey" (2006) 40 *Law and Society Review* 3 653, 668, and especially 679.

[65] At the same time, Belge, "Friends of the Court" 669, backs up her own skeptical views of this invalidation through a reference to Article 9 (the entrenching article of the 1961 Constitution) by referring to the critical comments of one Orhan Aldikacti, "a conservative law professor who authored Turkey's illiberal 1982 Constitution."

[66] Özbudun, "Secularism in Islamic Countries" 137–43.

argument, one that should not insist that interpretation is only negative legislation, must always concede that the interpretive act is not final. While it preserves the past, this must be done also in the name of a future that can reverse both the past and the interpretation itself. Thus, the Court's appeal should not and need not have been interpreted as referring only to the past, but much more to a future constituent power that should not be seen in similar terms to the Bonapartists of 1980 or even 1960. Admittedly, the Court did not help with this more progressive interpretation of its headscarf decision.

There was a basis of such progressive interpretation in the text of the 1982 Constitution, if not in the original intent behind the document. It is not just the amendment rule (Article 175) that contains the already-mentioned consensus requirements, which until 2002 no party alone could even hope to bypass; so does in a much less noticeable manner Article 148 on the Constitutional Court. This rule provided standing to political parties wishing to review amendments only if supported by one-fifth of the deputies, 110 members in all. Conversely, any amendment having the support of four-fifths of the deputies, as well as the president (who automatically had standing) could not be brought to the Court for review. The Constitutional Court could not initiate such a review on its own. For this reason, in light of the Court's assumption of strong amendment review, the four-fifths rule established in principle yet another track of change.[67] This track was not equivalent to the revolutionary ruptures implied by the Court's misleading reference to the "original constituent power." It was the track of consensual as against revolutionary power. More importantly, this was the track implied by the practice of All Party Reconciliation commissions in the 1990s and early 2000s, a practice the AKP abolished, but whose normative power remained significant even for interpreters on its political side.[68]

I have strongly implied that denying the Court's amendment review would have left the eternity clauses of the constitution defenseless, and unenforceable. Fortunately, or rather unfortunately, even the narrow textualist interpretation of the constitution leads to a different conclusion. The repeatedly amended power to close political parties was explicitly connected, among other things, to threats to the eternity clauses,[69] and both Islamist and Kurdish parties were repeatedly banned under this clause. Very much in the tradition of militant democracy, this meant that even and especially if amendments challenging the eternity clauses could not be substantively reviewed, parties attempting to enact such amendments could be closed for just that reason. Indeed, they could be closed pre-emptively for advocating them. In my interpretation, one that I shared in a

[67] Curiously a four-fifths rule represented the highest track of change in the Hungarian Constitution as amended in 1996, before abolished by FIDESZ by a two-thirds amendment, in my view unconstitutionally. See Chapter 4 above. The figure of four-fifths needed for enactment first surfaced in the making of the *Grundgesetz*.

[68] Özbudun and Gençkaya, *Democratization and the Politics of Constitution Making in Turkey*, *passim*.

[69] Article 68 (as amended in 1995) and Article 69.

controversial interview with the readers of the newspaper *Milliyet*,[70] the assumption of strong amendment review made recourse to militant democracy not only dangerous, as always, but also without function. Strong amendment review was the answer to Carl Schmitt, who was the first to argue for the effectiveness of militant democracy, in contrast to the constitutional guardianship exercised by a court.[71] In Turkey, in contrast to Schmitt's advice, it was the Constitutional Court that was the main agent of militant democracy, having closed about twenty-six parties by 2008.[72] That Court was therefore well positioned to see the connection between its amendment review and state guardianship functions, and to shift the balance from the second to the first, both in the name of constitutionalism.

Chief Public Prosecutor Yalçinkaya, however, was not interested in that functional connection when he opened a party closing case against the AKP, in part because it had advocated and passed the headscarf amendments, and had allegedly threatened secularism. This case constituted a second round of the horse race, but it was quickly ended by the fortunately correct decision of the Court, avoiding a potentially very destructive outcome. There is no need here to detail the very poor and dysfunctional case of the Public Prosecutor, which by its very existence made its big contribution to further political polarization in Turkey. It is enough to note that under the constitutional amendment of 2001 that required three-fifths of the members of the Court to decree a party closed, the still embarrassing 6:5 narrow majority was not enough to force the dissolution of the AKP. Thus, the result of the AKP case indicated a partial, obviously not yet complete, evolution of the Constitutional Court from a guardian of the state to the guardian of the constitution.[73]

Needless to say the critics of the Court did not see matters in such a positive light. They focused on the vote of just six out of eleven in favor of closing, and the equally unfortunate vote of the ten who fined the AKP for having become "a center for anti-secular activities." These votes helped to validate the views of those who claimed that the Court represented nothing more than the old tutelage or guardianship. Thus, many supporters of the AKP seemed to act almost as if a party closing did take place. They spoke of the re-establishment of a tutelary or a state-dominated regime, which put the AKP in a straightjacket, making

[70] See http://www.milliyet.com.tr/Siyaset/HaberDetay.aspx?aType=HaberDetay&Kategori=siyaset&ArticleID=982363&Date=25.08.2008&b=AKP accessed December 3, 2015.

[71] C. Schmitt, *Hüter der Verfassung* (Berlin: Duncker & Humblot, 1928).

[72] Shambayati, "The Guardian of the Regime: The Turkish Constitutional Court in Comparative Perspective"; The European Court of Human Rights ruled against some of these party closings, but upheld others, most famously that of the Welfare (Refah) Party. D. Kogacioglu, "Dissolution of Political Parties by the Constitutional Court in Turkey" in S. Arjomand (ed.), *Constitutionalism and Political Reconstruction* (Leiden: Brill, 2007).

[73] The widely and rightly criticized subsequent dissolution of the Kurdish Democratic Society (DTP) in 2009 certainly indicated that this evolution was hardly complete.

it incapable of doing anything, and especially of constitutional innovation. Neither the wrong (but ultimately minor) part of the Court decision nor the political situation at that time, nor even the imagined absence of available options, justified any such interpretation. But it was true that the favorable decision on the closing of the party only returned the AKP government to where it was before the case, with the Constitutional Court's limitation on the amendment and in their view the constituent power. Thus, even if the AKP government won the second round of the horse race, this success did not cancel out the results of the first round.

V CONSTITUTIONAL CRISIS RESOLVED? THE 2010 AMENDMENT

In my view, again, the Court's message in that first round should and could have been interpreted as insistence on consensual requirements restraining majoritarian constitutional politics. Accordingly, if the project of democratic innovation were to go on, whether on the road of constitutional amendments, or preferably a new constitution, these could be legitimately achieved in a divided society, where there was no political revolution, only by a highly consensual approach. Unfortunately, even in the face of earlier historical evidence, many supporters of the AKP, and its main leaders, seemed to believe that no consensus was possible. Thus they chose a path of confrontation, leading to the third round of the horserace between government and Court.

More exactly, after the 2008 decision of the Turkish Constitutional Court invalidating amendments to Articles 10 and 42 of the Turkish Constitution, but the refusal of the same Court to dissolve the AKP, the government led by that party had three choices. The first, indicated by the Court's return to the language of the original constituent power, namely to sponsor a program of revolutionary transformation where the constitutional regime of 1982 would be replaced *outside its own rules of change*, was entirely unrealistic, and to me (and most Turks) undesirable. The point of the conservative Court even raising this idea was merely logical and rhetorical. When it said that certain kinds of change altering the eternity clauses, namely Articles 1–3 of the constitution, as entrenched by Article 4, would require a return to the original constituent power, and thus by implication a revolution, the point was to indicate all the more strongly *what could not* be done through ordinary amendments. Yet to tell the Turkish people that they must make a revolution if they wish to make an entirely new constitution was, to say the least, unfortunate and in fact erroneous. Nevertheless, the same type of rupture in a toned-down version was actually recommended by the noted constitutional scholar Serap Yazici in a book[74] where she claimed that a democratically elected assembly need not be bound by

[74] S. Yazici, *Yeni Bir Anayasa Hazirligi ve Turkiye* [Preparation of a New Constitution and Turkey] (Istanbul: Istanbul Bilgi Üniversitesi Yayinlari, 2011). I thank Dr. Ertug Tombus for translating parts of this book.

either the eternity clauses, nor even the procedures indicated by Article 175, the amendment rule of the Turkish Constitution. While she was very right in suggesting that the highly undemocratic 10 percent threshold in elections should be abandoned, we can still be grateful that the AKP has so far at least not imagined that it could take the road of explicit legal rupture in constitution making.

The second option was to return to a consensual form of constitution making, at least implied by the Constitutional Court in the same 2008 decision, a method that could have led to the creation of a package with which all Turkish political forces could identify to some extent.[75] Such a solution would also have meant that perforce there could not be 110 deputies to apply to the Court for a review of the amendments or of the new constitution. In any case, at that time, the AKP government did not show any interest in any consensual alternative, including a return to the parliamentary All Party Accord Commissions of the epoch before.

What the AKP government has chosen instead was the third option, namely a return to the method of majority imposition, which has been its method in constitutional politics since 2007, the crisis over the presidency. Of course the Constitutional Court *did allow* (in spite of the leading narrative about the quorum affair) that imposition in 2007 by opening the way to a referendum that would predictably enact the election of the president of the republic in national referenda. Since that time, however, the Court has stood in the way of a repeat performance, as indicated in 2008 with its headscarf amendment decisions. These decisions seemed to renew the activist jurisprudence of the 1970s, when constitutional amendments were repeatedly reviewed—a jurisprudence that as we have seen was very much disliked by the military, which tried to block it at several junctions including the new wording of Article 175 of the 1982 Constitution. Given the increasingly monolithic nature of Turkish politics, such a renewed role for the Court was not the rise of juristocracy, but the attempt to establish at least one check and balance in an increasingly monolithic system desperately in need of it. Those democrats who in that context attacked the Court for historically understandable reasons were nevertheless fighting the battle of "yesterday," not seeing the very possible if not inevitable dangers of "tomorrow" that, as I then predicted, have now become the struggle of "today."[76]

[75] This was the position I represented in several debates, in the Press, on CNN-Turk and at a conference at Koc University. See A. Arato, "Democratic Constitution-Making and the Unfreezing of the Turkish Process" (2010) 36 *Philosophy and Social Criticism* 3–4 473–87. My idea was to draw the non-parliamentary parties into a consultative assembly (a "convention") elected by straight proportional representation without a cut-off, which would present an initial draft for a civilian constitution to a new Grand National Assembly still structured by the (otherwise undesirable) undemocratic 10 percent threshold.

[76] A. Arato, "The Constitutional Reform Proposal of the Turkish Government: The Return of Majority Imposition" (2010) 17 *Constellations* 2 345–50. See also the interview in Milliyet: http://www.milliyet.com.tr/soganin-cucugu-anayasa-mahkemesi/devrim-sevimay/siyaset/siyasetyazardetay/26.04.2010/1229780/default.htm accessed December 3, 2015.

But let us forget earlier predictions. Clearly the AKP government was following the pattern of other populist and especially authoritarian leaders and governments in attacking the supreme or constitutional courts that stood in their way. On the democratic side, Franklin Roosevelt, and Indira Gandhi[77] come to mind, while on the undemocratic side lie Peron, Fujimori, Chavez, and now Viktor Orbán.[78] But whether democratic or not, these attacks are always wrong headed. Their logic, whatever the specific intentions of the leading protagonists, is the establishment of the kind of monolithic power that no government should have. Indira Gandhi aimed at a social revolution much needed in India, but we should recall that she became the ruler of a destructive period of emergency rule in the 1970s, one that, after weakening the Court temporarily, almost destroyed Indian democracy. And even Roosevelt, the creator of the American welfare state (as deficient as it still is today), was also the jail master of 140,000 Japanese Americans, mostly citizens, an entirely unnecessary and repressive policy allowed by a cowed Supreme Court in *Korematsu v. the U.S.*, a case where the dissenting opinions are far more significant today than the controlling opinion itself. What all these leaders, including in earlier periods the Turkish military and now the AKP, have in common is that they have seen Court decisions interfering with their constitutional and political plans. Instead of modifying their plans they chose to move in various ways to transform the membership of constitutional courts, or greatly limit their jurisdiction, or both, so the same thing could not happen again. On the basis of the record, we can say that only in non-democratic countries or in countries where democracy is being lost can such a project fully succeed.

The court packing in 2010 took a highly sophisticated form, more so than any previous attempt elsewhere.[79] The AKP in 2010 still had over three-fifths of the seats, and this meant the ability to pass amendments if it was willing to ratify these in a referendum. That mode of ratification required a broadly popular amendment package. The fundamental trick, however, was forcing the population to vote on the package as a whole, rather than clause by clause. In the end an amendment of twenty-six articles[80] was settled on with provisions attractive to many constituencies, including and especially European institutions and governments.[81] The bulk of the amendments' content very much resembled the

[77] See G. Austin, *Working a Democratic Constitution: A History of the Indian Experience* (USA: Oxford University Press, 2003).

[78] See Chapter 4 above.

[79] Yet to interpret it as unpacking rather than packing was nothing short of absurd. A. Bâli, "Unpacking Turkey's 'Court-Packing' Referendum," Middle East Research and Information Project, November 5, 2010: http://www.merip.org/mero/mero110510 accessed November 19, 2015.

[80] Secretariat General of Turkish European Affairs, "Draft Constitutional Amendment Proposal," April 30, 2010.

[81] For a summary, see Bâli, "Unpacking Turkey's "Court-Packing" Referendum" 5. Bâli's remarks concerning the procedure of a single vote on the whole package appear rather disingenuous. On the contrary, see my paper, Arato, "The Constitutional Reform Proposal of the Turkish Government: the Return of Majority Imposition."

attractive packages from the 1990s and early 2000s, and was meant to be so regarded by Turkey's European interlocutors, as well as friendly scholars. This very fact, however, points to the hazards of interpreting legitimacy solely in terms of results. As opposed to the amendment process from 1995 to 2004, the procedure that generated these amendments was majoritarian rather than consensual, and the results of the referendum were badly manipulated by the structure of the proposal. That consensus was possible at the time is indicated by the proposal of D. Baykal, the then leader of the CHP, to pass twenty-three or so amendments from the government's list together, if the AKP was willing to dispense with the articles dealing with the reorganization of the courts and especially the Constitutional Court until the next elections.[82] That suggestion, angrily rejected by Prime Minister Erdoğan, may have been merely rhetorical, and could have reflected the links of the CHP to the judicial bureaucracy and profession. Nevertheless it did reveal what the whole project was mainly about.

In light of the horse race between Court and government, and the repeated diagnosis of a frozen constitution among scholars defending the AKP at that time, there can be little doubt that the Court reorganization plan, and the related project revising party closings were the really important main structural features in the AKP government's proposal. Within a new and properly negotiated constitution even these provisions could have been unobjectionable and even desirable. But here is my thesis: When the cart is put before the horse, as it already was in the case of the headscarf amendments, the new amendment package stood very much in the way of properly negotiating such a consensual, civilian constitution. However, it did open the way to a government potentially free of court interference in the rest of its constitutional plans—that seemed to be the very point of the exercise.

Thus even if the package had many random liberal and progressive features anticipating elements of a future, better constitution, here their purpose was entirely instrumental. It is of course a good idea to promote affirmative action, collective bargaining, and the abolition of an amnesty for the perpetrators of the bloody coup of 1980, even if the statute of limitations will not be thereby overcome. Even more importantly, it was a good idea to finally establish the possibility of "constitutional complaints" giving standing to ordinary citizens whose rights are adversely affected by a law or regulation at the Constitutional Court. But would any of the gains for rights and liberties truly matter in the face of a much more monolithic form of government, one that now at worst absorbed or at the very least significantly weakened the highest judiciary?

The most important defense of the government's plan thus had to deal with the features that critics such as myself have described as court packing. The

[82] "Premier Erdoğan Describes the Proposal of Baykal as Too Diluted and Unserious," *Today's Zaman*, April 18, 2010.

simplest defense was based on what I have called the Frankenstein argument.[83] Joost Lagendijk is certainly right: such provisions are to be found in democratic countries, and Turkey's existing rules very much needed revision. But what may be good as part *of a whole liberal democratic constitution*, as in the European countries he is thinking of, may not have the same meaning when enacted in the context of a constitutional crisis and especially during a struggle between government and Court. And what may be good and fair in one democratic setting may be unfair and authoritarian in another. One could indeed put together quite an authoritarian system by choosing some particular mix of regulations from various liberal democratic states. In Turkey the issue was very particular, however, and not all elements were stitched together from precedents elsewhere. Yes, the size of the Constitutional Court has been expanded in other settings, as in Turkey from eleven to seventeen. The question was only how the new justices would be appointed. It is true that the idea of parliamentary election of constitutional judges exists elsewhere (in Turkey: three in all) but generally it is tied to some consensus, beyond the vote of a single party. Here, as in Hungary under Orbán's reform, the parliamentary vote would be majoritarian.[84]

The idea that it would take a two-thirds vote of the Court to dissolve a political party only brought Turkey closer to places without this element of militant democracy, but tying the invalidation of constitutional amendments to the same two-thirds made amendment review, a key weapon in combating replacement under the guise of mere alteration, nearly impossible. Finally, a key provision found only in other court packing schemes was the immediate addition of six judges to the existing eleven, each for twelve-year terms. Two of these would be picked by parliament where the AKP had the required majority, and four would be the current substitute members whose identity and predilections were well known before the crafting of provisional Article 19 of the amendment.[85] The aim was obviously to dramatically and immediately change the majority of the same Court that had invalidated two amendments in 2008, had a six-vote bare majority to dissolve the AKP, and a ten-person majority to fine it for anti-secular activities. Along with retirements, this move promised to lead to the almost complete replacement of the old Court, in a new process under the control of the government.[86] But more importantly, its relevant majorities would be immediately altered. Thus, from the moment the amendment entered into force, in

[83] I have often jokingly described the logic involved as constructing a Frankenstein regime, with parts culled from different living organisms. I have applied the figure to the types of argument used not only by Erdoğan, but also Viktor Orban in Hungary.

[84] Provisional Article 18.

[85] Astonishingly, Bâli, "Unpacking Turkey's 'Court-Packing' Referendum," leaves out provisional Article 18 from her defense of the plan, and thus omits the feature of immediately adding six members under the government's control.

[86] As of 2015, three current members appointed by the secularist President Sezer remain on the Court. The other fourteen have been appointed by presidents Gül, Erdoğan, and the AKP dominated Grand National Assembly.

light of the two-thirds threshold required, no Constitutional Court would judge any of the government's future amendments unconstitutional, nor would rule that the party itself dissolve.

Note again that most of the individual parts of the amendment package were not the problem, but rather the package as a whole. Even the feature of court packing could be dismissed as likely providing in the end just another organization for the Constitutional Court whose decisions could not in the long run be predicted. What I would stress rather is the majoritarian procedure through which these changes were accomplished, and the likely strategic intention behind them. As to the procedure itself, it could serve as a precedent for how constitutional change would operate in the subsequent period. As to the intention, this was in part at least already decipherable in 2010. No government ever packs courts just for the sake of it. Thus without political plans that an old court could and might very well have interfered with, it would not have been packed. At stake in the horse race in Turkey was constitutional change. The old Court's composition and procedures represented a threat to the government's scenario of change. Thus, the amendments of 2010 should not have been regarded merely in their own terms, but as the first step of a potential two-step strategy the aim of which was to change and most likely replace the constitution.

The question then was what would likely happen when the constitution was changed as the result of this first step, namely after the passing of the amendment package, after a precedent has been established for a constitution-making procedure, and the Constitutional Court was effectively neutralized. There are two answers to this question. One was obvious at the time, and the other was possible to foresee for those who took the trouble. The obvious answer was that, in line with the expectations of many, constitution making would be resumed, as the second stage of the process initiated in 2010. Given the possession of three-fifths of the votes of parliament until 2011 at least, the issue for the moment was what would be the character of the constitutional innovations of that second stage. This could not be predicted on the basis of looking at the provisions of the first stage that were needed to get impediments out of the way. Nor would the necessary clues be provided, as some interpreters assumed, by the quite acceptable constitution of the expert team of 2008, including Professors Köker and Özbudun. That constitutional draft was produced in the midst of all the existing constraints: (i) a constitution with three "eternal" clauses; and (ii) a Constitutional Court having already taken its stand on these clauses in 2007 and capable of reviewing amendments, and indeed dissolving a party such as the AKP. The constraint of the existing Court enforced the constraint of the eternal clauses. After 2010 there would be no enforcement without the Court. With these constraints gone, the AKP would not be able to say to its militants, its hardliners: boys, (indeed not girls!) we cannot do all we wish to do in our hearts, you and I, because there are all these constraints.

In a phone interview with the *New York Times*,[87] Professor Özbudun, who supported the package, was asked why more has not been done by the government planners (apparently he was not among them or advising them) to liberalize and democratize the Turkish constitution. His answer was that "deep in their hearts" the AKP government would have done more, but because of their fear of the opposition and the Court this is all they dared to do. The experience in 2008 indicates the opposite. Then, instead of negotiating a civilian constitution in a process where the draft of Özbudun and his colleagues could have been one among many proposals, they tried to push through what was apparently really important to them, or at least amendments dear to their special constituency. But I agreed with Özbudun in 2010: If they got away with this, the government might indeed get a chance to show Turks what was really deep in their hearts, and this is rarely a good thing to find out in the case of any government—this is the basic liberal insight. In this case, too, I am afraid the result was not likely to be as beautiful as many of my liberal friends in Turkey then seemed to believe. Liberation from military tutelage had been a slow and painful process, and while it was not yet over, it was important that the process of extrication should not expose Turkey to even the possibility of another authoritarianism, one that could become an equal threat to both liberalism and democracy.

The second answer to the question of the character of the likely second stage was more difficult to discern—but not impossible. In 2007 the CHP had already campaigned against the introduction of the direct election of the president by constitutional amendment followed by referendum, charging that this move would open the road to a presidential regime. While inconsistent with Turkey's history of parliamentary government, there have been previous attempts in that direction by Presidents Demirel and Özal.[88] Admittedly, with A. Gül as the candidate for the office in 2007 when the amendment for direct election was successfully passed, and the fact that he was still elected by parliament, the threat of presidentialism seemed remote. Nevertheless, Prime Minister Erdoğan revived the prospect months before the referendum on the 2010 amendments was passed.[89] In a confusing and rambling interview, he spoke of the introduction of a presidentialist system of the American type that would supposedly make legislation easier, and would not have to deal with the recalcitrant constitutional review he had faced in the previous two years. The obvious contradictions of these ideas with American reality need not be detailed. I had a chance to argue at the time at several forums that the only new executive structure that would serve the two purposes he mentioned would be what has been called "hyper-presidentialism" in the Latin American context, and "executive presidency" in Africa. Indeed, Erdoğan and his closest allies were to soon redefine the project

[87] S. Tavernise and S. Arsu, "In Turkey Proposed Changes Aim at the Old Guard," *New York Times*, April 2, 2010.

[88] Özbudun and Gençkaya, *Democratization and the Politics of Constitution Making in Turkey* 47, who link that early attempt of 1999 to enact direct election with semi-presidentialism.

[89] "PM Warms to Presidential System Switch," *Today's Zaman*, April 19, 2010.

as presidentialism *à la Turque*. What in the world would this mean in a country that has experienced only absolute as well as constitutional monarchies, and also parliamentary republics?

In the absence of a published plan, we can only speculate concerning Erdoğan's intentions and meaning. The change to "presidentialism" would be valuable to a future incumbent only if some combination of strong foreign policy leadership, powers over the cabinet, significant decree and veto powers, strong appointment powers, and the power of parliamentary dissolution could be achieved. In such a scheme, a prime minister would depend on the confidence of the president first and foremost and not that of parliament. Indeed, it is important not to automatically regard the provision for a prime ministership as the institutionalization of a semi-presidential system, especially in the form that was inaugurated with Mitterand's first co-habitation. In most of the world where there are strong presidencies, prime ministers are dependent on the president, as are all other ministers.[90] This is the meaning of hyper-presidentialism, and we can safely assume that Prime Minister Erdoğan convinced his AKP colleagues to seek some relevant combination of its elements.

To sum up: the amendment proposal of 2010 aimed at neutralizing the Constitutional Court and to begin to use majoritarian procedures coupled with referenda to produce a new constitution. That constitution most likely entailed at least some and possibly many features that only the AKP and not the other parties were willing to support. Presidentialism or rather hyper-presidentialism was the most important such feature. But there were still hurdles to jump before that project could be consummated.

VI THE CRISIS RENEWED

The two hurdles facing the constitutional project of the AKP and Prime Minister Erdoğan were the old Court and the electorate. The first of these was overcome. Victory over the second was far less certain.

As to the first, the CHP had the necessary number of MPs to challenge the 2010 amendment in front of the old Constitutional Court that was going to be packed. It was argued in Court that the changes to the structures of the Constitutional Court and the Supreme Board of Judges and Prosecutors were in violation of the constitutional principle of separation of powers, which under the rule of law was supposedly permanently entrenched by Articles 2 and 4 of the constitution. The CHP claimed in other words that the AKP was attempting to change one of Turkey's constitutional articles that could not be amended. Formally these arguments were relatively weak. But there was reason to believe that the Court might resist its own packing, and since the amendment constituted one huge package there was the option of invalidating it as a whole. Moreover,

[90] Even in France the system remains strongly presidential when the party of the president controls the national assembly. In other words, a French president who has a parliamentary majority is domestically much stronger than the American president and when he does not, he is weaker.

the Court could have made the argument that significantly weakening its own powers in amendment review, the limits concerning Articles 1–3 became unenforceable. At the same time, the Court had never invalidated amendments that were about to be voted on in referendum, creating the appearance of reticence when dealing with an arguably higher level of change, supposedly involving the popular sovereign. The case involving the amendment enacting the direct election of the president in 2007, which was connected to the unamendable articles even more tenuously, was an important precedent here. That was the first time the government was forced to rely on ratification in a referendum, and the Court chose not to interfere with that process.

In the face of the challenge, both legal and political, the Court chose a traditional strategy of many courts elsewhere. It claimed the jurisdiction while avoiding invalidating the substance involved. This was done by judging a few, rather technical parts of the large amendment package unconstitutional, while explicitly affirming the right to do so, and allowing all the rest of the package including the court packing scheme to go to a referendum where it predictably passed by a large majority.

In spite of its pedigree of a strategy in comparative constitutional history, in Turkey it was, I think, mistaken if the Court was still interested in remaining an important actor in constitutional politics. The purely legal argument that it did not have jurisdiction over the substance of amendments was already previously disposed of by turning substance into procedure. If the lack of connection to the eternity clauses was the main factor in the decision, that connection was even less relevant in the case of the parts declared unconstitutional than with respect to the court packing provisions. Moreover, the strategy of deference while at the same time asserting jurisdiction was not going to work with new constitution making on the agenda. Even if the aim was to be able to protect the eternity clauses against future amendment packages or a new constitution, these did not necessarily come under threat in the emerging constitutional plans of the AKP. The project of presidentialism was less obviously in violation of clauses on the integrity of the republic, or secularism, or even rule of law, than the attacks on the Court itself. More importantly, there was going to be little chance to undertake strong amendment review subsequently. Once the 2010 amendment was ratified, it would be a packed court that would inherit the jurisdiction thus saved, one that was also made more difficult to exercise by the new two-thirds vote needed to invalidate amendments. At least that hurdle should have been disposed of or rather invalidated. The strategy of combining assertion of jurisdiction and substantial deference might have been appropriate in 2008 in the headscarf case, when the Court chose instead to confront the government more directly on an issue of very much arguable substance. In the changed context of 2010, the strategy amounted to an act of surrender by the Constitutional Court. The government decisively won the third and last round of the horse race.

But there was also the second hurdle for the government to pass, that of the electorate. The 2010 parliament with its three-fifths AKP majority had less than one more year to go before new elections. There was no longer enough time to undertake another amendment round or make a new constitution ratified by referendum. Thus, in the 2011 elections Erdoğan's main goal was attaining a constitution-making majority of two-thirds or at least retaining the three-fifths majority. While the AKP certainly won these elections, its results represented a significant setback for the party, and especially the Prime Minister, whose ambitions for a presidential regime, headed by himself, were now open. It would be inaccurate to say that the electorate rejected the AKP, Erdoğan, or his constitutional plans. That was indeed to happen in 2015. In the crucial elections of 2011 the AKP still managed to increase its share of the vote, from 34 percent in 2002, and 47 percent in 2007, to a figure just under 50 percent. Nevertheless, in the same three elections the party's number of seats attained actually dropped from 363 to 341 in 2007 and then to a total of 327 in 2011, which was slightly under the three-fifths needed to amend the constitution, even with the help of referenda.

The 10-percent threshold worked paradoxically in these three elections. What was involved was not a direct loss of support for the AKP, nor even learning by parties that had no chance to pass the threshold, of which ten, more or less, continued to compete in all three elections. Citizens were the ones who learned not to throw their vote away, and Kurdish constituencies and parties also learned that by running independent candidates they could gain representation bypassing the threshold. Citizen learning was indicated by the progressive reduction of the "lost votes," and along with it the index of disproportionality D, in the three elections: from 35 percent to 12.5 percent, to the relatively small 4.7 percent in 2011. Whether or not the voters were trying to avoid benefiting the largest party, the AKP, is not clear. The small parties that dramatically lost votes were in the majority secular. But it is clear that in 2007 the seats gained were to the benefit of the nationalist MHP, and to Kurdish candidates running as independents who did not have to meet the 10 percent cut-off; while in 2011 it was the secular CHP and again the "independents" who gained.

The AKP of course had no difficulty with 59 percent of the seats to form a government after the elections of 2011, and could even emphasize that it had received its largest ever support of nearly 50 percent. But unlike in the case of FIDESZ in Hungary, and quite unusually, increased support was coupled with a loss of a constitution-making majority. That was a highly important matter, because it strongly interfered with the party leader's very serious project of constitutionally providing for a new presidential regime.

VII RETURN OF CONSENSUS?

Thus, amazingly enough, demands for inclusion, consensus, compromise, and an institution of consensus creation, based on Turkish traditions and international precedents, were suddenly heard again, and from the advocates of the

AKP and the government, moreover.[91] The elections were in June 2011. In the following October, formally at the initiation of the AKP Speaker of the Grand National Assembly, the four political parties (the AKP, the Kemalist CHP, the nationalist MHP and the Kurdish Peace and Democracy Party (BDP)) were invited to participate in a new parliamentary Constitutional Conciliation Commission based on an equal representation of three members each. Subsequently the new forum met and produced its own rules.[92] These were:

1. All decisions would have to be made by the agreement of all four parties, meaning at least two members of each (though the parties may always vote as blocks in practice).
2. Meetings required at least one member from each party.
3. The Commission would be dissolved if any one party ceased to participate.
4. There would be technical committees of experts, each of which would solicit input from civil and political organizations.
5. A draft constitution would have to be presented by the end of December 2012.
6. It would be presented to the parliament's standing Constitutional Committee and then to the parliament, with neither having the power to amend the text unless with full consensus of all four parties.
7. The final approval would have to be under one of the present Constitution's amendment rules.

In principle this was a fair procedure, though not without serious problems. In the end it was deadlocked and eventually broke down altogether. Even in comparison with the failed consensual effort in Hungary in 1996–97 detailed in the previous chapter, there were serious procedural weaknesses in Turkey. The new rules, as against Hungary, were not constitutionally entrenched. The consensus requirement of unanimity was obviously too high (in Hungary it was only five out of six, which was indeed attained for a draft); three out of four would have been a better option. There was no fall-back position in the case of individual articles the parties could not agree on (in Hungary, the articles of the constitution of 1989–90 represented just this fall-back position). Perhaps most importantly, unlike Hungary there was no moratorium on ordinary amendments, which could still be made in Turkey with the support of a single additional party, as in 2008. That option could be used as a constant threat over the process, and reduced the need for the AKP representatives to come to a consensual agreement.

[91] The following section of the chapter draws on a joint study with Dr. Ertug Tombus: "Learning from Success, Learning from Failure: South Africa, Hungary, Turkey and Egypt" (2013) *Philosophy and Social Criticism* 39 4–5.

[92] For the working principles of the Conciliation Commission: https://yenianayasa.tbmm.gov.tr/calismaesaslari.aspx accessed December 3, 2015.

But the reasons for the breakdown were as much political as functions of the design of the process. There have been a variety of disagreements in the Constitutional Conciliation Commission. As opposed to the optimism at the beginning, the Commission could not reach agreement on most of the issues regarding basic rights and freedoms. In many cases the parties in the Commission have rigidly insisted on their "red lines." On the issues of the definition of citizenship, of secularism, on sexual orientation and the equality principle, on education in the mother tongue, and on the constitutional protection against social exclusions, the parties strongly disagreed, especially the Kurdish-led BDP (the new party after the DTP was dissolved) and the nationalist MHP. Yet, undoubtedly the biggest roadblock to the possibility of consensus was the proposal of the AKP (the details of which were never published) to execute a shift to a presidential and most likely hyper-presidential government. As already indicated, they had already achieved in 2007 the direct election of the president, but one whose power had been reduced in previous constitutional reforms. The aim now was certainly to increase these powers, and to elect Prime Minister Erdoğan as the new president in 2014. The goal could not be achieved through the Conciliation Commission, in the face of opposition by at the very least two and maybe three parties out four. Thus concurrently there were statements by the prime minister that implied the desire to revive the parliamentary majoritarian amendment route. Major figures from the AKP have insisted that they would introduce the party's own constitutional draft to parliament if the Conciliation Commission failed to come to a consensus.

These statements can have different interpretations. A more positive one would suggest that the goal of the AKP leadership was only to stimulate and motivate the members of the commission to achieve consensus. But two successive moves, both aiming at the voting potential of the Kurdish BDP, pointed in more problematic, if contrary, directions. First, the move by the prime minister to take away parliamentary immunity from ten Kurdish deputies (nine BDP and one independent) seemed to be an indirect attack on the Commission. Had the BDP collapsed as a result, so would the Commission according to its own rules. No Commission members were directly involved, but the BDP could very well have chosen to leave the process if its members faced arrest. If that happened, the AKP could return to the majoritarian option held in reserve, maybe make a deal once again with the most likely candidate, the nationalist MHP. Fortunately, Prime Minister Erdoğan did not have the full support in this effort of even his own party, and notably President Gül disagreed.

The second move, clearly inconsistent with the first, was potentially more positive. The AKP lacked only four or five parliamentary votes to resume a constitutional amendment process. The Kurdish deputies, whose issue was not primarily the issue of presidentialism, could under some conditions yield some of the needed votes. Several commentators have suggested that if indirect negotiations, mediated by members of the BDP, with the imprisoned Öcalan had succeeded, these votes would have been available.[93] There was thus a deep tension between two options, the majoritarian and relatively consensual[94] ones, but unless really significant concessions could be offered to the Kurds, the majoritarian one, even if a mirage, was the only remaining option. In that case, if the AKP could not gain even a single partner, the issue would have to be decided in the next presidential election, and perhaps under its influence in the next parliamentary contest.

My hypothesis is formed partially by comparison with the Hungarian case. Because of the very high consensual requirements for the Commission in Turkey too much veto power remained in the hands of any two members (or even one member) of each of the four parties. Second, too much opportunity was given to the ruling party to itself veto, deadlock, and wait out the consensual process. Finally, the assumption of genuine parity between forces that are politically and even in terms of the rules are fundamentally unequal was an illusion. The more powerful had to have more share in the constitutional outcome if it were not to use its power, as in Hungary in 1996–97, to bring it all down.

Unfortunately in Turkey no fundamental concession was acceptable to at least two parties on the issue of strong or hyper-presidentialism, and the possible compromise that would provide for a weak presidential government was quite contrary to the prime minister's or the AKP's interests. All the parties knew in advance that on the issue that really mattered, no compromise was possible. Thus they entered the consensual arrangements with the knowledge that it was likely to break down unless the AKP backed down. Yet there was never any sign that the AKP, under the domination of its leader, would abandon or even water down its project. Thus, in the AKP's case it is even possible that the consensual process was accepted, only to have it break down, thereby demonstrating to the electorate that no consensus was possible.

At least this seemed to be the case with the CHP, always considered the main antagonist. Thus, it seemed for an all-too-short period that the AKP chose the Kurds with which to ally itself. This could have been in line with Erdoğan's ambitions, but also followed from the Islamic assumptions of the AKP, according to which it was religion that mattered, not ethnicity.[95] As is well known, until 2015

[93] See the obviously knowledgeable commentator of *Today's Zaman*, H. Gulerce, "Presidentialism on the Horizon" (February 1, 2013); the same author previously spoke only of "Semi Presidentialism on the Horizon?" (May 15, 2012). See also S. Alpay, "Theories about Erdoğan I and Erdoğan II" in *Today's Zaman* (December 31, 2012).

[94] Here I would describe a two-party agreement structure as consensual (though obviously less so than if other parties were included), because it bridged a fundamental divide in Turkish society, the conflict between the two main ethnicities, Turk and Kurd.

[95] The majority of the Kurds followed the Shafi school of Sunni Islam, as against the Hanafi school of most Turks. Today at least this is rarely understood as a very deep division.

the party received many Kurdish votes, because of this potentially conciliatory attitude, more open to settlement than the nationalist MHP and even the secularist CHP. In any case, the settlement process of the civil war was launched in late 2012, and it is hard to avoid the impression that there was a link to the constitutional plans of Erdoğan. While significant concessions to the Kurds on their minimum demands of amnesty, cultural autonomy, and regional self-government would have been extremely positive, there were significant dangers too in going down this particular road, especially if a grand bargain was struck between the AKP government and the BDP alone. In other words, if the provisions the BDP bargained for were achieved, together with strong presidentialism, without the concurrence of either the other two parties, Turkey could have wound up with an exacerbation of an already violent conflict. On the one hand, inevitably it would be charged that Turkey had moved toward a more authoritarian system with the help of the Kurds. On the other hand, it would be claimed that the Kurdish deputies gave away more important rights (as they inevitably would) merely to make limited gains for themselves and perhaps for their titular leader. The extremes on both sides would have very strong points to make, and this would favor the eventual collapse of the deal except for the authoritarian elements, which could very well be called into play as the polarization was exacerbated.

This was the worst-case scenario. In the best-case scenario, the Kurdish issue could have played the same role as Algeria did in the making of the Fifth French Republic. In that case, de Gaulle successfully linked together peace making and regime transformation, and used his old and new powers to overcome all the radical challenges he faced. As the biggest prize for his efforts, he achieved the presidential regime he had long wanted (hardly semi-presidential in its initial workings) with himself as president, a solution that certainly Erdoğan would have preferred to any American variant. There is thus no doubt that de Gaulle could have served as a viable model for Erdoğan given the deep desire on both Turkish and Kurdish sides for peace and reconciliation. But to play de Gaulle's role in Turkey, Erdoğan had to be ready and able to offer really significant concessions to the Kurds, if not independence, than high levels of autonomy along with a general amnesty. As it turns out he was not ready, or was not able, or was perhaps neither ready nor able. And then, in Gezi Park, in the late Spring of 2013, the Turkish de Gaulle encountered his May '68, before he had his 1958.

VIII CONSTITUTIONAL POLITICS WITH OTHER MEANS

After the collapse of the parliamentary Conciliation Commission late in 2013, formal constitutional politics in Turkey came to a halt. There were no attempts to resume either the process of constitution making or amending. The packed

Constitutional Court has perhaps been somewhat less quiescent than I feared,[96] but is certainly no longer a major factor in Turkish politics. Yet the struggle over the Turkish constitution continued by informal means. Among these was the legal struggle in elections by both sides, one seeking to re-achieve an amending majority, the other trying to block the same. The rhetorical use of presidential elections by Erdoğan for this purpose was certainly legal, though the subsequent claims of popular mandate to establish a de facto presidential regime were far more questionable. That claim could be realized only if the AKP's majority in parliament was maintained, and the first parliamentary elections of 2015 also put that in serious doubt. More authoritarian means were resorted to in dealing with that problem, namely the subversion of the process of forming a coalition government, forcing parliamentary dissolution and new elections, as well as the re-launching of the military conflict with the Kurds. That form of constitutional politics through other means meant the very reversal of de Gaulle's model, one that was formal rather than informal, and involved peace rather than war making. It can succeed only if allowed to do so by both internal and external actors.

The repression of the largely peaceful Gezi Park mobilization and civil disobedience, using the old discredited methods of the dualistic state, subsequent corruption scandals involving Erdogan's family and close associates, and the mass purges of police and judiciary personnel, undoubtedly had more to do with the relative decline of support for the AKP than the party's manipulation of the constitution-making process. Similarly, the imprisonment of journalists, the conflict with the previously allied Hizmet movement led by Fetullah Gulen, and the showy reconciliaton with the military were probably more noticed by the voters than the AKP leader's relatively unpopular presidentialist ambitions. The decline was real in any case, as indicated by 2014 local elections when the AKP received only 43 percent support, dropping 7 percent from the previous parliamentary elections in 2011. For the moment, this fall in support could be masked by the subsequent presidential elections mandated by the amendment of 2007, but not held until August 2014, when as expected Erdoğan became the AKP's candidate. Because of his own strong, hard-core plebiscitary support, and the colorless candidate jointly sponsored by the CHP and MHP, Erdoğan won this election handily with 52 percent of the vote, against E. Ihsanoglu's 38 percent and S. Demirtas, the candidate of the reorganized Kurdish People's Democratic Party (HDP), successor to the BDP, who received almost 10 percent.

The presidential election result seems to have implied both a promise and a threat for the newly elected president. The promise involved two inherent possibilities. Either the high level of support could be converted into a new constitution-making parliamentary majority in 2015, or it could be claimed as a mandate to change de facto the way the presidency has functioned under the reformed Constitution of 1982. Initially, it was the first possibility that was

[96] M. Akyol, "Turkey's Constitutional Court stands up to Erdoğan," *Al Monitor*, July 2015: http://www.almonitor.com/pulse/originals/2015/07/turkey-constitutional-court-last-stronghold-rule-of-law.html# accessed November 19, 2015.

openly pursued, though simultaneously, without at first saying so, Erdoğan began to turn to the second. In other words he was increasingly tempted to use the remaining authoritarian powers of the dualistic constitution, and to even legislate new ones. He treated his prime minister, as is common in many presidential regimes, as merely one of his ministers, with Erdoğan presiding over all important sessions of the cabinet.[97] Contrary to the constitution, which required his neutrality, the president played an active role in the electoral process as the AKP's top politician.[98]

At the same time, he took the threat implied by the relatively strong showing of the HDP's Demirtas in the presidential elections very seriously, and used his office to try to diminish the dangers involved. It is hard to say now whether the settlement process with the Kurds was gradually abandoned because of the threat represented by Demirtas, or whether the new HDP launched such a strong challenge because they believed that nothing serious was happening in the settlement process. Most likely both scenarios were real, and they interacted to reinforce one another. On the one side, there were more and more signs, including statements of Erdoğan that there never was a Kurdish problem,[99] and his rejecting procedural steps already agreed upon by the government,[100] that pointed to the stepwise abandonment of real negotiations. On the other side, the HDP made a sustained effort to attract democratic and liberal non-Kurdish voters, and this entailed among other things (and because of earlier suspicions in this context) the determined and open rejection of a turn to presidentialism. This was a head-on challenge to the project of Erdoğan, as well as to his authority, to the extent that he was informally introducing a new type of presidency. Thus Erdoğan's rather fantastic and undemocratic post election rationalization that the settlement process was abandoned by the HDP through its challenge concerning presidential government was not entirely without substance, though of course without justification.[101] Whoever struck the first blow, the principled attitude of the HDP on questions of democracy undoubtedly helped its vote totals in 2015. The party received 13 percent of the vote, passing the threshold, with 80 deputies increasing its previous total as independents by forty-five seats. This time undoubtedly the HDP's success was the most important factor behind the dramatic weakening of the AKP, going from 50 to 41 percent of the vote, and with a reduced number of seats of 258 well below the threshold enabling it to form a single-party government.

[97] This was permitted by Article 104b, an authoritarian residue: "To preside over the Council of Ministers or to call the Council of Ministers to meet under his/her chairpersonship whenever he/she deems it necessary."

[98] Article 101: "If the President-elect is a member of a party, his/her relationship with his party shall be severed and his/her membership of the Grand National Assembly of Turkey shall cease."

[99] "President Erdoğan says Turkey never had a Kurdish Problem," *Today's Zaman*, March 15, 2015.

[100] "Erdoğan Rejects Dolmabahçe Blueprint, Slams HDP as 'Extension' of PKK," *Today's Zaman*, July 17, 2015.

[101] "Gov't says HDP's campaign of opposition to presidential system ended settlement process," *Today's Zaman*, July 29, 2015.

The defeat of the AKP in the June elections of 2015 not only said farewell to the possibility of an amending majority, but was in principle incompatible with the establishment of a de facto strong presidential government. The latter required a pliant parliamentary majority controlled by and supporting the "executive" president, which was now gone. For a brief period a caretaker government too could have played this role, and possibly a state of emergency under which the president and the cabinet could rule through extraordinary means. Yet, reminiscent of earlier authoritarian episodes, a state of emergency would not be easy to institute. It was thus at a time when both options became more precarious that Erdoğan openly admitted that while a formal establishment of presidential government was his preference, a de facto version such as the one he already exercised was also satisfactory.[102]

In my mind, this claim involved, initially at least, not so much a presidential coup as an attempt to utilize possibilities still present in the constitution of 1982, only reformed in part. Erdoğan was seeking in other words the restoration of an earlier regime in which one institution, the presidency, both at the head of the state and of the executive power would be the fulcrum around which all governmental powers were organized.[103] But unless he wished to carry out the constitutional coup he was immediately accused of,[104] or declare a state of emergency or martial law that would seem to amount to the same thing, he could exercise the de facto executive presidency only under the AKP's post election (but not pre-election) caretaker government, or if the party reversed its fortunes in new elections.[105] To achieve the latter, Erdoğan chose to do two things that were legal only in the narrow sense but deeply illegitimate. He prevailed on the leaders of his party, still the biggest in parliament, to deliberately sabotage coalition formation and thus move toward a situation where the constitution's Article 116 required a new election. When this move succeeded, he refused to offer the second-placed party, the CHP, the option to try its hand at coalition formation, as is customary in every parliamentary republic. Instead, he paradoxically appealed to the will of the people to decide the issue. Indeed, the Turkish voters had already spoken, but since what they said was not liked, they were asked to speak again. To make sure that this time they would say the right thing and allow the AKP to have at least a simple majority, a new factor was introduced: national security. That pertains to the second move within Erdoğan's strategy.

[102] "Erdoğan says Turkey's Government 'a De Facto Presidential System'," *Today's Zaman*, August 14, 2015.

[103] Under surviving parts of the dualistic constitution, the president has considerable powers to use this restoration, those under Articles 104b and 105 among them.

[104] "Opposition Decries 'Coup' after Erdoğan's Regime Change Remarks" and "Jurists: President Erdoğan's remarks against Constitution," both in *Today's Zaman*, August 16, 2015. Colleagues Özbudun and Köker both make the appropriate comments in the second article.

[105] According to Articles 114 and 116 of the constitution, if he dissolved parliament because supposedly no coalition could be formed, on the road to a new election, the president had to name an interim government composed of all the parties. However, the CHP and MHP had already announced that they would not participate in such government, and while the HDP announced the contrary it could hardly play much of a balancing role.

Here the interweaving parts of constitutional politics by other means become visible. Since the HDP was blamed, as it turns out partially correctly but unjustly, for the electoral weakening of the AKP, a main feature of Erdoğan's strategy was directed against the HDP. The existing links of that party with the guerilla PKK, actually a huge advantage if one sought a peace process, were now denounced as cooperating with terrorism. The possibility of lifting parliamentary immunity for deputies and even legal processes against them was seriously threatened. This was so far only the rhetorical part of the electoral strategy. Another related part, however, was much more than rhetorical. It involved the re-opening of the armed conflict with the PKK. Again, it is not so interesting who struck the first blow.[106] Under the partial deception of entering a war against so-called ISIS, the pliant Turkish government has begun an air campaign against PKK in Iraq, openly disregarding the fact that the PKK along with its allies and affiliates was currently the major ground force fighting ISIS.[107] Anticipating the bloody retaliation that one did not have to wait for long, President Erdoğan has generated a new rationale for electoral support. Coalition governments cannot deal with political emergencies, he claimed, and therefore he and the AKP should be given the voter's support to enable the putting together of a really strong government. The war-like acts were thus meant to dramatically diminish the HDP and improve the status of the AKP.

New "snap elections" took place early in November after the first draft of this book had gone to the publisher.[108] Before then, the declaration of either a state of emergency or of martial law in parts of the country by the president and the NSC were contemplated.[109] But such moves needed to be supported by the cabinet and at least one oppositional party, so that parliament would not have been able to rescind the declaration.[110] As it turned out, such a move was also unnecessary, especially after several terrorist attacks that played a similar role, by making the political campaigns of the CHP and especially the Kurdish-led HDP nearly impossible.

Erdoğan's overall strategy worked exceptionally well, and the AKP regained the majority needed to form a single party government. It was precisely the strategy of a protection racket. The Turkish people were put under serious threat by the government itself, and it was strongly implied that only the same AKP government could control and eliminate the same threat. While a governmental majority has been retained, the AKP is nevertheless again short of the

[106] See N. Mert "Is it a 'war coalition'?" *Hurriyet Daily News*, August 23, 2015.

[107] I leave out of consideration the fact that the American government has allowed this to happen, based on the entirely mistaken view that Erdoğan's Turkey is a more important ally than Kurdish irregulars. Turkey may be; Erdoğan is not.

[108] Thus the following last lines of this chapter amount only to a post script.

[109] See Articles 120, 121, and 122 of the constitution.

[110] Indeed, the nationalist MHP was the first to call for martial law to be declared in parts of the country, a call that was then rejected by Prime Minister Davotoglu. "Turkish PM rejects MHP call to declare martial law," *Today's Zaman*, August 20, 2015.

three-fifths constitution-amending majority. Thus the other parties may again face a choice, whether they are willing to trade some of their votes for concessions in the areas of their interests. But the biggest choice faces the AKP itself. Given their parliamentary strength, it will be up to that party and its other leaders to decide whether they formally wish to underwrite the executive presidency of an obviously dangerous and narcissistic leader. Their interests, I should note, are not the same as Erdoğan's, who has already cost the party many votes. Yet, even if they decide against formally supporting a new constitution of a presidential regime, Erdoğan could and probably would still try to govern as a de facto executive president. Then too it would be up to AKP leaders to stop him, but so far there is little evidence that they would even try. Of course a society and its social institutions, associations, and initiatives have other means to resist authoritarianism than relying on parliamentary votes. It is almost certain that there will be attempts by the other parties and their supporters in civil society to try to bring the epoch of Erdoğan finally to a close. If the major politicians of the AKP finally choose to resist Erdoğan, they could participate in and even lead such an effort. But whoever leads, it will be important to resume the task of making a new constitution, which is the only way to put an end to the dual regime of 1982, of which Erdoğan has become hopefully the last authoritarian inheritor.

PART III

POPULIST CONSTITUENT POLITICS

6

Political Theology, Populism, and the Constituent Power

I INTRODUCTION

Some of our significant political concepts are secularized theological ones. Not all of them. Some major religious-political concepts are theologized profane ones. What is crucial is that non-theological concepts like territory and population can also be theologized, as in "sacred homeland" or "the People." Such is the main effort of political theology, the preservation and imposition of concepts and figures of thought in political theory, inherited from monotheism, however transformed. It can only be countered by the further secularization and disenchantment of political concepts, the preservation or the re-establishment of their secular and rational character.

Why should we engage in this secularizing effort? This chapter will first argue, using the example of Carl Schmitt, that positive reliance on political theology can have a profoundly authoritarian meaning and is also helpful in disguising and misrepresenting that meaning. Second, I will try to show that taking this topos seriously does not commit a thinker to a political-theological posture. As demonstrated by Claude Lefort, political theology can be thematized in order to go beyond it. Lefort is important for my argument, because his concept of democracy as the empty space of power clearly draws the line of distinction not only with totalitarianism, as he stressed, but with all modern forms of dictatorship. I have made use of this concept throughout this book to help solve the problem of democratic beginnings where there is no democracy before.

Next, I will argue that without uttering the word itself, a political conception can be deeply theological, without admitting it. At a time when one can no longer openly argue for dictatorship as Schmitt still could in the 1920s, disguising the authoritarian disguise itself, namely political theology, can preserve its meaning and function. I will try to develop this point through a critique of populist politics in the version introduced by Ernesto Laclau, who explicitly advocates not only the construction of "the people" in an entirely voluntaristic manner, but filling the empty space of power by leadership incarnating a subject that does not exist.[1] Finally, relying on the conception of populism so introduced, I will end by presenting and criticizing one attempt to justify populist constitution making in Latin America, one that also uses radical democratic ideology to disguise the authoritarian danger that the conception cannot eliminate.

By political theology I do not mean only a politics that preserves the entire substance or structure or substantial contents of theology in secularized forms.[2] Mindful of Hans Blumenberg's powerful if ambivalent critique,[3] I do not identify political theology with the assertion of causality for theological origins, even a hypothetical one as in Weber's "protestant ethic" thesis.[4] nor with the claim of substantial structural identity of theological and "secular" concepts as in Karl Loewith's *Meaning in History*.[5] Neither Weber's nor Loewith's conceptions are primarily political. Not being theories of politics, they are not political theologies. Causality or substantial identities are neither sufficient nor necessary to indicate the presence of political theology. I find Blumenberg's idea of "re-occupation" of only the questions and not of the answers of theology powerful, but only with the proviso that for this re-occupation the "transformed" linguistic resources and structures of monotheistic religion play a key role (as he is forced to admit).[6]

Thus I believe one can speak of partial identity of substance, in addition to the re-occupation stressed by Blumenberg. This step leads not to a rehabilitation of political theology that he feared, but to a diagnosis of its presence in modern and contemporary political thought. In his fear of political theology, Blumenberg went too far toward trying to argue that there is really no such a thing at all. With this reservation, the shift of emphasis from substantial identity to the legitimating function of re-occupation remains important—this was already the role of the king's two-bodies doctrine in the variety of forms explored by E. Kantorowicz.[7] The famous Schmittian thesis concerning the secularization of theological concepts too implied the mobilization of political theology in the sense of "re-occupation" for purposes of legitimation.[8]

[1] Or exists only as myth. See the outstanding work of M. Canovan, *The People* (Cambridge: Polity, 2005), which is admittedly less hostile to mythology in modern politics than I am. I do believe that her critique of the equally excellent E. Morgan's *Inventing the People* (New York: Norton, 1988) is unfair and incorrect.

[2] Nor do I mean every possible use of religion and theology proper in politics, the broad meaning implied by H. de Vries and L. Sullivan (eds), *Political Theologies. Public Religions in the Post-Secular World* (New York: Fordham University Press, 2006). With the proviso below, I am using the term in Carl Schmitt's sense of the secularization of monotheistic religious concepts for political theory and practice.

[3] H. Blumenberg, *The Legitimacy of the Modern Age* (Cambridge, MA: MIT, 1983), Part One. See also the strong introduction by R.M. Wallace, 3.

[4] *The Protestant Ethic and the Spirit of Capitalism* [1905] (New York: Norton, 2009).

[5] Chicago: University of Chicago, 1949.

[6] M. Foucault, *Society Must be Defended* (New York: Picador, 2003) 74–80.

[7] E. Kantorowicz, *The King's Two Bodies* (first published 1957; Princeton, NJ: Princeton University Press, 1981).

[8] Certainly a better example than Blumenberg's two other targets: Loewith's theses concerning the origins of "progress" or Weber's ideal typical derivation of the spirit of capitalism.

II CARL SCHMITT'S CONSTITUENT POWER AND POLITICAL THEOLOGY

"All significant concepts of the modern theory of the state are secularized theological concepts."[9] This statement of 1922 cannot be taken literally, at least as a description, in light of *Die Diktatur* published a year earlier.[10] In that work, Carl Schmitt based his understanding of one of the two key concepts, commissarial dictatorship, directly on the Roman model linked to republican practice, rather than any theology. The very concept of dictatorship is Roman of course, and even the idea of sovereign dictatorship, if not the concept, made its appearance in Rome in the traditional treatment of the *decemvir* episode as recounted in Livy, as well as in the dictatorship of Sulla.[11] Schmitt's use of the word "all" is therefore revealing. I believe the reason to insist on it may very well have been a normatively charged justification for his own turn to political theology and his transformation of originally republican concepts into theological ones.

It has been argued that this turn had not begun even in the 1921 work that has been represented as a critique of sovereign dictatorship.[12] That interpretation is difficult to accept, since it implies a radical shift in the 1922 *Political Theology*, which is hard to explain or justify. In any case, after 1922 the issue is moot, and it is certainly incorrect to claim given the text of the 1928 *Verfassungslehre*[13] that Schmitt could adopt the concept of the constituent power of the people only as he freed it from the connotations of his earlier notion of sovereign dictatorship.[14] In the *Verfassungslehre* Schmitt adopted the very concept of constituent power worked out in *Die Diktatur*, linked to sovereign dictatorship and, equally important, to political theology.

There is little question that Schmitt understood the historical introduction of sovereign dictatorship in political theological terms. The key figures in *Die Diktatur* were Cromwell and Rousseau. One of these figures is theological in the traditional sense, but on the borderline of the sovereign dictatorship already hinted at by radical Protestant thought in England. The other breaks with the tradition and turns to political theology. The appeal to divine authorization is sincere in Cromwell and the clue to his quasi-monarchical sovereignty, while in Rousseau (following Machiavelli), religious justification proper is only a noble lie. It is

9 C. Schmitt, *Political Theology* vol. I (Chicago: University of Chicago, 1985) 37.

10 C. Schmitt, *Die Diktatur* (Berlin: Duncker & Humblot, 1928)—I am using the 6th edition.

11 In Latin: *dictator legibus faciendis et rei publicae constituendae causa* or: dictator for the making of laws and founding the republic.

12 See John McCormick, *Carl Schmitt's Critique of Liberalism* (Cambridge: Cambridge University Press, 1997) Chapter 3 and especially 133.

13 C. Schmitt, *Verfassungslehre* (Berlin: Duncker & Humblot, 1928).

14 A. Kalyvas in *Democracy and the Politics of the Extraordinary* (Cambridge: Cambridge University Press, 2009) 92ff, 97, 133. The term sovereign dictatorship and the emphasis of the dictatorial pattern of constitution making do return in Schmitt, *Verfassungslehre*, even if less frequently given the change of topics. See especially 59–60.

otherwise with *political* theology. Here in Rousseau, according to Schmitt, "the politicization of theological concepts, especially with respect to the concept of sovereignty, is so striking that it has not escaped any true expert on his writings."[15] According to *Die Diktatur,* Rousseau's general will has godlike dignity, uniting power and justice; it is an unlimited and illimitable legislator, the source of the laws of the state as God is of the laws of nature; it is undivided, and indivisible, indestructible, morally pure, incapable of error or even of willing a wrong.[16] This is distinguished from the will of all, the empirical will, and the people who can err, and thus the whole construct is an implicit transposition of the language of the king's two bodies (if, *pace* Blumenberg, not the precise substantial structure!) from the monarch to the people. Both the figure of God the Father and the Christological *metaphor* of Kantorowicz are present in this theologically mixed depiction. Nevertheless, the sovereign of Rousseau's political theology, whose will is the General Will, is said to surpass the theologically legitimated absolute monarch in its legislative capacity, unlimited by either a law of succession or divine and natural law.[17]

Rousseau's conversion of theological to political (-theological) omnipotence or at least unlimited legislative power was not the final form of the political theology of the constituent power, as far as Schmitt is concerned. As he correctly noted, Rousseau does not fully unify the will, and has a need to distinguish the authority of the wise *législateur*, one with a divine mission but without power, from both the power of the people that may not be wise and the power of the dictator that relies on external authority.[18] Schmitt thought another step was essential: the unification of dictator, *législateur* and, I would add, sovereign(ty) in a concept of sovereign dictatorship,[19] a step that he sees fully developed in Sieyès' notion of the *pouvoir constituant*.[20] Here, all the theological motifs are restated with full force and are even radicalized: absolute creativity, absence of limits, priority to all organization, infallibility, persistence. The relation of the *constituant* to the *constitué* is said be exactly analogous to Spinoza's pantheistic distinction of *natura naturans* and *naturata* with its *immanent* rather than *transcendent* conception of the divine.[21] The *constituant*'s power is an infinite, inconceivable, inexhaustible ultimate foundation (*Abgrund*) that produces ever new forms and organs.

At the same time, however, the very lack of clarity of the will of the people as the constituent power is interpreted theologically as expressing a hidden and never fully accessible divinity.[22] Since the will of the nation or the people is unclear, it can be misinterpreted and distorted, and therefore it takes an agency

[15] Schmitt, *Political Theology* I 36.

[16] Schmitt, *Die Diktatur* 118–19.

[17] This is still called omnipotence in Schmitt, *Political Theology* I (German text, 43) but to be replaced already in that work by a theology of the miracle, understood as the exception.

[18] Schmitt, *Die Diktatur* 125ff.

[19] Ibid. 126.

[20] Ibid. 137ff.

[21] Ibid. 139. This formulation is slightly altered in Schmitt, *Verfassungslehre* 79ff.

[22] Schmitt, *Die Diktatur* 142.

to rightly construe it, one that has not only the authority to interpret it but the power to impose it as well. The role of such a church-like entity is all the more necessary because the empirical people is not the ideal one, and thus needs regeneration, and as Lefort shows with respect to the Reign of Terror, this idea is then reduced to another: "the people must be extracted from within the people."[23] Many years before Schmitt popularized his concept of the political, his political theology anticipates the friend and enemy polarity, parallel to even if not identical in substance to the saved and the damned.[24] This political theology could be said to be immanent; both friend and enemy are worldly actors. Admittedly, there is only partial identity of substance. While the friend is identical to the ideal people, the enemy is not identical to the empirical one, which in part can be regenerated. The empirical people, however, are seen as contaminated by the enemy. Thus, while the external enemy can be excluded even from the empirical people, the internal one represents an entirely different task.[25] The purified body of the elect is a not yet, an absence rather than a real presence. It cannot act, and must be represented, as the visible church represents the invisible one.[26] Thus the idea of a "hidden God" appears in spite of Schmitt's repeated criticism of the deist political theology he sees in the German *Staatslehre*, one that he describes derisively as a cloak and dagger drama assuming an entity incapable of action behind a variety of political functions and institutions.[27] Yet he himself has noted the absence of a personalist and decision-making quality in his central concept of the people.[28] Where he differs from the German *Staatslehre*, is that, unlike Jellinek et al.,[29] he posits the need to have an entity that can successfully identify itself with the people in order to have a popular decision at all.[30] This is where the largest trouble lies.

"Extraction" and "regeneration" (and therefore: proscription) as the production of the supposedly constitution-making subject are the highest task of sovereign dictatorship in Schmitt's original interpretation, higher than even the production of the constitution. As I will show below, this idea will be taken over by Ernesto Laclau. In Schmitt's case, dictatorship is still in the name of the true sovereign, or rather its placeholder, the *pouvoir constituant*, and in appearance it

[23] C. Lefort, "The Revolutionary Terror" in *Democracy and Political Theory* (DPT) (Minneapolis, MN: University of Minnesota Press, 1988) 79.

[24] He has made this point himself in the *Concept of the Political* (New Brunswick: Rutgers, 1976), after again denouncing the "superficial political theology" of the omnipotence of the state. C. Schmitt, *Der Begriff Des Politischen* (Berlin: Duncker & Humblot, 7th edn. 2002 (1932 version of the text)) 42–3. Also see Schmitt, *Political Theology* I where he presented the theological conception of universal guilt, implying the division (*Einteilung*) of the saved and the damned, a model for the friend enemy concept of the political. Ibid. 63–4.

[25] In Schmitt, *Concept of the Political* 46–7 this idea is maintained in terms of the declaration and proscription of the internal enemy.

[26] C. Schmitt, *Roman Catholicism and Political Form* (first published 1923; Westport, CT: Greenwood Press, 1996).

[27] Schmitt, *Political Theology* I 38; *Die Diktatur* 27 and 138.

[28] Schmitt, *Political Theology* I 46.

[29] G. Jellinek, *Allgemeine Staatslehre* 3rd edn. (Berlin: Springer, 1920).

[30] Schmitt, *Political Theology* I 10 and 49.

is commissioned by the people. There is not, however, nor can be, an actual act of commissioning by the ideal body of the people, whose general will is identified not as the fallible will of all, but as one that cannot err. This will must be represented, empirically speaking, by the will of a minority, or even of one man.[31] If there is commissioning, or authorization, it comes close to self-commissioning or self-authorization. The empirical people is either not a person, unlike the monarch, with a will,[32] or, less likely, has a will that only corresponds to that of the monarch's natural body, which could be in error. This is perhaps why the *pouvoir constituant* of the people is not initially identified with sovereignty as such implying that the ideal unity is not a person with a will. Its sovereignty is at best latent, and its powers are given to, or rather taken by, the sovereign dictator. While the *pouvoir constituant* and sovereign dictator may not be omnipotent, they are both unlimited and incapable of limitation.[33]

Thus, in sovereign dictatorship, absolute power is exercised also over the entity that supposedly commissions it and is the source of its legitimacy.[34] How much difference does it make that this is supposed to be only dictatorship, not sovereignty itself? The temporal limitation Schmitt implies may turn out to be illusory as already in France in 1793 and then in Russia in 1918. It is true that with the regeneration of the people as expressed legally speaking by the full enactment of a constitution even sovereign dictatorship is supposed to come to an end. Here, however, the classical concept of dictatorship is under strain, because regeneration may be time consuming, and who is to say when it is completed. Even the enactment of a constitution, as in 1793, need not have meant full regeneration, since the emergency definition of the *gouvernement révolutionaire* as in place "till the peace" refers to both the external and the internal enemy. The difficulty is even more clearly illustrated by the example of the dictatorship of the proletariat that has no strict time limits in any Marxian version. I should add that even this motif is theological, with the sovereign dictatorship exercised by a quasi-church waiting for "the end of time."

In my reading, the two Schmittian works that treat the constituent power are not fundamentally different in their conception. First, in both the theory of constituent power is understood as secularization of the notion of God as the "*potestas constituens*."[35] Yet, well before Blumenberg, both texts comprehend that political theology is not simply theology, since the people can neither fully replace God, nor has the ability to alone create a constitution, nor is a constitution the whole of social life. And second, because here, as elsewhere,[36] Schmitt

[31] Schmitt, *Die Diktatur* 120.

[32] Schmitt, *Political Theology* I 48–9.

[33] The difference between omnipotence and being unlimited is that between theology and political theology, or between superficial and serious political theology.

[34] Schmitt, *Die Diktatur* XIX. Lefort points to a triple absurdity in "The Revolutionary Terror" 79.

[35] Schmitt, *Verfassungslehre* 77.

[36] C. Schmitt, *The Crisis of Parliamentary Democracy* (Cambridge, MA: MIT Press, 1988).

sees no tension or fundamental contradiction between dictatorship and democracy, and it is even stated that dictatorship is possible only on democratic foundations,[37] as distinct from the republican (but hardly democratic) earlier theory of the commissarial dictatorship. The key here, obviously, is an understanding of democracy in plebiscitary terms as fundamentally public possibility of acclamation. But most importantly, third, because the newer conception of constituent power is such that all the elements are still there that require dictatorship: the friend and enemy conception of the political requiring "the extraction of the people from the people," the unclarity of the will, the disorganization of its agent, the possibility of error and falsification on the one hand, and the indivisibility, purity, creativity, incapability of error of the people's ideal body on the other. I would even say finally that the need for a disguise for a fundamentally authoritarian politics was there in both texts, even if there is in this context a slight shift between them. Originally this need was answered by the Roman concept of dictatorship, but, in spite of Schmitt's notable and sophisticated scholarly effort, it remained suspicious because of his own new concept of sovereign dictatorship, as well as the stubborn, more modern meaning of the same term as a permanent regime, which Schmitt was in any case closer to conceding in *Verfassungslehre*.[38] There, the theologically constructed democratic language replacing the republican one is the main answer to the need for disguise. That it is a disguise still can be shown in the very terms of Schmitt's own theory, his discussion of representation and government. In all states there must be some who can say *l'état c'est nous*.[39]

III POLITICAL THEOLOGY AS A LADDER TO THE POLITICAL

Political theology generally accomplishes the move from the king to the people within a two-bodies doctrine. In the case of monarchy, the doctrine was developed primarily in a constitutionalist, or at least anti-absolutist direction, through the postulate of an abstract body transcending the will of an individual man, namely the king. Transferring the model to the people, its immediate implications are, however, anti-democratic.[40] As the distinction between general will versus will of all shows the point here is to devalue and abstract from what the population actually and empirically wants, to the benefit of another will. For Claude Lefort, this transference is accomplished by "the phantasmagoria of

[37] Schmitt, *Verfassungslehre* 236–7.

[38] See F. Neumann, "Notes on the Theory of Dictatorship" in *The Democratic and Authoritarian State* (New York: Free Press, 1957) and my piece, A. Arato, "Conceptual History of Dictatorship (and its Rivals)" in E. Peruzzotti and M. Plot (eds), *Critical Theory and Democracy* (London: Routledge, 2012).

[39] Schmitt, *Verfassungslehre* 207.

[40] As already it seems to be the case in Marsilius of Padua, who was perhaps the first to inaugurate the synechdochal move *pars pro toto* in his concept of the *pars valentior*. See F. Neumann, "Types of Natural Law" in Neumann, *The Democratic and Authoritarian State* 78.

popular power,"[41] contemporaneous with but in contradiction to the invention of democratic politics in modern revolutions.

In no other author does the two-body scheme taken from Kantorowicz play a more important role than in the work of Lefort. However, this should not be understood as Lefort's clinging to a medieval form of thought, to a political theology.[42] In Lefort's instance, the effort produced not a political theology, but a process of learning from it that goes beyond its limits: "rather than seeing democracy as a new episode in the transfer of the religious into the political, should we not conclude ... that the theological and the political became divorced."[43] For Lefort, political theology is a ladder to use and to leave behind. It is neither an instrument to disguise or justify domination as for Schmitt, nor the ever-present condition of possibility of liberal democracy. The key here is the insistence on the symbolic dimension and the idea of the empty space of (symbolic) power that political theology helps to discover, but under democratic regimes also to misconstrue. The insights nevertheless gained can be abandoned in a democracy only at the cost of authoritarian populism (if the space is filled), or worse: totalitarian re-incarnation (if the spatial position is entirely obliterated).[44] The scheme is one of a no longer theological dualism, in other words, it is the affirmation of transcendence without a transcending entity that could be imagined as a body.[45]

Lefort first relies on political theology to show that, historically, the model of what he calls political science cannot account for the workings of power that require symbolic projections of legitimacy. Without this level, *politics* may be possible, but not the understanding of *the political*, defined as the activity and interpretation that establish and reproduce the most fundamental institutions of society.[46] These institutions are founded in never fully accessible metanormative structures: deep-seated, unconscious assumptions that, without being normative themselves, determine the meaning of truth, justice, and law within a social-political order as a whole. For Lefort, this idea of the political, very different than Schmitt's friend-enemy polarity, is the key to different political forms or regimes. Lefort consistently maintains throughout that pure immanence, in other words a purely human world, or even society, is ontologically and

[41] C. Lefort, "The Revolutionary Terror" and "The Permanence of the Theologico-Political?" in DPT 77ff; 236ff.

[42] The criticism would be right in the case of an author such as L. Barshack, "Constituent Power as Body: Outline of a Constitutional Theology" (2006) *University of Toronto Law Journal* 3–56.

[43] C. Lefort, "Permanence of the Theologico-Political?" in DPT 255.

[44] I agree with Laclau that Lefort tended at times to operate with the rigid alternatives of democracy and totalitarianism, leaving no room for anything in between.

[45] This transcendence is similar in my interpretation to the lifeworld of Habermas, with the proviso common to both authors that while any of its dimensions will be potentially open to reflection, there will always be others that must fundamentally elude us.

[46] The best treatment of Lefort's political thought is B. Flynn, *The Philosophy of Claude Lefort: Interpreting the Political* (Evanston, IL: Northwestern, 2006).

historically impossible.[47] The two-bodies metaphor is important to him in order to establish the space where counterfactual norms or symbolic meta norms that transcend the real could be located within a political model of legitimacy, initially a political theology. Even the will of a sacerdotal monarch thereby comes under what this will ought to be, in other words under law. Thus in the case of the king, the two-bodies metaphor leads in the direction of the rule of law and even constitutionalism, as Kantorowicz strongly implied. For the efficacy of the symbolic, in the case of kingship, both the identification of the symbol with a body, and their constitutive difference are important. The king can represent unity both because he stands for much more than simply a concrete human body, and because he is *also* a human body. In other words, as the figure of Christ he mediates between the bodily and the symbolic, though as Blumenberg would stress for a different, more immanent end. Lefort is above all concerned with the survival of the modality of thinking that we have already seen in Schmitt, the replacement of the king's by the people's two bodies.[48] Here he notices, however, that the lack of an identifiable unitary body, as in the case of the king, can lead in the opposite direction: the search for a new embodiment.

Lefort's analysis of Michelet in particular shows that in the case of the people as well as the king, it was possible to postulate both symbolic embodiment and physical incarnation, and thus symbolic meaning as well as the presence of the symbol, but without the full identity of these dimensions. The empirical people are again seen, as in Rousseau, as fallible and open to manipulation, but here also open to demagogy and capable of senseless violence. Yet "the people" are seen as a subject and an actor in the streets and assemblies of Paris, moving the revolutionary process forward with intense energy. To Lefort, this construct represents adding yet another figure to the dualisms reconstructed by Kantorowicz, preserving a partially overlapping theological structure. It is Michelet who clings to a medieval figure of thought. According to Lefort, in spite of Michelet's attacks on the theologians of politics, both monarchical and popular, his conception *is* a political theology. But he explicitly does not stay with Michelet and the people's two bodies. Lefort speaks of the obvious weakness of Michelet's argument, which starts with but is not restricted to an "outrageous simplification of Christianity." It is this very simplification that helps to produce the mistaken impression that democracy involves a mere repetition of historical forms.[49]

[47] Lefort, "Permanence of the Theologico-Political?" 229, 254; and Flynn, *The Philosophy of Claude Lefort, passim.*

[48] On this also see E. Morgan, *Inventing the People* (New York: Norton, 1988); P. Pasquino, "Constitution et pouvoir constituant: Le double corps du people," unpublished lecture (May 2004).

[49] Lefort, "Permanence of the Theologico-Political?" 248.

While learning from the genealogy of the two bodies, Lefort insists that democracy represents a fundamental break with it.[50] The gap between the symbolic and the real is now much greater, and can no longer be mediated by a single subject with two bodies. The transcendent space is still there, but it cannot be occupied as long as democracy survives. This means two things. First, that there is no democracy without symbolic reference, one that cannot be reduced, as in the realistic theory, to the concrete description of its workings. Thus the lessons learned from religion and political theology should not be forgotten. Second, it also means that instead of replacing God with people, the theological notion of *the* people must be abandoned altogether. Thus we must break with all political theology.

The key to the last step is Lefort's analysis of the concept of the people in the French Revolution.[51] "No more God-People" he exclaims, twice quoting Edgar Quinet.[52] Lefort, while not entirely consistent in his usage, sees the people and popular sovereignty as paradoxical: in the moment of their emergence they either lose their identity and become anonymous, or dissolve in mere number and more importantly division.[53] Given an only "latent" identity, as well as empirical multiplicity, and multiple dimensions, as a subject or subjects, the people can be defined only in a "juridical construction."[54] By juridical, I think he means more than the legal equality of the members of democratic society, but also various more active possibilities: the people as the majority of an election according to various rules, or a referendum, or any other participatory process procedurally provided for including the diffuse processes of the public sphere that also must be legally constituted. As he has argued in several pieces dealing with the French revolution, to insist on the people as the (pre-legal, pre-constitutional) subject of *revolutionary* politics leads to some absurd paradoxes we have seen in Schmitt, such as the idea of "the extraction of the people from the people," or the project of the regeneration of the agent that is the very source of the authority of this operation, its own midwife.[55] Or, "the people ask their delegation to give birth to them but the delegation is part of the people." Lefort calls this idea "triply absurd" because it presupposes that the operation is needed because the people are crushed, yet able to delegate and imagine a freedom that they have never experienced.[56]

It could be said that the people in its very indeterminacy and latency as well as divisions means empty space, but Lefort's own analysis shows that it is difficult

[50] Ibid. 255.

[51] See the 1980 essay, C. Lefort, "Interpreting Revolution in the French Revolution" in DPT. This analysis relied on F. Furet, *Interpreting the French Revolution* (Cambridge: Cambridge University Press, 1978), both predating Morgan's partially parallel treatment in *Inventing the People*.

[52] E. Quinet, "The Revolution that Failed" in DPT 134.

[53] Lefort, "Interpreting Revolution" 227, 230–2.

[54] Ibid. 230.

[55] Lefort, "The Revolutionary Terror" 79 as well as C. Lefort, "Interpreting the Revolution" 107–8. Beyond Francois Furet, the most important source of this argument is Quinet, "The Revolution that Failed."

[56] Lefort, "The Revolutionary Terror" 79.

to restrict it to this merely negative meaning. Nor is it easy to replace normative foundations by an ontological conception of the symbolic. While the difference is subtle, Lefort does not simply restate the formulation of the German *Staatslehre* and Carré de Malberg of popular sovereignty as national, as merely another, symbolically elevated face of the state where the people or the nation appear as a hidden God incapable of any embodiment by any political organ. Following Furet, for Lefort while the space is empty, in the revolution at least there was a continual struggle to occupy it. Edmund Morgan[57] has documented the same process for the English and American Revolutions. According to Lefort, it becomes impossible to say "which group, which assembly, which meeting, which consensus was the trustee of the people's word." At the moment when the existence of a new legitimate power is declared, fully united and self-identical, it becomes impossible to identify. Yet the attempt is made, and made possible by assertions of identity and unity. The failure of each claimant and the revolutionary terror directed at all of them is testimony that all such claims can only be usurpations in a democracy.[58] I think Lefort is forced to admit this struggle not only on historical grounds, but also because he is not satisfied with a purely negative principle of legitimacy that would make modern democracy too precarious. Thus his rejection of the notion of popular sovereignty is equivocal. Yet these very semantics produce the conflicts with and within the democratic principle as he has defined it. Emptiness is in itself not a normative desideratum, and popular sovereignty on the face of it implies a stronger normative figure: the rule of the whole people only by itself.

Lefort I think neglects the question of democratic legitimacy, because to him it is the symbolic that on a deeper level determines which type of legitimacy is possible at all for a given regime. He puts the idea of popular sovereignty in doubt, without seeking to replace it. The empty space of power means the symbolic establishment of division and contestation rather than unity and absence of conflict. As the key to the integration of democratic politics, it is defined above all by a discourse of a power that belongs to or is embodied by no one, and that defines the exercise of power as a periodic contest.[59] This symbolic structure leads to a scheme of plural legitimating possibilities, rather than the monistic scheme of populism based on popular sovereignty and identification. But he knows that only institutionalization allows the distinction of the democratic contest for power, from the use of violence on behalf of as well as against attempted usurpation. Is such institutionalization possible without some at least implicit consensus on legitimacy?

[57] See Morgan, *Inventing the People*.

[58] Thus Lefort, I think mistakenly, and in a contradictory fashion, at times sees the reign of terror as ultimately democratic (Flynn, *The Philosophy of Claude Lefort* 138, 244–5) because it is directed at keeping the place of power empty, as against usurpations. But he equally says that the logic of the terror springs from the need to extract the people from the people (ibid. 135), which highlights the authoritarian dimension.

[59] Lefort, DPT 226.

Division and conflict as ultimate principles no longer belong to political theology. Beyond the still theological dualism of ideal unity and empirical division, Lefort's proposal involves an ideal framing of conflict, where plurality rather than even duality is the fundamental principle. This step can occur only with the defeat of the revolutionary imaginary in processes of transformation and institutionalization.[60] As against a certain Schmittian interpretation of Lefort,[61] I would argue that this notion is not incompatible with the ideas of Rawls and Habermas. Conflict has to be institutionalized if it is not to mean dualistic friend-enemy relations or a pluralistic war of all against all, which, given the notion of popular sovereignty in the French Revolution, led to the Terror. Each faction, seeing itself as the people, sought to eradicate all others defined as the enemy, whatever the appearances. To avoid such a logic requires fundamental rights and the separation of powers, as Lefort repeatedly states, and not only de facto social pluralism. But the model also presupposes a constitutionalist constitution, though not necessarily a written one. It requires a constitution having at least a minimal symbolic consensus, in any case more than a mere modus vivendi that may be the way it is first established, for example, after revolutionary struggles or pre-empting these, but remains contingent on given constellations of power.[62] The constitution presupposes and seeks to conserve social diversity rather than aiming at unity and unification.

As for popular sovereignty, if one still wishes to retain the idea of bodies, than it must be the multiple[63] rather than the two or even three bodies[64] of "the" people. It must involve the legalization of each supposed body. But the survival of the definitive article "the" even here indicates the danger that a temporary incarnation expressing one valid perspective will be propagated and accepted as the only valid one. Even if Lefort is right that the claim itself is not a problem, claims and counterclaims of this type if taken sufficiently seriously, each claiming to be judge in its own cause, can be adjudicated only by violence. Thus it may be best to go beyond incarnation altogether, as Lefort and Habermas both repeatedly suggest,[65] and replace the idea of popular sovereignty by that of a

[60] See A. Arato, "Lefort, the Philosopher of 1989" (2012) 19 *Constellations* 1 23–9.

[61] E. Laclau and C. Mouffe, *Hegemony and Socialist Strategy: Towards a Radical Democratic Politics* (London: Verso, 1985).

[62] See J. Rawls, *Political Liberalism* (New York: Columbia University Press, 2005), whose notions of modus vivendi and overlapping consensus remain unsurpassed.

[63] See N. Walker, "Post Constituent Constitutionalism? The Case of the European Union" in M. Loughlin and N. Walker (eds), *The Paradox of Constitutionalism* (Oxford: Oxford University Press, 2007) 247–68.

[64] The two-bodies conception becomes one of three bodies when the representation of the ideal segment of the people, "the plebs" or "underdog" in Laclau becomes a problem. This happens with Lukacs' theory of the party, and Laclau's concept of leadership.

[65] For one of the many places in Lefort see "Permanence of the Theologico-Political?" 255. For Habermas, see J. Habermas,"Popular Sovereignty as Procedure" in Habermas, *Between Facts and Norms* (Cambridge, MA: MIT, 1996) where what is left of popular sovereignty is only decentered and temporally disaggregated, multiple procedures of largely informal democratic communication. Its formal preconditions are fundamental rights, and its organizational bases are the associations of civil society. Habermas repeatedly rejects the idea that popular

democracy that can be defined only in procedural terms, the notion of *the* people in the singular by a model of pluralistic legitimation. Such a model would have learned from political theology the importance of the political without replacing one theological scheme by another.

IV POPULISM AS DISGUISED POLITICAL THEOLOGY

There is little question that Schmitt, both an analyst and expert of political theology, is partially right: sovereignty and the constituent power are commonly used as political-theological concepts. But he neglects the possibility that these now secular concepts can be further secularized and thereby de-theologized. The theory of populism of Ernesto Laclau heads in precisely the opposite direction. Taking a political category, namely "populism," which despite its well-known ambiguities and multiplicity of forms describes a shifting set of very real and very stubborn empirical phenomena, he theologizes it and strongly affirms the theological structure he secretly introduces.[66] This can be shown precisely in relation to Schmitt's political theology, which Laclau either assumes, without a single citation, or rediscovers in his desire to justify and disguise his own version of authoritarian politics. The frontier of antagonism of Laclau is Schmitt's friend-enemy conception of politics. The stress on symbolic representation is a return to Schmitt. Above all Laclau's populism involves the extrication of the people from the empirical people by an evidently plebescitarian form of leadership. This conception is also squarely rooted in the theological two-bodies conception, one that is explicitly affirmed.[67]

With Schmitt not mentioned, Laclau only seems to be relying on Lefort's version of the people's two bodies, traced in turn by the latter back to authors such as Michelet. But contrary to Lefort, Laclau refuses to leave this construct behind. While the two-bodies conception applied to the people represents to Lefort only a ladder that must be thrown away once fully ascended, Laclau formulates his model of populism exactly in terms of double or triple incarnation. Thus in spite of important points of contact, Laclau reverses Lefort's emphasis precisely on the question of political theology.

sovereignty should refer to a collective body, will, or even a subject of any kind: ibid. 472–3; 486–7. His communicative, de-substantialized translation of "the people" is convincing, but it is unclear why this should be called sovereignty at all. See also repeatedly in Habermas, *Between Facts and Norms* 136, 185, 300–1. The concept of decentering in Habermas is similar to Lefort's empty place. They both explicitly reject embodiment, which Habermas ascribes to "republican" conceptions.

[66] Admittedly, the use of religious metaphors and pseudo-rituals is characteristic of many populisms themselves. This is well demonstrated with respect to Latin American cases by C. de la Torre, *Populist Seduction in Latin America* (Ohio: Ohio University Press, 2010) 11–12; 15; 65; 207 and elsewhere. Curiously, Laclau entirely neglects the religious or quasi-religious appeals of many populist movements. In reality, the theological turn in his thinking universalizes this phenomenon, to all populisms, and indeed the political.

[67] E. Laclau, *On Populist Reason* (London: Verso, 2005) 126.

The positive link with Lefort is not the trivial one having to do with equality and equalization mentioned by Laclau.[68] In fact, the notion of *the political* (*le politique*) as the activity that consciously aims at the institution of society, constantly redefining it, is inherited from Lefort (and with a slightly different terminology from the more radical, revolutionary version of Castoriadis). Just as Lefort, Laclau has little theoretical interest in *politics* (*la politique*), which he identifies with social action ultimately, defined as rule following or acting within unchallenged rules or what he refers to as merely institutional action. The political on the other hand is seen as foundational and creative. But, and this is a big but, Laclau identifies the political with populism[69] even if occasionally and inconsistently populism appears as *only one* of its forms.[70] It is in this context that Lefort is attacked for tending to identify populism with totalitarianism and both with the obliteration of the political. Note, however, that populism is not mentioned by the cited Lefort text, and it is Laclau himself who, rightly, applies to populism some of the features of Lefort's totalitarianism: "power is embodied in a group ... in a single individual ... the development of the fantasy of the People-as-One etc."[71]

Laclau is undoubtedly right: populism and totalitarianism should not be conflated even if there are "totalitarian" forms of populism.[72] Lefort's concepts allow us to make the distinction between occupying the empty place of symbolic power and obliterating the distance between the symbolic and the real. Totalitarianism does both, while populism only the former. But Laclau is also right to suspect that for Lefort the populist move in itself represents a threat to democracy. It is on this point he wishes to refute Lefort.

Here it is not only a question of populist inclusion that can have the democratic effect of broadening the community of "citizenship," the achievement of a democratic result by non-democratic means.[73] Laclau wishes to treat the means itself as a fundamentally democratic one, in the sense of the construction of popular subjects. But this move represents insistence on a concept of popular sovereignty that Lefort subjected to serious critique, rather than democracy. It is meaningless to say that democracy need not be understood as a form of regime. More deeply, Laclau abandons Lefort's definition of democracy as the emptiness of the place of power and the process of institutionally securing

68 Ibid. 165. 69 Ibid. 99, 117, 222, 231–2.

70 He is quite explicit about this move: see E. Laclau, "Populism: What's in a name?" in F. Panizza, (ed.), *Populism and the Mirror of Democracy* (London: Verso, 2005). On page 47 he asks if populism becomes synonymous with politics, and replies that "the answer can only be affirmative. Populism means putting into question the institutional order by constructing an underdog as an historical agent – i.e. an agent which is an other in relation to the way things stand. But this is the same as politics." (I thank Carlos de la Torre for this reference.)

71 Laclau, On Populist Reason 165–6.

72 It even goes too far to see populism, as Žižek does, as a "long term Fascist tendency." In S. Žižek, "A Leninist Gesture Today: Against Populist Temptation" in S. Budgen, S. Kouvelakis, S. Žižek, and D. Fernbach (eds.), *Lenin Reloaded: Toward a Politics of Truth* (Durham, NC: Duke University Press, 2007) 83.

73 This is the dimension stressed by many authors otherwise not sympathetic to populism, such as de la Torre, *Populist Seduction in Latin America* 125–6.

its emptiness. The political space can be and even must be filled, at least "partially" (whatever this means) and emptiness reappears only on the ideological level as the "empty signifier" that only superficially—on the level of naming—keeps something of Lefort's conception. The empty signifier's stress is on unity rather than plurality. In all versions it refers to the unification of heterogeneous demands around admittedly vague, symbolic contents that obliquely anticipate a utopian condition of total social unity, homogeneity, and reconciliation. The content can be an idea such as justice or equality, or a person such as Boulanger or Perón, but in all cases they must be carried and promoted by a partial social reference group, "the plebs" or the "underdog," that identifies itself with "the people as a whole," the populus.

The concept of a part that represents the whole is inherited from the Marx of 1843,[74] who most likely was reflecting on and radicalizing the conception of Sieyès in *What is the Third Estate?* But in Laclau it is no longer the logic of history that will turn the exclusion of "the plebs" or of the "underdog" into the representative of the people as a whole. In effect, the alternative concept of democracy we have is one of the empowerment of a weakly identified subsection of the population through rhetorical devices bereft of rationality. Moreover, given the likely heterogeneity (at times confused with mere difference) even of the partial group, unification by an abstract utopian reference is depicted as insufficient. An empty signifier is a reference point, a name that constitutes reality, but is not an agent or a subject capable of decision and action. Thus even when a populist movement is not immediately identified with the empty signifier of a leader's name (as in "Peronism"), leadership seems essential.[75] Here we have an example of double embodiment, or the application of the king's two bodies to the ideal body—redoubling it and bringing it back to a physical incarnation. Thus while the partial group embodies the whole; the leader embodies the partial group, with a three-bodies conception as the result.

Clearly, Laclau explicitly rejects Lefort's ban against embodiment. The king's two bodies continue to operate in democratic societies, but now in terms of a triple scheme: the leader, the extracted groups, and the universal reference that is an empty name.[76] He understands embodiment not only as an empirical phenomenon necessitated by the inability to identify the people or the *pueblo*, "a profoundly vague" concept.[77] For him embodiment in leadership is the highly desirable constitution of a popular subject, one that otherwise would fall back

[74] K. Marx, "Critique of Hegel's Philosophy of Right. An Introduction" in F. Engels and K. Marx, *Collected Works* vol. I (Moscow: International Publishers, 1975).

[75] Laclau, *On Populist Reason* 99–100. Thus the basically leaderless U.S. version of populism does not fit into Laclau's theory even though he refers to it as a case.

[76] Ibid. 170. This is not to be confused with a multiple-body scheme such as in Walker, "Post Constituent Constitutionalism?" where each "body" of the people is given an organizational form, and where action is not understood as that of a hierarchically dominant body, as in Laclau.

[77] de la Torre, *Populist Seduction in Latin America* 78; 139; 207.

into mere difference.[78] Why the filling of the empty space by leadership in this conception is said to be only partial remains unclear. Laclau does not have in mind the highly precarious and inevitably temporary nature of empirical attempts to embody; these remain open to critique precisely in the name of democracy. This was a logic described by Furet, Lefort, and Morgan, consistent with the concept of emptiness. The emptiness of the democratic space, reproduced by institutions and discourses, is deeply inhospitable to all and any efforts at embodiment. However, Laclau, unlike Morgan, is not only an analyst of the fictional use of the concept of the people, he is an advocate of the fiction and of the political construction of fictions.

As this conception is developed, the model of the political is contaminated. The process of "the extraction of the people" is incompatible even with the process of inclusion stressed by all ideologists of populism: some are included, while others are immediately excluded, and worse. What Laclau constructs as equivalence among those who are different, and even heterogeneous, is possible only if a radical "frontier of antagonism" is constructed within society. Equivalence is attained only in common opposition to those who would deny otherwise heterogeneous demands. The political as the foundational is replaced by the idea of friend-enemy relations. The vagueness of the ideology is compensated for by the intensity of antagonism. The absence of real identity is made up for by affective, libidinal ties, "love" for the leader and love for all those whom the leader supposedly loves.[79]

The conception is Schmittian also in its reliance on Hobbes. As sociology from Durkheim to Parsons has been pained to point out, Hobbesian atomism excludes the notion of the social. The social is absent in Laclau as well. Atomized individuals (even if replaced by atomized "demands") are only united politically. Referring to Hobbes, Laclau's notion of leadership has exactly this function, even if he supplements the Hobbesian sword[80] with what he presents as Freudian love. This can be most clearly seen through his notion of representation. After calling Hannah Pitkin's "still the best theoretical treatment of the notion of representation" he proceeds to reduce her complex, five-fold theory of representation to primarily one of its dimensions, namely symbolic representation, reinforced by an element of Hobbesian "authorization view."[81] It is thus that he cites the notion that a dictator can be as good or even a better representative than an elected member of parliament because of his emotional, that is, charismatic powers.[82] As he knows, this was hardly Pitkin's final word on the subject, and indicated rather her critique of the reduction to symbolic representation. This critique is explicitly rejected by Laclau who, in spite of a feeble

[78] This does not describe the situation of Solidarity with respect to Walesa, or what Laclau produces as one of his examples, Mandela with respect to the ANC (Laclau, *On Populist Reason* 100).

[79] Ibid. 53–6, 82–3. [80] Ibid. 88, 100. [81] Ibid. 159.

[82] H. Pitkin, *The Concept of Representation* (Berkeley, CA: University of California, 1967) 106–7.

attempt[83] to repeat Pitkin's view of Fascism as "the extreme form of symbolic representation" in fact returns to precisely Schmitt's proto-fascist understanding, derived from both the symbolic and institutional practice of the Catholic Church, and derisively juxtaposed to mere interest representation, or *Vertretung*. The idea is that of a symbol or an official symbolically incorporating an absence, for instance, the cross for Christ, or the pope for the Church's ideal body. When reinforced by Hobbesian absolute authorization, this position combines unlimited power of the "representative" with the emotional attachment of the represented.

Laclau rejects Pitkin's idea that an empirical case of representation can be judged according to normative criteria (whether there are good reasons for accepting a given leader), and produces the purely Hobbesian counterargument that the criteria can be formed only within and by representation, and never outside it.[84] This argument, however, is false for any but the most closed and least differentiated society. Given Laclau's denial of asking normative and critical questions concerning the validity of a form of representation, his implication that there is a spectrum of possibilities between purely top-down and purely bottom-up forms of representation, that representation is a two-sided phenomenon, is futile and self-contradictory. The point is right, but he has no way to judge any option within this scheme preferable to any other, especially as he abandoned Pitkin's other forms of representation. With the assumption of Hobbesian "radical disorder" or radical heterogeneity, order and homogenization can only move from the representative to the represented. Since the latter's very identity and unity is said to be constituted by representation, the idea of a two-way movement is a subterfuge. A reverse movement, from the represented to the representative, could only be satisfied by missing links such as accountability, whether electoral or judicial, or similitude, or public pressure and influence, and most radically by direct democratic devices such as imperative mandate and recall. All such mediations, well discussed by Pitkin, are missing—if not in all populist movements, then certainly in Laclau as he follows the paths of Hobbes and Schmitt.

Hobbes is Laclau's key move, not only forward to Schmitt, but also back to Lenin in his most voluntaristic version. Laclau abandons not only the Marxian notion of class, as he should, but any plausible sociological alternatives (whether stratum, group, association, corporate entity, movement, and so on) seen as

83 What makes it extreme, exactly, if it does what symbolic representation is supposed to do, namely produce unity and identity? Pitkin has the answer, as opposed to Laclau, namely the neglect of the interests and opinions of the represented.

84 Laclau, *On Populist Reason* 161. This argument was already implausible in the case of Hobbes, whose sovereign could not be in the position even according to him to rule over the conscience of the subject. It is all the more ridiculous for Laclau, who is focusing on modern settings.

concepts with a content juxtaposed to empty but constitutive names.[85] Thus we are left with what Merleau-Ponty called ultra-Bolshevism, in reference to the early Sartre.[86] In the 1950s, Sartre argued that, in light of what he took to be the empirical situation of the working class, only the party can produce unity and universality where there is empirically only heterogeneity and particularism, a heap of dust particles or of sand, separated rather than unified by primitive need.[87] Reproducing the Hobbesian argument that Laclau too will use, Sartre argued that the least division within the organ that unifies would reproduce the dispersion. The splitting up of the proletariat would mean the "breaking apart of popular sovereignty."[88] Thus leadership becomes essential, logically of one person ultimately, leadership that according to Sartre must incarnate the unity of the group that is an unattainable ideal even with the suppression of dissent and minorities he sees as essential.[89] Collective consciousness is impossible as "group mind"; to exist it must necessarily be incarnated in leadership. Leaders are dictatorial because the group has supposedly chosen them to exercise dictatorship over each member.

As Sartre had a real point against orthodox Marxism's economistic or historical deterministic or even neo-Hegelian derivations of the unity and consciousness of the proletariat, Laclau has one against Žižek and Negri as well. A political theology of immanence based on a Hegelian identical subject object, or a Spinozian agency (proletariat or multitude) has no plausibility anymore, whether sociological or political. He is right in suspecting that the invocations of the proletariat or the multitude are not based on any coherent sociology of groups and movements. But the answer, to constitute exactly the same type of actor now called "the people," a historical subject, entirely voluntaristically, by uttering a name, as in magic, and embodying that name in a leader with emotional ties to the masses, is only somewhat less implausible and is definitely more dangerous.[90] It is in any case a political theology.[91] More importantly, politically, the construct reeks of manipulation, what Rosa Luxemburg as well as the young

[85] This is the point made over and over by Žižek in his polemic against Laclau. Žižek, "A Leninist Gesture Today" 83 and 89. And, they are very much right against each other. Žižek's class, which Laclau wishes to leave behind, is an objectivistic myth, while Laclau's people is a voluntaristic one that does not convince Žižek.

[86] In M. Merleau-Ponty, *Les adventures de la dialectique* (Paris: Gallimard, 1955). In English: *Adventures of the Dialectic* trans. by Joseph Bien (Evanston, IL: Northwestern University Press, 1973); Merleau-Ponty here followed a critique of Sartre by his student, the young Claude Lefort, whom he went on to call "Trotsky's Trotsky."

[87] J.-P. Sartre, *The Communists and Peace* (New York: Braziller, 1968) 130; 216.

[88] Ibid. 228. [89] Ibid. 216–17; 222–3.

[90] Through the medium of Freud, Laclau adopts some assumptions of earlier crowd and mass society theories even though modern studies of social movements have demonstrated that it is the already organized and associated who are the constituents of major movements.

[91] That point was not made by either Lefort or Merleau-Ponty vis-à-vis Sartre. Castoriadis did make it with respect to Lukacs: "the Party here appeared as the embodiment of actual class consciousness. As always, spiritualism ended up by finding a concrete historical subject in which to embody the transcendental entity, which would otherwise have to remain what it really is: a ghost. So God becomes the Catholic church." P. Cardan (Cornelius Castoriadis), *Modern Capitalism and Revolution Solidarity* pamphlet (London: 1974). The piece was from 1965.

Trotsky strongly criticized as "substitutionism," radicalized in Sartre's "ultra-bolshevism" of a certain period.[92] Trotsky already accurately foretold the likely result in 1905: one-person dictatorship. It does not help that, contra Hobbes, the unification by the leader in Laclau's version is supposed to be linked to the constitution of a revolutionary subject of action, rather than a final outcome, namely "actual ruling" or regime. Here Lenin was more consistent and frankly admitted that the point of constituting a political vanguard was to establish a dictatorship (whether first the "democratic dictatorship" of workers and peasants, or later the party). At least he believed that there was a logic in history that would make such a regime eventually obsolete along with the state. Laclau neither shares this optimism nor tells us why the elective affinity between dictatorial movement and dictatorship as regime should not be seen as very strong, even if the linkage is said to be not "automatic."[93]

How do we sell such ultra-bolshevism[94] today, in an age when dictatorship seems to be fully discredited? One certainly cannot do so in terms of the language inherited from Lacan, such as the concepts of *objet petit a* and *mother's milk*, that seem to me unnecessary even in Laclau's conception.[95] These are, politically speaking, only curiosities that most readers will quickly forget. It is otherwise with the language of political theology, with deep roots in some versions of Marxism, and capable of mobilizing strong, religious-type sentiments. It is indeed striking that religious movements and mobilizations do not already play a significant role in Laclau's conception, though they would eminently qualify at least as long as they were carried by subaltern agents. Political theology, however, treats all movements on which it focuses as religious. Moreover, there is not a critical word concerning religion in Laclau's text, and the political theologists he criticizes, mainly Žižek and Negri, are attacked only because they have the wrong political theology, one based on immanence rather than transcendence.[96] It is their followers, along with other leftists, who are the main target of a work the language of which evidently does not seek to speak to populist movements and their potential participants: the addressees are intellectuals who are open to the secularized religious character of (some) movements, and who are invited to give up one political theology for another.

[92] R. Luxemburg "Organizational Questions of Russian Social Democracy," [1904] in *Rosa Luxemburg Speaks* (New York: Pathfinder, n.d.); Leon Trotsky "Our Political Tasks," in R.V. Daniels (ed.) *A Documentary History of Communism in Russia: From Lenin to Gorbachev* (Burlington, VT: U. of Vermont, 1993).

[93] Laclau, *On Populist Reason* 100.

[94] Of course, I am using this concept only in an abstract sense—I do not mean to imply that Laclau speaks for any Marxist-Leninist groups. On Laclau's contemporary political commitments and role see V. Palermo, "Intelectuales del Príncipe: Intelectuales y Populismo en la Argentina de Hoy' (2011) 2 *RECSO*, Montevideo Uruguay 81–102. (I owe this note to Carlos de la Torre.)

[95] Žižek, as a Lacanian, pays precious little attention to these constructs in Laclau, and rightly so. They violate Occam's razor, or the principle of the economy of thought.

[96] Laclau, *On Populist Reason* 239ff, 242ff.

Laclau's political theology as one of the transcendent type is already indicated by his revival of the king's two-bodies metaphor. The old image drawn from Sieyès and Constant—repeated by Arendt and Lefort—is one where absolutism put the king in the place of God, and the revolution similarly replaced the king by the people. It is repeated here, but this time with a positive evaluation. The people as a whole is a transcendent God, never present or visible in its full universality and completion. It is an absent or a hidden God, "an absent fullness" It does not matter a whole lot that this is seen as a failed or non full-fledged transcendence.[97] Since Laclau assumes Kantorowicz's Christological metaphor, he also assumes that that which is absent is and must be made present by incarnation. The people's three bodies are present as different levels of embodiment. The plebs and the leader are representative symbols that make present the "fullness" that must remain transcendent. "The fullness of communitarian being is very much present for them as that which is absent." [98] It is in and by the name of the transcendent that the levels of incarnation are constituted, but only through incarnation can constitution through a name be successful. The ontological argument for the existence of God is reinvented in a nominalist form, "the people" a name the uttering of which establishes its reality.[99] However, for this reality to be active, mediations are needed, and this is possible only through representative symbols that produce affective identification with bodies that can act. The invisible Church must be embodied in the visible one.

Act to do what? In this conception populism, as already mentioned, shares the logic of the political, or rather is that logic, and consists in confronting and challenging the established institution of society. However, this is a critical function, not yet a theological one. The step to theological expectation, already contained in Marxian theories of revolution as shown by Karl Loewith, lies in the notion of a transcendent place, a new ordering of the social realm. "The fullness of the community is merely the imaginary reverse of a situation lived as *deficient being*." What Laclau shares with his forerunners is the idea of this political transcendence as a rupture with all previous orderings. Where he departs from them is the frankly assumed sociological emptiness of the anchoring notion, and the rather Kantian idea that transcendence can never be achieved: "a just society … exists only ideally."[100] The goal is nothing, the movement is everything, even if Laclau would not appreciate the reference to Eduard Bernstein. That there is no concrete political project here (unlike in the case of Bernstein) is certainly not due to Laclau's inability to conceive of one, but to the ideological heterogeneity of populisms, as well as the sociological heterogeneity of each populist movement, each drawing on incompatible demands that can never be reconciled in his own presentation. The vagueness of populist ideologies is one result, one that Laclau affirms without declaring his allegiance to any of them. The easy possibility of moving from one populism to another, even from left to right, is

[97] Ibid. 85 and 244. [98] Ibid. 94 and 223. [99] Ibid. 105–6ff, 108.

[100] Ibid. 86 and 94.

explicitly admitted by Laclau's theory of the *floating* signifier.[101] This conception shows that on Laclau's grounds it is impossible to normatively distinguish among different populist movements as long as, I suppose, they organize the underdog. From the point of view of any of them, the only defense against "floating" is rhetorical and emotional success. The very vagueness of the empty signifier, of a mere name, means scant mobilizing power without being embodied in groups and leaders with whom affective, rhetorically produced ties can replace the missing rationality. This is all the more important when key segments of the movement discover (as he is forced to admit) that their interests cannot be represented, that their demands must be suppressed.[102]

V POPULISM AND THE CONSTITUENT POWER

Ernesto Laclau has given us a sophisticated reconstruction of the logic of populism. To those who do not share his obvious normative commitment to populist politics, he has provided a convincing characterization of the danger in spite of his intentions. In one respect, however, his analysis remains suggestive but undeveloped. He has insisted on the populist character of *the political* as against mere *politics*, and has defined the former, following Lefort, in terms of orientations to the foundations and re-foundations of states. While empirically we may very well doubt that all founders have relied on the myth of the people as their ultimate source of authority,[103] it is clear enough that in the modern world, historically, many of them have, and still do. The idea is radicalized by populist constitution makers, whose paradigm is populist constitution making with a stress on ever-present embodied popular sovereignty. While Carl Schmitt remains the classical theorist of the populist constituent power, until Joel Colón-Ríos[104] no one had made a full attempt to step into his shoes. As both a constitutional theorist and a comparativist, Colón-Ríos was in a good position to try to accomplish this task. I find it hard to criticize him, because I agree with his attempt to rescue the actual making of constitutions from orientation toward mere results, or imputation based on the contents of a basic law.[105] I also agree with a lesson he drew from Castoriadis, Lefort, and Habermas, that constitutions should be understood as ongoing democratic projects involving wide publics, rather than either eternalized or assigned to governments or any of its branches as one of their tasks.[106] Thus I agree with his critiques of Waldron's

[101] Ibid. 88, 129–38.

[102] This is documented by de la Torre, *Populist Seduction in Latin America* for Velasco in Venezuela and Correa in Ecuador.

[103] Machiavelli as well as Rousseau still stressed, empirically, claims of divine authorization.

[104] J. Colón-Ríos, *Weak Constitutionalism* (London: Routledge, 2011).

[105] See Introduction and Chapter 1 above.

[106] Colón-Ríos, *Weak Constitutionalism* 58–60ff.

parliamentary absolutism and Dworkin's result orientation, though I do not think his critique of Ackerman is quite fair.[107]

Nevertheless, criticize Colón-Ríos I must, not because he has a different theory than mine, with a focus on a largely different set of cases, but because of the elective affinity of his theory (revealed by some of his positive examples) to democratic dictatorship that he may try to break with, or at least conceal, but cannot. This problem of course is inherited from Schmitt, who was not shy about his preference for plebiscitary forms of authoritarianism. Hannah Arendt, who in the path of Jefferson and Condorcet sought not only the constitutionalization of public freedom, but also the domestication of revolution, noticed this. She attempted to accomplish the above task through a radical critique of Sieyès, partially misunderstood because seen through the lens of Carl Schmitt. In reality, the object of her critique, consciously or not, was Schmitt himself. On the contrary, Colón-Ríos chooses to fully return to Schmitt, along with the latter's one-sided version of Sieyès. All the key themes of Schmitt are positively insisted on: the priority of the sovereign constituent power *to* constitutions, and its *survival* under them; the impossibility and undesirability of any limitation of the constituent power of the people, the absence of any definite procedure by which the constituent people must act, the sovereign dictatorship of the constituent assembly; the limitation of the amending power; the depiction of representation as democratically deficient; and, as against Lawson and Locke, the absence of any need to justify the activation of the constituent power.[108]

I do not claim that Colón-Ríos is consistent on all or even any of these matters. He seems to think that without freedoms of speech, assembly, and press, the popular constituent power cannot be activated. But, given their common assumptions, Schmitt is on firmer ground here, since in revolutions such rights are likely to be missing, or at least disregarded by the revolutionaries. Colón-Ríos also credits parliaments with at least some democratic credentials, rather than seeing them as aristocratic, and in any case deems them preferable to entrenchment and to the constitutional review linked to it. Finally, he does seem to suggest a very specific procedure or set of procedures that are to satisfy his two democratic desiderata: "openness" and "participation." Instead of the revolutionary reactivation of the constituent power in Schmitt, he imagines legal institutionalization in the form of new amendment rules. While derived from actual constitutions, these additions at best lead to an antinomic theory, in which the populist dimension is never dispensed with and even remains dominant.

[107] Unfair because their positions are often very close, and since Ackerman abandoned the position he is criticized for, his own fiction of the people, in the second volume of his work.

[108] Quite implausibly, he argues that Lawson and Locke only have a theory of resistance and not that of the constituent power.

Populism cannot work without popular sovereignty imagined as the real presence of the people.[109] Colón-Ríos takes note of claims that real presence is inevitably mythological, but seeks to move beyond them and goes on a search for the empirical embodiments of the popular sovereign. He tries to do so using a claim by Edmund Morgan that the counterfactual or fiction of popular sovereignty works only when it comes closer to reality.[110] To Colón-Ríos, this means first that a perfect embodiment of the people is not possible, but second that there can be successively higher forms of embodiment of the popular subject. Thus parliament is the lowest level of embodiment, however superior to an unelected court, a referendum is higher but still deficient, an extraordinary constituent assembly is higher still, while a process involving triggering, initiation, and enactment by ordinary citizens is perhaps the highest. That these are very often either self-authorizing minorities or elected bodies, hardly more representative than parliaments, does not seem to bother him. Note, however, that with this last move he has wound up finding three "peoples": the mobilized or even revolutionary multitude as "the trigger," direct democratic bodies charged "to initiate," and the drafting assembly defined as "the executor." This move could have been made compatible with a democratic conception.[111] However, the dominance of the Schmittian version means that each of these, in their various contexts, are said to be sovereign, and somehow it is assumed that a single united *voluntas* will be expressed. That Colón-Ríos has some doubts about that kind of identity is indicated by his rather quiet acceptance of Schmitt's sovereign dictatorship,[112] which can, as it is well known, exercise dictatorship over its commissioning instance, the empirical people.

Colón-Ríos is well aware of the dangers of adopting Schmitt's doctrine of the extra-constitutional, unlimited constituent power, which has been rightly regarded by many as a sword of Damocles hanging over constitutionalism. Yet he dismisses these rather negligently. There is little danger, he claims, that popular mobilization will attack the rights that sustain it, apparently for logical reasons, though evidence to the contrary has been and remains plentiful since the French Revolution. Constituent assemblies will not seek to perpetuate themselves or even greatly extend their tenure, he says, in spite of the example of the great *Convention nationale* of 1792–95 as well as the recent Venezuelan *constituyente* that has very much impressed him. Popular constituent process will not establish dictatorships—and why? Because that would be incompatible with

[109] H. Lindahl, "Constituent Power and Reflexive Identity: Towards an Ontology of Collective Selfhood" in Loughlin and Walker, *Paradox of Constitutionalism*; and H. Lindahl, "Sovereignty and Representation in the European Union" in N. Walker (ed.), *Sovereignty in Transition* (Oxford: Hart, 2003, 2006).

[110] I agree with Morgan's conception, but think that relevant legitimating ideas, rather than "bodies," express closeness to reality.

[111] See Walker, "Post Constituent Constitutionalism?"

[112] Colón-Ríos, *Weak Constitutionalism* 87.

democratic legitimacy. But perhaps other sources of legitimacy would be available, for example, religious, national, or plebiscitary charismatic forms, all compatible with authoritarian rule.

The problem of legitimacy returns with Colón-Ríos' treatment of parliamentary sovereignty. As already said, he considers parliamentary sovereignty interpreted in a majoritarian manner as superior to "strong constitutionalism" based on entrenchment and the constitutional review that enforces it. But parliamentary absolutism is said to be deficient because it suppresses the possibility of both democratic origins and democratic openness, each understood in terms of direct democratic participatory constitution making and remaking. If these elements were added, or even just openness alone, irrespective of original origins, we would apparently get a good example of "weak constitutionalism." Then ordinary laws and "non-foundational" constitutional provisions could be enacted by majority rule, while foundational norms could be altered or replaced only by a special process. But one would not need an entrenched fundamental law to accomplish this differentiation, nor judicial enforcement, both to various extents incompatible with weak constitutionalism.

Let me express double astonishment concerning this thesis, which was perhaps influenced by New Zealand's constitutional traditions. First, I note that the differentiation of foundational and ordinary constitutional provisions is even more difficult in a Westminster-type regime, rather than the one between the constitution and ordinary laws. A constituent assembly is already a foreign entity within such a system. If it were established, it is not clear what it would enact or constitute if it were not to codify forms differentiated by entrenchment, in this case not necessarily a whole constitution as elsewhere, but only its fundamental part. For example, the constituent assembly could establish that a statute enacted by the majority of parliament cannot undo a new, participatory process regarding some matters. If it were not to do this, one could not even reliably identify the parts to be changed through the two different methods. Let us assume that Colón-Ríos will concede this necessity. But then what happens if parliament does nevertheless pass a statute repealing just this rule? It would be legal, he says, but illegitimate. That helps about as much as the traditional British "legal, but unconstitutional" does. Schmitt's *bon mot* regarding the impossibility of the enactment of a Soviet regime in the United Kingdom by parliamentary majority may be true enough, but the same may not be equally true regarding more technical, though fundamental, parts of the constitution. Ordinarily we respond to this option by pointing to judicial review, a topic discussed by Colón-Ríos using examples from India and Colombia. In fact he even claims that the identification of a basic structure in a vast legal universe of homogeneous statutes, an uncodified basic structure within a documentary constitution would be as easy to find as it was in India, a claim we are entitled to very much doubt.

But, and here is my second source of astonishment, at this point Colón-Ríos doubles down on Schmitt's hardly inadvertent neglect of the possibility that a court should enforce limits on the amending power. Unfortunately, however, he seeks to improve on Schmitt, who has left the matter unresolved, by sketching an alternative. According to Colón-Ríos, while the legality of parliaments' unconstitutional statutes cannot be challenged, this can be done politically, apparently by a combination of a minority (parliamentary or popular) complaint confirmed in a referendum. Thus the outvoted minority, partially modeled on the type of review present in some Kelsen courts, would play the role of plaintiff, and the people in referendum would play the role of a constitutional court. Colón-Ríos does not seem to realize that with the intervening domain of *constitutional but not foundational laws* missing, such a device may lead to every law of any importance being challenged in referenda, and thus the replacement of parliamentary government by a plebiscitary one. Unfortunately, even legal but illegitimate was a more workable formula, leaving accountability entirely to the ordinary political process. Yet, in that case, the two tracks insisted on by Colón-Ríos would have to be sacrificed.

The deeper problem is that he seems to consider illegitimacy, as he defines it, to be an argument with almost automatic causal effects. This is surprising, because he in fact presents us with an interesting three-part concept of legitimation that adds a separate category of the "legal" to what I myself have tended to see in terms of only the contrast of the "sociological" and the "philosophical." While the sociologist can treat legality as a form of empirical legitimacy claim relevant only with the probability of significant acceptance, to the jurist or lawyer (as Weber knew) the meaning is different, and is based on the relationship of a norm to a framework of norms, one that may or may not reflect justice from the philosopher's point of view. Thus three things are involved: empirical acceptance, legal validity, and normative justification. After this interesting exposition, however, Colón-Ríos fails to explore the relationship of these three levels in processes of legitimation of political rule and decision making. Instead he presents us with what he takes to be a fourth form, democratic legitimacy, as a function of two related principles, democratic origins and democratic openness. These two normative principles are indeed important, and link together constitution making and the contents of constitutions in an interesting way.

However, this is not a fourth type of legitimacy, but one that remains analyzable under the other three. For example, we can say that an amending process is democratic, because the legal rules for elections and procedures have been followed. To the lawyer, that kind of openness would be all that can be demanded, given a particular legal order. Or, alternatively, we can diagnose that a process is accepted because the citizens, or a considerable proportion of them, do actually believe that the acts of their freely elected representatives are democratic. Finally, we can indeed say with Colón-Ríos that a process was democratic because it was triggered and initiated from below and was completed by an elected, extraordinary assembly. This would be an interesting argument, justice based, belonging to the philosophical concept of legitimacy. But unless it is already legally established and empirically accepted, the fact that we may consider it right and just would have little to do with the legitimacy of the process as a factor in political conflicts. There the legal and sociological meanings are more important, and these may not reflect any given philosophical perspective, whether based on openness, deliberation, or a veil of ignorance. Unfortunately, after his elegant differentiation of the three levels, their apparent confusion mars the analysis of Colón-Ríos. The reason why he is not aware of a problem here is perhaps because in several Latin American countries, something approaching his understanding of the philosophical level has indeed, at least at particular historical moments, coalesced with the empirical and the legal.[113]

The main value of Colón-Ríos' book is that he is the first to try to provide a normative theory of recent adventures of constitution making in the Andean republics. He finds them especially instructive, because in Colombia and Venezuela at least the Schmittian theory of the constituent power was explicitly articulated by supreme courts to justify a new democratic enterprise involving elements of popular participation. In line with his assumptions he very much prefers the opinion of the Colombian Supreme Court that denied, in a curious reversal, the attempt of the president of the republic to formulate limitations on the work of the *constituyente*.[114] In Venezuela, the Supreme Court also did allow a referendum providing for the election of a constituent assembly outside the amendment rule, but tried, in vain, to impose limits on what it wished to consider the derived constituent power. Colón-Ríos does not tell the full story in either case, and thus unfortunately omits the active role of the plebiscitary presidency in Venezuela that helped to generate the incredibly disproportional electoral rule and to intimidate the Supreme Court. He also omits, for that matter, the role of negotiations in Colombia in producing the type of proportional representation rule he otherwise seems to favor. In general we get not a single word about the dominant role of the presidency in any of the Andean republics. It may be a fair assessment of his argument to say that he wishes to disguise this role, of which he must be entirely aware. Thus two points are emphasized, in addition to the sovereign status of the constituent assemblies: one of these is the role of popular, grass roots initiatives along with referenda, confirming the democratic pedigree of the process; the other is the production of amendment rules making future popular initiatives to convoke constituent assemblies again possible, and, I would add, unambiguously legal. Thus, the recent Latin American processes are seen favorably in comparison to the later experiment in Iceland, where, according to his presentation, popular forms of participation were the most developed, but where the drafting council was not sovereign, and

[113] Empirical because of the popular mobilizations behind the idea of participation; legal because of the decisions of Supreme Courts. Given the absence of the revolutionary overthrow of the previous constitution, both of these dimensions were important.

[114] Indeed he claims that, as a result of the Court's decision, a "constitutional" assembly, implying under law, was renamed as the constituent one.

where the proposed constitution (which was ultimately rejected by parliament) did not provide for future reliance on the same participatory principles.

The idea that the constituent assembly should be sovereign is typical for the populist conception, even though it is much older than any populism. But it is quite inconsistent with the notion proposed by Colón-Ríos that the assembly should only execute what the true sovereign wishes to enact. He cites Sieyès ("a substitute for the whole nation" etc.) and fails to see the difficulty.[115] The idea of an executive constituent assembly, however inconsistent with the notion of a sovereign one, conjures up imperative mandates, and the idea of a non-deliberative assembly of ambassadors. No modern constituent assemblies have or can work on these bases, converting lay instructions that are likely to be contradictory into legal syntheses. Yet the fear that a deliberative representative assembly can detach itself from influence from below, and indeed even the specter of sovereign dictatorship, should certainly be taken into account. This cannot happen with inconsistent ideas of the absence of limits attributed to each level of constitution making.

Nevertheless, one dimension of the idea of "executive assembly" is right, namely that when the principles of a constitution are agreed upon, there must be sufficient power to enact and establish the new rules. A short discussion of the Arab Spring and subsequent mass mobilizations in Europe and America helps to make the point clear, although Colón-Ríos does not draw the right conclusions. With the exception of Tunisia, whose negotiated process he does not explore, these mobilizations resulted in authoritarian constitutions (Egypt), civil wars (Syria, Libya), or the absence of constitutional change (recently in Spain and Greece). Colón-Ríos remains enchanted with the mobilized and revolutionary multitude, and proposes that movements such as these must be "the trigger" of foundational constitutional change. He does not seem to understand that such triggers led to a negotiated process, as in Colombia and Tunisia, or to a plebiscitary one, as in Venezuela, only when organized political forces helped to move things in these alternative directions. The participation he wishes for on the level of initiation requires action on the level of politics as well as the political, and it is because of populist blinders that the former is de-emphasized in favor of the latter.

Populist leaders and organizations of course do completely understand the need for politics with a small "p" and without the definitive article "the." This is why there are not only populist movements but also populist regimes, a point often neglected by analysts such as Canovan, Laclau, and Rancière. But part of their politics is ideology, an ideology that disguises a particular brand of power politics of new leaders and elites, as the political acts of the imagined or claimed unitary subject, the people. There is nothing wrong with an analyst such as Colón-Ríos demanding democratic legitimacy of the constituent process, during the making of constitutions and also their re-foundation. But it is wrong to

[115] Colón-Ríos, *Weak Constitutionalism* 85.

help disguise the forces that help to manufacture unity from above, or, for that matter, to produce compromises on the intermediate level. As a result all we get is popular processes, triggered, initiated from below, and carried out by a merely executive assembly on the higher level. The latter has representation, as does Rousseau's "prince" or "government," but it is not supposed to legislate. That is the myth. In reality, constitutions are made precisely on this level. How they are made does matter, and legitimacy in all of its senses does depend on it, but neither the process nor the legitimacy should be presented as carried by none other subject than the united people.

Admittedly, by translating the populist message of Schmitt in terms of democratic legitimacy, Colón-Ríos is heading in two directions at once. He may be in effect saved by his contradictions. On the one hand, his model for democratic openness is the Schmittian, unlimited, ever-present constituent power, mythologically ascribed to revolutionary constitutional origins, none of which have ever been democratic. Here the reference to the unorganized multitude, a remnant of philosophical vitalism, is meant to demonstrate the primordial, unlimited status of the constituent power in the state of nature, but wrongly assumes that it is possible in a society to be in a normatively, indeed legally empty space. In any case, in this version new or reconceived amendment rules, however democratic, can have no place. From the radical populist point of view, the basic structure argument would apply to all or any of them, and the renewal of the constituent power would be possible only in a revolution or a coup.[116] On the other hand, he proposes a type of openness that could be provided for only by a multi-leveled democratic revision rule, as in the cases of the Latin American amendment rules he reconstructs. If they are to work as intended these in fact presuppose, as he admits, constitutions that establish and protect freedoms of association, assembly, speech, and press, as well as personal security. While they are meant to be *constituant* they thus presuppose a *constitué*. As specified rules, they are moreover procedurally limited by definition. In principle, they can be even limited in substance by "eternity rules" protecting the rights essential to any democracy whatsoever, thus enabling rather than disabling limits,[117] without being undemocratic. All depends on whether this type of constituent power *derivé* could also become the normative model for the *originaire.*

In fact the antinomy penetrates to a slight extent even to Colón-Ríos' understanding of the original constituent power. When he finally discovers the identity of "the" people, he comes up with three very different entities in three stages of action. Arguably none of these can exist or act outside normative rules, even if they are not provided for by the legality of a given constitutional regime, or a dictatorship for that matter. While in the triggering stage civil disobedience and revolutionary insurrection are two very different things, which should not be

[116] That was the very Schmittian argument of the Turkish Constitutional Court in its headscarf decisions of 2008.

[117] In terms of the important distinction of Holmes, cited but misinterpreted.

conflated under a Schmittian concept, the former is clearly under and defined by rules.[118] This was the very point of Gandhi's as well as Martin Luther King's teaching. In the initiative stage, democratic forms may vary, but on an abstract level their deliberative nature is sustainable only on the basis of rights and democratic procedures. This is eventually conceded, as Colón-Ríos follows Kalyvas in adding (Habermasian or Arendtian) public discussion and plurality to Schmitt's model of plebiscitary acclamation. Whether such things can be simply added to an entirely foreign conception is another matter. Finally, to establish democratic constituent assemblies, electoral rules are needed. While models for these exist either under the inherited regimes, or at the very least internationally, one must choose among models and there may be good reasons as in Colombia[119] to break with the electoral rule in place. But the choice must be made somehow, by someone, and neither elections nor grass-roots influence will be able to make the choice, for two different reasons, logic and technicality. And some normative principle or another must justify the choice. Moreover, to sustain what is misleadingly called the executive quality of democratic constituent assemblies, procedural and perhaps substantive limits are required as well, considerably short of imperative mandates. These limits ought to be enforceable and, as the South African case (neglected by Colón-Ríos) shows, this is best done by a court when all democratic actors, including participatory democrats, support its independence.[120]

Finally, the politics of democratic amendment rules can be highly sensitive to the question of power, without wishing to imagine away *politics*. In all the Latin American efforts at reconstitution elections did play an important role. In modern societies, however, parties are the key actors in democratic elections. It is not enough to merely try to use representative and direct democracy in complementary ways, as does Colón-Ríos. In our resistance to the elite model of democracy we should not go so far as to eliminate the role of parties, which are the only way to mediate between influence from below and power exerted above. When the level of democratic initiative is presumed to be able to produce a constitution on its own, as in Iceland, the effort can completely fail. Even worse, when the level of triggering seeks to decide things on its own, as in Egypt, the result is chaos and an opening for authoritarians. From Nepal's panchayats[121] to Mugabe's popular

[118] Much more controversially, even revolutions are arguably under normative rules, derived from natural law or the customary rules of a political community. Thus the initial explosion of freedoms under most revolutions are almost always suppressed by the revolutionaries.

[119] G. Negretto, *Making Constitutions: Presidents, Parties, and Institutional Choice in Latin America* (Cambridge: Cambridge University Press, 2013) 166–95.

[120] But the futile struggle of the Venezuelan Court does as well, which he also astonishingly neglects, thereby avoiding either siding with the presidency, or accepting his own deviation from the Schmittian position.

[121] J. Whelpton, *A History of Nepal* (Cambridge: Cambridge University Press, 2005) 86, 99ff.

consultations[122] these authoritarian forms often use participation as an excuse to eliminate parties and affirm the power of one party alone. The amazingly uniform and disproportional constituent assembly of Chavez too emerged through an electoral rule that eliminated all parties except the coalition behind the president.[123] If we are to insist on a Colombian-type electoral rule as the proper way to elect an inclusive constituent assembly, as Colón-Ríos does,[124] we should be more conscious of the type of meta-process that is likely to produce such a rule, namely inclusive negotiations of parties or proto-parties. The fundamental contrast between Colombian and Venezuelan constituent assembly elections should not go unmentioned. Both solved the problem of power, one in a form of imposition legitimated by plebiscite, the Bonapartist way, the other by taking party pluralism seriously, and expanding rather than displacing it.[125]

The idea of democratic openness under constitutional regimes, already insisted on by Hannah Arendt, is too important to allow populists to hijack it. Paradoxically, it is this idea that should be used as the foundation for legitimate, original constitution making as well.[126] The choice is clear: we should decide whether it is the democratic amendment rule under law or the primordial, unlimited, theologically conceived power that represents the core of democratic constitution making. Democratic theory insists on the first choice, while populism, openly or not, advocates the second.

Even as we refocus on amendment rules, we cannot forget the problem of original constitution making. The post sovereign paradigm implies two gains in this context. First, it helps solve the problem of how the amendment process can be applicable even where we wish not to preserve, or even reconstitute, but transform. Second, this paradigm has the best chance to produce democratic openness in the new constitutions. While in principle reform, revolution, and their relevant constituent procedures too could produce constitutionalist as well as open constitutions, there is at the very least an elective affinity between democratic multi-track amendment rules and the post sovereign paradigm of constitution making.[127]

[122] M. Ndulo, "Zimbabwe's Unfulfilled Struggle for a Constitutional Order" in L.E. Miller (ed.), *Framing the State* (Washington, DC: USIP, 2010); A. Saati, *The Participation Myth. Outcomes of Participatory Constitution Building Processes on Democracy*: http://umu.diva-portal.org/smash/get/diva2:809188/SPIKBLAD01.pdf accessed November 20, 2015.

[123] A.R. Brewer-Carías, *Dismantling Democracy in Venezuela: The Chávez Authoritarian Experiment* (Cambridge: Cambridge University Press, 2010).

[124] Colón-Ríos, *Weak Constitutionalism* 92–3.

[125] R. Segura and A.M. Bejarano, "¡Ni una asamblea más sin nosotros! Exclusion, Inclusion, and the Politics of Constitution-Making in the Andes" (2004) 11 *Constellations* 2 217–36; Negretto, *Making Constitutions*.

[126] See my presentation of Carré de Malberg's conception of amendments in Chapter 1 above.

[127] A. Arato, "Multi-Track Constitutionalism Beyond Carl Schmitt" (2011) 18 *Constellations* 3, 324–51, where I argue that either post sovereign form is required to achieve a multi-track, open constitutional democracy, or a process that has incorporated its normative lessons.

Conclusion

Even as I finish this volume constitution making and altering political projects are fought over in many parts of the world. These cannot be reduced to a single type, and they will have many different outcomes. They will be more or less democratic, constitutionalist, or stable. As in all important areas of political life, the sheer empirical complexity and variability involved could easily overwhelm us. One way of dealing with this great difficulty is to collect a very large number of cases and isolate a few abstract variables around which some regularities and causal linkages can be reconstructed. I do not doubt that important discoveries can be and have already been made this way. But I do have some serious qualms about such an endeavor. First, I am not sure that what is or will be discovered by such large-scale research is or will be genuinely new knowledge, not already known to sophisticated practitioners in the field. Admittedly, confirming the greater generality of what is already known can be worthwhile. But I also fear that the method often winds up comparing apples and pears, and in this case the very different types and meanings of constitution under differing regimes. Finally, I fear excessive formalism because what can be most easily measured and quantified are formal, documentary constitutions that by no means exhaust the meaning of constitutions in the material sense. But the latter are the real governing institutions of society, and in many places have little to do with the documentary constitution. If the method of large N research is to make any sense at all, in my view it must be complemented by comparisons of fewer cases and individual case studies focusing on history rather than formal analysis.

My project represents another way of introducing order, and, even more, normative standards into the complexity of constitutional phenomena. As more or less traditional at the New School for Social Research, it is inspired more by the methodology of Max Weber than by contemporary American social science. Thus I do undertake comparison but in terms of abstractly constructed ideal types, rather than a very large number of cases. I attempt to constantly move back and forth between abstract analysis and history. I assume that the self-understanding of important participants is as important as reconstructions by historians and the analyses of jurists and social scientists. The history of ideas is just as crucial from my point of view as the history of institutions.

The main ideal type that I have constructed is that of post sovereign constitution making, represented by the title of the book. It is based on one class of cases from the 1970s to the present, from Spain to South Africa and beyond, that in my view have important advantages in facilitating learning and legitimacy. The ideal type is derived not only from these cases, but also from the contrast with another type, sovereign constitution making where one institution or set of actors presumes to speak in the name of what I take to be a fiction, "the people," before and outside the constitution. In post sovereign constitution making no actor is recognized as taking the place of the absent or fictional sovereign. Based on actual cases, but reducing their internal complexity, the post sovereign ideal type is then linked to other more or less common features, such as the importance of the central institution of the round table, a two-stage process, an interim constitution, and legal continuity. These features are not all present in every single case. Spain did not have a round table. Poland's process was multi-stage rather than two-stage. In Iraq a revolution occurred, if one externally imposed. In Nepal legal continuity was broken. Only Hungary, Poland, South Africa, Iraq, and Nepal had developed interim constitutions. These differences can be accounted for by the development of the paradigm through time and by national specificities and constraints. But the contrast with the sovereign form and its central institution of the unlimited constituent assembly around which it is organized remains clear in spite of divergences from the constructed type.

Even the world of democratic constitution making, on which I exclusively focus, is not exhausted by my ideal sovereign and post sovereign types. I also use a four-part model of types, consisting of revolution, reform, revolutionary reform, and regime change, to indicate other possibilities. The link of revolution (the rupture of legality and legitimacy) to the sovereign type and of regime change (the rupture of legitimacy only) to the post sovereign type is historically demonstrable. Reform and revolutionary reform, both involving intact forms of legitimacy are more complex. They can, as recent reform in Hungary did, assume the sovereign and unlimited power of a legislature, or submit to constitutionalist constraints, as more commonly elsewhere. Revolutionary reform, first utilized in the United States, also allows a choice. Even the main actors of its key institution of the constitutional convention can assume that this body has only limited powers to recommend or ratify. But without a break in institutional legitimacy, this form, as often in Latin America, can convert a constitutionally limited power into a sovereign unlimited form. One important goal of this study is to promote a post sovereign turn also within reform and revolutionary reform. While in Hungary for the time being such a better alternative has lost out, in Turkey, my second important case study, the two options, sovereign and post sovereign, are still available. Hopefully the elections of November 2015, with their authoritarian outcome, have not definitively decided this very issue.

I consider the post sovereign option, because of the necessarily elite-dominated first stage, to be more sensitive to the problems of legitimation than all other forms. Empirically, I have reconstructed the response in terms of several normative desiderata: pluralistic inclusion, relatively consensual decision making, an empirical veil of ignorance, public openness, generosity, and legality. Not all of these are relied on in every round-table setting, of course, and some of these norms can be adhered to under reformist and revolutionary reformist models of constitution making as well, and perhaps even in revolutionary settings. I have equally insisted on the facilitation of learning, not only from the negative lessons of sovereign constitution making and among the round-table countries, but also within each post sovereign setting. It is above all the multi-stage character and the institution of the interim constitution that are the key learning devices. But learning, especially across international divides, is possible also under the other forms of constitution making.

In spite of its advantages in legitimacy and learning, I have been forced to depict the post sovereign paradigm as path determined. All the important cases represent transitions from authoritarian forms of rule, and thus cannot be fully relevant where the task is to change one constitutionalist form into another. Moreover, even under authoritarian forms, the model presupposes relative equality, or at least perception of equality between regime and opposition forces. Where the regime forces are much more powerful, they may opt for reform from above even where the old constitution has entered into crisis. Conversely, where new actors are in a dominant position, and understand themselves as such, they generally do not choose to negotiate with forces in old regimes. Nevertheless, learning is possible from the post sovereign paradigm even where the ideal typical structure cannot be fully applied. I try to show this in the case of reform in this volume, while a subsequent book will explore the possibility in the cases of revolution and revolutionary reform.

Finally, adopting a post sovereign path does not guarantee success. As all constitution-making methods, the new one assumes the existence of a state, or in the case of federations-to-be, states for whom the constitution is to be made. When the state collapses in the middle of a process, as in Czechoslovakia, or is absorbed in another state, as in the case of the German Democratic Republic, the round-table-led process cannot succeed. I think it is fair, however, to counterfactually argue that in these settings sovereign claims by constitution-making bodies would have failed even more certainly, and produced far greater disasters. In both cases reference to "the people" as author would have been entirely untenable, because of the two different forms of division within the actual or the projected political community. The case of Hungary is apparently more difficult for my conception, because there, in my country of origin, the structure of the state was not in doubt. Yet, in the end, sovereign imposition nevertheless displaced the post sovereign scenario. My explanation has to do with two important issues: time and the need for completion. The two- or multi-stage process definitely extends the time of post sovereign constitution making. But it is not by logic a completely open-ended process, such as has been described and even advocated for polities as different as Israel and Iraq.[1] The legitimacy problem of which many of the participants of the round tables were fully aware cannot be addressed without democratic elections, mid-way rather than in the very

[1] H. Lerner, *Making Constitutions in Deeply Divided Societies* (Cambridge: Cambridge University Press, 2011); H.A. Hamoudi, *Negotiating in Civil Conflict: Constitutional Construction and Imperfect Bargaining in Iraq* (Chicago, IL: University of Chicago Press, 2013).

beginning of the process. If the first stage of round tables does produce constitutions, as in Hungary and South Africa, these should have an interim status only because of the problem of the absence of full democratic legitimacy. This means that the two- or even multi-stage process must have a final stage, in which the more permanent constitution is enacted. This happened in Bulgaria, Poland, and South Africa, but not in Hungary where the attempt of 1995–97 was a failure. While constitutional development in that country was in the end completed, I argue this was done in 2011 by violating all the normative desiderata of the round-table-led paradigm. As revolutions have been historically challenged by counter revolutions, post sovereign regime change too has now met its counter process.

Even the completion of the two- or multi-stage process of course is no guarantee against unlearning what has been learned. Between 2005 and 2007, under the Kaczynski twins, Poland also came close to reversing many of the results of post sovereign constitution making. With the surviving Polish twin's electoral victory in 2015, the same danger has reappeared, with court packing and jurisdiction weakening as its most important sign. Even in South Africa the negotiated process and its results are constantly challenged and will remain precarious for a long time. What is behind these efforts are versions of an alternative project, populist constitutionalism, a model always claiming embodied popular sovereignty realized through elections rather than revolutions. My last chapter seeks to explain the seductiveness of populist politics as a political theology and to warn against its dangers in the domain of constitutional politics. I believe the secret of Orbán's success so far in Hungary, and Erdoğan's apparent victory in Turkey lie in their ability to mobilize the "empty signifier" of the people on behalf of authoritarian goals. The post sovereign democratic paradigm represents today the best alternative to populisms, both on the left and the right. The defeat of populism, however, will not be possible without improving the quality, the responsiveness, and the accountability of contemporary democratic politics well beyond the constituent process.

Index

The manufacturer's authorised representative in the EU for product safety is Oxford University Press España S.A. of El Parque Empresarial San Fernando de Henares, Avenida de Castilla, 2 - 28830 Madrid (www.oup.es/en or product.safety@oup.com). OUP España S.A. also acts as importer into Spain of products made by the manufacturer.
Printed and bound by CPI Group (UK) Ltd, Croydon, CR0 4YY
14/09/2026
02216307-0011